THE

CONSTRUCTION

OF MEMORY IN

INTERWAR FRANCE

THE

CONSTRUCTION

OF MEMORY IN

INTERWAR FRANCE

Daniel J. Sherman

————

THE UNIVERSITY OF CHICAGO PRESS

CHICAGO AND LONDON

DANIEL J. SHERMAN is professor of French studies and history at Rice University. He is the author of *Worthy Monuments: Art Museums and the Politics of Culture in Nineteenth-Century France*.

The University of Chicago Press, Chicago 60637
The University of Chicago Press, Ltd., London
© 1999 by Daniel J. Sherman
All rights reserved. Published 1999
08 07 06 05 04 03 02 01 00 99   1 2 3 4 5

ISBN: 0–226–75285–2 (CLOTH)

Library of Congress Cataloging-in-Publication Data

Sherman, Daniel J.
   The construction of memory in interwar France / Daniel J. Sherman.
      p.   cm.
   Includes bibliographical references and index.
      ISBN 0-226-75285-2 (alk. paper)
      1. France—History—1914–1940—Historiography. 2. World War, 1914–1918—France—Influence. 3. War memorials—France—Psychological aspects.
4. Memorial rites and ceremonies—France—Social aspects. 1. Title.
DC389.S437 1999
940.4'6544—dc21   99-13677
                                                         CIP

Parts of this book have been previously published as follows: portions of the introduction and chapters 1, 4, and 6 in "Monuments, Mourning, and Masculinity in France after World War I," *Gender & History* 8 (1996): 82–107, © 1996 Blackwell Publishers Ltd.; portions of the introduction and chapter 2 in "Bodies and Names: The Emergence of Commemoration in Interwar France," *American Historical Review* 103 (1998): 443–66, © 1998 American Historical Association; portions of the epilogue in "Objects of Memory: History and Narrative in French War Museums," *French Historical Studies* 19: 1 (Spring 1995): 49–74, © 1995 Society for French Historical Studies.

⊗ The paper used in this publication meets the minimum requirements of the American National Standard for Information Sciences—Permanence of Paper for Printed Library Materials, ANSI Z39.48–1992.

introdroduce D.sherman

For Edward and for Paula

>

). Present book
    - research aim
    - main questions   ] — how I read it
    - memo. approach

) Dan sherman's intro
    2) state of field
    3) comment on our presentation ←
    +) intellectual history, way to book

) Introduce History of Memory (or ask D. Sherman)

Intro
①
4
5
6

CONTENTS

ABBREVIATIONS

AC   Archives Communales de

ADL   Archives Départementales de Loir-et-Cher

ADM   Archives Départementales du Morbihan

ADMe   Archives Départementales de la Meuse

ADV   Archives Départementales du Var

AFC   *L'art funéraire et commémoratif*

AM   Archives Municipales de

AMV   Archives Municipales de Vannes

AN   Archives Nationales

BM   *Le bulletin meusien* (Verdun)

CM/D   Délibérations du Conseil Municipal

ED   Extrait des Délibérations

GBA   *Gazette des beaux-arts*

JO	*Journal officiel*
JO CD	Chambre des Députés, Débats Parlementaires
JO CD/A	Chambre des Députés/Annexes (Documents Parlementaires)
JO S	Sénat, Débats Parlementaires
JO S/A	Sénat/Annexes (Documents Parlementaires)
JP	*Journal de Pontivy*
LeF	*Le Figaro*
LeT	*Le temps*
NM	*Nouvelliste du Morbihan* (Lorient)
OR	*L'ouest républicain* (Lorient)
PV	Procès-Verbal
RDM	*Revue des deux mondes*
RE	*Le républicain de l'est* (Commercy)
RLC	*La République de Loir-et-Cher* (Blois)
RM	*Le réveil de la Meuse* (Bar-le-Duc)
RTC	*Revue mensuelle du Touring-Club de France*
SAVT	Société des Amis du Vieux Toulon, Archives
SEACVG/SM	Archives du Secrétariat d'État aux Anciens Combattants et Victimes de Guerre, Sépultures Militaires
UNC	Union Nationale des Combattants

ILLUSTRATIONS

ACKNOWLEDGMENTS

In an age of diminishing funding for the humanities, I am fortunate to have a number of agencies and foundations to thank. Without the support of the National Endowment for the Humanities, I could never have written this book. An NEH Summer Stipend, together with a Grant-in-Aid from the American Council of Learned Societies, enabled me to begin work on the project in 1988; an NEH Travel to Collections Grant in 1989 supported additional preliminary research. The major part of the research was carried out with an NEH Fellowship for University Teachers in 1990–91. In addition, funds from the Endowment supported my membership in the School of Historical Studies at the Institute for Advanced Study, Princeton, in 1993–94, where I completed the research and began writing. I am also very grateful to the Dean of Humanities at Rice University, for supporting additional research in France as well as the production of photographs, and to Rice's Center for the Study of Cultures, which funded a teaching release in the fall of 1996 that allowed me to complete work on the manuscript.

In France, the directors of the departmental and municipal archives where I worked were unfailingly helpful: they include, in the Loir-et-Cher, Thérèse Burel (Archives Départementales), Mme. Benoist (Vendôme), and Mlle. Vallon (Romorantin); in the Meuse, Gérard Mauduech and J. Mourier (Archives Départementales) and Françoise Allorent (Ligny-en-Barrois); in the Morbihan, Vivienne Miguet (Archives Départementales), M. Poupard (Vannes), and Guy Primel (Lorient); and in the Var, Mme. Martella (Archives Départementales). I also wish to thank Serge Barcellini and Jean-Claude Carlier, directors of the Délégation à la Mémoire et à l'Information Historique, Secrétariat d'État aux Anciens Combattants et Victimes de Guerre, for allowing me access to archival materials in their care. A number of private associations and companies graciously made space and photocopiers available to me, and also took the time to offer advice and assistance, for which I am deeply grateful: Mme. Mireille Rougier at the Union Fédérale, M. Marcellin and Mme. Creac'h at the Union Nationale des Combattants, Col. Giroux at the Souvenir Français, and Adeline Rispal at her architectural firm, Société Repérages. My thanks also to M. Gensollen and Mlle. Groffal of the Société des Amis du Vieux Toulon; to Hugues Hairy, Véronique Harel, and Thomas Compère-Morel of the Historial de Péronne; to Col. Léon Rodier of the Mémorial de Verdun; and to Joseph Hue and Laurent Gervereau of the Bibliothèque de Documentation Internationale Contemporaine, for allowing me access to their collections and archives. Among the many librarians who assisted me, special thanks to Maryvonne Bonnet and Mme. Daniel of the Bibliothèque Nationale's newspaper division, formerly in Versailles, and to Carol Leadenham of the Hoover Institution Archives.

Writing is necessarily a solitary business, but research need not be, and over the years a number of people have helped make it an extraordinarily lively and stimulating experience. Antoine Prost, Jean-Jacques Becker, and Stéphane Audoin-Rouzeau offered good advice; Jean-François Sirinelli and Jean-Pierre Rioux kindly invited me to attend their seminar on cultural history at the Institut d'Histoire du Temps Présent in 1990–91. Marjorie Beale, Barry Bergdoll, Laura Frader, Carla Hesse, Anne Higonnet, Mary Louise Roberts, Aron Rodrigue, David Rodowick, Vanessa Schwartz, Todd Shepard, Tamara Whited, and Michael Wilson have all been good companions on both sides of the Atlantic. In France, I have enjoyed many afternoons and evenings with Félix and Jacqueline Collin, Anne and Alain Cornet-Vernet, Jean-François and Hélène Eck, Michèle Fogel, Marie-Hélène and Moifak Hassan, Marie and Guy Pessiot, François and Denise Petit, and Dominique and Monique Poulot. Vivienne Miguet welcomed me into her home during my research in the Morbihan, and Jan and Nancy Brumm generously lent me their *mas* in the Var, where Ellen and Olivier van der Heijden were extremely hospitable. A special thanks to all those who led or accompanied me on visits to monuments in various parts of France, including Louis Cooper, Eduardo Douglas, Jean-François Eck, Carla Hesse, Isabelle Lemaître, Vivienne Miguet, the Pessiots, the Petits, and Leonard Smith.

It has been a privilege to try out my ideas and findings in a variety of settings, including American University; the Institute for French Studies at New York University; Oberlin College; the Rutgers Center for Historical Analysis; the University of California, Irvine; the Alliance Française de Chicago; the University of Washington; the Center for Twentieth-Century Studies at the University of Wisconsin, Milwaukee; and, in Australia, the Australian War Memorial; La Trobe University; the University of Melbourne; and the University of Technology, Sydney. In Berkeley, Susanna Barrows, Thomas Laqueur, and Sarah Farmer helped stimulate my thinking about memory. At the Institute for Advanced Study and subsequently, Joan Wallach Scott has been an astute critic and a generous friend; I am fortunate to count myself among the many who have learned from her. I am also most grateful for advice, information, and assistance from Bernard Aresu, Barry Bergen, Laird Boswell, Nancy Deffebach, Sarah Fishman, Tara Fitzpatrick, Hélène Lipstadt, Philip Nord, Peter Paret, Lou Roberts, Bonnie Smith, and Len Smith. At Rice I have been part of an extraordinarily close and supportive intellectual community, which has nourished this project in a number of ways. Lauren Bernard, Caroline Harris, David Harvey, and Shane Story provided able research assistance; my thanks to the departments of French studies and history for funding their work.

Nélia Dias, Eduardo Douglas, Robert L. Herbert, Helena Michie, Carol Quillen, and Joan Scott shared with me their reactions to various chapters, much to the book's benefit. I owe more thanks than I can say to Judy Coffin, friend and comrade of long standing, who read every word of the first draft, some of them more than once, and offered her comments with enormous patience and good cheer. Susan Bielstein is the editor all authors dream of: critical, gracious, and supportive in equal measure. I am also grateful to Carol Saller for her superb copy editing and to Jean Williams Brusher for her invaluable editorial assistance. My first teachers—Claire Richter Sherman, Stanley M. Sherman, and Stanley Hoffmann—remain inspiring models. Diane Van Helden and Paula Sanders helped me keep my life together. Eduardo Douglas, above all, made it worth living.

INTRODUCTION

The Emergence of Commemoration

By common consent, the postmodern age is obsessed with memory. The novelist Mary Gordon has observed, "Everyone's talking about memory: French intellectuals, historians of the Holocaust, victims of child abuse, alleged abusers."[1] The sense that the modern nation-state in particular has a deep connection to memory is of course not new: in his 1882 essay "What Is a Nation?" Ernest Renan called "the possession in common of a rich legacy of memories" one of the two constitutive elements of the nation, the other being a shared purpose growing out of this heritage.[2] More recently, Benedict Anderson has explored the way memories, themselves highlighted by selective forgetting, help to fashion and perpetuate the "imagined communities" of which nations consist.[3] Yet the inability to confront or master certain kinds of memory can haunt nation-states, exposing the fragility of their construction, crippling their politics, even destroying them entirely.[4] At a more philosophical level, the obsession with memory becomes a central characteristic of modernity, and the distinctness of the modern world finds expression in forms of memory proper to it. Within intellectual history, the long-standing question of the relationship between history and memory has recently received new attention.[5]

The conception of the term "memory" varies widely, but even, perhaps especially, at its most metaphorical the use of the term reflects the influence of two forebears, one of the acknowledged masters of twentieth-century thought, Sigmund Freud, and a more obscure figure, the sociologist Maurice Halbwachs. Freud's notion of the unconscious as a repository of repressed memories, inaccessible to normal consciousness, but capable of disrupting our conscious lives,[6] lies at the heart of the persistent belief that the past continues to inflect the present. Freud's phylogenetic theory of the psyche offered a way of moving from the individual to the social level, but it has never enjoyed the influence of his psychoanalytic writings.[7] Thus in recent years Halbwachs's concept of collective memory has played a greater role in constructing memory as a cultural metaphor. The resonance and utility of the term has tended to conceal the sharp difference, even incompatibility, between Freud and Halbwachs. Halbwachs regarded *all* memory as collective, in the sense that memories endure only through the frameworks provided by social groups and the spaces they occupy.[8] Halbwachs affirms that "it is individuals as group members who remember," but only to the extent that they belong to and draw ideas from those groups.[9] In Halbwachs's conception, collective memory has little room for the individual unconscious.

For memory to serve as more than a metaphor in historical analysis, we need to retain a sense of both its individual and collective dimensions. We can agree that individual memories exist at several levels, including the sensory, the habitual, and the semantic, and are not all accessible to our conscious minds. Collective or social memory, meanwhile, can be defined as the ideas, assumptions, and knowledges that structure the relationship of individuals and groups to the immediate as well as the more distant past.[10] This book explores the relationship between these two types of memory, individual and social or collective, with particular attention to the emergence, from their dynamic interplay, of the form of social memory we know as commemoration. I take both forms of memory to be representations, which Richard Terdiman defines succinctly as "the function by which symbols, or simulacra, or surrogates, come to stand for some absent referent."[11] Just as individual memories constitute a fund of images and impressions—sensory as well as conceptual, auditory and tactile as well as visual—through which we seek out and recast our pasts, the discourses of collective memory and the practices of commemoration represent a society's past to itself. Recent scholarship leaves little doubt that the construction of memory as a form of representation is a political and social process,[12] but the materials, operation, purposes, and consequences of that construction have only just begun to receive the theoretical and historical attention they merit. As a place and a historical moment intensely focused on memory, France after World War I offers promising ground for an exploration of these questions. The central artifacts of commemorative practice, the monuments to the war dead built in towns and villages across the country, form an appropriate centerpiece to it.

In both its historical specificity and its concerns, this study bears some relationship to Pierre Nora's massive project *Les lieux de mémoire*, seven volumes of essays, by multiple authors, published between 1984 and 1992. *Les lieux de mémoire* seeks to elucidate what Nora has called the "points of crystallization" of the French national heritage;[13] it thus extends well beyond the artifacts and practices at issue here. In popular usage in France (where the term has become so widespread that it has entered the dictionary of the Académie Française) *lieux de mémoire*, literally "sites of memory," has come to refer primarily to material and monumental sites.[14] But for Nora the term has a much broader meaning. The subjects covered in the series range from historiography to Impressionist painting to gastronomy to features of the natural terrain; the concept encompasses, for Nora, "any signifying entity, of a material or ideal kind, which has through human will or the work of time become a symbolic element of the memorial patrimony of a given community." The essays in this complex edifice (Nora likens it to a giant Meccano set) have in common not a particular object of inquiry but a common approach: "What counts . . . is not the identification of the site, but the unfolding of that of which this site is the memory."[15] As a historical project the distinctiveness of *Les lieux de mémoire* lies in its interest in the construction of France as a symbolic reality and its consequent refusal to take "Frenchness" as an inherent quality of the phenomena it studies.[16]

Nora and his contributors have placed salutary emphasis on the constructedness of society's relationship to its past, and the proposal that scholars attend to the artifice involved in the manipulation of national symbols obviously has a bearing on cultural histories such as this one.[17] But in one important way the objective of this book is the reverse of Nora's. Rather than "unfolding that of which the site is the memory," broadly speaking the First World War and the enormous loss and dislocation it caused in French society, I seek to analyze the way in which the war and its consequences became *en*folded in a discursive site cast as memory. My concern, then, is with the set of representations that constituted, and were constituted by, the commemoration of the Great War in the decade or so after the war ended, rather than with the lasting place of the war in French national memory.

Despite the diversity of its subjects, *Les lieux de mémoire* proposes not only a new approach to historical scholarship but a distinct schema of modern French history and a critique of contemporary French culture. One of Nora's contributors, Mona Ozouf, argues, indeed, that the notion of *lieux de mémoire* entails, on the part of the historian employing it, a preoccupation with the present-day world.[18] One is tempted to reply that all historical writing constructs the past from the perspective of the present; that is the nature of interpretation. But my own presentist concerns have to do more with the general workings of commemoration than with France's relation to its past at the end of the twentieth century. Nora's overall schema, moreover, is too broad and, in a literal sense, too categorical to illuminate the dynamics of interwar commemoration in any detail. He regards the end of the Great War as both the apex of the national and civic form of commemoration developed by the Third Republic, with its affirmation of the values incarnated by the secular nation-state, and the beginning of a long period of decline. Today, he argues, a patrimonial form of commemoration has replaced the national, characterized by a pluralist interest in the history of the groups composing the nation rather than by an assertion of its unitary values.[19] Yet a close examination of commemoration at one crucial moment may yield a somewhat more nuanced view of its long-term evolution.

With respect to commemorative monuments, both Nora's methods and his schema draw on the pioneering work of two distinguished historians who contributed to *Les lieux de mémoire*, Maurice Agulhon and Antoine Prost. In a series of articles published in the 1970s, Agulhon constituted the figural monuments of the nineteenth century as a field of historical inquiry. He demonstrated that statues of Marianne, the female allegory of the Republic that first appeared during the Revolution, grew out of popular images and practices reflecting the ardent political commitment of certain small-town and peasant communities. Like the parallel movement that became known as "statuemania," the erection of statues and busts to the great men of the past, the diffusion of images of the Republic in the late nineteenth century grew out of both the maturation of republican civic pedagogy and the proliferation of serially produced monuments for a burgeoning market.[20] Agulhon's two monographs on Marianne offer a comprehensive survey of the changing iconography and political significations of the allegory of the Republic from 1789 to 1914, the moment he identifies as the high point of the regime's self-representation in monumental form.[21] Monuments to the dead of the 1870 Franco-Prussian War had a role in this democratization of commemoration, but, for the most part limited to eastern France and to major cities elsewhere, they never dominated the civic landscape to the extent that World War I monuments would come to do.[22]

Prost, in his magisterial 1977 history of the post–World War I veterans' movement, established the significance of monuments to the war dead as "a system of signs, complex but coherent, which convey the meaning that each spiritual, ideological or moral family claimed to find in the war."[23] Prost presents a typology of war memorials based on their iconography, inscriptions, and location within a town. These types range from the two most frequent, the civic and the funerary (the former usually in town squares and featuring republican symbols, the latter often in cemeteries and incorporating signs of mourning), to the rarer monuments that celebrate victory or protest the war.[24]

Hybrid "patriotic-funerary" types also exist. But beyond the diversity of their forms and meanings, Prost makes clear the important role monuments played in a new type of civic ritual. All monuments, he believes, became the focus for a secular "republican cult" in which the memory of the dead served to reinscribe republican values, notably a selfless devotion to the cause of freedom.[25]

This conception of Great War commemoration as the apex of republican civic pedagogy coincides with the conclusions of recent French scholarship on World War I. Historians both of the home front and of combatants argue that France's ability to endure four years of invasion, devastation, and unremitting loss had to do with the strength and solidity of French society. For Jean-Jacques Becker, the Republic's educational system had done its work well, and its leaders were able to mobilize the population in the national cause.[26] Just as Prost dismisses the once common view of war memorials as artifacts of the nationalism of the extreme right, Stéphane Audoin-Rouzeau rejects as ex post facto legend the portrayal of French soldiers as cynical, uninterested in the progress of the war, even defeatist. Despite their strained relations with civilians, soldiers' ties to the "national community," Audoin-Rouzeau asserts, were never broken, and "cohesion was able to triumph over divisiveness."[27] This cohesion continued, in Prost's view, in the ideology of the French veterans' movement. Veterans' pacifism and antipathy to politicians and the parliamentary system, he stresses, for the most part remained consistent with loyalty to the Republic.[28]

This historical consensus has behind it both solid research and persuasive historical argument, and it is not my purpose to challenge it. But the portrayal of a resilient republican culture sustaining both the war effort and its subsequent commemoration raises a number of questions.[29] First, how did a war that had so severely tested the French and their institutions become the basis for a renewed affirmation of republican values? This question involves not the ultimate efficacy of postwar reconstruction in France, of which commemoration formed only a part, but the construction of commemorative culture itself. Which aspects of the war predominated in the discourses, imagery, and rituals of commemoration, and which ones fell by the wayside? What kinds of contestation did commemoration produce, how did the commemorative process deal with them, and with what consequences? How did commemoration use, reinforce, or question existing distinctions within French society, notably those of class and gender, in its efforts to activate a vision of harmony?

In exploring these questions, my approach differs from those of Agulhon and Prost in a number of respects, above all in refusing to privilege coherence over difference. Prost acknowledges that the construction of war memorials, and the commemorative rituals that developed around them, did provoke contestation. Yet he sees such discord not only as less important but as less interesting than the overall ideological coherence of interwar commemoration. Agulhon makes a conceptual distinction between "ideology," which for him pertains to basic philosophical conceptions of society, and "politics," referring to conflicting choices within an ideological context accepted by both sides. The urge to commemorate through monuments stems from ideology, briefly a kind of Enlightenment humanism, whereas disputes over the modalities of commemoration take place at the pettier level of politics.[30] Such a distinction effectively informs Prost's work as well, as it does that of scholars who would qualify the view that monuments to the dead of the Great War constituted the apex of republican civic culture. Jay Winter, for one, sees commemoration of the war not as political but as an existential response to universal bereavement. Annette Becker, who also regards commemoration primarily as a public form of mourning, stresses the way in which it facilitated a reconciliation between the Republic and the Catholic church.[31]

But the emphasis on unitary meanings, whether republican, consolatory, or Christian, risks distracting attention from a deeper dynamic at work in the commemorative process after the Great War, one that arguably constitutes its most lasting legacy to the twentieth century. Whatever strains and tensions can be perceived in interwar commemoration only hint at a more profound conflict, the result of the process fundamental to commemoration's emergence. For commemoration to have the larger political and social resonance with which historians credit it, it must subsume individual memories and other cultural materials into a larger narrative about the commemorated event, in this case the Great War. To the extent that commemoration grew out of and sought to reshape both individual and collective knowledge of the war, moreover, knowledges with a direct bearing on the future cast of French society, the oppositions it entailed were central to its larger stakes, power.

The contention that commemoration represents a struggle over power obviously draws on the work of Michel Foucault. For Foucault power does not emanate from a single location, but is multiple and mobile; power is immanent in other relations, including those of knowledge, not exterior to them; there is no binary opposition between rulers and ruled, but "manifold relationships of force" throughout society and its institutions.[32] The Foucauldian nexus of power/knowledge thus provides an essential foundation for understanding the dynamics of commemoration. A number of other terms and concepts, from a variety of methodological perspectives, will also prove helpful. Though many of these terms will receive further elaboration at the beginning of the relevant chapters, a few need to be set out in advance, along with the contours of the historical situation they illuminate.

To summarize the terms outlined so far, *commemoration* mobilizes a variety of discourses and practices into a representation of an event or epoch; this representation contains within it a social and cultural vision it casts as inherent in the "memory" of the commemorated event. *Discourse* may be defined, summarily, as a group of statements linked by their object;[33] *representation*, we will recall, is an operation, and the artifacts of that operation, that causes signs to stand for an absent referent. Representation constitutes a potentially endless process of the production of meaning. In this process, subjects construct new signs with which to interpret those at hand, but at a certain point, which C. S. Peirce conceptualized as the "final interpretant," the specificity of meaning attached to a sign becomes habitual, and leads to some form of human action.[34] When a number of these signs converge into a set of interpretations and actions common to a social group, small or large, the representation has become a *culture*, a repository for the beliefs and values of a group of people and for signs and interpretive strategies they share. Culture as a collection of signs has a conventional rather than definitive status; it always remains subject to the play of representations.

As a form of representation, commemoration seeks to reinforce the solidarity of a particular community or set of communities. It does so by forging a consensus version of an event or connected series of events that has either disrupted the stability of the community or threatened to do so. This narrative of the past usually, although not necessarily, reflects the interests of the community's leading social and political groups, and thus constitutes what some scholars have referred to as a ***dominant memory***. I use this term advisedly, to characterize not simply, as Henry Rousso puts it, a "collective interpretation of the past that may even come to have official status," but a set of narrative explanations emanating from dominant groups.[35] Such elites label these narratives "memory" as part of an effort to assert the inherence of what is, in the first instance, their construction.

In the aftermath of war, societies both enact and attempt to displace individual *mourning*, which Freud conceives as the process through which a bereaved person transfers desire to some new object. Like the lost object, the object of commemoration can be either a person or "some abstraction which has taken the place of [a loved one], such as one's country, liberty, an ideal, and so on."[36] The political dimension of commemoration resides in the way it channels mourning in a direction that conforms to dominant perceptions of the national interest. But the work of commemoration is also cultural: it inscribes or reinscribes a set of symbolic codes, ordering discourses, and master narratives that recent events, perhaps the very ones commemorated, have disrupted, newly established, or challenged.

The construction of a commemorative culture is a form of what Jane Tompkins has called *cultural work*, the process through which texts of various kinds at once describe the social order, providing society with ways of thinking about itself, and offer projects for transforming it.[37] The concept of cultural work takes as its starting point the similarity of different kinds of texts, including commemorative speeches, legislative debates, novels, memoirs, and guidebooks, without attempting to classify them in terms of some originary influence. Regarding texts as bearers not only of meanings but of interests, cultural work offers a way into the problems these texts grapple with, and the solutions they propose, through their form, their substantive content, and the symbolic codes that tie them together. In the operation of these symbolic codes, *gender*, not only as a construction of sexual difference but as a means of representing other power relationships, plays a crucial role.[38] During and after World War I in France, gender served as a primary figure both for the social disruptions of war and for various forms of social renewal and retrenchment. Commemoration, in turn, not only reinscribed gender codes that World War I had disrupted in France, but also played out, in gendered terms, a pervasive cultural unease in which nothing less than the masculine cast of politics and of national citizenship was at stake.[39]

The post–World War I years in France emerge in the latest scholarship as a period of retrenchment and retreat in gender relations. Unlike Britain, Germany, and the United States, France did not accord women the vote until after World War II. The progress in women's employment during the war proved only temporary, as employers hastened to hire veterans and send women workers home. In a climate of pervasive anxiety about demographic decline, heightened by the magnitude of the country's losses, state policy placed an overwhelming emphasis on women's roles as wives and mothers. This policy involved not only inducements, such as medals and financial incentives for large families, but coercion, notably the draconian repression of abortion and family planning.[40] Thus summarized, this history can take on an air of inevitability, as though the gender anxieties that the war produced led "naturally" to the reassertion of male authority. But as Mary Poovey has written of Victorian Britain, "Representations of gender . . . were themselves contested images, the sites at which struggles for authority occurred," and also sources of legitimacy in such struggles.[41] Commemoration mobilized representations of gender, and gendered representations, for the most part on behalf of the dominant memory of the war, thus reauthorizing a masculinist vision of French society. But it could not entirely suppress memories of greater female independence during the war, a layer of latent contestation that lurked beneath the surface of commemorative discourse.

The elements of representation, cultural work, and contestation come together in Michel Foucault's concept of *emergence*, a component of his genealogical method. Foucault employs this term in preference to "origins" because it avoids the latter's suggestion of a continuous evolution from an ideal prototype and attends to "the details and accidents that accompany every beginning."[42] Since it involves a particular configuration of forces, "the isolation of different points of emergence does not conform to the successive configurations of an identical meaning; rather, they result from substitutions, displacements, disguised conquests, and systematic reversals."[43] These terms capture the basic workings of representation and the range of possible relations between sign and referent. At its most basic, representation involves one thing standing for or taking the place of another, as in a "substitution," but it can also entail a more forcible transposition, or "displacement," which it can conceal behind apparent continuity or seek to render virtually automatic ("systematic reversal"). The idea that a practice can emerge at "different points," moreover, suggests the complexity of this process, which generally does not conform to a precise chronological sequence. Because the stakes of commemoration include consolation, the affirmation of core values, and a larger social and political vision, it proceeds simultaneously on a number of fronts. Its success depends in large part on its ability to effect a basic displacement: to cast commemoration not as a political and cultural construct but as inherent in a domain of memory enjoying unique access to the "real." Conversely, the conflicts that ensue from commemoration reflect the difficulty attendant on such an ambition.

In exploring the complexities of commemoration's emergence in interwar France, this book takes a largely synchronic approach, focusing on the relatively brief period, from the end of the war to the mid-1920s, in which the constitutive elements of commemorative culture were most intensely in play. The narrative structure derives not from the standard chronology of French political history, though concurrent events do impinge on it, but from the stages that individuals and communities typically passed through in the practice of commemoration. The typical is of course both a subjective and an imprecise category; I employ it only to convey the principle adopted in selecting materials and organizing the narrative, and the lack of any pretense to exhaustiveness. Many artifacts of commemorative culture—paintings, films, and religious objects, including the memorial plaques in churches that were almost as pervasive as secular monuments—fall outside the scope of this study. A focus on the complexity of commemoration as cultural process requires selectivity, and while visual imagery, narrative prose, and religious discourse occupy an important place in the analysis, a survey of all their traces in various media would require another book, of a very different kind.[44]

The book begins with some of the central materials, structures, and assumptions, many of them arising before and during the war, that provided the basis for commemoration's emergence. In chapter 1, close readings of a number of influential literary texts, battlefield guidebooks, and visual representations of the war demonstrate how memory, constructed as an extension of experience, acts to privilege and exclude as well as to preserve. In particular, accounts focusing on the experience of the common soldier or poilu, while potentially subversive in wartime, could easily take on a conservative valence as they became part of a dominant memory. Chapter 2 looks at the many connections between local commemorative practice and the great national ossuaries on the battlefields. Both, crucially, grew out of the enormous physical task of

selectivity

privilege, exclude preserve

local vs. nat'e

locating and accounting for the war dead, and their competing claims led to intense contestation over both the physical and the discursive disposition of those remains. The inscription of names, one of the characteristic forms of modern commemoration, emerged in counterpoint to this struggle, affirming the worth not only of individuals but of the cause for which they ostensibly gave their lives.

The second part of the book, chapters 3–6, explores the central commemorative practice of the interwar years, the construction of monuments to the war dead in nearly all of France's 36,000 communes, the basic units of local government. Ranging in size from major cities to villages with their rural hinterland, communes are grouped together, in ascending order, in cantons, *arrondissements*, and departments, of which there were ninety in metropolitan France in the interwar period. In post–Revolutionary France, the state assigned a prefect to supervise and approve the actions and finances of the communes, as well as those of an elected *conseil général*, in each department (each member of the *conseil général* represents a single canton). Following this administrative division, historians of modern France have customarily selected regional samples at the departmental level. So, in an effort to disentangle local particularities from more general patterns, the analysis in chapters 3–6 considers four departments, in very different parts of France. Many of these particularities became inscribed in the language and iconography of local commemoration, but for the most part they will form a backdrop to an analysis that highlights the structural polarities of commemoration itself.

One could hardly consider the emergence of commemoration without looking at its construction in an area directly affected by the war. The department of the Meuse was the scene of some of the most bitter fighting and most savage destruction of the war; it includes the city of Verdun, which became the symbol of the war's horrors and of the courage and resistance of the French soldier. Mostly rural before the war, the department tended to the mainstream or republican right. The three other departments, at some distance from the front, present a mosaic of French diversity. The Morbihan, a society of fishermen and small farmers with one substantial industrial town, Lorient, typified the Breton variety of Catholic conservatism. In the Loire valley, the Loir-et-Cher (like the Cher, the Loir is a tributary of the much longer Loire) mixed prosperous market farming with more isolated forests and marshes favored by hunters. Politically, the department inclined to the blend of fiercely secularist rhetoric and fiscal conservatism that characterized the center-left Radical party, pivot of Third Republic politics, though it had some pockets of deep conservatism as well. The Var, finally, had long been in the advance-guard of the republican left, from the busy naval port of Toulon and its industrial suburbs to the bustling market towns of the Provençal hills.

The chronology of these chapters follows the stages in the construction of a typical local monument, from fund-raising to dedication. In chapter 3, we examine the combination of private contributions, local government appropriations, and state subsidies that funded monument construction, with an eye to both the claims and the silences of the fund-raising process. Chapter 4 concerns monument design and the emergence of a set of critical attitudes that distinguished between monuments' aesthetic and commemorative functions. Considering the similarities as well as the differences between artist-designed monuments and the serially produced versions available from entrepreneurs, the chapter also examines how and why local communities continued to insist, against the critics, that their monuments were works of art. Chapter 5 then explores the insertion of monuments into local communities, notably issues of location; symbolism, including religious iconography; and materials and labor. The purposes and methods of commemoration entailed an effacement of politics in favor of an assertion of local harmony, but, even as "local" artifacts, monuments bore many traces of political conflict. Chapter 6 surveys the civic rituals that took place around monuments, focusing on the dedication ceremonies that set the pattern for annual observances on Armistice Day, the *11 novembre*. The elements examined in earlier chapters, including commemorative naming, monumental forms and spaces, and both local and national politics, came together in commemorative ritual to construct and secure an account of the war consistent with a conservative vision of French society. An epilogue seeks to bridge the interwar period and our own time by examining shifts in commemorative culture in the 1930s and 1960s and a number of recent representations of the memory of World War I.

No consideration of memory in France since 1945 can ignore the effects of World War II, the Vichy regime, and the Resistance. But by offering an epilogue rather than a conclusion, and situating it in the context of current attitudes toward memory and commemoration, I want to circumvent the too-frequent temptation to reduce all histories of the interwar period to the fall of France in 1940.[45] Omer Bartov has argued that evocations of the war and its lessons by interwar political parties deepened France's internal divisions, leaving important segments of popular opinion unwilling to contemplate an external war.[46] Ultimately, however, that question has to do more with the deployment of competing historical interpretations within the realm of high politics than with the construction of memory per se. That it could be posed in terms of "memory" demonstrates the importance of the rather different politics at issue in this book. For the belief that overtly political discourses about the "lessons" of the Great War constituted a form of memory can be traced to the discursive maneuver at the heart of commemoration. The efficacy of commemoration lies in its ability to convince people that the discourse it constructs out of their memories can itself be called "memory"; that rival versions of the same event may so qualify only indicates the power, mobility, and versatility of commemoration as a form of representation. In different guises, with different materials, and with different stakes, commemoration today retains much of its persuasive power. We cannot hope to understand why without a sustained and critical examination of the intricate and intimate politics of its own emergence.

EXPERIENCE AND MEMORY

At some instinctive level, most of us probably associate memory with images, particularly with photographs. Individual memories, in French *souvenirs*, are like snapshots; the sum of those memories, the French *mémoire* (the word also designates the faculty of memory) we may liken to a collection of photographs, or, in a more contemporary simile, to a videotape with soundtrack. Some memories, like photographs, fade with age, or become lost in a larger collection, requiring extraordinary effort—perhaps, to extend the figure further, the effort of psychoanalysis—to unearth. Also like snapshots, memories differ in their sharpness, their precision; some may be blurry from the moment our mind captures them, while others retain their vividness over the course of a lifetime.

In Western thought the conceptualization of memory in visual terms, as a store of images, goes back as far as antiquity, to the legendary mnemonics of Simonides.[1] Yet as technologies of reproduction have proliferated in the past two centuries, cultural and scientific understandings of memory have grown more complicated. Although the influential philosopher Henri Bergson referred to the components of memory as "images photographed upon the object itself," he conceived of memory-images as part of a temporal continuum involving not only perception but the movement of the body.[2] Bergson's construction of memory in terms of action rather than vision secures the philosopher an important place in Martin Jay's history of the "denigration of vision" in twentieth-century French thought. For Jay, Bergson's well-known comparison of memory to early cinema expresses not an embrace of modern technology but a profound critique of fin-de-siècle theories of cognition and temporality. In Bergson's view, the eye of the camera epitomized a misconception of memory as localized, a set of images that the mind has captured as though on

[handwritten marginalia: indiv vs. collective memory]

[handwritten marginalia: Diff. types of memory]

film, rather than a combination of such images, bodily sensations, and less palpable intuitions.[3]

But neither Bergson's work nor subsequent scientific analyses likening memory to electronic circuitry rather than to the visual archive[4] have disrupted the basic assumption underlying the photographic metaphor of memory: that memory involves the recording of experience. Indeed, if one can find a Bergsonian strand in constructions of memory in the aftermath of World War I, it arguably lies in an emphasis on participation in the war, rather than observation of it: memory as rooted in action, not simply spectatorship. In this way, memory inheres in the physical body of the remembering subject. Whatever the source of this emphasis, even if it is, in Jay's terms, an "anti-ocularcentric" strand of theory, it has the paradoxical effect of strengthening the hold of a visual conception of memory. For, as Joan Scott has observed, "Knowledge is gained through vision; vision is a direct apprehension of a world of transparent objects. In this conceptualization, the visible is privileged; writing is then put at its service."[5] Constructions of memory, then, privilege the visual because of its traditional association with cognition.[6] Sight is the only sense powerful enough to bridge the gap between those who hold a memory rooted in bodily experience and those who, lacking such "experience," nonetheless seek to share the memory.

In this reasonably common view, it is taken for granted that authentic memories have a unique purchase on individual experience. The articulation of memories connected to the experiences a society deems important accords the holders of those memories special status and a claim on the social conscience. In a society in which the critique of visual sensation was still embryonic, and largely confined to the intellectual elite,[7] the criteria for testing the validity of such memories, and the modalities through which memories contest each other, were largely visual. Even today, one could argue that, whatever the prevailing scientific and intellectual consensus on the nature of individual memory, the notion of collective memory continues to be articulated in terms of images, a term in which, as W. J. T. Mitchell has shown, visual connotations have remained primary.[8]

Understood as offering unmediated access to some foundational or transformative experience, the concept of "memory" has much the same effect that, in Scott's argument, a reified notion of experience has on historical writing. "When experience is taken as the origin of knowledge," Scott writes, "the vision of the individual subject (the person who had the experience or the historian who recounts it) becomes the bedrock of evidence on which explanation is built. Questions about the constructed nature of experience, about how subjects are constituted as different in the first place, about how one's vision is structured—about language (or discourse) and history—are left aside."[9] As we will see, discussions of memory during and after World War I tended to divide memories into categories based on the life-experiences of the remembering subjects: front-line soldiers versus staff officers, combatants versus civilians, men versus women. The categories themselves are taken as given, immutable, and largely determinant. But just as, in Scott's formulation, "it is not individuals who have experience, but subjects who are constituted through experience,"[10] images or language acts construed as memories play a vital role in constructing the categories into which they ostensibly fall. These categories draw their substance and legitimacy from their claim faithfully to transcribe a fully experienced reality. When several incompatible or contradictory sets of categories emerge at the same time, they give rise to inescapably political contests over whose memory "counts," that is, has social value and merits retention at a collective level. Since, however, memories can be judged or evaluated only in terms of their accuracy, their fidelity to the ostensibly neutral ground of "experience," such struggles seek to mask their political investments and those of the very categories they employ.

At certain times, individuals understand the situations and perspectives they construe as experience in terms of categories of preestablished historical importance such as "war." In such instances the simultaneity of the construction of experience and of memory emerges with particular clarity and a special edge. Fictional and autobiographical narratives published during and after the war suggest that soldiers were obsessed with being forgotten; for most, the surest means of avoiding that terrifying prospect involved replacing preexisting notions of the nature of war with their own constructions of the war as experience. Yet in this respect the prevalent concept of memory posed a challenge that amounted almost to a trap. The genre category "war narrative" created a set of expectations in readers that war writers made it almost a point of honor to subvert. For if individuals truly remember only their own experiences, and if soldiers' claims to the gratitude and perpetual recognition of the nation thus depended on the uniqueness of their memories, how could they hope to convey those memories to those who, by definition, had not experienced them? Both combatants' feverish attempts to narrate their memories and their almost ritual despair at the gap between the home front and the battlefield grew out of this paradox. The institutionalization of commemoration, and the reduction of memory to a set of common images at its heart, had the effect of reifying the paradox—literally setting it in stone—but in no sense resolved it.

Three registers of experience played a crucial role in constructing memories of World War I in France and endowing them with a collective dimension: war narratives, battlefield tourism, and visual imagery. In each of these domains, albeit in different ways, patterns of discourse and imagery offered themselves as both the product of experience and the basis of memory. Whether as readers, as tourists, or as spectators, individuals had the opportunity to form their own memories out of cultural materials that by and large masked their collective dimension. Soldiers did not wait until the war's end to publish their accounts of it: trench newspapers, expertly surveyed by Stéphane Audoin-Rouzeau, both offered a running, soldier's-eye view of the war and contested the versions of official bulletins and the civilian press that were more likely to reach the civilian public. Many trench newspapers consciously sought to provide a record for posterity, so that subsequent accounts, whether commemorative or historical, might, as soldiers had, identify the "Great War" with the experience of the common soldier as they had constructed it.[11] At the same time, both autobiographical and fictionalized accounts by former soldiers, many published in book form before the end of the war,[12] made truth claims militant in their exclusivity. Not only did their experiences authorize soldiers to speak, they denied that right to those who had not shared them. Yet even noncombatants could join soldiers in what many authors described as their primary motivation for writing: the desire, even a sort of primal need, to pay tribute to their dead comrades. Memory, first constituted in the textuality of soldiers' experiences, thus became a social and cultural imperative for a nation seeking to assimilate the pain of war and move on.

War narratives offered readers access, ostensibly direct and unmediated, to soldiers' "experience"; they thus offered themselves as the ground for a collective memory of war centering on the combatant experience. But veterans and noncombatants alike had another potential avenue both to recollection and to the acquisition of primary knowledge about the war: visiting the battlefield. Many would undertake such a journey in search of communion with the dead, or, as we will see in chapter 2, of more direct contact with the remains of a loved one, a body either buried in a marked grave or, all too often, lost. Such a "pilgrimage," in the then-current parlance, offered the safest and most widely approved motive for a journey to the front, the desire to pay tribute to the dead. "Tourism" in the sense of sight-seeing was another matter: although it had its boosters, notably the Touring-Club de France, they already seem to have been fighting against the pejorative connotations of the term, the familiar charge that, as Dean MacCannell puts it, "touristic experiences fall short of 'understanding.'"[13]

Whatever visitors' reasons for being in the former war zone, however, various agencies, from civic and religious leaders to the publishers of guidebooks, promised that not merely the sight but the experience of seeing the ruins and vestiges of war would offer them both indelible impressions and valuable lessons. Just as the denigration of vision was in its early stages at the end of World War I, so too much of the modern cynicism about tourism that Mac-Cannell has described lay in the future. If visits to battle sites did not always

Sight = experience

come with the authoritative voices of soldier-writers (though veterans often served as guides for tour groups), they did offer discernibly "real" traces of war experience. To behold scarred landscapes, ruined towns, and innumerable graves firsthand, rather than simply as images, offered visitors an opportunity to construct memories out of their own "experiences." Seeing becomes experience through physical presence; thus tourism both draws on and reinforces the privileged status of sight.

Combatant literature and battlefield tourism, then, offer those who partake of them vicarious experiences of war, but they do so on radically dissimilar premises. Most war narratives construct the experience of soldiers as radically other, fundamentally different from those not only of civilians but of military personnel who did not serve in the front lines. The narratives themselves could offer noncombatants some understanding of soldiers' experience, but could not entirely bridge the gap those experiences created; indeed, the texts served, among other things, to make that gap a (discursive) reality, mapping its contours, probing its limits. Tourism, on the other hand, rests on the proposition that knowledge, largely visual but supplemented by written and oral information, can transmit the essentials of experience. If this effort is always, as Mac-Cannell asserts, "doomed to eventual failure,"[14] it nonetheless rejects in advance the notion that some experiences are incommensurable.

As we analyze the process through which both concepts of memory and particular memories found expression in interwar France, we need to attend to another level at which the contesting claims of war literature and tourism were largely irrelevant. Both literature and tourism required active engagement, whether of time, money, or both. Yet a whole set of images of the war presented themselves on a regular basis to the public whether it sought them or not: the mass-cultural images of postcards, caricatures, posters, and the like. A brief survey of these media will suggest something of the complexity of the interaction between stock images and the construction of memory. For commemoration drew from the visual field not only specific images, but a whole mode of representation in which the visual sign offers itself as a substitute for what cannot be seen or pictured directly. Images bore the trace both of their sources and of their own status as representations. At the same time, their resemblance to individual memories allowed commemoration to carry out its cultural work without overtly challenging the paradox of incommensurability at its heart.

Narrating War

Discourse, to remain effective within a culture, must continually develop new standards of inclusion and exclusion. This is cultural work at once at its most technical and its most open, the work a society normally assigns to the editors of dictionaries, the givers of prizes, the authors and judges of professional examinations. These cultural workers evaluate other cultural work, though usually on the basis of a narrow and specific range of criteria. In 1920s France, the discourse of war experience had no more ardent enforcer than an expatriate French literature professor at Williams College. Jean Norton Cru's critique of French war narratives still commands the respect of historians,[15] but for our purposes its primary interest lies in the cultural work it performs. Norton Cru's methods and opinions thus provide a window into the ways war narratives themselves both helped to construct commemorative discourse and functioned within it.

Published in 1929 and running to over seven hundred pages, Norton Cru's *Témoins* (Witnesses) presented, as its subtitle put it, "an analysis and critique of combatant memoirs published in French between 1915 and 1928."[16] By "memoirs" Norton Cru meant any form of literature presenting a first-hand prose account of the war by one who had participated in it: the book considers diaries, letters, meditative essays, even fiction, as well as actual autobiographies. Evaluating these works, over three hundred of them, solely on the basis of their fidelity to the combatant experience as Norton Cru, himself a veteran, understood it, *Témoins* finds many of the best known wanting. The book sparked considerable controversy, and some hostility, not only from writers Norton Cru had criticized but from other veterans who found his judgments too severe.[17]

For Norton Cru, *Témoins* had a fairly simple purpose: responding to a 1921 article in the *Revue de synthèse historique*, one of the leading avatars of the new scientific history in France, he offers the study as a guide to historians of the future in their search for reliable evidence about the war. The present moment, he writes, does not offer sufficient perspective for the writing of real history, but is ideal for "the preparation of materials."[18] But *Témoins* had another goal as well, almost as frankly acknowledged: to establish the experiences of front-line soldiers as the basis for the subsequent history of the war. By the end of the war, Norton Cru asserts, all combatants agreed that "If anyone knows the war, it is the poilu, from the common soldier to the captain; what we see, what we live through, *is*; that which contradicts our experience, *is not*," no matter where the claim comes from.[19] The flatness of this assertion bolsters Norton Cru's choice of the word *témoins*, "witnesses," with its cognate *témoignage*, "testimony," as his title; the paratactic linking of vision and experience (what we see, what we live through) reminds us of the epistemology sketched by Scott. As Shoshana Felman has written, "The specialness of testimony proceeds from the witness's irreplaceable performance of the act of seeing—from the witness's seeing with his/her own eyes."[20]

Norton Cru's definition of the combatant excludes not only, as in the quoted passage, all ranks higher than captain, but staff officers and support personnel who did not take part in battle. "The fundamental idea of my work," he writes, was to "bring together the accounts of narrators who acted and lived through the events [*qui ont agi et vécu les faits*], excluding the stories of spectators, whether they were at headquarters a few kilometers from the scene or in their offices in Paris."[21] The distinction between observers and participants certainly coincides with the Bergsonian emphasis on action and "individually endured time," as opposed to mere perception, as the basis for memory.[22] But not all participant accounts had equal worth. What qualified Norton Cru to evaluate them? On the one hand, he claims only that, "as a witness myself, I judge acts of witness [*témoignages*]." Though at the outbreak of the war he was almost thirty-five, and had been teaching at Williams for six years, Norton Cru returned home and volunteered; he served at the front for over two years as a corporal and then a sergeant, before being sent to work as an interpreter with the British and American armies. But, conscious that service alone might not grant him sufficient authority, he also claims that intensive reading of everything related to the war gave him the special expertise available to researchers. Norton Cru makes the latter claim with even greater force in *Du témoignage*, a version of *Témoins* for a general audience published in 1930.[23]

As a reader, Norton Cru sought above all precision, notably about topographic details, the frank expression of soldiers' reactions to their experiences—"the suffering, the anguish, the anger, the hatred, the desires, the judgments"—and a lack of heroics.[24] He lists a number of myths about war that the poilus' experience had disproved, ranging from clichés ("war is a struggle," for example) to legends to images of rivers of blood or mountains of corpses, which he felt exaggerated a reality that was sufficiently horrific on its own.[25] Norton Cru's target is clear: the old mythology of war as glorious combat, a view of war "from on high," based on strategy, tactics, conquests, and losses, what the French call *faits militaires*.[26]

For Norton Cru the absence of *faits militaires* demonstrated the "sincerity" of an eyewitness account, the "fidelity of the image" it paints of war.[27] He had no interest in traditional accounts of battles, like the so-called battle of the Marne, for

in the current state of knowledge, the battle of the Marne is scarcely more than an abstraction; it is a convenient idea that allows us to conceive more clearly of the totality of the battles of the Ourcq, of the two Morins, of Vitry, and so on. Those battles themselves have a reality only to the extent that they sum up the engagements of army corps, divisions, regiments, companies, and so on, coming down finally to the individual soldier who is the primordial reality, the one that gives life to the abstract notion of the battle of the Marne.[28]

The introduction to the later volume, *Du témoignage*, takes on a second target, the argument, advanced in response to *Témoins*, that "art" grants writers more freedom with facts and details than Norton Cru had acknowledged. Norton Cru retorts that art has only as much freedom as the public grants it, and that in any case much of the prestige attached to works like Henri Barbusse's prize-winning *Le feu* (1916) derived from their authors' reputations as witnesses. Moreover, Norton Cru points out that his primary concern was establishing a historical record, and history has the right to establish its own criteria.[29]

It would be superfluous to critique Norton Cru's premises on the basis of more recent developments in theory and epistemology, for these have made the limitations of positivism and empiricism quite familiar. Nor should one gainsay the important contribution of *Témoins*, both at the time of publication and subsequently, to a more nuanced understanding of "war" as a sociocultural category.[30] Of more particular interest here are certain problems in Norton Cru's analysis that result from his conceptions of memory and of narrative. In *Du témoignage*, Norton Cru expresses a fundamental distrust of memory, which, in good Bergsonian fashion, he sees as a form of invention, intimately linked to forgetting.

The witness forgets, but if he were satisfied to lose track of the facts the problem would not be so serious. In reality his memory tricks him: it recreates as much as his forgetting obliterates, and this creation never conforms to the original reality. It is inspired by long-held notions of the [human] spirit, in this case by the traditional, legendary image of war.[31]

"Legend" here functions as the sign of a discredited discourse, one that cannot convey the truth of experience; that it can shape "memory" indicates the magnitude of the critical task Norton Cru has assigned himself. Norton Cru favors above all narratives based on diaries, day-to-day notations of events the author lived through. But unless a writer actually takes notes continuously and instantaneously, unlikely in the midst of an attack or bombardment, memory, even if short- rather than long-term, always enters into play. Maurice Genevoix, one of Norton Cru's favorite writers, would have been the first to admit this: at one point he portrays himself writing with the phrase "I jot down some memories [*souvenirs*]."[32] If memory inevitably deforms experience, in other words, no account could be entirely free of its effects.

Norton Cru also recognizes writers' tendency to invent and exaggerate, whether for ideological purposes, notably pacifism, or, more problematically, because of the powerful persistence of the legendary view of war. He implores the veterans among his readers to confine their writings to what they actually saw and experienced, but expresses some doubt that they would do so.[33] For Norton Cru, "only the most lucid, the most independent" of writers had been able to resist the legendary in their writings. But this argument poses problems for a critic who elsewhere dismisses works or episodes that stray too far from "general cases, the facts common to several accounts."[34] If one puts these strands together, Norton Cru is essentially arguing that only exceptional writers, those able to resist the pull of legend, could relate the most common facts. Nor does he pause to consider *why* the traditional heroic account of war should endure despite its obvious irrelevance to the common soldier's experience of World War I. To do so would confront him with the ways in which preexisting assumptions, not only about war but about the structuring norms of society—gender, class, language, culture—played a part in shaping first soldiers' "experiences," and then their accounts of them. For Norton Cru such an insight was quite literally unthinkable, yet it emerges, unwelcome and unacknowledged, in the gaps and contradictions of his texts, a kind of political unconscious.

These contradictions, and his pessimism about the waning of a realistic view of the war, did not keep Norton Cru from his main task, an evaluation of some three hundred texts and a categorization of them in terms of their documentary or "truth" value. His classification encompasses six categories, ranging from "practically nil" to "excellent."[35] We will consider three texts in the highest category: Genevoix's *Ceux de 14*, Charles Delvert's war diaries, and Jean Bernier's *La percée*, as well as two best-selling novels Norton Cru ranks much lower: Barbusse's *Le feu* and Roland Dorgelès's *Les croix de bois*.[36] Three novels that fall outside Norton Cru's scope, Jean Schlumberger's *Le camarade infidèle*, Genevoix's *La joie*, and Joseph Jolinon's *La tête brûlée*, are also of interest to the extent that they deal with the fate of veterans and their memories after the war. Their differences notwithstanding, certain thematic similarities among these works lend insight into the ways in which narratives construct both the experience and the memory of World War I.

Charles Delvert's *Carnets d'un fantassin* (Notebooks of a foot soldier) nicely fit virtually all of Norton Cru's desiderata.[37] Written in a diary format, the text includes numerous indications that the author simply transcribed the notes he took at the time; a later edition provides a precise physical description of the notebooks, and prints in italics passages composed from memory, a year after the events they cover.[38] Genevoix, of whom Norton Cru writes "of all the war authors, Genevoix indisputably occupies the first rank," offers a similarly plotless narrative of the war. His texts, arranged chronologically but with chapter titles as well as diary notations, follow the first-person narrator and his comrades for seven months as they move back and forth between the front lines to their rest billets, sparing the reader none of the wearying monotony of military life.[39] *La percée* is a novel, but its autobiographical dimension and detail are clear enough to convince Norton Cru of its accuracy, and he considers it "from the documentary point of view" the best of the war novels.[40]

Themes that Norton Cru stresses in his introduction run through the works of all three writers. Though they recount military engagements, they do so from the perspective of common soldiers and low-ranking officers, who hear about impending attacks first through rumor and can assess their outcome only through the new positions they are assigned afterward.[41] Rich in detail, all emphasize the physical sufferings and psychological responses of soldiers, not *faits militaires*. Both Genevoix and Bernier describe, after the anguish of long periods of waiting, a strange exultation when the moment of attack actually comes, followed by a momentary calm, almost detachment, during the engagement itself.[42] All three writers, like the trench press, relate the miseries caused by rain and mud, which never diminish.[43] Yet the detachment of battle gradually extends to a matter-of-factness toward the death of comrades, as though the perpetual horror of war has dulled reactions to its grimmest consequence. In his first month of battle, Genevoix's "heart skips a beat" when he encounters a dead man in a trench, but a few months later, when he learns of the death of his closest friend, he feels only "a hard coldness, a dry indifference, a kind of shrinking of the spirit."[44] Nonetheless, all write admiringly of the loyalty and solidarity that prevail among front-line troops, another trope of the trench press that Audoin-Rouzeau considers a form of myth-making.[45] Such a vision of comradeship, is, of course, a precondition for the notion of a typical or common experience that undergirds Norton Cru's analysis, the typical being the opposite of the "legendary."

Certainly these texts provide considerable evidence for the uniqueness of the ordinary soldier's experience, its difference from preexisting notions of war, and its inaccessibility to outsiders. Speaking of the heroic notion of war, Delvert writes that in August 1914 "our ideas about combat were so wrong that we all thought we would soon be fencing with sabers against German bayonets!"[46] While front soldiers quickly realize that this war does not correspond to the legendary version of it, others, notably staff officers, do not. All three writers regularly lambast the officer corps for their ignorance of conditions at the front and their heedless disregard for the lives of their soldiers. When Genevoix dispatches a report on German defensive activities at Les Éparges, requesting authorization to fire, he knows it will receive little attention, because the general staff "knows better than we what is going on. . . . They have plans, and ideas that they're attached to. Old ideas, solid ideas, and which have the admirable characteristic that reality must submit to them or risk being no more than a myth." Bernier describes the sudden arrival, one evening before an attack, of a general with his staff; on horseback, forming a "very Napoleonic group," the party gallops up to a high point, peers into the distance through binoculars, then departs, without any contact whatsoever with the soldiers present.[47] Delvert's notes bristle with savage invective directed at the high command, though his caricature of a punctilious staff officer, more concerned that he be consulted on every detail than with the safety of his men, has if anything even more bite.[48] Like Delvert, Bernier attacks the generals' "obstinate" attach-

Tropes in war narratives (trench press)

ment to an offensive strategy, despite its patent ineffectiveness and high cost in human life; late in the novel, his hero, Jean Favigny, reflects on how little commanders know about the experiences of ordinary soldiers. Despite Genevoix's effort, in a chapter entitled "The Others," to empathize with those who have not seen action, he falls in with the common opinion that "the people at headquarters are odious."[49]

The remoteness of staff officers from the "reality" of the war extends, in another theme prevalent in the trench press, to civilians' total lack of comprehension of military life. For Delvert the two are connected: when letters from home and civilian newspapers refer to the generals' compassion for their troops, this simply indicates how little they know.[50] In *Ceux de 14* the gap between soldiers and civilians emerges chiefly through the narrator's persistent inability, which he does not entirely understand, to write honestly about his experiences to his family. "So dry and so cold, my letter," he writes at one point. "So detached, after only a few days. . . . But what is a letter? What are the words one can write?" Bernier puts the same dilemma more bluntly, in a formula Audoin-Rouzeau finds often in the trench press: "I am torn between the desire to confide in others and the fear of not being understood."[51] Though a third-person narrative, *La percée* contains many such passages ostensibly taken from the hero's letters or diaries. This confessional mode, like Genevoix's throughout, functions as a certificate of authenticity, one that Norton Cru, among others, clearly found quite convincing.

Of the three authors, Bernier constructs the gap between soldiers and civilians most starkly, devoting an entire section of *La percée* to Favigny's home leave. The soldier shocks his parents' bourgeois friends with his frank condemnation of politicians, the high command, and civilian illusions about the war. One woman begins to cite the more positive comments of her son, an artilleryman, but he cuts her off: "Your son's not a foot soldier, ma'am, so he can just shut his trap. He has no right to talk. He knows nothing, nothing; he's got no idea of the war!" In a more meditative iteration of this theme, Bernier tells his readers, "He who has not understood with his body cannot speak to you. You yourselves, having read me, will not understand. But I have to devote myself to the impossible task. I have to for my peace of mind."[52] Norton Cru calls this "the alpha and the omega of all war literature written by witnesses," and considers Bernier's account of a soldier's relations with civilians far superior to those of Barbusse and others.[53]

Norton Cru knew, of course, that the public could also find many of the themes of "authentic" combatant literature in works he disparaged. Soldiers' hostility toward civilians and the general staff pulses through *Le feu* and *Les croix de bois*. In the latter, Dorgelès characterizes poilus as the only true soldiers, while both books supply considerable psychological detail.[54] Barbusse, moreover, frames the gap between combatants and civilians in much the same way that Genevoix does, albeit far less subtly. On leaving a café where the narrator and his friends have listened to civilian idiocies about the war, they "scarcely speak. It seems to us that we no longer know how to speak."[55]

Yet Barbusse's self-construction as spokesman for the combatant experience fails to impress Norton Cru; indeed, he attributes Barbusse's reputation entirely to the author's successful self-promotion as the sole repository for the soldier's "truth." Norton Cru condemns Barbusse for having "filtered his memories to purify them of all heterogeneous elements, distilled them to retain only the essence of his prejudices, of his preconceived opinions, sublimated them to reduce beings, things, and feelings to abstractions." The critic attacks precisely those qualities that give *Le feu* its literary feel: condensation, the construction of a distinctive space and time, a self-conscious preoccupation with form.[56] Dorgelès, whose novel Norton Cru considers entirely derivative of Barbusse, comes off even worse, since the critic at least credits Barbusse with sincere convictions, whereas, when Dorgelès "imitates *Le feu*, it is above all the book's success he wants to imitate."[57] Norton Cru supports his evaluations with lengthy and detailed (though, he claims, hardly exhaustive) lists of the writers' errors.

Whatever the utility of Norton Cru's assessments for more empirical studies of the war, his preferences also have to do with other, less obvious aspects of war literature, and with the structural effectiveness of the cultural work war narratives perform. Both Norton Cru's self-presentation and a posthumous account of his life by his sister stress his impartiality, meaning a lack of interest in partisan political quarrels. But when, in *Du témoignage*, he dismisses pacifist commitment as a justification for inaccuracy, he does so on the grounds not that combatant experience leaves no room for ideology, but that the "truth" would better serve the cause of peace.[58] Throughout *Témoins*, Norton Cru never attacks a writer on the basis of ideology alone, but, as in the case of Barbusse, for subordinating "accuracy," signified by precise detail and conformity to a consensually defined norm, to ideology. The problem is not the writer's point of view, but his method of persuading readers of its accuracy. We have already seen that Norton Cru approved of the methods (by no means identical) of Bernier, Delvert, and Genevoix; does it not stand to reason that he found their points of view congenial as well? A closer examination of those texts may yield some insights into their larger assumptions, and, beyond that, into the cultural work they perform.

Recall that, for the purposes of delimiting the genuine combatant experience, Norton Cru's category of "poilu" extended from the common soldier to the rank of captain (this was much broader than some combatant definitions, which restricted the term to common soldiers).[59] Bernier, Delvert, and

Genevoix, as well as Bernier's hero Favigny, cluster toward the top of that range: not career officers, at the outbreak of hostilities they were mobilized at ranks ranging from corporal (Bernier, the youngest) to lieutenant (Delvert) on the basis of their age, education, or background. All three were promoted over the course of the war, Delvert to the limit of Norton Cru's definition, captain; Genevoix from second lieutenant to lieutenant; Bernier, in stages, to second lieutenant.[60] Audoin-Rouzeau has noted that this group, the top level of non-commissioned officers and lower-level officers, dominated the trench press as well: soldiers with some authority, however minimal, yet in close enough contact with common soldiers to share in their rotation in and out of the front lines.[61] Such positions gave both authors and readers the opportunity at once to identify with the common soldier and, subtly, to affirm the class hierarchies that gave the narrators, or their heroes, authority.

All three narrators make mildly patronizing references to the soldiers under their command. Delvert, for example, refers to "my little privates [*mes petits troupiers*]," Bernier describes the awkwardness and inarticulateness of his "simple men [*bonhommes*]," while Genevoix at one point wishes he were a "simple poilu" so he could sleep a little later in the morning.[62] As we have seen, all three praise the courage and devotion of common soldiers, but they also validate their own authority by portraying themselves as compassionate and understanding. After a battle in which he shouts at his troops to keep them from fleeing in panic, Genevoix feels enormous regret, and relief to be back among them: "Every time I meet the glance of one of my soldiers, it is confidence and affection that are exchanged. That's all that is true. The anger, over there by the road, the threats, the rude gestures, that . . . that was a misunderstanding." Bernier's Favigny, now a sergeant-major, feels he must keep from his men his "personal opinion, my certainty that it will be a sterile sacrifice, because they— they're my section, my section, my section!"[63]

The markers of class range from the subtle to the unmistakable. After struggling to give his men some rest on a march, a lament from *Tosca* comes to Delvert's lips. When Genevoix wants to help his men dig shelters for the night, his orderly gently tells him that he lacks the experience of manual labor and will need assistance. More directly, Bernier has Favigny feel conscious of class differences when he arrives at the front, although the friendliness of his men soon dispels his fear that they would resent him.[64] Note that, however subtle, the marker of class never occurs alone, but always comes paired with an indication of the narrator's freedom from class prejudice. Genevoix refers to the expression on the face of his orderly, Pannechon, as "an irreverence in which I measure my inferiority"; elsewhere he insists on the social diversity and solidarity of the men he serves with. Examples of paternalism more heavy-handed than the narrators' own—in Genevoix, for example, a captain's pompous reference to "the obscure suffering" of the common soldier—inevitably come in for mockery.[65] The narrators want to be their soldiers' big brothers, not their fathers, as on the occasion that Genevoix's fellow lieutenant, Porchon, persuades one of his men to marry the mother of his child. But they claim the right to speak for their soldiers, in their name: when Genevoix assembles Porchon's men after his death, "We speak of him together; I am the one who speaks, but we speak of him together because their looks answer me."[66] This simple ceremony comes after a disastrous engagement that leaves Genevoix numb with shock, empty of both feeling and memory. His reassumption of authority the next day thus has a dual function, reassuring the reader as well as his men that a simple humanity lies at the heart of both his resilience and his reliability as a narrator.

The realism of these texts thus serves to reassert the validity of traditional social hierarchies in a way far more plausible, because more subtle, than outright praise for the high command could accomplish. The narrators of *Le feu* and *Les croix de bois* are common soldiers, their authors far less concerned with bolstering the social order; indeed, after the war Barbusse became one of the leading intellectuals in the French communist party. Norton Cru has little to say about the way his preferred narrators perform their command functions, but he does criticize Barbusse for obscuring the social diversity of the front-line troops, making them more proletarian than they actually were and practically eliminating the bourgeois and petit-bourgeois elements. In his introduction, Norton Cru provides statistics from the *Almanach du combattant* to demonstrate that "men from the liberal professions were sent to and kept at the front in a greater proportion than those from the other professions."[67] Is it simply coincidence that he favors works that, whatever their other merits, represent the service of such men as enlightened and humane?

If Barbusse and Dorgelès neglect signs of class difference at the front, they do, like Bernier and to a lesser extent Genevoix, use another sign of difference, gender, as a figure for the gap between soldiers and civilians. Audoin-Rouzeau has shown how women became, in trench newspapers, the emblem for everything the war was not. Mary Louise Roberts argues that stereotypes like the devoted mother or the adulterous wife in wartime and postwar literature provided a way of expressing moral responses to the war in culturally accessible, gendered terms.[68] Women as symbol of the decadence of the home front, of civilians' lack of gratitude for soldiers' sacrifice, recur in *Les croix de bois*. One soldier returns from orderly duty calling the front superior because there are no mocking women there; the death agony of a second is also an agony of indecision over whether to send an accusatory or forgiving message to his unfaithful wife; a third, invalided out, looks forward to his return home, then learns his wife has left him.[69] In *Le feu*, a soldier slips behind the lines to catch a glimpse of his wife in German-occupied Lens, and is shocked to see her smiling at the German officers she is lodging. Though few women appear in *Ceux de 14*, they nonetheless serve to emblematize the differences between civilians and soldiers. The unattractiveness of the female characters, whether shrewish, venal peasant women, a prostitute attached to a shady bomb defuser, or a group of women who recoil in horror from the wounded, accentuates the virtues of common soldiers. The rare exception, a model wife and mother, also serves to point up difference, when Porchon teases Genevoix for imitating her skills as a provider.[70]

Although *La percée* includes an extended home leave, Bernier offers a somewhat narrower range of female types: aloof, foolish, supportive (the hero's mother and grandmother) and pliant. Favigny seduces a young woman with bold talk about the war, then leaves her without regret to return to the front. The entire novel, however, constitutes a paean to masculine prowess and male bonding, with regular references to virile self-mastery, the boldness of the *peuple mâle*, and "the goodness of our male hearts" as soldiers accept civilian tribute for their willingness to risk their lives.[71] The tribute involves mostly male noncombatants, chaplains and nurses, bidding farewell to soldiers about to march to the front, but Bernier genders the image by transposing gratitude into the "love" of France, both linguistically and in traditional imagery female, for her soldiers. When a little later Favigny reflects that if everyone shared the combatant experience, the war would end, the first figures he uses to represent civilians are women.[72] Thus the gendering of the divide between home front and battlefield, while retaining some degree of moral ambiguity, leaves the uniqueness of the combatant experience intact.

Without contesting the claims of *Ceux de 14* to be "one of the most faithful acts of witness [*témoignages*]" to the First World War, Maurice Rieuneau has called attention to the "novelistic" skills Genevoix brought to its composition: dramatization, counterpoint narratives, scene-setting, and so on.[73] It would be superfluous to apply such an analysis to other texts that, whatever their truth-claims and the generic conventions they follow, clearly employ the artifice of narrative to construct experience. Of greater interest, although ignored by Norton Cru, are the ways in which these texts, across the critic's evaluative categories, thematize issues of perception, testimony, knowledge, and memory. The "performance," to recall Felman's phrase, of the act of witness proves in these accounts to involve a complex layering of gestures and reflection.

In the introduction to *Témoins*, Norton Cru devotes some pages to refuting the "paradox attributed to Stendhal," the idea, derived from Fabrice del Dongo's confused passage through the battle of Waterloo, that soldiers taking part in a battle cannot really understand it.[74] Yet many of the war writers emphasize the limits of their knowledge, sometimes amounting to a kind of sensory deprivation. At one point in *Le feu*, soldiers reflect on how little they know about the battle in which they have participated; like Dorgelès's narrator, some risk their necks to obtain a better view of the battle.[75] Genevoix shows an acute sensitivity to the sense of sight, and his usage endorses the unique access to experience that vision confers: of a sudden shelling that kills three cardplayers, "I looked, and I saw this thing in its brutal horror"; of an officer hit by a missile, "I saw it, saw it clearly." A good officer he describes as having "eyes everywhere."[76] But in battle, or marching in the rain, he feels as though blinded; he refers to one battle, which he can judge only by sound, as "this invisible drama."[77] The most one can derive from visual sensation in battle, Genevoix implies, is what happens as the Germans launch a surprise attack: "Everything was confused in a single impression."[78]

In a crucial way, moreover, these descriptions depend on knowledge either prior or subsequent to "experience," and external to it. Genevoix does not have simply an "impression," but an "impression of an unforeseeable and nasty attack," the latter a category that, in effect, transforms his multiple sense-impressions into a single experience. One of the prime sources of such ordering categories consisted in the stories soldiers told each other. The war narratives cast storytelling as a basis of soldiers' solidarity, a habitual act responding to a basic need to wrest order out of multiple sensations. These stories did not always have to do with the war: at a slack moment, the soldiers in *La percée* "developed their friendship by telling each other about their lives." For Dorgelès, the stories told during periods of recreation have a ritual aspect, and are "always the same," while those recounted by cooks, supposedly in the know, could not always be trusted.[79] Barbusse and Genevoix do not comment much on storytelling, but both incorporate many acts of narration into their own stories, making clear the way in which secondary narratives work their way into memories of first-hand experience.[80]

With varying degrees of explicitness, all these texts convey a considered sense of the mental processes that form impressions, convey knowledge, and construct memories. Certain events, according to Dorgelès, "inscribed themselves in [their] thought in precise strokes, brutally, without emotion," although we might note Norton Cru's extreme skepticism that the related incident, a kind of fistfight in the middle of a battle, could ever have taken place.[81] More often, as Genevoix puts it, many events become confused in single impressions. In *Le feu*, after some soldiers on kitchen detail, searching only for matches, have a bizarre encounter with a German soldier, the French soldiers "reconstructed, hastily and in confusion, the drama from which they were awakening without really knowing it."[82] Frequently, the people in these narratives have difficulty making sense of the situations in which they find themselves. The problems range from a simple disparity between reality and sensation, as when Genevoix writes, "It must be cold. Nonetheless, my head and my hands are burning," to a kind of mental paralysis. On the train returning from his home leave, "Favigny, bewildered, could not understand himself, life seemed a mystery to him, he could not conceive of [*réaliser*] the war in which he was again immersing himself."[83] Understanding could sometimes come from unlikely sources, whether a cliché-ridden official bulletin in Genevoix or, in Bernier, a troop review that, for all its traditionalism, Favigny and his men find oddly reassuring.[84] Seeing, however, does not always promote understanding; for Genevoix it may produce only the illusion of knowledge. Reflecting on some excesses his men have committed, he reflects: "I watched them make war, and I thought that I saw them, perhaps even that I knew them." Or again, "I wanted to be close to them, and for them to feel me close to them; because of that, sometimes, I believed that their eyes betrayed them, and their thoughts. . . . But do I really know? What moved me in their eyes, was it not a reflection of myself?"[85]

What ultimately come between Genevoix and his men are his own memories, "this hidden world of memories and hopes, this prodigious world that will die if I die." From the earliest days of the war, memory plays a crucial role in all the narratives, but not a uniformly positive or reassuring one. As in the passage just cited, memory divides as much as it unites; memory interferes with current perception; like all precious things, memory constitutes a burden that sometimes becomes too heavy to bear. Repeatedly over the course of Genevoix's narrative, "memories flare up" as he comes across the scenes of earlier experiences. But this means, in good Bergsonian fashion, that he cannot always distinguish between the past and the present: "I did not see, at my feet, the slope of the hill, nor the Longeau in the valley, nor the battered houses of Les Éparges. But I saw before me other desolate slopes whose color, even in that light, was that of mud."[86] A salvo from the German artillery "stings with the memory of our last night on lookout, in this very place." Similarly, in *La percée*, Favigny, when under attack, relives the disastrous first battle in which he took part.[87] All these impressions fall into Freud's category of "screen memory," one that "owes its value as a memory not to its own content but to the relation existing between that content and some other, that has been suppressed." The formation of screen memories, Freud tells us, involves "conflict, repression, substitution involving a compromise," readily apparent in the emotive energy with which the writers endow them.[88] Indeed, in an engagement at Les Éparges toward the end of *Ceux de 14*, an exhausted Genevoix is assailed by "feverish images" of dead comrades, so vivid and so frequent that he has trouble focusing on the battle at hand.[89]

If memory constitutes a burden, forgetting, *oubli*, offers a respite, a tactic of survival. To a fellow lieutenant who has just returned to the front after being wounded, Genevoix tells of some of the horrors he has missed, and says, "You

memory + forgetting

*can we seperate memory and
experience*

can't know how much the sum of these memories weighs, some evenings. And then, above all, when they come back, they are never, never alone: regrets weigh along with them."[90] Forgetting, as Favigny realizes when he first arrives at the front, has to be learned, and can be accomplished most easily during periods of rest behind the lines.[91] This odd dialectic, of course, serves to set up a distinction between voluntary and involuntary memories, one that parallels the structuring difference between soldiers and civilians. The burden of memory comes from those memory-images—and Genevoix uses the words *souvenirs* and *images* more or less synonymously—that a soldier cannot repress: "Oh! to have to see that, and to keep it forever in one's memory," Dorgelès writes of the sight of a soldier's execution by firing squad.[92]

But poilus also retain certain voluntary memories, chiefly those of their dead comrades, not only out of duty but out of self-regard. Though they would prefer to forget much of what they have experienced, they fear being forgotten themselves, above all by civilians. Walking among some graves from the first stage of the war, one of Genevoix's fellow officers foresees "a misfortune worse than these massacres: perhaps those unhappy souls will be forgotten very quickly. No, listen: they will be the dead of the beginning, *ceux de 14*. There will be so many others! . . . Decidedly, since the war is settling in like a canker, who knows if there won't come a time when the world will have become accustomed to going on with this abomination upon it?"[93]

That Genevoix later chose a phrase from this passage as the collective title for his war narratives makes explicit the way in which writing itself functions as an act of commemoration. We have already seen that combatants despaired of communicating the reality of their experience to civilians; the idea of paying tribute to their dead comrades thus supplies a purpose for the exercise of writing. "My dead friends back there call me every day," Favigny reflects in *La percée*. "'Have you told, you who have come back? or are you too forgetting? Are you betraying us, you too?'" Not long after, the "immense memory" of his comrades at the front both inspires and empowers him to tell the truth to the arrogant bourgeois he encounters during his home leave.[94]

Yet none of these texts takes a very optimistic view of memory as a collective activity. "People will forget," Dorgelès writes in his typically melodramatic conclusion. "The mourning veils will fall like dead leaves. The image of the dead soldier will slowly disappear from the consoled heart of those they [*sic*] loved so much. And all the dead will die a second time."[95] But for Bernier the problem has a different dimension, involving the uniqueness of experience; he expounds on it with an almost poetic bleakness.

> The dead for whom they weep, the mourners did not see them die; they did not hear their cries and were not horrified at their wounds. They do not know the white faces, the tan turning green.

So they do not grasp the final separation at all. . . .

To relieve their suffering, they attribute to dead fighting men their poor noncombatant feelings, stupidly possessed by society and its "proprieties."[96]

Those who have no one to mourn come off even worse, for they will understand the dead only as a statistic. Bernier's sober reflections recall Genevoix's construction of memory as a kind of solitude, the indissoluble ground of every soldier's individuality. Yet here the individuality of memory becomes a figure for the breach between soldiers and civilians, a gap of experience that memory cannot hope to bridge.

The sense of difference that separated veterans from noncombatants carries over to postwar literature, where, along with the fragility of memory, it becomes one of the principal themes. Joseph Jolinon's *La tête brûlée* (The daredevil), the second volume in an autobiographical tetralogy in which the author takes the name Claude Lunant, typifies the genre.[97] The book recounts the difficulties Lunant encounters in publishing his first novel, like Jolinon's *Le valet de gloire* a fictionalized memoir of the war. Again and again publishers tell him that the public has lost interest in the war, that he would have better luck with adventure fiction; the firms who do indicate some interest try to cheat him out of his royalties. Meanwhile, Lunant's immediate circle shows no gratitude for his war service. By the time Lunant's novel is published, after many delays and to mixed reviews that he attributes to commercial motives, the veteran is sustaining himself by working the land, writing only on the side.[98]

Because most veterans who wrote tended to idealize wartime solidarity among soldiers, as, indeed, they had done during the war itself, class tends to appear in their works as an unwelcome reassertion of social norms that soldiers had managed to slough off. In *La tête brûlée*, Jolinon disposes of the issue by having Lunant, from a family of prosperous farmers, embrace a former comrade who is only a gardener.[99] Gender, on the other hand, was freely available as a signifier of difference, if anything intensified from wartime precedents. For Jolinon, gender provides an answer to a tricky problem of characterization: how to portray Lunant (that is, himself) as seeking commercial success and fame while protecting him from the taint that veterans normally attached to such ambitions.

In the novel, Lunant's ambition derives solely from a need for a material base from which to reclaim his wartime lover, the mother of his child, who has married an odious newspaper publisher. The character Madeleine is oddly ambiguous: her features are described as "masculine," and in most scenes she displays a chilly self-assurance, entirely free of sentiment.[100] Clearly, however, Lunant has no hope of winning her without the ability to support her in the lavish manner to which she has become accustomed. At one point he reflects that all women are demanding: "Their heart descends to their shoes. Anyone who wants to please them must be good enough for their shoes or show up dressed in fine shoes himself."[101] In line with common perceptions at the time, "woman" both causes and emblematizes the corruption of poilu idealism. Though the pair never break off relations, Lunant never wins her outright either, and the distance between them, reduced to the male incomprehension of fashion— Lunant can never remember to compliment Madeleine on her hat, which vexes her—becomes a figure not only for the postwar gender divide, but for the gap between veterans and civilian society in general.[102]

The first half of *La tête brûlée* has remarkable parallels with Genevoix's novel *La joie*, also published in 1924. The heroes in both novels campaign for Parliament without any faith in politics, and feel contempt for the politicians on their party lists; both are in love with women who had married shirkers during the war; both find the complacency of their rural hometowns stifling. But in the second half of *La tête brûlée* Jolinon subordinates issues of politics and memory (though not of gender) to an obsessive account of the corruption of the Paris publishing world, while in *La joie*, a more successful if more conservative novel, politics, memory, and gender remain tightly intertwined. *La joie* tells the story of a young wounded veteran (he has lost a foot) who, shortly after being elected to Parliament in 1919, returns to his native village, St. Gervais, to recuperate from tuberculosis.[103] Illness and depression force the hero, Pierre Andrianne, to reconsider his past life and commitments; as the story develops, Pierre grows increasingly impatient with the stale rhetoric of politicians, with the pettiness of local politics, and even with the internal divisions of the veterans' movement.[104] These reactions accurately reflect those of most well-educated veterans and former officers at the time, groups to which both Genevoix and his central character belonged.[105] But the plot revolves around Pierre's relationship with a young widow called Hélène, whose troubled past epitomizes the gender uncertainties of the new France. During the war, while living in Paris with her husband, an older man she did not love, she had an affair with an old schoolmate of Pierre's, a medical student he considers a shirker (*embusqué*).

On one level, Genevoix presents Pierre's personal crisis—at one point he actually strikes Hélène, causing a temporary breach in their relationship—as the straightforward result of jealousy.[106] Yet the character feels this jealousy not toward Hélène's dead husband, whom he had never liked, but toward his own friend, the shirker; at one point, referring to the latter, he says to her accusingly, "As I was fighting, as I was shivering in Boche-land [*Bochie*, in a German prisoner-of-war camp], this man set himself up at your place and didn't leave." Pierre wants, quite simply, to possess Hélène; after they first make love he reflects, "This woman was his, absolutely," a sentiment echoed by Claude Lunant after his first postwar tryst with Madeleine. Yet her previous liaison with a shirker makes that possession virtually impossible by implicitly devaluing the masculine sacrifice in which the soldier had been engaged.[107] Sexual jealousy here instantiates a crisis of masculinity; as it does in much postwar fiction, this crisis flows directly from the male protagonist's tortured memory of the war years, when, as Roberts has put it, "female infidelity symbolized the isolation, alienation, and emasculation of the male combatant."[108]

In a significant way, moreover, Genevoix makes Pierre's frustration, and its eventual resolution, indissoluble from his political maturation. In the first dramatic step in this process, Pierre resigns his seat in Parliament and sends a long, rambling denunciation of contemporary politics to a local socialist newspaper. But when the newspaper's editor comes to congratulate him personally for his courage, Pierre tells him that he would never have written as he did if he had had a woman at his side to comfort and console him.[109] At the end of the novel, safely married to Hélène and expecting their first child, Pierre writes a letter to the same man. Now that Pierre has obtained from Hélène "the divine maternal tenderness of which a woman's heart is capable," his crisis of masculinity has resolved itself into a patriarchal vision.[110] "I wish only," Pierre writes, "for my life to unfold, according to its own norm, on its own terms, in harmony with the heritage of my race, along with the men of my native soil, from my dead parents to my children who will one day be born."[111]

From his election to Parliament at age thirty-four, to his illness, to his ideological uncertainty, Pierre's entire situation results from his wartime experience. In this respect alone, *La joie* participates in the construction of a discourse and a culture of commemoration. But commemoration itself, in the form of the building and dedication of a local war memorial, plays an important, indeed a crucial, role in the novel. For Pierre's disgust at the petty bickering that marked the construction of the monument, and his revulsion at the hollow rhetoric of the dedication ceremony, prompt him to resign from Parliament and launch an attack on contemporary politics. At the dedication he remains unmoved, like Norton Cru's image of the war writer, "a dispassionate observer, his own master." By the end of the novel, however, after he has conquered his inner demons, Pierre finds the recollection of the ceremony immensely moving. Indeed, through his belated understanding of the monument dedication ceremony, he comes to find in the sacrifice of his comrades and the suffering of their families the basis for a new creed, a simple love of humanity.[112]

On one level, official commemoration of the Great War in France sought to present the war dead as examples of devotion and self-sacrifice, much as Pierre construes them at the end of the novel. Yet more is at stake in this internal conflict, this prolonged crisis of masculinity: the gendering of commemoration itself, and beyond it of postwar politics. By undergoing this painful transformation, Pierre effectively reenacts the war experience, which Genevoix, at the very end of *Ceux de 14*, casts as fundamentally life-altering: "Oh, my friends, is it my fault if I have changed so much?"[113] He thus proves himself a true poilu, a worthy object of commemoration. Leaving aside, although hardly resolving, the questions about memory he raised in *Ceux de 14*, Genevoix effectively naturalizes commemoration not so much as a masculine activity, since as a responsibility it involves the whole community, but as a tribute to masculine sacrifice.[114] Genevoix has little use for the old political class that the war left in place, but the alternative he offers is simply a new type of man, one whose sacrifice has qualified him for leadership—and earned the support of a loving, domesticated woman.

Jean Schlumberger's *Le camarade infidèle* (The unfaithful comrade, 1922) lacks both the corrosive irony of Jolinon and the lyricism of Genevoix, who was to become celebrated for the evocations of nature in his prose.[115] Yet the discursive connection between memory and gender is just as central to *Le camarade infidèle* as to the works of Genevoix and Jolinon. In the opening dialogue a war widow, Clymène Heuland, challenges her uncle, a general under whose command her husband had died. The general insists that it is best not to speak of the sufferings of the dead. Perhaps, Clymène says simply, survivors could help civilians understand the war simply by talking about their own feelings.[116] Thus the novel begins by undercutting the basic distinction between veterans and noncombatants, the latter, as usual, represented by a woman.

The central character in the novel, Vernois, a captain who had served with Heuland, dislikes General de Pontaubault and sympathizes with the widow. Respecting her devotion to her husband's memory, despite the contempt in which her aristocratic family had held him, Vernois has no interest in curing her of it, as her uncle desires. Yet the more he learns about the dead man, the more troubled he becomes. Heuland had had an affair with his children's governess, his war record had been undistinguished, his work as an inventor before the war almost completely without merit. Yet Vernois resists telling Clymène any of this, and like the general, avoids telling her about Heuland's lingering, painful death on the battlefield.

Despite the narrator's sympathetic portrayal of Clymène, *Le camarade infidèle* in the end preserves the gender gap that other texts had constructed around memory. Early in their acquaintance, Clymène tells Vernois that, while she had viewed her attachment to her husband's memory as a manifestation of feminine weakness, he had given her hope that memory could take a more virile and reasoned form.[117] Yet while Vernois manages to speak honestly about Heuland's death to the governess, who in his eyes forfeited the respect due womankind when she betrayed her mistress, he cannot do so with Clymène. Vernois's brother chides him for placing a higher value on the emotional bonds of wartime comradeship than on truth, but he clings to his sense that sacrifice in

Gender gap in memory

war sanctifies the memory of otherwise unworthy men. "How can we separate our innate worth from what the war has put into us?" he asks, and adds that Heuland's death alone merits that he not be forgotten.[118] By the end of the novel neither Clymène nor Vernois has any illusions either about Heuland or about their feelings for him; Clymène even implies that the love she declared in a letter found on the dead man's body was in part feigned. Vernois, who admires Clymène but is not in love with her, proposes marriage to her out of respect not so much for Heuland's memory as for memory itself, the last vestige of the code of masculine solidarity he had practiced during the war.[119]

Does Schlumberger, then, share the belief of his character Clymène in a distinctively masculine form of memory? Only partially. The "masculine" memory of former combatants, like their "vision" of the war, has an astringency and self-consciousness that denies memory any external value: memory will not make remembering subjects better people, it will not moralize politics, it will not redeem the loss of so many lives. Memory's value comes only from the ethical commitments it instantiates in individuals—male individuals, for women lack the kind of memory that would prompt such commitments. In this way, Schlumberger's altogether cooler and more philosophical account joins in the cultural work performed by *La joie*. For despite the latter's sentimental conclusion, Genevoix hardly suggests that the commemorative ceremonies in St. Gervais had any value in themselves: only Pierre Andrianne's new-found commitment to perpetuating the patriarchal order grants them a kind of retrospective redemption. Skepticism about collective forms of memory would prove an enduring subtext for the interwar culture of commemoration, and at some level all commemorative efforts had to combat it. Ultimately, this attitude lay rooted in competing claims to authority over memory, a contest in which all victories were doomed to be partial and impermanent.

Seeing Memory   Battlefield tourism

When Vernois informs General de Pontaubault that he plans to take Clymène to the Chemin des Dames, site of the bloody 1917 battle in which her husband had died, the general tells him not to bother, since he had already taken his niece there. In a voice that recalls Norton Cru's, Vernois replies, "I was more closely involved than you were, general, in the details of what happened. I can convey them to her in a livelier fashion."[120] At the site, however, Vernois is struck by how small the hill that had been their objective now seems. When Clymène admires the panoramic vista, he admits that from the trenches the soldiers' view had been considerably more restricted. Above all, he had not anticipated how the place "would lack a language for those who did not know [it] in its original state." When he points to the spot where the shell that killed her husband struck,

Clymène staggers and falls to her knees "like a soldier who has been hit," taking a clump of earth in her hands; her emotion is so patent that her son turns away in embarrassment.[121] Whether consciously or not, the widow here performs the act of seeing as a bodily experience, yet she has trouble conjuring up memories of her husband. In the end, Clymène and Vernois, unable to master their own faculties of memory (*mémoire*), go looking for objectified memories, *souvenirs*. They fail to find Clymène's objective, a helmet, but turn up numerous cartridges, containers, and flares. Even in the absence of a distinct memory-image, the trip provides the emotional closure both had desired, and at its end Clymène is no longer haunted by the tragic inadequacy of her husband's life.[122]

As Schlumberger pictures it, the visit to the battlefield does not overcome the gendered memory gap, for that is unbridgeable. Yet nothing in his description contradicts the fundamental claim of those promoting such visits, that they would develop an empathic understanding of the war "par la vision même des choses et des vestiges" (the actual vision of things).[123] Clearly such claims rest on the familiar privileging of vision as a form of knowledge, even if the sites in question required what Dean MacCannell calls "markers"—guidebooks, plaques, monuments, a guided tour—both to make clear the kind of knowledge on offer and to transmit it.[124] Many visitors were, like Clymène, seeking above all personal knowledge, and public and private agencies went out of their way to assist those seeking information about dead or missing relatives. Yet texts that construct tourism as a source of understanding offered experience of two kinds, both symbolically present in Clymène's tour of the Chemin des Dames. One urged visitors to "see what the victors saw" by looking down, at the debris of equipment, uniforms, and personal effects they could still find on the battlefields.[125] A second approach offered a more panoramic view: as the *Indicateur du tourisme* put it in 1921, it had no pretension of enabling, or compelling, visitors to relive the battle of the Marne; it simply wanted to point out the salient points that all good French citizens should know and remember.[126] The difference between these types of tourism had to do not so much with their fundamental assumptions, which were broadly similar, but with their points of view, both literal and metaphorical.

The term "battlefield tourism" encompasses various activities that had their roots in the war years. Visits to the front lines by civilians, notably politicians and journalists, often crop up in the trench press. Soldiers did not welcome such tours of inspection—in *Le feu* Barbusse refers to "trench tourists," who he says make soldiers feel like zoo animals—and disparaged the claims to knowledge that returning visitors made, but they served as a precedent for less official visits.[127] Barely a year after the end of the most active phase of the battle of Verdun, a former mayor of Verdun, Péquart, described for a Lorraine newspaper the atmosphere in the city, still within earshot of German guns and just a few miles from the front lines. From the ruins of an old rampart, Péquart could observe several groups of between twenty-five and thirty people, including primary school and lycée students, touring areas of the old town destroyed in German shelling. On each street the state had stationed a wounded veteran of the battle to provide commentary, and it was also taking pains to preserve the ruins. "It is a great historical event," Péquart writes, "that the visitors are for a few moments attempting to relive in their minds." Though Péquart gives few details about the visitors, he notes that some were speaking foreign languages.[128] A phrasebook and summary guide for British visitors to France published in 1916, though it did not list the war zone as an attraction, offered a four-page glossary of "military vocabulary," including the French equivalents for such terms as "howitzer," "martial law," "rifle cleaning rod," and "wound," which it mistranslates as *blessé*, actually the masculine noun or adjective meaning "wounded."[129]

It is hard to believe that private tourism to Verdun could have been extensive before the war's end, given that visitors could have found shelter only in makeshift dormitories—even in 1919, the town had only three functioning hotels—and would not have had much freedom of movement. But in another sector, the Marne, the possibility of fairly independent tourism seems to have arisen as early as 1917. At a luncheon that year in Chantilly to launch the Michelin series of battlefield guides, which after the war would grow to twenty-five titles in several languages, the eminent historian Ernest Lavisse hailed the appearance of the guides as a way of promoting serious-minded inspections of the battle sites, which he envisioned as living lessons in "present history."[130]

Within a few months of the armistice, the Office National du Tourisme, a semiautonomous government agency established in 1910, was working to establish tent hotels and practicable roads for visitors to the battle sites around Reims, Verdun, and Arras.[131] The enormity of the destruction, however, made the task difficult, and the majority of travelers who depended on trains and buses faced particular hardships. The Touring-Club de France had to scale back ambitious plans for student tours of the battlefields in the summer of 1919 because of problems with transportation and catering; that June one association official reported seeing posters advertising train excursions to the "devastated regions" covered over or torn away.[132] As late as the following spring one veterans' newspaper was appealing to the railroad companies to restore local train service in the Aisne for families wishing to visit cemeteries at Easter. The Michelin guide to the Chemin des Dames published in the fall of 1920 advised travelers to pack a box lunch for at least part of the itinerary, since no restaurants were available. Visitors to Verdun and the Artois had to wait until late 1921 or 1922 for regular train or train-bus service to battlefield sites, as well as guided bus tours.[133]

Many of these problems, of course, stemmed from the dimensions of the devastation: 62,000 kilometers of roads and 5,000 of railroad tracks to rebuild; 11,000 public buildings (schools, town halls, churches) to restore or replace. At the same time, returning refugees had to be sheltered, but 350,000 houses in the ten departments of the war zone had been destroyed or rendered uninhabitable. The main priorities in clearing the battlefields involved recovering human remains and, where possible, restoring the land to cultivation (2.5 million hectares had been lost); making these areas safe for tourists did not rank high on the list.[134]

But beyond these practical difficulties, the notion of tourism itself provoked certain resistances. One type of visitor that everyone agreed should be accommodated was the "pilgrim," a widow, parent, or child coming to pray or grieve at a loved one's grave, or, even more poignantly, to try to locate a missing body.[135] At the other extreme, both those promoting tourism and those hostile to it opposed what one veteran called *pèlerinages à grand spectacle*, or show-business tours, a vague notion that seems to have encompassed smoking, picnicking, loud talking, and the sale of merchandise at sites.[136] But between these two types, there was much disagreement over what constituted a true "pilgrimage." Writing in 1921, the bishop of Verdun, Charles Ginisty, argued that "to see and walk through these tragic places . . . so that one can form an exact idea of the great war" constituted a kind of civic duty for all French men and women.[137] Lavisse had put forward a similar notion in his 1917 speech at the launch of the Michelin travel guides. He hoped that after the war tours would not turn into "pleasure trains," the battlefields into "fair grounds," but asserted that soberly conducted, informative tours would communicate to visitors the "truth" about the war. The preface to those guidebooks characterized their itineraries "not as a simple run through the devastated regions, but as a real pilgrimage."[138]

Groups like the Touring-Club and the Office National du Tourisme had to tread a fine line in presenting their argument—now familiar, then relatively new—that tourism offered important economic benefits. "Profit" was a delicate word in a society that made the term "profiteers" signify the polar opposite first of soldiers, then of all those who had suffered during the war. In a pamphlet on the potential contributions of tourism to the postwar economy, Léon Auscher, vice president of the Touring-Club de France, noted that the country needed to remedy an unfavorable balance of payments and boost a declining franc, both consequences of wartime indebtedness. Auscher described tourism as a kind of "internal export," since it brought foreigners and foreign currency to France with minimal investment at home. Sensitive to the pejorative connotations of the word, Auscher declared that if tourism had formerly signified "the egoistical art of traveling well," henceforth it should be "the national industry of fine hospitality." The idea of the "internal export" implies that France would market its own best qualities for the consumption of travelers; the commemorated, in other words, become a tangible asset. In the wake of war, people from all over the world would want to visit France to pay the "tribute of admiration that the best of our blood sacrificed to the best of causes has earned us." Taking such visits for granted, the pamphlet principally addresses the problem of providing incentives for travelers to prolong their stays elsewhere in France. But Auscher made regular trips to towns in the war zone as well, and he had his work cut out for him.[139]

Like the poilus before them, residents of the devastated areas did not want their privations to become a spectacle for curious strangers. Another Touring-Club official noted that even businessmen in the war zone had been reluctant to invest in hotels and tourist infrastructure, unaware that "not only was there a patriotic task to accomplish, but also an excellent opportunity, a safe, remunerative investment." Local government officials were even more resistant:

The municipal authorities in the great martyr-cities have seen this project [tourist development] as a response to some kind of unhealthy curiosity, and they have fled from it in horror. "No tourists here!" cried a mayor, one of the most courageous and meritorious, but poorly informed about the ideas that guide the leaders of the Touring-Club in this instance. To show our ruins to our children, to our friends is, on the contrary, sacred work, and at the same time useful work, because all these travelers will leave behind some beneficial manna that will help restore our beloved cities.[140]

The words *pie* (pious, sacred) and *manne* (manna), the latter with its biblical overtones, contribute mightily to performing the work of this text.

In 1921 Parliament passed a law providing free transportation to war cemeteries for relatives of the dead, thus ensuring the continual flow of "pilgrims" to the former war zone. Whatever their doubts, towns did expand their hotel resources and made efforts to welcome visitors. When a new hotel catering to tourists opened in Verdun in 1923, the Touring-Club praised its owner, declaring that while Verdun would always be "the city of glory," it was fitting that it should also become "one of the great tourist centers of France."[141] Although in 1921 the prefect of the Aisne responded to reports of inappropriate behavior by visitors by putting up signs urging respect for the dead at one of the principal sites on the Chemin des Dames, most such reports could not be confirmed. In 1920 the prefect of the Nord wrote that he saw no need for special battlefield regulations in his department.[142] After 1921 even rumors of disrespectful tourists tapered off, suggesting a general level of satisfaction about visitors' conduct, but whether this involved a change in behavior or modified standards is less clear.[143]

Certainly texts that attempted to structure the visitor's experience made every effort to vaunt their seriousness of purpose. Indeed, all the Michelin guides published before 1920 cast themselves as memorials, bearing on the title page the dedication "To the memory of the workers and employees of the Michelin factories who died gloriously for the fatherland."[144] The books made clear the difference between idle curiosity and what a "notice to the reader" in the Marne volumes called "a true pilgrimage," for

seeing is not enough, the visitor must also understand: ruins are more impressive when coupled with a knowledge of their origin and destruction. A stretch of country which might seem dull and uninteresting to the unenlightened eye, becomes transformed at the thought [*souvenir*] of the battles [*lutte*] that raged there.[145]

"At once a practical guide and a history," each guidebook would contain a comprehensive history of operations that precedes the actual itinerary, precise accounts of the battles in each sector described, and many sketch maps to connect the narrative to the sites. Michelin also made a fairly stringent truth claim, declaring that the reader would find "no attempt at literary effect; the truth [*la réalité*] is too beautiful and tragic to be altered for the sake of embellishing the story; therefore the author has carefully sifted the great volume of evidence available, and selected only that obtained from official documents or reliable eyewitnesses."[146]

The Michelin's use of the word *lutte*, in such close proximity to *souvenirs*, would be sufficient to taint its project for Norton Cru; when he presents his list of "false ideas about war," the notion that "la guerre est une lutte" (war is struggle) comes first.[147] Another clue to the series' orientation comes in a sentence describing the verbal and visual information offered: "In the course of the description, a brief military commentary is given on the numerous views and panoramas contained in this book."[148] Recall that none of the war writers we have examined had much interest in so-called *faits militaires*, which Norton Cru considered vestiges of the legendary, heroic account of war. But the Michelin guides, like most of their competitors, consistently emphasize military history of a traditional kind, with generals and commanders as the major players, strategic decisions and attacks the key events, and few details below the divisional level. It is, quite literally, history from above. As the introduction to the third volume on the Marne, *La trouée de Revigny*, puts it:

The study in detail of this stupendous event will continue for centuries. But its main lines, which we have been at pains to trace, already stand out clearly. They recall all the old French traditions. The clearness of the plan, the suppleness of maneuver, and the bold use of reserves, remind [one] of the Napoleonic era. The enthusiasm which galvanized soldiers and chiefs alike, dates back to the Revolution.[149]

The guidebooks covering the first battle of the Marne are divided geographically into sectors corresponding to the successive phases of battle, and take special pains to situate the reader both spatially and historically. Visual aids include two-page color route maps, smaller schematic maps, and a number of orienting photos. At the beginning of the battlefield itinerary in volume 1, one reads the following, keyed to a photograph of burned houses in the village of Chauconin, just west of Meaux: "After having had a peep at the little country church, we take a few steps along the path shown in the *view below*. The houses which border it still show traces of the incendiary fires of September 1914."[150] Photographs could offer evidence as well as direction: the tour of Senlis illustrates virtually every building and street mentioned, with the text decidedly secondary. We see the same views before and after German damage, photographs of German soldiers in the town, with the note that they forced the photographer to take them, a shot of a fire in progress, and a picture captioned "Marks of German Bullets in the Hospital."[151] The guide provides a detailed account of the arrest of several civilian hostages including the mayor, Odent, who was eventually executed on charges of ordering civilians to fire on the Germans. A reproduction of a painting depicting the execution of hostages in Senlis during the Hundred Years' War comes with the comment: "Six centuries have elapsed, but it will be seen that the Germans still retain the mental attitude of the Middle Ages."[152]

Throughout the guidebook, the tourist has the opportunity to view the war from the perspective not of common soldiers but of commanders and VIPs. In Chantilly, the guide pauses at some length in front of the house that Joffre occupied as commander-in-chief, commenting reverentially on his "strict routine" and praising the rigorous isolation on which he insisted in order to keep his mind clear.[153] Precisely this kind of isolation, of course, would later attract the criticism of many war writers and of Norton Cru. At Barcy, north of Meaux, the visitor can retrace the steps of former British prime minister H. H. Asquith, shown in two photographs (fig. 1.1). Here Michelin invites the tourist to participate in the construction of a memorial landscape. Asquith had come to lay a wreath at a mass grave, and at the entrance to the village "the tourist will see the site of the great commemorative monument which is to be raised by subscription." Outside of Étrépilly, the guide points out, and illustrates, "the memorial raised by the engineers in front of the cemetery, at the place where the battles of Étrépilly reached their climax." Throughout, cemeteries and isolated graves are scrupulously pointed out.[154]

But the perspective most typical of Michelin's approach to the Marne is the panoramic. Visitors receive precise instructions on how to reach strategic views of former battlefields: "Turn to the right at the foot of the slope into Étrépilly, and on leaving the village, take the road to the left; cross the river, turn again to the left and follow the track which climbs the plateau. After a few hundred yards the right slope disappears. It was at this point that the Panorama D was

FIGURE 1.1. H. H. Asquith visiting the battlefield. *Michelin Guide to the Battlefields of the World War*, vol. 1, *The First Battle of the Marne*, pp. 104–5. © Michelin from *The First Battle of the Marne*. Permission no. 9808388.

taken, showing, from the German side, the battlefield seen from the French side in Panorama B" (fig. 1.2).[155] From this spot visitors can trace the German forward lines and the progress of a French attack. Broken lines leading from the photograph to captions identify points described in the text. Not only in this view but in others, however, one cannot but notice that the points of interest, including roads, farms, and natural features, lie at a considerable distance from the observation point. The reader, and presumably the viewer, has no choice but to take the identifying captions on faith. In the photograph, at least, the marked sites are too small and indistinct to be matched definitely with the words describing them.

Michelin presents, in effect, a general's-eye view: only a visitor on horseback, like the ones in *La percée*, or equipped with map and binoculars, could make sense of this "panorama." The aphorism "Seeing is not enough, the visitor must also understand" here takes on a new significance, for the knowledge that provides understanding lies, if not completely outside of vision, certainly at its limits, available only to those with special training and authority. The

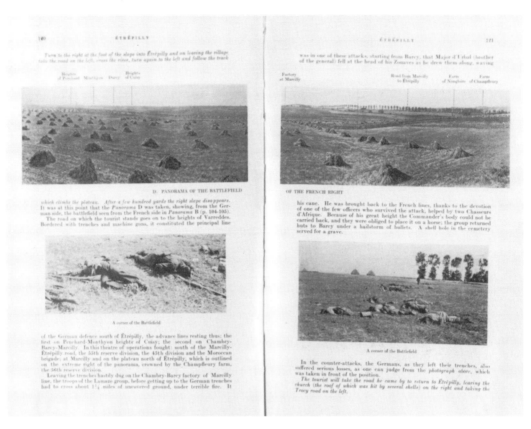

FIGURE 1.2. Panorama of the Marne battlefield from Étrépilly. *Michelin Guide to the Battlefields of the World War*, vol. 1, *The First Battle of the Marne*, pp. 120–21. © Michelin from *The First Battle of the Marne*. Permission no. 9808388.

guidebook offers the visitor both knowledge and vision to which few ordinary soldiers would have had access, and the vicarious experience it promises involves a degree of abstraction, and of temporal extension, far removed from the moment-by-moment notation that Norton Cru favors. "In the course of the excursion," the guide to the Ourcq states, "the tourist will relive the pathetic moment when the Germans, now within cannon range of the capital, had to decide if they would continue their thunderous march on Paris or, beforehand, try to eliminate the French and English armies from battle; then, he will reconstruct that tragic five-day struggle between Gallieni, Maunoury, and von Klück."[156] The smooth transition from a moment to a number of days parallels in the temporal dimension the book's typical spatial strategies.

The Michelin panoramas, in other words, urge visitors to ignore what lies directly before them—in most of the Marne photographs, the somewhat incongruous sight of grain stacks laid out in neat rows. Soldiers attending films while on home leave had had occasion to note the disappointment of civilian spectators with the few visible traces the battle of the Marne had left on the landscape.[157] This could explain the guidebooks' meticulous detail about damage from fire and shelling, which, together with the emphasis on the overview, encourages visitors to use the information provided to visualize the scene of battle. In effect, they invite the tourist to invent a set of images in his or her imagination, and then to call them "memories." This invitation, like all constructions of memory, entails the selective use of forgetting, *oubli*, in both the spatial and the temporal dimensions. The bracketed or overlooked foreground corresponds, in this schema, to the intervening *time* that visitors must forget as they try to reconstruct the selected scene. In this way a common set of images can come to supplant the timeframes of individual lives.

Subsequent volumes in the Michelin series, published after the end of the war, do not offer such minute instructions to orient the reader's vision, though topographical directions perforce remain precise: the Verdun guide, for example, published in 1919, notes the points at which shell holes make passage difficult, and includes a photograph of a spot near Vaux where cars needed to make a U-turn.[158] But the visual and textual strategies pioneered in the Marne series do not change very much in the postwar titles. In the volumes on Verdun and the Chemin des Dames, covering much hillier terrain than the Marne, the panoramas feature not only more extensive vistas but the dramatic signs of war that civilians were looking for, whether the barren tree stumps along the Chemin des Dames or the devastated, almost lunar landscape visible from Esnes, on the right bank of the Meuse northwest of Verdun.[159] But the points of interest marked on the panoramas remain just as indistinct as in the earlier books. Knowledge about these points of interest, and the ability to connect them to the visible foreground, depends if anything even more heavily on the authority of the guidebook than in the initial volumes.

Although virtually all the Michelin guides offer detailed tours of the cities in the various sectors, some devote far more attention to art and architecture than to the war. The Strasbourg volume is particularly notable in this respect: Strasbourg remained well behind the German lines for the duration of the war, and French troops did not occupy the city until ten days after the armistice. After a historical summary that passes rather quickly over the Great War, the guidebook proper deals exclusively with the city's churches, museums, and historic buildings.[160] A note to the reader at the beginning of the Marne volumes justifies the occasional detour from the war: "In visiting a place that is interesting either from an archaeological or an artistic point of view, the tourist halts even if the war has passed it by, that he may realize it was to preserve intact this heritage of history and beauty that so many heroes fell."[161] Though they would undoubtedly have snickered at this rationalization, former soldiers probably would not have minded the attention the Michelin guides pay to conventional tourist attractions. For in their narratives authors like Genevoix and Delvert oc-

guide's authority

casionally played tourist—and, in effect, tour guide—themselves, commenting for example on the architecture of a noteworthy church they had come upon in a moment of repose.[162]

But another tendency of the guidebooks, their focus on the personal and material sufferings of civilians, would certainly have angered many veterans, as such accounts in the civilian press had during the war. The trench press habitually disparaged accounts of civilian hardships as in no way equal to those of combatants, and even expressed a kind of grim satisfaction when cities behind the lines were subject to aerial bombardment.[163] Yet as part of their demonization of the enemy, the Michelin guides devoted considerable space to accounts of German hostage-takings (as in Senlis), mistreatment of civilians, and destruction of civilian property. The guide to the Somme, for example, includes numerous photographs of the ruins of Albert, Bapaume, Péronne, and smaller towns, but very few illustrations of trenches, though numerous trench networks in the Somme have been preserved to this day. The few trenches pictured tend to be German ones, and thus serve as further examples of German barbarity. In Péronne, for example, "The cemetery . . . was devastated. Many graves were desecrated, and trenches dug among the violated sepulchres. A battery of artillery was even posted on the site of ancient vaults. These profanations did not prevent the Germans from burying their dead in a corner of the cemetery, or erecting funeral monuments to their memory." The guide to St. Quentin, Cambrai, and the Hindenburg Line deplores at some length the German destruction of venerable old trees, flower beds, and statues in the Cambrai public gardens.[164]

Even when it came to the front lines, combatants had a distinct conception of the sites that really mattered, a notion that did not always correspond to those of tour guides and officials. Debates about the preservation of sites of course had important ramifications not only for tourism, but for commemoration in general. As early as the fall of 1916, a journalist who had toured the site of the previous year's battle of Champagne lamented the disappearance of key features of the battlefield, like the elaborate German barbed-wire defenses. Writing in *L'illustration*, he urged readers to visit them quickly, while it was still possible "to take in their fierce and bitter beauty. Within a few months, they will again have become like those sad, dead sites, those places that were so moving a short time ago, immediately after the battles that destroyed them."[165] In 1917 the government established an interministerial commission on war remains and relics (*vestiges et souvenirs*). As a first step toward preserving visible traces of the war, the commission undertook a survey of military structures, ruins, and other sites in inactive sectors, considering the possibilities of preserving them. It concluded that the need to return land to cultivation and property to its owners would allow the physical conservation of only a "small number of especially typical structures." The "memory" of the remainder, however, would be preserved through exhaustive "graphic and photographic documentation."[166]

In 1921 a bill came before the Chamber of Deputies to make possible the classification of war remnants as "historic monuments." That status accorded structures legal protection against demolition, alteration, the posting of unauthorized signs, and, within limits, against new construction in the immediate vicinity. Veterans followed the proposal with interest.[167] In the fall of 1922, A. Thomasset, president of an association of former prisoners of war, challenged the criteria the commission had used to establish its initial list of sites to be protected. He asked rhetorically,

What, in fact, is a "*vestige de guerre*" for a combatant? Is it the house (whatever it might be called) that almost swallowed him up under its roof or, on the contrary, is it the trench, the dugout, the underground shelter that were his daily share? Whenever one of us speaks of these war memories, these things are always what we mean. It is they that are "our" war remains.

The official list, however, included only constructions in "cement or stone. Which of our infantrymen lived in these paradises of safety, given that this construction was uniquely Kraut [*Boche*]?"[168] Veterans did not advocate, Thomasset added, the neglect of ruined churches and other monuments, but he insisted that conveying the lessons of Verdun, the example he had chosen, required the preservation of typical sites like trenches. A glance at the six-page list of sites appended to the report on the preservation bill confirms Thomasset's characterization: the commission selected above all cement and concrete shelters, lookout towers, and fortifications, especially German ones, and the ruins of French villages; the only trenches on the list were German. Unsurprisingly, this official notion of preservation closely parallels Michelin's "general's-eye view" of the war.

Michelin had competition in the guidebook business, ranging from summary brochures offering little more than lists of sites and suggested itineraries to full-scale guidebooks from the French pioneer in the market, Hachette's *Guides bleus.*[169] Indeed, the extensive Michelin series seems not to have been profitable (profits were supposed to be donated to a pronatalist charity, which instead received a gift from one of the Michelin brothers),[170] perhaps because, in price and in organization, the guides clearly targeted the very small sector of the market that owned automobiles. But even a cursory glance at other guidebooks reveals little difference in orientation. In his *Circuits des champs de bataille*, Gabriel Hanotaux, a member of the Académie française and former foreign minister, even more than Michelin presents a chronicle of military operations linked through barely described panoramic vistas. Despite the book's claim to be "not only a History, but above all a Guide," sites per se do not really interest Hanotaux except as jumping-off points for historical facts. Comments and directions rarely have much specificity: "The panoramic view from Mont-girmont allows us to situate in a few moments the most important events that took place over four years in the northern Woëvre."[171] The book contains no photographs, only maps and schematic bird's-eye views such as might have been available to aerial reconnaissance.

In the *Guides bleus* series, the 1934 guide to Verdun and Metz, like the Michelins, offers detailed information on various sites, but its narrative of military operations refers exclusively to commanders' strategy and tactics. The guide also repeats the legend of the Tranchée des Baïonnettes at Verdun, where an entire squadron of soldiers was supposed to have been killed by a missile that buried them standing up, their bayonets protruding from the earth.[172] Norton Cru demonstrates persuasively that this story reflects a complete misunderstanding of the physical effects of shelling, of standard burial practices at the front, and of the original combatant account from which it derives. Yet the site had powerful resonance for visitors, and legislators used the notorious disappearance of the bayonets (the ones now visible there are reconstructions) as the principal example in their report on battlefield preservation. The theft of the bayonets prompted a wealthy American, George Rand, to pay for construction of the concrete structure that covers the site, and the monumental gateway leading to it; dedicated in 1920, it was one of the first war sites to receive such "markers."[173]

Yet despite their command perspective and their highly conventional understanding of the war, in one basic sense the Michelin guides and others like them reinforce rather than challenge combatants' construction of the war "experience." Unintentionally, but nonetheless effectively, the Michelin guides leave soldiers' fundamental claim, to the uniqueness of their experience, intact. For the construction of visitors as tourists preserves the distinction between soldiers and civilians as the basis for memories of the war. There was no risk of confusing the memories of a tourist, in which a visit to a cathedral or museum jostled with vistas of battlefields and occasional close-up views of ruins, with those of soldiers. The discerning tourist, squinting at the far distance and looking for the points indicated on one of the photographic panoramas, might even have grasped Norton Cru's distinction between staff officers' knowledge of war and that of eyewitnesses. The former, Norton Cru argues, derived solely from the faculty of "intelligence," comparable to the sort of external knowledge the guides provided, whereas the latter drew on "all the emotions felt" at the front.[174] In this view, the perspectives of tourists and commanders did not fundamentally differ, and while some tourists might have been troubled by this realization, the majority undoubtedly did not probe far enough to let it bother them.

As Clymène's attempt to see through her body suggests, many visitors to battlefields did seek a more authentic experience, something that would bring them closer to what they imagined soldiers had endured, than guidebooks had to offer. Veterans, of course, often revisited the battlefields; a journey to Arras in 1922 by members of the Rouen chapter of the Union Nationale des Combattants, numerous enough to occupy a special train, gave one of the chapter's officers an opportunity to vaunt its devotion to the "cult of memory" and to attack those who, "having shared neither their suffering nor their glory, would welch on their debt of gratitude by letting [soldiers'] sacrifice fall into oblivion."[175] Boy scout troops and school groups often camped out on the battlefields; each spring during the 1920s, a Catholic secondary school in Tourcoing sent a group of boys to bicycle around the Verdun battlefields and gather fragments of remains, which they turned in to the provisional ossuary at Douaumont.[176] Nothing better exemplifies the desire to gain understanding through close contact with the war's fragments, rather than by mastering the "main lines" inscribed in panoramic views from above. Yet such attempts at closeness carried risks: in 1929 a priest and a student from the Tourcoing group were killed, and two other students seriously wounded, when their campfire ignited an old missile buried in a shell hole.[177] The Union Nationale's newspaper paid tribute to the students, contrasting the "fervor and generous devotion" of their search for remains with the materialism of those who scoured battlefields for usable metal or who amassed fortunes in the "commerce of corpses." At a time when veterans were fearing that they and the relatives of the dead were the only ones to remember, the schoolboys had shown that they too had not forgotten.[178]

Everyone knew, of course, that the former war zone was dangerous; much of *La voix du combattant*'s tribute was directed at those who reproached the Tourcoing group for imprudence. Newspapers in towns close to the front regularly reported on accidents, often fatal, that befell workers trying to dispose of shells or farmers who encountered one while tilling the fields: one such incident occurred at virtually the same time as the Tourcoing explosion.[179] But the poignancy of the latter incident had to do with the way in which the schoolboys' search for authentic experience had so horrifically repaid them. In that respect it recalls an episode that took place near Verdun some years earlier, in December 1921. According to a lengthy report in a local newspaper, Yvonne Breuillard, the twenty-two-year-old daughter of a distiller in Melun, had had frequent bouts of depression since her brother was killed in the line of duty at Fleury, near Verdun. After dispatching three notes from a café in the Verdun train station the young woman rented a car, dismissed the driver, then proceeded to her brother's grave at Fleury. The next morning her body was found in a shell hole near the cemetery, a pistol in her hand and a single bullet hole in her head. "Her hat had been laid at the edge of the hole, as well as her handbag, indicating the sangfroid with which the victim had operated." The suicide's father, who had come to look for her, had her buried in the cemetery of Bras, not far from the place where her brother had fallen.[180]

Yvonne Breuillard's gesture did not earn her the kind of tribute the young men from Tourcoing had received. The story in the *Réveil de la Meuse*, framed in the breathless, voyeuristic tones of the *fait divers*, treats the event as a pathetic spectacle, "poignant" for the grieving father, but of no special significance. The account comes with all the markers of class—the hat and handbag, which no bourgeois woman in public would be without, the rental car and driver, the presumably lucrative family business—but also with those of gender. The story begins by noting, "Numerous are the examples of elder sisters who have sacrificed their own existence to devote themselves to the welfare of younger brothers and to lavish on them an affection almost as sweet as maternal love." That this was not such a case we learn only in an offhand reference in the last sentence to Yvonne Breuillard's "older brother," but the mention of her *crises de désespoir* suggests a distinctively female malady. Parallel phenomena among soldiers and veterans—shellshock, amnesia, other psychological disorders—do not enter into the account, for they might suggest too much commonality between the young woman's psyche and those of troubled veterans.

At the outer limit, Yvonne's suicide could be understood as a form of female tribute to male sacrifice, just as *La joie* characterizes commemoration itself. But the most disturbing aspect of this incident, the young woman's insistence on dying violently, as her brother had done, and as close as possible to his remains, could not be acknowledged, for it challenged the basic construction of the war experience as dividing, not uniting, soldiers and civilians, men and women. The teacher and schoolboy had stumbled unwittingly into the soldier's "ultimate sacrifice," and they were men, so it cost veterans little to recognize that equivalence. In the case of Yvonne Breuillard, even the hint of equivalence belonged to the realm of madness.

Lasting Impressions

In his article on war remains, the veteran leader Thomasset declared that

what will be needed to represent, from far off, a little of the life of the poilus to an outsider is a trench surrounded by sandbags, with a lookout slit on top; the dugout, in which we'll see the famous little table and its little bench, the bunk beds, the barrel with fresh water, the ventilation slot, the observation post and the straight ladder leading to it. That's what those who come to our battlefields should be shown.[181]

Thomasset here sketches a kind of ethnographic museum installation, at once authentic and a representation, generic and precisely detailed. Like the official proposal to photograph sites that could not be preserved, this vision reflects a desire for a visual record of war remains, a kind of image bank to "engrave in memory" what time would inevitably alter, and indeed, as Thomasset noted, had already begun to.[182] This desire for the visual would find one kind of response in the many kinds of exhibition spaces created to preserve objects related to the war, from trophy cases in village schools to full-scale museums. Although many of these institutions, such as the Bibliothèque-musée de la Guerre established in 1917, were ostensibly dedicated to furthering historical knowledge, and thus put more emphasis on documentation than on display,[183] their beginnings owe much to the visual conception of memory.

If, for writers of war narratives and even guidebooks, experience involves more than just seeing, the visual nonetheless played a crucial role in the construction of memory during and after the war, although not always at a conscious level. We need only think of the way, in recent American culture, certain images have resonated as signs of particular events or eras: marines hoisting the flag at Iwo Jima for World War II, a terrified girl hit by napalm and running naked toward the camera for Vietnam, Martin Luther King in front of the Lincoln Memorial for the civil rights movement. The photograph of marines raising a flag on Mount Suribachi has particular relevance here because it both conveyed a somewhat misleading impression (the photo captures not the initial flag-raising at the culmination of the battle, but the subsequent replacement of that flag with a larger one) and, regardless, was later transformed into a monument and a widely diffused popular image.[184] Probe any image, however, and one will find complexity: the child in the 1972 Vietnam photograph, Phan Thi Kim Phuc, survived, left Vietnam for Cuba and eventually Canada, and in 1996, on a holiday originally created to commemorate the end of World War I, visited the Vietnam Veterans Memorial in Washington in a gesture of reconciliation.[185] In our own time aural impressions also make the passage from the individual to the social level, for example, King's voice proclaiming "I have a dream"; but in the 1920s, when radio and the commercial diffusion of recorded images were still in their infancy, the visual arguably played a larger role in the social transmission of memory-images.

The importance of visual images in commemorative culture had to do not only with their polyvalence, their availability to many kinds of appropriations, but also with their complex structure. For the casting of an image in memory takes place simultaneously with its construction as a sign in Roland Barthes's sense: "the associative total of a concept and an image." Retrieval of an image either through individual memory or through the discourses and practices that represent memory at a collective level may change the sign, for example, by turning it into myth. Even at the initial moment of its insertion in memory, however, an image is a sign in that it "is full, it is a meaning."[186] Consider, for example, the way in which clothing resembling a French poilu's uniform constructed various bodies as signs for individuals who, as well, obviously committed them to memory. For Émilie Carles, a young would-be teacher in the Alps, her brother's filthy, lice-infested uniform long remained a figure for the disillusionment with the war he expressed while on an unexpected home leave in 1916. Simone de Beauvoir distinctly recalls, from forty years' distance, the admiration she, not yet ten, and her younger sister received when their mother paraded them around Paris during the war in coats made of the same blue cloth, and in the same style, as a soldier's great-coat.[187] That such an idea had some currency is clear from a pattern for converting a soldier's coat into a lady's published in a fashion magazine after the war (fig. 1.3). That the creative use, or reuse, of military fabric for civilian garments could have multiple significations emerges from a story by Colette in which a soldier on home leave finds himself quite disturbed by the "patriotic" soldier's coat in which his wife greets him.[188] In his wife-turned-image, he sees not so much tribute as the gap, almost an abyss, between experience and representation.

All kinds of visual images offered raw material for this dual construction, of memory and of cultural signs. Types of images historians have plumbed for insight into the cultures of the war and postwar eras include postcards, children's games, devotional objects, *images d'Épinal* (mass-produced lithographs destined for a popular audience), and posters.[189] Though the traditional, heroic vision of war and conventional formal languages tended to predominate in

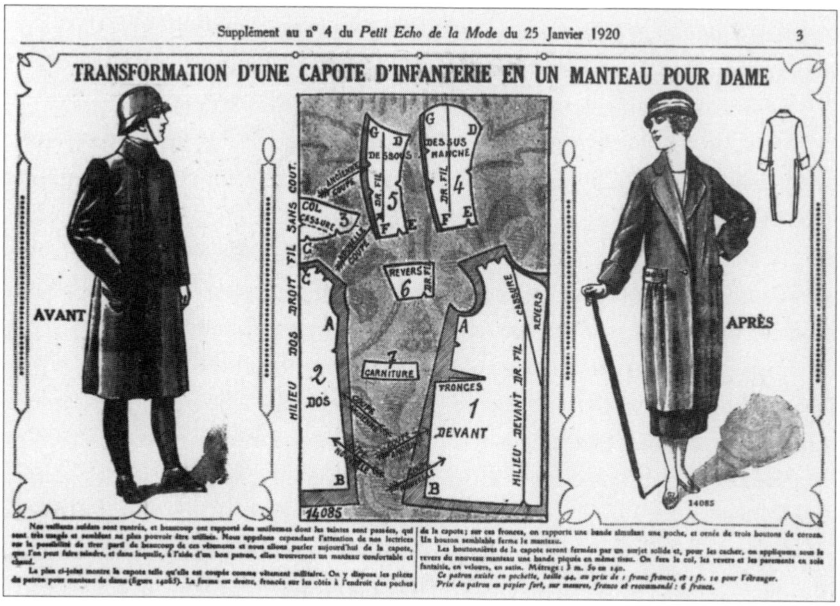

FIGURE 1.3. "Transformation d'une capote d'infanterie en un manteau pour dame." *Petit écho de la mode*, 25 January 1920. © Cliché Bibliothèque Nationale de France, Paris.

certain genres, others offered a wide range of subjects. Postcards featured ruined villages, sometimes with before and after views, cemeteries and monuments, battle sites. Until at least a few years ago it was possible to buy many such cards at flea markets in Paris and elsewhere, some with messages conveying the complexity of the memory-work they performed.

On the back of a scene of a military cemetery in the Argonne (fig. 1.4), a note dated 5 April 1916 and addressed to *ma chère petite femme cherie* (my dear little sweetie wife) hopes that the card will please her; the husband admits that the scene "is not beautiful, but it's to give you some idea of what is happening at the moment." A card (fig. 1.5) depicting the ruins of the church in Rembercourt-aux-Pots (Meuse) comes with a few brief lines, headed "1914–15 Campaign": "I'm sending you this card showing a terrible battlefield where the 54th covered itself in glory. Kisses from your brother." Another postcard (fig. 1.6) showing the ruins of the village of Lacroix-sur-Meuse bears a scribbled message, full of misspellings, to the effect that a friend evacuated to Lyon would soon be sending the recipient an inkwell made from the top of a German missile. But, the message cautioned, the inkwell should not be taken to school because, made of copper, it would not preserve the ink; it would be better to put a small ink bottle inside.[190] Each of the three messages takes a different attitude toward the image it accompanies: the first gently disparages it, the second takes it as an unproblematic sign of "glory," the last ignores the image altogether. Each takes a different kind of distance from the depicted scene, using, respectively, codes of gender, geography, and the everyday. Yet in different ways each augments the image, making it a sign of the distinctness of the (individual) soldier's experience, thus, we can imagine, fixing it in recipients' memories.

Civilians seeking a more systematic visual record of the war had many options, including, as we saw earlier, documentary films. For most of 1916, the army published, on a biweekly basis, large-format collections of photographs, each fascicule covering a topic such as soldiers' daily lives, arms and armaments, and the naval war.[191] *L'illustration,* France's best-known illustrated magazine, included photographs among the many images it published on a weekly basis for the duration of the war, along with narrative accounts of the latest operations. Like the army photograph series, *L'illustration* produced a highly polished publication on glossy paper, clearly destined for a bourgeois readership. The editorial tone was as relentlessly positive as one would expect for such an establishment publication, yet it did not completely spare its readers painful topics. A drawing by one of its staff artists serving at the front, Georges Scott, depicts an entrance to a first-aid post during a battle (fig. 1.7). Though it does not approach the hellishness of Barbusse's description, it conveys far more physical suffering than the photographs of clean, tidy surgeries, calm patients, and relaxed doctors and nurses in the army compendium. A photograph

LES MORTS POUR LA PATRIE SONT UN LEVAIN DE GLOIRE
PLUS COUTEUX EST L'EFFORT PLUS BELLE EST LA VICTOIRE

473. La Grande Guerre 1914-15 - En ARGONNE (Meuse) - Un cimetière militaire.

Visé Paris 473   R. P.

FIGURE 1.4.
Postcard: "La Grande
Guerre 1914–15. En
Argonne (Meuse)—
Un cimetière
militaire." Private
collection.

436. La Grande Guerre 1914-15
REMBERCOURT-aux-POTS (Meuse). — Ruines de l'Eglise après la bataille   A. R.

FIGURE 1.5.
Postcard: "La Grande
Guerre 1914–15.
Rembercourt-aux-
Pots (Meuse).—
Ruines de l'Eglise
après la bataille."
Private collection.

LACROIX-SUR-MEUSE — Bombardement 1914-1915

Propriété de M. l'Abbé Dubois pour l'érection d'un monument aux héroïques défenseurs du Fort de Troyon
Cliché J. Corret

FIGURE 1.6.
Postcard: "Lacroix-
sur-Meuse—
Bombardement
1914–1915." Private
collection.

FIGURE I.7.
Georges Scott,
"L'entrée du poste de
secours: arrivée des
blessés." *L'illustration*,
6 January 1917, 9.

published in July 1916 of diggers (*sapeurs*) at Douaumont pays tribute to their industry, but shows them asleep in the trenches they have dug, literally collapsed with fatigue (fig. 1.8).[192]

Perhaps more surprisingly, *L'illustration* regularly evoked the gap between soldiers and civilians, chiefly through the drawings of Lucien Sabattier. In November 1915, the magazine published a full-page drawing (fig. 1.9) by Sabattier called "Le récit de la bataille" (The story of the battle), showing a soldier in a café listening skeptically to a civilian's account of a battle at which the soldier had been present. Another drawing published six months later, "Réflexions de permissionaires" (Home leave thoughts, fig. 1.10), has more of an edge: two soldiers on home leave comment with "a good malicious smile" on the latest Paris fashions.[193] In both cases, the soldiers' expressions show bemusement rather than anger or hostility, so that the breach between the battlefield and the home front hardly seems unbridgeable. Yet the editorial comments below each drawing indicate some unease about their critical overtones. Both texts suggest, the later one explicitly, that the civilians pictured represent a kind of extreme, and they effectively present the soldiers' tolerance as another form of heroism. Together, the texts and drawings clearly come down on the side of the poilus, in an obvious attempt to alleviate their anxieties about civilian ingratitude. A drawing somewhat more typical of *L'illustration*, Lucien Jonas's "L'arrivée du permissionnaire" (The homecoming, fig. 1.11), makes the point far more directly, and thus needs no textual comment.[194] Jonas's drawing, however, might not have resonated with soldiers, because its uncomplicated sentimentality scarcely leaves room for any anxiety about the home front, an anxiety Sabattier acknowledges while simultaneously attempting to defuse it.

Of all the visual media providing source material for memory, none, arguably, had a wider distribution than posters. Contemporaries made much of

FIGURE 1.9. Lucien Sabattier, "Le récit de la bataille." *L'illustration*, 20 November 1915, 534.

FIGURE 1.10. Lucien Sabattier, "Réflexions de permissionnaires." *L'illustration*, 27 May 1916, 503.

L'ARRIVÉE DU PERMISSIONNAIRE

FIGURE 1.11. Lucien Jonas, "L'arrivée du permissionnaire." *L'illustration*, 17 July 1915, 69.

the impact of posters on morale, in part because their ambiguous status between art and publicity lent them a certain prestige, or at least fascination, but
in part simply because of their ubiquity. On opening in 1924 the Bibliothèque-
musée de la Guerre held 11,000 posters, 6,000 of them illustrated; the Imperial
War Museum in London contained nearly twice as many.[195] A review of the
Bibliothèque-musée in the *Mercure de France* wrote that "More than any other
esthetic form, perhaps, [posters] provide the psychologist a precious contribution to the study of national characters and ethnic particularities."[196] A month
before the end of the war, *L'illustration*'s cover (fig. 1.12) showed a wall plas-
tered with posters as evidence for continued public support of the war effort.[197]

Like postcards and caricature, posters offered a surprising diversity of subjects and idioms. On the civilian side, one could see peasants making their contribution to the war effort or a mother hugging her baby under the picture of an
absent soldier father. But the majority of posters featured images of soldiers
themselves. Two of the most prominently displayed on the *Illustration* cover
show French soldiers fighting the eagle of German imperialism; in the Crédit
Lyonnais poster (fig. 1.13), only the helmet makes the soldier, otherwise depicted as a classical heroic nude, recognizable as a poilu. The allegorical strain
continues in another celebrated image, by Sem (fig. 1.14), in which the Grande
Armée of the Napoleonic era, led by the Rude sculpture known as the *Marseillaise*, comes alive on the Arc de Triomphe to inspire French soldiers to victory.

FIGURE 1.12. Anonymous, "La réponse est sur les murs." *L'illustration*, 12 October 1918, 333.

FIGURE 1.13. Abel Faivre, "Souscrivez au 4e emprunt national." Poster Collection, FR 425, Hoover Institution Archives. © 1999 Artists Rights Society (ARS), New York/ADAGP Paris.

FIGURE 1.14. Sem, "Pour le triomphe, souscrivez à l'emprunt national." Poster Collection, FR 428, Hoover Institution Archives. © 1999 Artists Rights Society (ARS), New York/ADAGP Paris.

Many images of soldiers, however, employ a more contemporary, if obviously stylized, idiom. One could see soldiers looking over the top of a trench onto the forbidding landscape of no-man's land (fig. 1.15), two soldiers at rest, one writing a letter (fig. 1.16), even a photograph of a jolly poilu on home leave juxtaposed with an informal, handwritten message.

The visual field thus offered a kind of template for the construction of the war "experience" in narrative texts, including the fundamental difference between the combatant and civilian domains. There was one major difference, however: the visual field contained very few depictions of dead bodies.[198] In the army photographic service's fascicule on the wounded, the only representation of death is a scene of a military funeral in which a blanket covers the corpse.[199] Among the many historical photographs in Michelin's Marne guidebooks, only three show dead bodies (see fig. 1.2); in none of these can one make out any wounds or distinguishing features of the dead, and in one dead horses outnumber soldiers. Later volumes display if anything even greater reticence: the Chemin des Dames and Ypres guidebooks contain not a single picture of a dead soldier, nor, amidst all the images of ruined towns, does the guide to the Somme.[200] Nor did *L'illustration* often risk disturbing its readers' sensibilities with graphic scenes of the battlefields after an attack. In 1918 the magazine reprinted a striking drawing by Jean-Louis Forain (fig. 1.17), first published in

FIGURE 1.15. Curtin (?), "Vous devez leur donner les moyens de hâter la victoire." Poster Collection, FR 578, Hoover Institution Archives.

FIGURE 1.16. Lucien Jonas, "La journée du poilu." Poster Collection, FR 648, Hoover Institution Archives.

LA BORNE
Dessin de Forain.   *(Figaro du 22 mars 1916.)*

FIGURE 1.17. Jean-Louis Forain, "La borne." *L'illustration*, 16–23 November 1918, 488. © 1999 Artists Rights Society (ARS), New York/ADAGP Paris.

the daily *Le Figaro* in 1916, in which a mass of dead bodies forms a kind of barricade at Verdun (the name on the *borne,* the boundary-stone, that gives the drawing its title), but, reduced to blurry outlines, the bodies work almost as a kind of abstraction.[201]

Of course signs of death abounded in the visual as in the textual field throughout the war: tombs, cemeteries, monuments, ruins. *L'illustration* published photographs of grave sites and memorial observances from the fall of 1914, and it recorded the erection of the first battlefield monuments as early as 1915;[202] all the Michelin guides to battlefield areas depict such sites as well. In the first volume of Genevoix's *Ceux de 14*, published in 1916, the narrator and his men come across a few primitive graves in the Marne, only a few days after they were dug in September 1914. "Not aligned or even grouped," crudely marked with two branches attached in the form of a cross, the tombs prompt this reflection: "Hasty tombs, formed with the same little tools that dig the battle trenches, I would wish you deeper and more possessive. The bodies you conceal form a slight rise in the surface of fields. The rain must have soaked them these last days and nights."[203] Elsewhere in *Ceux de 14* the narrator encounters or discusses various forms of memorialization, from the neatly

JOURNÉE DES RÉGIONS LIBÉRÉES
QUE VOTRE AIDE À NOS FRÈRES MALHEUREUX SOIT GÉNÉREUSE!

aligned rows of military cemeteries to an unrecoverable body left to rot on the battlefield, but the most frequent image is that of the primitive grave marker, the *croix de bois* or wooden cross.[204] By the end of the war, the *croix de bois* had become the privileged sign of French loss, serving as the title of Dorgelès's 1919 novel and as the subject, both familiar and emblematic, of Théodore Steinlen's well-known poster for the relief of war-devastated regions (fig. 1.18).

The gravestone in the poster looks somewhat more solid, the planks of wood thicker and more substantial, than those in the photograph on a *L'illustration* cover at the end of July 1915 (fig. 1.19). The caption to that photograph

FIGURE 1.19. Anonymous, "Les tombes dans les blés." *L'illustration*, 31 July 1915, 99.

explains that a farmer went around the graves when laying out the furrows the previous September, so that a path through the wheat now connects them. "Devoted hands" planted the flag on the fourteenth of July. The crosses also bear wreaths in tribute to the dead, just as a strand of "withered laurel"[205] adorns the cross in the Steinlen poster. There the dandelions in the barbed wire, the glowing sun, and the robin in full song replace the flag as signs of regeneration. The cross, of course, represents one dead individual—Genevoix notes, when he first sees the *croix de bois*, the handwritten inscriptions of names—though in the image the specific becomes general, and refers to all the dead. Laurel or other wreaths stand for mourning and imply the presence of mourners, those paying tribute to the dead and ensuring that they will not be forgotten. The flags, and in the poster arguably the robin as well, generalize the tribute and underline its connection to the ongoing national effort.

But beyond this basic level of signification, the two images constitute what Barthes would call a "second-order semiological system," or myth.[206] In both, we see the visual doubling back on itself, asserting its own value and utility. For in representing these signs of commemoration, Steinlen and the *Illustration* photographer demonstrate the potential of visual signs to fix memory and focus mourning, very much in the Freudian sense, even in the absence of the dead. Of course much traditional funeral practice in the modern West involves signs that compensate for the absence of the dead, but the war had deprived the bereaved of many of these rituals and of the images they customarily produce in memory. As a consequence, in these images memory moves in an unaccustomed direction, from the collective or social to the individual level. For the bereaved who could not visit a loved one's grave, for the many without even a grave to visit, the *croix de bois* offers an image that can merge with their private memories and endow them with a larger, structural meaning, encompassing both a reassurance of national gratitude and an assertion that the remembered death had a purpose.

Images like the *croix de bois* offer the visual not only as an adequate means of representation, but as the basis for a whole range of practices, commemoration, that would seek to channel mourning in a socially productive direction. Ironically, the *croix de bois*, although here appropriated on behalf of official commemoration, became a symbol and rallying point for those who resisted and challenged the commemorative project. As the ensuing chapter will show, commemorative practices did not take hold in French culture without a struggle, and the question of where and in what configuration to bury the dead constituted one of the first and most emotional theaters of that contestation. For many veterans and families of the dead, the *croix de bois*, in its very simplicity, stood for the private, individual nature of the tribute they wished to bestow. Yet the polyvalence of this sign, its availability for multiple appropriations, gave commemoration a powerful tool in its continuing effort to meld individual memories into a collective narrative of the war.

2

BODIES AND NAMES

Near the end of his autobiographical narrative *Ceux de 14* (1916–23), Maurice Genevoix describes himself as in a state approaching complete disorientation. As he marches toward an obviously doomed engagement near Les Éparges, visions of earlier battles and of dead comrades run through Genevoix's mind, so fragmentary and detached that "I no longer remember who I was only an hour ago; I don't know who I will be in another hour." He cannot understand or interpret the memories that haunt him: "I no longer reason, no longer imagine; I come and go, and the minutes run along beside me, without hurrying, without stopping." Suddenly, however, Genevoix's memories take on a different form:

> Names keep passing through my memory: Butrel, Sicot, Liège, Biloray, Beurain . . . And every step seems easy to me, the mud less heavy, the sky lighter. Other names, a gray thread [*trame*], a murmur without an echo: Timmer the Deaf, Compain the Chatty, Perrinet, Montigny, Chaffard; nothing but names. Still more, which leave me weary and panting: Durozier, Gerbeau, Richomme . . . I keep walking, rocked by a vague, regular, swinging. I don't find this hard; I don't try to escape; it seems to me that it's good [*bien*] like this.[1]

The key word in this passage is *trame*, which can mean a number of things: the thread of life or of memory, the texture of a speech, a plot or conspiracy, or a grid interposed between the original and a light-sensitive surface in photography. Names indeed constitute the texture of Genevoix's narrative, but they also serve as a kind of grid that transposes his memories into textual form. Virtually all the names in *Ceux de 14*, with the exception of Genevoix's own and that of his best friend Porchon, are fictitious; Genevoix's private papers include a master table that keys the pseudonyms to the names of actual people.[2] After orienting the composition of the text itself, within the text this thread of names imposes calm and order on Genevoix's thoughts, so that the situation in which he finds himself becomes no longer absurd, irrational, confused, but simply *bien*. In this passage, Genevoix invests names with at once the reassuring concreteness of the real and the ordering power of the abstract. Yet since the names he lists are his own inventions, they also stand for the arbitrariness of the sign, the contingency of the relationship between memory as a social construct and the images that comprise it.

In his novel *La tête brûlée*, set a few years later, after the war, Joseph Jolinon comments on this contingency in a more ironic vein. After a memorial service in the hero Claude Lunant's native village, his old comrade the gardener asks him if he knows "what happened to the corporal of the 4th. I don't remember his name any more. Haven't you noticed how quickly we forget the names?" Lunant replies, "Yes, but I think the names fade so we can better remember everything else."[3] For the veteran, both the arbitrariness of the name and its universality make it suspect as a form of memory. Anyone could remember a name, and the host of associations that names summon up; only veterans could remember "everything else," the experiences that set soldiers apart from civilians. The irony of Lunant's remark comes in the phrase *les noms s'effacent*, for in postwar France, the names of the dead served as the keystone of commemorative practice. The claim that veterans were forgetting the names of their dead comrades creates an implicit contrast with the proliferation of names in civilian commemoration; the contrast sows doubt about the adequacy of commemoration to the task of collective memory.

Recent studies have overlooked this skepticism about commemorative naming and have retrospectively endowed it with a curious kind of modernist sensibility. At least since the work of Philippe Ariès in the 1970s and 1980s, we have seen lists of names as the fruits of mass democracy, fundamentally different from earlier memorial forms that paid tribute to generals and rulers while leaving common soldiers forgotten in mass graves. In this dichotomy, names constitute signs of mourning, and express an individual and communal grief indifferent, if not actively hostile, to the ideology of patriotism and military glory.[4]

Maya Ying Lin's Vietnam Veterans Memorial in Washington, D.C., completed in 1982, spurred a number of critical interventions that cast the inscription of names of the dead as a distinctively modern form of commemoration. Writing about the Vietnam Memorial itself, Marita Sturken observes that the inscription of names on monuments enacts a kind of resistance to totalizing discourses that would subsume individuals into some larger meaning.[5] Standing alone, signifying as much in conjunction with each other as with the body whose double absence, physical as well as temporal, they signify, names point to and embody discontinuity, rupture. Thomas Laqueur, writing of British monuments to the World War I dead, argues that the serial inscription of names

is commemoration adequate for collective memory?

names = signifies against universalizing commemoration

epitomizes the way in which, in the modern, "semiotically arid world, a solution is to eschew representation and the production of meaning as far as possible and to resort to a sort of commemorative hyper-nominalism."[6] The meaning of this form of commemoration resides in the very lack of meaning, the reduction of signification to a vast aggregation of names.

It has become a commonplace that "the principle and production of memory that is so characteristic of our time may be said to date from the Great War of 1914–1918."[7] Lin's monument makes the move back from our own time to World War I appear both seamless and natural. If her design conspicuously lacks the conventional pieties associated with representative sculpture, so do some of the most celebrated monuments of the Great War. Lin herself has acknowledged a conceptual debt to Sir Edwin Lutyens' Monument to the Missing of the Somme at Thiepval (fig. 2.1).[8] Like his contemporaries, Lutyens was struggling to find a way to represent a war of which human loss had become the paramount sign. Like Lin's memorial, his multiple arch surrounds the visitor with names in a pattern of complex repetition that resists attempts to assign that loss a simple or a single meaning. Even the historian Jay Winter, who rejects a political reading of Thiepval and emphasizes the traditionalism of commemoration after the Great War, calls the monument "an embodiment of nothingness, an abstract space unique among memorials of the Great War."[9] Thus Thiepval and the Vietnam Memorial together establish a lineage in which modern commemoration, with the listing of names as its central practice, has its roots in the Great War's aftermath.

FIGURE 2.1. Edwin Lutyens, Monument to the Missing of the Somme, Thiepval. Photo: Author.

Yet to cast commemorative naming as a spontaneous reaction to, and inscription of, the meaninglessness of the war's slaughter neglects the ways names served (as in Genevoix's text) to order memory, thus enabling a search for meaning in the conflict. Such an interpretation also overlooks the resistances, like Jolinon's, that effort provoked. A speech delivered at the dedication of a war memorial in Villerbon, in the Loir-et-Cher, in 1921, exemplifies the discursive formation that Jolinon implicitly disparages. The town's mayor, Lesourd, observed that although the town's dead had proved themselves the equals of the heroes of recorded history, "for history they are, alas, anonymous, because too many." The monument's list of names thus became for Lesourd a kind of alternative history:

> The tribute to the unknown soldier in Paris, offered in the name of all France, is a tribute to all, but if history cannot preserve the names of those hundreds of thousands of brave men who fell in defense of the sacred soil of the fatherland, those who knew them, at least, must retain an imperishable memory of them. Their names must be synonymous with glory and abnegation, with patriotism and duty fulfilled, in the countryside [*pays*] where they were born and lived. Finally, future generations must be able in case of need to reinvigorate themselves through the reading of these valiant names.[10]

As in so many texts from the immediate postwar years, names here represent a supplement, not a rival, to traditional historical writing. They construct a bridge between collective tribute and the memory of individuals, claiming to offer a catalog of patriotic virtues and a permanent inspiration or example for future generations. For many, names in themselves constitute a lesson that will perpetuate memories of the war. In the spring of 1919, a group of eighty members of Parliament urged the government to supply towns with marble plaques on which they could inscribe the names of their dead: "All [the dead] . . . have the right that their name not be buried in oblivion, and that their example serve as a lesson for the generations that will follow us."[11]

Questioning the identification of World War I as a decisive step in the "onward ascent of modernism," Winter has argued that postwar commemoration actually employed more "traditional" motifs in order to respond to individuals' need for consolation. Commemoration, in this view, is simply an extension of mourning, the "acts and gestures through which survivors express grief and pass through stages of bereavement."[12] Yet these "acts and gestures" also have a social and cultural derivation and, as with any form of representation, take on a set of purposes that extend beyond those of its primary cultural materials. The First World War did introduce practices of commemoration that often sought to replicate, and thus seem merely to reproduce, the private practices they appropriated. But this appearance is an illusion, for it conceals both the ways in which commemoration seeks to naturalize particular versions of history and the conflicts to which its appropriations of individual practices give rise. Indeed, since the Great War commemoration has embodied a continual struggle between the desire to find meaning as part of some larger collective "history" and the attempt to find meaning at a more local and personal level. Names play a central part in this struggle not because they inherently resist meaning, but because their resonance for individual mourners enhances their value as commemorative signifiers.

Foucault's concept of "emergence" is helpful here, for an emergence consists of both conflict and the recasting of that conflict in new terms. The struggle out of which commemoration emerges, in other words, involves not simply the appropriate means of honoring the dead or of comforting survivors but the nature of the French polity itself. Besides the individual versus the collective, another dichotomy structured this emergence, one familiar in French history since the ancien régime: that between the state and local communities. We should take care, however, not to superimpose these dichotomies on one another or to assume that they are the same. Whatever the power of the French state, as a parliamentary republic it had, at least formally, to acknowledge the priority of local rights. One of the peculiarities of the Third Republic, indeed, with its weak party system and executive and strong bicameral legislature, lay in the importance of legislators' roles as representatives of local communities.[13] Moreover, since one of its principal tasks involves the reinscription of a polity's core values in the aftermath of some traumatic disruption, commemoration is an arena in which informal structures of power could not easily trump a regime's more abstract principles. Composed as it was of a frequently changing executive, a noisy and fractious Parliament, many of whose members also held local office, and a corps of dedicated and powerful civil servants, the French state encompassed the full complexity of the debate over commemoration rather than any one side of it. The stakes of that debate went beyond the nature of commemoration or, in particular, the way in which France would incorporate the Great War into its official histories; they also touched on the internal dynamics of the polity itself, the relationship between the state, constituent communities, and individual citizens.

Seeing commemoration as a struggle or negotiation between competing narratives helps to elucidate the formal complexities of monumental representation. Most local monuments combine lists of names with a sculptural or architectural motif, typically a statue of a poilu or a simple obelisk or shaft, thus conjoining the collective and the individual dimensions of commemoration. In the war zone, the commemorative landscape includes not only cemeteries and largely abstract monuments like Thiepval but many figural monuments as well, ranging from a caribou, the Newfoundland memorial in the Somme, to a defiant skeleton at the aptly named le Mort-Homme in the Verdun theater (fig.

FIGURE 2.2. Sixty-ninth Division Memorial, le Mort-Homme (Meuse). Sculptor: J. Froment-Meurice. Photo: Author.

2.2).[14] From the beginning, the fabric of commemoration so tightly interwove the local and the national, the individual and the collective, that the weave itself, the negotiation between the elements, must occupy a central place in any analysis of commemoration's emergence.

In the cities, small towns, and villages of France, names stood for bodies that lay, often in pieces, entangled with the debris of war on the battlefields. These were names without bodies; in contrast, bodies without names littered the war zone. Like the isolated graves and primitive monuments pictured in

L'illustration, local monuments thus literally *embody* a discourse of commemoration centered on grief and individual loss. But battlefield cemeteries and local communities had different claims on the bodies of the dead, and the inevitable contest between them offered fertile ground for the appropriation of this discourse by more overtly political narratives. As the literal struggle for bodies became enmeshed in more philosophical debates over the nature of commemoration, the canniest spokesmen for particular interests found ways of cloaking their plans in more intimate mourning practices, for which names served as the privileged sign. The tense relationship between bodies and names crystallized the emergence of commemoration as a distinctive form of representation, one that simultaneously subsumed individual memories into collective ones and sought to mask that appropriation in the guise of intimacy.

An Immense Necropolis → war cemetaries

Virtually from the moment of the war's outbreak, few doubted that the memories it spawned would find large-scale public expression. "No effort will be needed," wrote one senator in 1916, "to initiate this cult of memory. It is instituted in advance in the hearts of all Frenchmen."[15] Many anticipated with intense unease the flood of new monuments that would follow in the war's wake. In the preface to a 1916 book presenting the views of a number of writers, politicians, and other notables on the question *Comment glorifier les morts pour la patrie?*, its compiler, Jean Ajalbert, wrote acidly, "The way in which our great men were glorified until very recently has nothing in it that could provoke today's *Saviors* to desire the hideous repetition of monuments obscuring the public thoroughfare all over France." The mass of the bereaved, Ajalbert continued, would probably prefer "silence alone to the kinds of demonstrations that attempt nothing less, under a patriotic cover, than to appropriate private grief and mourning to make them the collective substructure of Committees of Profiteers of all sorts."[16]

Politicians, of course, could hardly take such a jaundiced attitude toward collective forms of commemoration. Yet they too saw monuments as embodying a form of commemoration distinct from private mourning. In May 1915 the deputy Petitjean introduced a bill on an issue that would prove highly controversial at the war's end, the transfer of the remains of dead soldiers to their hometowns. Justifying his proposal that the state undertake such transfers at its own expense, Petitjean wrote, "Later on, our cities and our countryside will build commemorative monuments to remind survivors how those who are no more fell. There must be room, alongside these collective demonstrations, for a pious and familial pilgrimage to other monuments or other tombs, which, really in their case, contain the remains of the valiant soldiers interred in the vaults or cemeteries of their elders."[17] The contrast here turns on the "real" bodies that graves and family vaults would contain, for their presence provides consolation and enables the private, intimate mourning rituals sanctioned by tradition.

Yet if one probes further, it is less clear of what the distinction between the private, individual and public, collective levels of commemoration consists. The former might be less subject to the kind of appropriation Ajalbert feared, although the insignia, figurines, and souvenir helmet cases advertised in veterans' newspapers suggest that no dimension of commemoration could escape the twinned lures of commerce and representation.[18] But in a speech to the Senate in 1920, Adolphe Simonet, one of the most ardent advocates of a liberal exhumation policy and thus of "private" commemorative practice, described private mourning as part of the *same* "culte" or system of devotion as public commemoration, "as moving in its simplicity" as the pomp and spectacle that mark "an entire people's gratitude."[19]

Beneath this apparent ambiguity lurks an awkward political reality. At the same time that they were asserting the primacy of the family in the matter of burial, legislators were attempting to offer some direction to the public commemorative effusion that Ajalbert so dreaded. The first bill to require localities to pay tribute to the war dead dates from May 1915, when the war was barely ten months old; the deputy proposing it, Revault, presented the measure as a powerful "encouragement" to soldiers, a promise that they would not be forgotten.[20] Other bills instituting various forms of commemoration, from plaques to registers of names to be deposited in town halls, cropped up at regular intervals throughout the war.[21]

Parliament began working on a definitive commemoration bill in May 1918; it took a year and a half for the two houses to work out their differences. Although the dispute involved details such as the precise location of a national war monument or the date of national commemorative observances, the main point of contention was whether the state should make some form of local commemoration obligatory. Several Senate versions of the bill would have required all French communes to put up a monument or at least a plaque in honor of their war dead, but the Chamber of Deputies consistently rejected them.[22] Barely a week after the armistice, a committee of the Chamber declared that "it is not necessary legally to prescribe to French municipalities the duty to honor and glorify the children of their commune who will have died in the defense of the fatherland; [we] are convinced that not a single one will fail in this duty."[23] In the end the Chamber prevailed: the bill that ultimately passed imposed no commemorative mandate on localities, while promising financial support for communities' own initiatives.[24]

Conducted largely in hypothetical terms, the debate on the 1919 law on commemoration effectively ignored the many monuments that had sprung up from the earliest days of the war. This commemorative apparatus included both individual graves and collective memorials; indeed, it often blurred the distinction between them. In the Michelin guide to the Marne, for example, the word *tombe* can apply both to individual graves and to a group of tombs that together constitute a memorial and pilgrimage site.[25] Yet the commemorative urge first manifested itself not only on the battlefield but also at the local level, as towns and villages throughout the country sought to compensate for physical absence with the symbolic presence a monument could project. The town council of Caro, in the Morbihan, voted in November 1914 to build a monument to its dead sons (eight had already been killed) at the end of the war.[26] Also in the Morbihan, Moréac had by the fall of 1916 drawn up plans and organized a public subscription to raise funds for its monument. Clearly, that monument was meant to function at least in part as a substitute tomb: it was built in the cemetery plot where the commune's dead soldiers were to be buried after the war.[27] Such practices as these—simple, small-scale, rooted in the locality—offered at once consolation to the bereaved and a compelling model for those seeking to legitimate far more ambitious forms of commemoration.

The competition among groups seeking support for various commemorative projects after the war was in many ways a ruthless one. Visiting the World War I battlefields today, we see a landscape saturated with monuments, yet many grandiose projects, such as the proposal for an Arc de Triomphe in Bar-le-Duc to mark the beginning of the Voie Sacrée, the main supply route to Verdun in 1916, fell by the wayside for lack of financial support.[28] Few interest groups had greater success on this contested terrain than the committees that took charge of the construction of ossuaries to house the remains of the unidentified dead on the battlefields. Although ossuaries exist in cemeteries throughout the former war zone, four major ones have the status of national monuments: at Douaumont (Meuse) in the Verdun theater, Notre-Dame de Lorette (Pas-de-Calais) in Artois, Dormans in the Marne, and Hartmannswillerkopf in Alsace. All, however, were the fruits of private initiative, built by specially constituted committees headed by bishops and including prominent generals, local politicians, and society ladies who had been active in war relief work. The state provided only minimal financial assistance—less than 10 percent of the 15-million-franc cost of the Douaumont Ossuary, for example—but except at Dormans it did grant the committees sites in the midst of national cemeteries, and their status derived primarily from these prestigious locations.[29] All consisted of actual repositories for bones as well as religious and commemorative spaces, although a variety of architectural devices kept the chapels separate from the strictly memorial areas. All proclaimed as their purpose the perpetuation of memories of the war and, especially, of the dead.

The ossuary committees owed much of their success to the effort and prestige of the clerics who led them. For two bishops, Charles Ginisty of Verdun, the head of the Douaumont committee, and Eugène Julien of Arras, for Lorette, the ossuaries represented a logical extension of their efforts on behalf of their flocks during four years of bombardment, evacuation, and privation.[30] No one could doubt the genuineness of their concern for the bereaved at the war's end. Yet they would not have been doing their jobs if they had not also been concerned with the larger interests of the Roman Catholic Church. The 1905 Law of Separation had unilaterally ended the church's official connection to the French state, and the church had long been the object of suspicion and hostility on the part of French Republican leaders. Out of patriotic as well as political impulses, the church had rushed to embrace the national cause during the war. Bishops organized patriotic prayer services and urged France's cause among Catholics in neutral countries, while thousands of young seminarians volunteered for military service, many at the cost of their lives.[31] At the end of the war, church leaders at all levels hoped that their record of service and devotion to the country would help not only to consolidate the position of the church but actually to restore it to its preseparation centrality in national life. But four years of conflict, and growing problems of morale, had reduced the credibility of virtually all large-scale institutions that had supported the war effort.[32] Thus, instead of memories fading with the passage of time, as the twenties progressed the church's need of its wartime reputation only increased.

Both ossuaries and local monuments grew out of the very practical need, physical as well as emotional, to bring order and resolution to the chaos of bodies that remained one of the most poignant legacies of the war. Under a law promulgated on 29 December 1915, the Ministry of War had the authority to expropriate terrain needed to bury soldiers not only, as one draft would have stipulated, when existing civilian cemeteries proved inadequate, but whenever it saw fit.[33] Over the next two years the military was able to replace mass graves with individual tombs and to regroup them in distinct military cemeteries. But the German offensive and the rapidly shifting fronts of 1918 disrupted much of this work, as cemeteries were attacked, abandoned, and sometimes destroyed. By the end of the war burial conditions once more verged on the chaotic.[34]

Two weeks after the armistice, a government decree transformed the burial services attached to each of the French army corps into a semiautonomous Office des Sépultures Militaires (military burial service) within the Ministry of War, with an independent high commission to supervise it.[35] But the burial service remained chronically understaffed, ill-equipped to cope with the disorder left by the last stages of the war, including masses of fragmentary, unidentifiable remains and an enormous number—a later report put it at 200,000—of isolated graves, many without proper identification, scattered throughout the former war zone.[36] Readers of early war narratives like Genevoix's *Ceux de 14* would have had a good idea of the dimensions of the problem. In one passage, set in October 1914, Genevoix is walking in the woods in the Meuse when he comes upon a makeshift cemetery. Already, he observes, the primitive crosses that marked the tombs of foot soldiers were sinking into the earth, rotting, or splitting, "And it was last month, only last month, that war came to this countryside!"[37]

Yet the familiarity of lost tombs as a trope of the war experience did not attenuate public concern about the fate of soldiers' remains, nor did it make families more tolerant of delay. Indeed, at the end of the war conditions in military cemeteries rapidly reached the proportions of scandal. Impatient with the slow pace of identification and regrouping, families of means hired private contractors to carry out clandestine (and illegal) exhumations and return the bodies of their loved ones to them.[38] Corruption among these contractors fueled further controversy, as did stories of incompetence and indecent profits among those officially hired to search for bodies. Rumors about the lack of respect for the dead shown by some workers and battlefield tourists also aroused indignation.[39]

Partially concealed under the noise of controversy and the common rhetoric of patriotism and mourning lay a divisive struggle over a fundamental question of policy: where to bury the dead. France's allies had managed to resolve the issue relatively simply, if not without controversy, the British by forbidding exhumations, the Americans by permitting them, while at the same time creating at Romagne (Meuse) a cemetery that became the envy of many French observers (fig. 2.3). Matters were not so simple in France. On the one hand, veterans, politicians, and families of the dead insistently called for a

FIGURE 2.3. Meuse-Argonne American Military Cemetery, Romagne (Meuse). Photo: Author.

liberal exhumation policy, in which the state would pay for the transfer to local cemeteries of all remains requested by relatives.[40] On the other hand, authorities in the still scarred battle areas, as well as some generals and a few politicians, urged that the dead be left where they had fallen.[41] Although both sides justified their positions in terms of the presumed wishes of the soldiers themselves, self-interest also came into play. One of the leading advocates of burial at the front, a periodical called *La voie sacrée* (the name here generalized to denote the whole front) was the organ of the national tourist board, which regarded visits to graves as an important element in reconstruction.[42] The wholesale removal of bodies might also have had undesirable symbolic overtones for residents of the devastated departments.

In other parts of France, however, the families of the dead, and the local officials they elected, felt keenly not only the absence of the dead but the lack of a place where they could mourn them. In August 1919, in a speech delivered at a ceremony marking a "Journée de la Reconnaissance Nationale" for French soldiers, the mayor of Blois spoke of the absent bodies in these terms: "But how many sons of our region [*pays*] lie far away, in cemeteries in the midst of ruins, enfolded by the land where their sacrifice stopped the invading horde? Though we cannot visit them, let their names remain engraved in our memories."[43] Monuments and names together filled the role played by bodies in traditional mourning rituals. The metaphor of "engraving in memory," with its obvious connection to the inscription of names on monuments, would become virtually a cliché of commemorative ceremonies. Its utility lay in the implicit parallel it establishes between the monument and the bodies it represents, not only the dead but the living whose memories the monument seeks to fix in stone.

In more ways than one, the state found itself in the middle of the debate over burials. As the state's representatives, ministers and prefects routinely presided over ceremonies, notably monument dedications, that implicitly claimed the locality as the privileged seat of patriotism and mourning. The government could not openly oppose the desire of relatives to reclaim the bodies of their loved ones, but it had too many demands on its own limited resources to encourage calls for universal reinterment in local cemeteries. On the other hand, the government could not ignore the increasingly insistent, even strident calls from members of Parliament for a liberal exhumation policy. When, in September 1919, the undersecretary responsible for this issue, Léon Abrami, told the Chamber of Deputies that "on a question of this nature and this magnitude, it is unthinkable that there should be a major difference between the Chamber and the government," he was giving voice not simply to a polite commonplace, but to stark political reality.[44]

The government's first inclination was to temporize. In February 1919 it introduced a bill that would have extended through 1921 the military's ban on the transfer of remains to private citizens. The proposed legislation cited the disorder of current burial arrangements, the need to locate and identify many unmarked graves, and the lack of available transportation, particularly in the war zone, where both train tracks and rolling stock had suffered severe damage.[45] The bill was greeted with near universal hostility. Even the stolid daily *Le temps*, usually close to the government, weighed in with a leader article highly critical of the government's position. Revealingly, the newspaper couched its opposition in terms of a contrast between collective and individual forms of commemoration: it had nothing against the former, *Le temps* declared, but the government had to stop regarding the bodies of the dead as "its property [*sa chose*]."[46]

In separate appearances before the two houses of Parliament, undersecretary Abrami described the government as caught between two incompatible philosophies, or as he called them "systems," of commemoration. Two prominent politicians, both of whom had lost sons in the war, had framed the debate as members of the National War Graves Commission.[47] The first system, identified with Paul Doumer, future finance minister and president of France, conceived of the front as "an immense necropolis of [grave] monuments." Imitating the British, this system would leave the dead on the former battlefields, assuring them, as they lay with their comrades, the perpetual care and attention of the state.[48] A second system, which Louis Barthou, a former prime minister and future foreign minister, had defended as "equally respectable," would return the dead to their hometowns for the devotion that only a family could provide.[49] The government, Abrami declared, could not impose a choice between these options; he thus conceded in principle that families who wanted to bury their sons at home should eventually have the right to do so, at the government's expense.[50]

Although Abrami insisted that the government was delaying for purely practical reasons, namely the devastation of the former war zone, he failed to assuage his critics. Following parliamentary elections in November 1919, the first minister of pensions in the new government, the distinguished veteran André Maginot, moved swiftly to conciliate veterans and the families of the dead. In the summer of 1920, the government announced that it would begin returning remains to families that requested them toward the end of that year. Maginot, however, expressed his personal view that the dead should be buried with their comrades on the battlefield. As incentives to families to choose that option, the government offered perpetual care and the promise—enacted into law the following year—of a free annual visit to the graves for parents, widows, and children.[51]

Proponents of the transfer of remains constructed the contest over them as a classic struggle between an overweening, insensitive state bureaucracy and powerless families. The terms of this construction were familiar ones: public versus private, collective interests versus individual rights, abstract policy versus concrete suffering. Both sides in the debate claimed to take inspiration from wishes they attributed to the dead; they could agree only that, in the absence of any clear and comprehensive statement of their desires, the preferences of their families should have priority.[52] It would be simplistic, however, to reduce this struggle to an opposition between the state and localities, or between collective and individualist notions of commemoration. Far more complex displacements, substitutions, and reversals, to use Foucault's terms, were involved.

Critics of the government, for example, stopping at nothing to make their case, occasionally found it useful to cast aspersions on their opponents in the highly charged language of the nationalist right. The monthly (sometimes semimonthly) newspaper *L'art funéraire et commémoratif* was, as we will see in chapter 4, essentially a publicity sheet for commercial monument manufacturers. At least in part to establish its own legitimacy within the commemorative arena, shortly after its initial appearance in the spring of 1919 *L'art funéraire* organized a petition drive in favor of immediate, government-funded exhumations, and eventually gathered 30,000 signatures.[53] The newspaper's articles on the burial question included an anti-Semitic attack on Abrami, a xenophobic comparison between French and Allied rates of exhumation (the Allies were much further along), and an attack on a supporter of burial at the front on the grounds that he was not a father.[54] Even in the more circumspect context of a parliamentary debate, politicians routinely couched their arguments for the return of bodies in the imagery of "villages" and "native soil" (*pays natal*).[55] Such language not only portrayed France as Arcadia, ignoring the many dead who came from cities, it also tapped into the rhetoric and ideology of the nationalist leader Maurice Barrès.[56]

In contrast, although some government officials undoubtedly lacked sensitivity to the concerns of families, one of their main arguments for delay rested on the basic republican principle of equality. Some, like Barthou, asked why families who knew where their sons were buried and could afford to reclaim their bodies should not be allowed to do so. Abrami and others replied that the government could not contemplate "two regimes, one of favor, that would benefit only the rich . . . and another that would apply to the poor, to farmers, to workers, to . . . the majority of citizens who lack the means to pay for illicit exhumations and are obliged patiently to await an agreement between the government and Parliament." Bureaucratic as it might be, this response had a certain stiff-necked justice to it. The government's opponents were reduced to arguing that in such matters there could be no equality.[57]

Nor did the proponents of immediate exhumation have a monopoly on moving or disturbing anecdotes. Abrami recounted how a family found nothing in a Meuse cemetery plot officially identified as their son's grave, then, after a prolonged search, witnessed the excavation of thirty to forty bodies intermingled in a single plot. "Can one reasonably envision," he asked rhetorically, "subjecting families to a sight of this kind?"[58] Other graves marked with the names of French soldiers had instead turned out to contain German remains. The government took seriously its responsibility to find and identify as many bodies as possible, and officials could turn the tables on those who claimed, as antistate rhetoric often did, that they were mired in abstraction. "We must not view these things in theory, in the light of sentiment," Abrami told the Senate. "They must be seen in the harsh and sometimes tragic light of the realities of the front."[59] One member of the War Graves Commission, originally convinced that families' demands deserved an immediate response, said that he returned from a tour of the battlefields "with my opinions completely changed."[60]

Maginot's compromise policy of course did not satisfy everyone. Some deputies, for example, objected that the state's offer of perpetual care over the graves of soldiers at the front unfairly discriminated against families wishing to bring their loved ones home. But the most controversial aspect of government policy, once it had agreed to permit the transfer of remains to private citizens, had to do with the transfers the state continued to carry out on its own authority. The state's effort to find and identify bodies went along with a project to regroup them in large battlefield cemeteries. This regrouping had a number of justifications. On a practical level, bodies could hardly be left scattered in fields and forests and by the sides of roads: such graves, Abrami suggested, would soon disappear without a trace.[61] Symbolically, battlefields offered more fitting sites of mourning than the cemeteries in small towns near the front where many soldiers had been buried. From the point of view of national pride, too, many felt the need in some way to match the tidy plots and the careful landscaping of the Allies' cemeteries. "When you see the admirable cemetery for 25,000 Americans at Romagne," Doumer told the national commission, "you will want us to have comparable ones wherever our sons distinguished themselves."[62]

But families and veterans found the regrouping wanting both in principle and in practice. In practice, they complained that they were often not notified of the transfer of remains, and thus risked a painful surprise if they went to visit the original site.[63] Moreover, criticism in the press and Parliament of the poor conditions of existing cemeteries suggests a persistent distrust of the state's competence in this regard.[64] The war cemetery, that "immense necropolis" that some saw not only as a sign of national pride but as guarantor of continued recognition of the dead, became for its opponents a figure for the soulless inhumanity of the war. L'art funéraire et commémoratif, somewhat incongruously for a publication peddling mass-produced monuments, even objected to the government's rumored bulk order of grave markers, calling them "posthumous

FIGURE 2.4. Muslim war graves, Douaumont Cemetery (Meuse). Photo: Author.

uniforms." The state, of course, justified this uniformity in terms of equality; in any case, regulations did permit variations in the shape of the tombstones according to the religious affiliations of the deceased.[65] The cemetery at Douaumont includes 592 graves of Muslim soldiers, grouped together and oriented toward Mecca (fig. 2.4). They do not disrupt the regularity of the cemetery, but do at least hint at the diversity of those, including an estimated 600,000 troops from the French colonies, who fought for France.[66]

The main grounds for opposition to regrouping, however, was that the displacement contradicted the very rationale for leaving bodies at the front: that the poilus had wanted to be buried as close as possible to where they fell.[67] In April 1922 a group of deputies even proposed giving families who had decided not to reclaim their loved ones' bodies a "second option" to do so, at such time as the state decided to transfer those remains to a new or different cemetery.[68] Though nothing came of this proposal—the deadline for families to request transfers, already extended several times, had passed several months previously—it demonstrates the extent to which large military cemeteries struck some families as a betrayal of the government's original promise.

In a sense, the most disturbing aspect of the national cemeteries lay in their very essence: the attempt to impose order on the chaos of war. This order is, of course, factitious, and masks even the complexity of the cemeteries' creation. Walking through the serried rows of graves, one finds no apparent order: neither alphabetical, nor chronological, nor by military unit. From the beginning, families have had to rely on registers of names kept by the cemetery staff to find the graves of their loved ones.[69] That is because the actual location of graves in the necropoles resulted from such chance factors as the pace of transfers from smaller cemeteries elsewhere, physical conditions in the new cemeteries, which could delay burials, and the number of subsequent exhumations requested by families.[70] The 20,000 bodies at Lorette came from many different cemeteries in Belgium and northern France; Douaumont gathered together bodies from twenty-two cemeteries in the Verdun theater, and a hitherto unknown military cemetery containing over fifty World War I dead was discovered near Verdun as late as 1949.[71]

Almost by default, the two sides to the burial dispute could agree on one thing, the treatment of the missing. Senator Simonet observed in presenting his bill to permit exhumations that the number of unidentified bodies made the rivalry between Abrami's two "systems" almost irrelevant. "When all is said and done," he wrote, "not every family will be able to obtain the restitution of their dead, even if all of them requested it, which will not be the case. . . . Alas, thousands of anonymous, unidentified heroes will not be lacking to populate the vast necropoles of the front with their shades."[72] In principle, the division was fairly simple: identified remains were entitled to individual graves, those that could not be identified were to be housed in ossuaries. The latter category constituted a potentially enormous number of bodies, but in 1922 a number of senators criticized the Ministry of Pensions for including whole bodies among the remains to be deposited in the ossuaries. Ossuaries, they declared, were intended to house only "scattered, jumbled remains"; all bodies intact enough to have been buried provisionally in individual graves should continue to receive one.[73] The many anonymous but individual tombs in the modern battlefield cemeteries indicate that the government eventually heeded the senators' wishes; even death had its hierarchies.

In 1922 the impressive monumental ossuaries were, like the battlefield cemeteries of which they would form a part, still largely in the planning stage. But the committees in charge of building the ossuaries had clear notions of the functions they would fulfill: not for them the modest guardianship of fragmentary remains. The ossuary committees had to work hard behind the scenes to secure the setting they desired for their monuments.[74] Local leaders of the associations, like Bishop Ginisty of Verdun, relied heavily on the support of such influential figures as Marshal Pétain, the honorary president of the Douaumont committee, General de Castelnau, a member of its patrons' committee, and Victor Schleiter, the mayor of Verdun and a deputy from the Meuse. The Douaumont committee also took full advantage of the prominence of two other Meuse politicians, Raymond Poincaré, president of France from 1913 to 1920 and twice prime minister in the 1920s, and his trusted acolyte André Maginot. Even without such powerful contacts, the Lorette committee had sufficient influence in Paris to force the Ministry of Pensions to realign the existing cemetery there around a new axis consisting of the basilica and ossuary tower. In order to avoid similar problems at Douaumont, the ministry encouraged field officials of its war graves service to cooperate with the ossuary committee in laying out the cemetery.[75]

The ossuary committees' stake in the debate over burial sites was clear. As the Douaumont bulletin put it, "We prefer—and who could reproach us for it?—to keep close to us, close to the front, along the line of battle, those who so valiantly defended us."[76] Only the repeated intervention of the Douaumont committee and its influential supporters could have brought about the creation of a cemetery on such an unpropitious site. State officials soon discovered that the ossuary association had grandiose designs for Douaumont. The architect wanted 30 hectares (nearly 75 acres) cleared for the cemetery, whereas the ministry anticipated no more than 10. Given the hilly terrain and its state of total devastation (the site chosen had been at the center of one of the most murderous battles of the war), the cost of clearing even 10 hectares bordered on the prohibitive.[77] As work on the site dragged on and its cost mounted, the ministry, responding to the continued flow of exhumations, and under pressure to preserve other cemeteries in the area, gradually reduced the size of the planned Douaumont cemetery.[78] Supporters of the ossuary waged a vigorous campaign to restore the cemetery to its originally planned size. In 1926 Ginisty, Pétain, Schleiter, and the Princesse de Polignac wrote to the minister of pensions, Louis Marin, stressing the need for a French military cemetery as impressive as its American counterpart nearby in Romagne.[79] The ministry, which had once made a similar argument, rejected the comparison, noting that the Americans had only five such cemeteries in France, whereas the French government had to maintain nearly four hundred. But by the time the ossuary was inaugurated in the summer of 1932, the cemetery contained more than 15,000 bodies, well above the ministry's low estimate of 9,000, in addition to the unidentified remains of an estimated 32,000 inside.[80] The tawny stone and gray metal nameplates used for French war graves are less imposing than the neoclassical grandeur, the dazzling whiteness of the tombstones, at Romagne. As the committee intended, however, it is virtually impossible today to think of the Douaumont Ossuary apart from its setting (fig. 2.5)—or, indeed, to think of the Douaumont cemetery as anything other than as the setting for the ossuary.

But to have argued in an open or partisan way for battlefield cemeteries would have damaged the committees' prestige, and perhaps even put off potential contributors. The brilliance of the tactic they chose to make their public case lay in their ability to appropriate the issue of burial for their own ends, while circumventing its most contentious points. By focusing on the emotionally resonant but spatially indeterminate names of the dead, yet portraying

FIGURE 2.5.
Ossuary and cemetery,
Douaumont. Photo:
Author.

their attitude toward bodies as one of sensitive concern, the ossuary committees defused potential controversy, guaranteed their prestige, and secured a position as one of the leading sites of postwar commemoration.

Inscribing Absence

Put off by the impersonality, the scale, or the remoteness of the new national cemeteries, many families did avail themselves of the opportunity to reinter their sons' and husbands' bodies in local cemeteries. In towns as different as St. Tropez and Levallois-Perret (fig. 2.6), the war memorial either stands near these transferred remains or incorporates vaults in which they are interred. But however much some may have preferred the presence of tangible remains to their simulacra, they had to face the fact that a large number of the dead would never be recovered as identifiable bodies. On the morning of the inauguration of the monument in Dieue, in the Meuse, in October 1922, the president of the local veterans' association observed that only seventeen of the town's fifty-two dead had been returned. Some of the remainder were buried in military ceme-

FIGURE 2.6. War monument, Levallois-Perret (Hauts-de-Seine). Photo: Author.

teries, but many, he sighed, "are forever buried in the mud of Flanders and of the Somme, the chalky soil of the Marne, the forests of the Argonne, in our own Lorraine region, and under the pines of the Vosges."[81]

In the absence of bodies, names served both to trigger memory and to construct it as a responsibility, and a right, of the local community. Again and again, speakers at dedication ceremonies stressed that the newly completed monument now belonged to the commune, which thereby assumed the responsibility to care for it and to preserve the memories it embodied.[82] At a city council meeting in Vannes, in the Morbihan, in December 1918, a returning prisoner of war said of the dead:

Their names should be glorified not only by the generations that have witnessed their heroism, but by all generations . . . They must therefore be forever engraved on our most durable monuments, so that they may be transmitted to our children, who will return to them in tribute what they receive from them in examples.[83]

Through an obvious process of displacement, which we will consider in greater detail in chapter 6, names become the vehicle for the transmission of meaning, a civic pedagogy in which they stand for "heroism," receive "tribute," and provide "examples" of imitable virtue.[84] A number of monuments offer a striking visual representation of this process, like the one in Guémené-sur-Scorff (fig. 2.7) where a mother, clad in recognizable Breton garb, shows her son the monument's actual list of names.[85]

But monuments demanded another kind of displacement, a transfer of emotion from the body of the deceased to the inscribed name, and this elision of bodies and names hardly proceeded without resistance. It was in effecting this delicate process of transference, clearly akin to Freud's notion of mourn-

FIGURE 2.7. War monument, Guémené-sur-Scorff (Morbihan). Photo: Author.

ing,[86] that the ossuary committees proved so wily. Their strategy had two distinct but related components, and both involved names. First, the associations' periodic bulletins, the subscribers to which constituted the only effective membership they had, characterized themselves as a kind of information bureau at the service of families searching for remains. They regularly printed the names of identified bodies found in their sector, inventories of the objects found on unidentified remains, and, later, notices of the transfer of remains. They also publicized their services in both local and veterans' newspapers.[87]

Lorette's bulletin included a section called "Spes contra spem" consisting of letters from readers who had found the remains of their sons or husbands on the basis of information they had read in the journal.[88] Going beyond the ossuaries' limited role as repositories for unidentifiable remains, the building committees made themselves, in effect, the moral guardians of all the dead of their respective theaters. Among other things, they sponsored annual religious pilgrimages for the families of the dead—buried or missing, identified or not.[89] Describing the 1931 exhumation of six bodies for return to their families, the bulletin of Notre-Dame de Lorette wrote pointedly, "God willing, may the night of forgetfulness never descend on their memory, and may their graves, carefully distinguished from other graves, always receive what the dead of the cemetery of Lorette will never lack: a special tribute of admiration, gratitude, and prayer."[90] Playing on the fear of forgetting at the heart of commemoration, the Lorette committee challenges the claims of localities that *their* monuments and inscriptions could secure memory for future generations. After all, the text suggests, that way is untried; the church has been in the memory business for centuries.

The second element of the ossuary committees' strategy played on the obsession with names that communal monuments all over France had made manifest. First Lorette, then Douaumont offered contributors the opportunity to inscribe the name of a loved one inside the ossuary. At Douaumont, the cost ranged from 200 francs for name and regiment number alone to 500 francs for a more prominently located inscription of first and last names, regiment number, and dates of birth and death; Lorette asked a more modest 100 to 250 francs.[91] At least at Douaumont, the idea met with all the success the committee could have wished. The Douaumont committee first proposed paid inscriptions not long after reporting a drop-off in individual contributions (as opposed to those gathered by parish or other groups). In the first months thereafter, the bulletin reported that a large proportion of the increased contributions received came from those wishing to inscribe stones.[92]

In the association bulletins, the lists of names form an uninterrupted sequence: names of the dead inscribed by contributors, names of bodies recently unearthed, the latter continuing through the 1930s. Publishing names inscribed inside the ossuaries as well as names found outside on individual tombstones established the associations' commitment to a generalized *culte du souvenir* that would perpetuate individual memory. In this way, the ossuary committees appropriated not only local mourning practices, but also a basic strategy of the state in its dealings with veterans and families of the war dead. Avoiding the shared responsibility of the state and of national institutions for the enormous *collective* loss, church and state officials cast themselves as the guardians and protectors of the dead as individuals. They thus effected a double reversal. At the level of commemorative practice, the individual dead became the touchstone of observances carried out in the name of a collectivity, whether the church or the nation. The narrative accompanying those practices, meanwhile, transformed compulsory service into voluntary sacrifice, obscuring the relationship of domination that had sent to their deaths the "heroes" whose memory both church and state vowed to preserve.

Annette Becker has argued that postwar commemoration grew seamlessly out of the revival of faith evident during the war.[93] All the ossuary associations, it is true, situated their activities in a framework of popular Catholic piety: novenas, pilgrimages, requiem masses, and the like. The devout could also earmark their contributions to the ossuaries' Catholic chapels rather than to the secular burial spaces.[94] Beyond this, the ossuary bulletins regularly published speeches and lectures that construed the war in terms of Christian sacrifice and patriotic devotion to country.[95] Yet the recourse to paid inscriptions points to the limits of a memorial discourse based on traditional notions of collective sacrifice and to its gradual elision, even in these spaces of high Catholic observance, with a discourse of individual loss. In 1928, a priest writing in the Lorette bulletin reflected:

Doubtless the cult of memory is not necessarily religious, and if purely touristic visits hardly seem compatible with the solemnity of the site, it is easy to imagine that even those who have neither faith nor hope in the afterlife will come to wander among the tombs as philosophers, patriots, and good Frenchmen, thinking human thoughts and offering the fallen heroes their share of human glory.[96]

Effectively acknowledging that commemoration did not afford the church the chance to vanquish its secular opponents, this text espouses an unabashed pragmatism; a live-and-let-live attitude gave the committees all the opportunity they needed to be major players in postwar commemoration.

The builders of the ossuaries undoubtedly sought to inculcate in visitors not only a commemorative discourse with which they were already familiar but also more traditional Catholic doctrine. In a self-consciously artless sermon to a group of children at the dedication of the Douaumont Ossuary, Bishop Ginisty took note of the cruciform shape of the tower walls, characterizing them as a giant tomb marker:

FIGURE 2.8.
Basilica and ossuary,
Notre-Dame de
Lorette (Pas-de
Calais). Photo:
Author.

The monument is a mausoleum: the most humble of graves has its monument, the little wooden cross that stands above it. And what a fine mausoleum this is: [it is] the cross of Christ, cross of the Redemption, the cross that has been set on every tomb, the cross placed on the chests of our brave heroes; the cross of honor to which everyone aspires, the cross of immortality, whose extended arms cry out unceasingly for the mercy of Almighty God.[97]

In a pastoral letter urging contributions to complete the ossuary at Notre-Dame de Lorette, Bishop Julien of Arras justified the construction of the huge Byzantine-style chapel by saying that the "Christian faith" to which most of the soldiers adhered, at least in death, "calls for a properly religious *ex-voto* that is a sign of true and felicitous immortality, the necessary crown on that perishable and impersonal immortality represented by the monuments of public gratitude."[98] The basilica opened in 1927, without most of its interior decoration, but with walls and columns ready for the inscription of names.

Visiting Lorette today (fig. 2.8), one notices first of all—one can hardly avoid it—the sheer massiveness of the religious structures and the insistently Christian decoration. Plans for the chapel/basilica included mosaic flooring reminiscent of the cathedral of St. Omer, this according to the architect, who was also responsible for the basilica of Ste. Thérèse in Lisieux. Stained-glass windows, the gift of the British Imperial War Graves Commission, depict two martial saints, George and Joan of Arc.[99] The monumental tomb of Bishop Julien, who died in 1930, stands in one corner of the chapel. Worshipers can pray not only to Notre-Dame de Lorette but to a mosaic representing the Black Virgin of Czestochowa, the gift of Poland. Only the eclecticism of the stylistic references and the luster of the materials risk distracting the visitor from the religious message.[100] The lantern tower that rises atop the ossuary proper marks the ostensibly secular portion of the ossuary complex. Yet the tower's raised cruciform stonework unmistakably evokes the traditional *lanterne des morts,* and was occasionally so described in Lorette's publications. Rooted in the folk custom of placing a lantern in the window of a recently deceased person's home, the *lanterne des morts* had long found architectural expression in cemeteries, particularly in western France, where they were of course Christianized.[101]

trad mourning

The Christian iconography at Douaumont (fig. 2.9) seems less insistent, in part because of the form of the structure, oddly reminiscent, as J.-M. de Busscher has remarked, of a submarine.[102] Still, the ossuary there also has its *lanterne,* funded largely by the American Knights of Columbus, with, as

FIGURE 2.9.
Ossuary, Douaumont.
Photo: Author.

Ginisty proclaimed, a raised cross on each of its four sides. And though the Catholic chapel was funded separately from the ossuary proper, it sits at the center of the monument, on axis with the main entrance.[103] Visitors may thus not realize its functional distinctness from the ossuary, which consists of a ceremonial space generally referred to as the "cloister," although it is a fully enclosed foyer running the length of the building. The Douaumont cemetery also contains monuments to the Jewish and Islamic dead of Verdun, the symbolic counterparts to the Catholic chapel, but they do not form part of the ossuary complex.[104]

We cannot assume, however, that visitors to the ossuaries between the wars reacted passively to their surroundings, assimilating the proffered religious imagery without resistance. Many, undoubtedly, were believers, visiting the ossuary and chapel as part of some larger religious devotion. But given the long history of conflict between the church and the French Republic, the religious character of the ossuaries was also bound to provoke resistance. Both before and after the completion of the Douaumont Ossuary, individuals ranging from prominent French Masons to radical politicians objected to the prominence of the Catholic chapel there and called for the creation of a "neutral" organization to administer the ossuary.[105] At Lorette, veterans' groups protested the committee's sale of religious objects inside the basilica, leading the state to intervene. Eventually, the sales were stopped. Although the veterans couched their opposition in terms of the unseemliness of "commerce" inside the cemetery, the state read their position as secularist as well.[106]

The associations' best efforts notwithstanding, moreover, the ossuaries could attract opposition simply as part of the "immense necropolis" that some politicians, and many veterans, continued to find distasteful. Writing in a veterans' newspaper in February 1922, a deputy from the Somme, Gontrand Gonnet, expressed his opposition to new plans for battlefield cemeteries. Ossuaries merited barely a glancing dismissal in this critique: "It is anticipated that unknown bodies will be buried together in a *single ossuary*. It's an idea; I find it unfortunate." Gonnet considered a "multitude" of grave markers with a "uniform inscription to 'An unknown French soldier'" far more moving than "a stela bearing a summary, official figure [*chiffre*]."[107] Ossuaries are here elided with the impersonality of collective representation, one that privileges numbers over the designation of individuals.

It is telling that Gonnet should have used as a figure for ossuaries a type of vernacular design, the stela, most commonly found on war memorials, to which ossuaries bore only the most superficial resemblance. He seems to be drawing a contrast between actual bodies and the monuments that stood in for them: the former, in the common view, offered far greater consolation to the bereaved than their symbolic representation. But the main signifying mark on local monuments was not numbers but names. In contrast to the ossuaries' sale of inscriptions, local officials went to considerable trouble to establish definitive lists of the dead, in general including all those who had been born in a town or whose death certificates listed it as the person's official residence.[108] Yet at the local level too, inscriptions operated as part of a larger economy of commemoration.

Most towns, as we will see in the next chapter, raised at least part of the cost of their monuments through public subscription; relatives of the dead were among those who typically solicited contributions. People who feared some lapse or oversight in the recording of a name, for example members of families who had left a commune before or during the war, often enclosed a contribution with their inquiry, though of course they were not obligated to do so.[109] When a soldier had been born in one town, married in a second, and mobilized in a third, it could be difficult to find any community willing to accept responsibility for inscribing his name. The evident distress of a baker in Morée (Loiret-Cher), whose brother-in-law's name was rejected by three different communes, testifies to the highly emotional investment that fueled this economy. Although the baker, Monsieur Redouin, wrote somewhat bitterly that the response he had gotten "is not likely to encourage patriotism," others in his situation might have been inclined to make a contribution to an ossuary, simply to ensure that the name would be inscribed *somewhere*.[110]

If, in other words, uncertainty was a problem for the builders of local monuments, it presented an opportunity for the ossuaries to carve a niche for themselves in the economy of mourning. In a fund-raising speech in 1924, Canon Collin, one of the clerics on the Douaumont committee, constructed the ossuaries' role as complementary to that of local monuments. Speaking of the missing, Collin said, "There is not a village in France that has gathered up the remains of all its dead: many names on funeral monuments are accompanied by a singularly sad notation: 'Missing.'" The cleric suggested that Bishop Ginisty's original proposal for a definitive ossuary had sought above all to give the missing a fitting memorial. In a passage from the 1919 speech that Collin quoted, however, the bishop had anticipated that the ossuary would inscribe the names of *all* the dead in the Verdun theater; Collin did not note that only those names whose families could afford to pay for them would actually appear on the ossuary's walls.[111]

At least in 1920–21, during the period in which families could reclaim bodies at the government's expense, names shared a certain portability with the bodies they identified. Under the decree of September 1920 that governed the operation of military cemeteries, however, fragmentary remains could be interred only in the relevant ossuary. The arrangement of these remains offered the ossuary associations an opportunity to create a new type of memorial site. Tombs had bodies and, usually, names, although many marked the resting place of unidentified soldiers. Local monuments had names and sometimes bodies, but they almost invariably included names without the bodies that corresponded to them. Ossuaries combined selective lists of names with fragments of bodies that might or might not correspond to them. The ossuaries' uniqueness, as Ginisty had anticipated in first sketching his vision of the Douaumont complex in 1919, lay in what they offered to the families of the missing: "the consolation or the illusion of believing that in that place there is something of their children."[112]

Consolation or illusion—we will return to this disconcertingly frank pairing shortly—the ossuaries attached considerable importance to facilitating this feeling of proximity to the remains, however fragmentary, of particular individuals. In March 1923 a jury chaired by Pétain chose the winner in an architectural competition for the Douaumont Ossuary. From that moment publicity about the design emphasized the attention it paid to the desires of private mourners. A full-page article on the competition in *L'illustration* featured two renderings by the winning architects, Léon Azéma and Jacques Hardy. One was an exterior view from the cemetery, the other an interior with the caption "Each of the sarcophagi, of which two will be housed in each bay, will rest above remains found in one of the 52 sectors of Verdun." The text of the article described a "special device in the crypt openings" that would permit the deposit of newly found remains in the appropriate section of the vault.[113] In other words, each of the symbolic tombs in the central nave of the ossuary thus sits atop a crypt containing remains found in a precisely delimited sector of the front. Lorette, with considerably less floor space in the ossuary, presents a similar if less elaborate arrangement consisting of eight coffins set over an open crypt; seven additional "ossuary" plots, containing the remains of an estimated 20,000 soldiers, are scattered throughout the cemetery.

The disposition of remains at Douaumont was so central to the ossuary's purpose that the Michelin guide to the Verdun sector mentions it even before the opening of the definitive structure. An article in *L'illustration* on the opening of the initial portion of the Douaumont Ossuary in 1927 (only the tower and six of the anticipated twenty-six bays of the "cloister" were completed) included a two-page photograph showing a procession of poilus carrying remains from the fifty-two sectors toward the new building. Two of the three smaller photographs that accompanied the article also feature the coffins.[114] For, as the builders never ceased to remind subscribers and potential visitors, the sectoral arrangement allowed those with no tomb to visit to feel that in kneeling before the appropriate catafalque, they might, in the words of the Princesse de Polignac, a war widow and co-president of the association, be close to *un peu de lui,* a little bit of him.[115]

Lest her meaning be mistaken, however, Madame de Polignac added that "it will seem to them [families] that since the mortal remains are closer, the spirit that has left them is nearer to them as well. The missing soldier is no longer entirely missing: between him and his survivors there is a more intimate communion, and thus consolation arises."[116] The word "consolation" leads us back to Bishop Ginisty's remarks, which the war widow's speech, steeped in Catholic devotion, helps to clarify. One might describe the link between "consolation" and "illusion" as theological, the gap between them as one that only faith can bridge. Both wary and disapproving of the wave of spiritualism and parareligious practices the war had fostered,[117] the church had to avoid suggesting that mere proximity to physical remains, in the absence of true belief, communicated anything of value. To think differently amounted to "illusion," whereas the faithful might find "consolation" through a spiritual "communion." Achieving such communion, however, required a prior acknowledgment that the "spirit" sought was only symbolized by the physical remains of a body. Above all the church wanted to avoid appearing to cater to more sensationalist interests or desires, desires suggested in de Busscher's account of how his family used to rush "greedily" into the ossuary at Notre-Dame de Lorette to gaze at the bones in the one coffin the authorities had left open. De Busscher attributes the subsequent closure of this coffin to the number of fainting incidents it caused, but we may also suspect that its obvious appeal to the morbid occasioned too much unease.[118]

Although no record of the dead of World War I could ever be complete, the inscriptions on local monuments, taken together, come closer to completeness than those in the ossuaries. But the peculiar combination of bodies and names they offer, as well as their location in a dense fabric of monuments and memorial sites, lends the ossuaries a stature and a durability in commemoration that few local monuments, more subject to the ravages of time, can hope to achieve. This is undoubtedly what Arno Mayer meant in writing that "Douaumont originated in civil society but soon became an official undertaking." Yet these massive and impersonal structures do not simply present, as Mayer would have it, "a civic religion of nationalism whose officiators were political, military and religious leaders with essentially conservative world views and agendas."[119] The ossuaries also embody a style of commemoration rooted in the emotion of individual mourning and given shape by small-scale, local commemorative practice. Whatever its claims to legitimacy, no memorial, no ritual, no sacred space could have taken root in postwar France without acknowledging and accommodating the enormous private loss the war had caused. Yet from that acknowledgment, virtually all memorial sites sought both to contain private loss and to channel it in particular directions. Wherever they appeared, names functioned as the instrument and privileged sign both of the initial accommodation and of the subsequent displacements it made possible.

"This Precious Patrimony"

The magnitude of their commemorative efforts exposes the ways in which both church and state sought to appropriate individual memories as the basis for collective narratives. By contrast, local commemorative practices appear closer to the Foucauldian category of "local knowledges." Genealogy, of course, seeks to rescue local knowledge from the marginality to which unitary or totalizing discourses, such as those of the nation-state and of Catholic dogma, consign it.[120] Yet even within the local community, commemoration does not simply reproduce such knowledge but transforms it. Even apart from the ceremonies they engender, monuments, through their use of inscriptions, engage in a public writing that commits individual names to a discourse construed in the process as collective memory. And Michel de Certeau reminds us that the urge to enact writing as a form of praxis is not ideologically innocent: "Scriptural practice has acquired a mythical value over the past four centuries by gradually reorganizing all the domains into which the Occidental ambition to compose its history, and thus to compose history itself, has been extended."[121]

How, then, can we understand the centrality of names in commemorative practice? Names constitute the first level of the ideology of a civil society organized on the basis of patrilineal descent. The inscription of a name attests to an individual's place in that society, without which a place in history would be literally unthinkable. A conservative veterans' newspaper articulated this social function of the name when it reported on a court decision that upheld a father's right to oppose the inscription of his son's name on a memorial plaque. The newspaper called the decision an "absolute error. . . . The patronymic is in no way a piece of property, but an institution of public order, even of security. To bear a name is an obligation as much as a right."[122]

In their role as social regulators, names have far less mobility than individuals, and the boundaries that names police starkly constrained the potential of commemoration to offer consolation. In 1921 a postal worker nearing retirement and thinking of returning to his native village of St. Maurice-sous-les-Côtes, in the Meuse, wrote to the town's mayor to ask whether the name of his son, who apparently had never lived in the village, could be carved on its monument. If it were not, he wrote, he would probably choose to move elsewhere, for even though he was in possession of his son's remains, "seeing this war memorial with its inscriptions, my son not among them, would be very painful to me."[123] We do not know the outcome of this plea, but in similar circumstances the petitioners invariably met with polite but firm refusals. If monumental inscriptions began with private loss, their recording was a collective act constrained by the arbitrary and largely inflexible ways in which society categorizes individuals.

Adopting de Certeau's schema, which locates a rupture in "scriptural practice" around the time of the Great War, we see names not as an absolute refusal of meaning but as a late stage in the modern scriptural economy dating from the seventeenth century. In this economy, "normative discourse 'operates' only if it has already become a story, a text articulated on something real and speaking in its name, i.e., a law made into a story and historicized [*une loi historiée et historicisée*], recounted by bodies."[124] Or, one might say, by names. Thus the heterogeneous character, and structural polarities, of commemoration in the period of its emergence. Indeed, local commemoration lent itself with sometimes startling ease to appropriations of various kinds. Despite its history of centralization, the French state, particularly in its republican manifestations, had long cultivated an ideal of the nation as rooted in local communities.[125] Such a discourse made possible a casting of commemoration, even at the local level, in a conservative, nationalist, and not coincidentally patriarchal mold. "The Fatherland [*La Patrie*], my dear friends," declared the mayor of Caro (Morbihan) at the dedication of its war memorial in 1923, "is that small patch of land that our ancestors inhabited, the land where you are, where your descendants will be; it is the earth you live off of, the field you cultivate, the house where you reside, your relatives, your friends, your churches, your beliefs, in short everything that surrounds you."[126]

The effort to make names the building blocks of the kind of "story" or narrative (*récit*) to which de Certeau refers sometimes produces a kind of catachresis, a strained or paradoxical rhetorical effect in which names seem to crack under the weight of two simultaneous dimensions of meaning, collective and individual. Two weeks after the dedication of the war memorial in Ploërmel a Catholic newspaper there published a long lyrical poem entitled "Leurs noms." The poem begins with an invocation: "Je vous chante, ô noms sacrés, gravés sur la pierre." It moves on to meditate on the functions of names at various stages of the lives of the town's dead, using the names as a device to address the dead directly. The sixth stanza is worth quoting in full (in French, since a translation could hardly do it justice):

Ils sont écrits, nimbés du hallo de gloire,
Car vous fûtes, sans peur, les modestes héros
Qui, sans fin brilleront au soleil de l'histoire
Dont les rayons très purs, éclairent vos tombeaux![127]

Written to provide consolation, the poem offers an implicit reply to the notion with which this chapter began, that for "history" the dead would necessarily remain "anonymous, because too many." The light of history, the poet suggests, would illuminate the tombs of individuals—including, presumably, the substitute tombs constituted by monuments' lists of names. The strain of this vision emerges in the awkwardly shifting pronouns and adjectives. Lurking in the gap between "they" (*ils*), the names, and "you" (*vous*), the dead, is all the ambiguity of a relationship between signifier and signified that has taken on mythic proportions, in this case the proportions of commemoration.

Perhaps to avoid overloading names with too many layers of meaning, speakers at dedication ceremonies normally constructed their individual and collective referents as, effectively, distinct stories. "To build monuments," declared the subprefect of Commercy, Toucas-Massillon, at the dedication of the war memorial in Sorcy in October 1921, "is to write the glorious history of France during the four terrible years." He continued, "to inscribe names on their [monuments'] granite is to give our heroes individual immortality, after they have attained collective immortality."[128] At first glance the "histories" evoked in such speeches seem for the most part to pertain to that collective dimension. Speakers compared the dead to great warriors of the past, from the Gauls to the Revolutionary popular armies, from the Napoleonic *Grande Armée* to the *mobiles* of 1870 whose loss, of course, they had now avenged.[129] Such analogies served a number of functions. They offered a ready-made set of images from which the qualities of the dead could be rhetorically deduced. As we will see in chapter 6, these qualities then served as examples for survivors to imitate, with their own highly contingent political meanings. As foils for the dead, the soldiers of the past also provided a basis for asserting the uniqueness of the experience of World War I. Speaking at Rouvrois-sur-Meuse in 1925, Toucas-Massillon evoked medieval pikesmen and harquebusiers, musketeers of the age of absolutism, the popular armies of the Revolution, and the soldiers of 1870. "If the rings in this continuous chain," he declared, "seem to be made of the same metal, the last was, without any doubt, forged and reforged tougher than any other."[130]

But these figures from the past also filled another function: they constructed a lineage, or in Foucauldian terms a descent, encompassing the soldiers of World War I and by implication continuing into the future. Thus, although they everywhere served the same general rhetorical purpose, many of the historical examples also had a certain local specificity. In the Meuse, one of the Lorraine departments never ceded to Germany, speakers tended to evoke figures like Joan of Arc, a native of the area, and the Revolution-era soldiers who defeated the Prussians at Valmy, in the neighboring department of the Marne. Dedicating a monument to the battle of the Argonne at La Haute Chevauchée in 1922, Poincaré neatly extended this lineage to the remote past by citing a phrase attributed to General Dumouriez, the commander at Valmy in 1792: the Argonne "'will be my Thermopylae,' Dumouriez had said, 'but I will not be killed there.'" Speaking in Commercy the following year, the prime minister used Joan of Arc as a figure for the native courage of Lorrainers in repelling repeated German invasions.[131]

Although such references crop up all over the country, in Brittany speakers also evoked distinctly Breton traditions of valor. Rhetorically addressing a number of Breton heroes including Bertrand du Guesclin, constable of France during the Hundred Years' War, a priest speaking at the dedication of the Ploërmel memorial told them, "Lean down to your sons and be proud. They are greater than you. You fought for a few hours, they fought for five years. You struck in shining armor, for a shield they had only the mud of the trenches. Like you, better than you, they carried out our motto, the old motto of our ancestors: 'Britanny to the fore!'" Emphasizing his own Breton background, the minister of public works, Yves Le Trocquer, said that on seeing the menhir, a traditional Celtic ritual stone that formed the war memorial in Quiberon, "anchored in the earth as the traditions of our Brittany are anchored in the past, it seems that centuries gone by join in with our own to cry out the memory of those who were the greatest among the great."[132]

Despite this gesture toward the memory of individuals, akin to that in the poem "Leurs noms," the lineage such references establish is almost entirely collective. Du Guesclin, Dumouriez, and Joan of Arc were all commanders, notable figures whose names—Joan's, of course, lacking the modern patronymic —emblematize the sum of individual displays of courage they were able to mobilize. A history or narrative constructed around these figures could cast only a reflected glory on the individuals whose names were inscribed on monuments. The verb *clamer* that Le Trocquer, oddly, chose to characterize the work of monuments, and of history, in transmitting memory, conveys the awkwardness of the connection he and the Ploërmel poet were trying to make. *Clamer* means to cry or shout, usually with violence, often in protest;[133] it is not a verb one would normally associate with memory or commemoration unless the imminent disappearance of memory provoked some kind of crisis. In this context its use verges on the aporetic.

The resonance of the name as bearer of memory extended beyond the contested realm of monuments and commemorative ritual. At the same time that ossuaries were appropriating that resonance on behalf of a religious vision of sacrifice and devotion to country, in the legislative arena others were using it to somewhat different ends. What passed for innovation, however—the first attempt to change the legal status of names since the promulgation of the Napoleonic code—also served a vision of French society rooted in notions of patriarchal order.

Existing law made it virtually impossible to change one's name, requiring an extraordinary decree of the Council of State to do so, and gave an individual the right to sue anyone who, by using his name, had caused him "pecuniary or moral" damage.[134] But in 1916 René Viviani, then the minister of justice, introduced a bill to allow collateral descendants to carry on a surname of which the last male bearer had died for his country. The proposal's *exposé des motifs*, or presentation, is worth quoting in extenso:

Transmitted, from male to male, to the members of a single family, the name is at each generation enriched by a tradition, an example, or a memory. Few of those who receive it in the cradle understand all its worth at first, for that appears to them fully only at the death of the men who bequeathed it to them. Then its value is increased by the tribute they pay to their memory, and by the faint but deep feeling, as old as mankind and just as eternal, that through the community of the name, they are connected to a whole mysterious past of which they are the tributaries. . . . Symbol of the past and the future, laden with the memory of the dead, as though impregnated with their joys and their sorrows, their efforts and their sacrifices, their disappointments and their hopes, from a simple abstract sign, born of use and custom, over time the patronym is, at least among the best of us, transformed, unconsciously and by a sort of instinct, into a living reality, animated by its own personal life, encompassing all the virtue of a race, humble or illustrious. Companion of our life, witness to our acts, it thus becomes our judge: it absolves or condemns, tolerates or defends. But in its turn, for honor alone, it too is defended. . . . It is in order to save this precious patrimony, for which so much blood is now being shed, that it is fitting to give our heroic dead the right to survive themselves, in a name transmitted as the sign of their sacrifice to those designated by the deceased's natural affection or free choice. It will cost them less to die if their name is saved from oblivion.[135]

Despite this lofty prose, which among other things portrays the transmission of names—as another wartime proposal had characterized monuments—as a compensation for soldiers' sacrifice, Parliament did not consider the bill during the war. In 1921 Viviani, no longer in government, reintroduced the proposal, which quickly won approval in the Chamber of Deputies. The committee reporting on the bill called the possibility of "nominative resurrection" an important legal innovation, one that would enlarge the significance of the name from "a distinctive sign of personality, a simple label" to "a symbol, a lesson in duty."[136] Thus the proposed legislation assumes the functions that in Viviani's text fall to the normal transmission of a family name through the generations.

When the bill reached the Senate the following year, however, the legal committee modified it, removing a provision allowing the last bearer of a name to bequeath it to any family member eligible to inherit property. The committee also excised a provision exempting claimants from court costs, on the grounds that such claims would "be inspired above all by a feeling of pride [*amour-propre*], no doubt legitimate, but not to the point of shielding them a priori from contributing financially to reach their ends."[137] In the floor debate, several senators insisted that the right to bequeath a name be restored, and the bill was sent back to committee. A year later it was passed in close to its original form.[138] The law's practical effects merit further study, but they were most likely limited to families of aristocratic descent. One of the few actual names cited in the debate on the measure had a particule: according to Senator Gourju, one Gabriel de Collomb had actually bequeathed his name to a relative before being killed in battle in 1917.[139] Yet the bill had wide support from veterans' groups, and they hailed its passage as an important innovation concerning that "element of the moral patrimony called the name."[140]

In its symbolic dimensions as well as its limits, the law of July 1923 opens a window onto the moral landscape in which the culture of commemoration was taking shape in the early twenties. One of the prominent features of this landscape, as we know from the work of Mary Louise Roberts and others, was a concern to shore up the structures of the family, which many felt the war had weakened.[141] Senators justified their initial excision of the direct bequest of names on the grounds that this might cause hard feelings within a family. The law as passed allowed other relatives to oppose an individual's claim to a name on the basis of his or her poor moral character. In a technical debate on the degree of consanguinity the law would recognize, Senator Morand, the bill's official reporter, called the name "a collective property, the property of an entire family, [that is] a group of citizens formed by ties of blood."[142] The legal definition of the family grew out of the fiscal code, which limited rights of succession to intestate estates to the sixth degree, and as such was admittedly artificial; prior to 1917 succession had been possible to the twelfth degree. If the name were, as Morand put it, "any old [quelconque] element of one's patrimony," it could be left to anyone. But, Morand argued, "if one grants the name this special, particular character of family property," it could be disposed of among members of a family only as defined by law.[143]

Family, law, blood—the name as intersection of these three terms clearly sums up the values that the French elites, at least, held dear. The term "family" designated not only the group that held a name in common, but also the beneficiaries of state-funded exhumations and the interest groups calling for them. One deputy tried to extend such benefits, in the case of soldiers without any surviving relatives, to friends who could prove their knowledge of the deceased's intent. The committee assigned to consider this proposal commented, in effect, that everything had limits, and the bill went no farther.[144] "Law," *le droit*, was, along with civilization, what the French, in the prevailing political discourse, had fought and died for in the war. "Blood," of course, was what French soldiers shed in the name both of this abstraction, the law, and of a larger one, their country. Yet the connection between blood and country also permitted the discursive construction of a more intimate purpose for soldiers' sacrifice, rooted in the double meaning of *pays*. A *pays* can betoken both one's country, that is France, the *patrie* or fatherland, and the more specifically familiar, and familial, area one calls home, "that small patch of land," in the words of the mayor of Caro, that soldiers were commonly thought to envision in their last moments.[145]

The name, "enriched by memory" and transmitted, following the provisions of the law, to a member of the "blood" group who would not otherwise have the right to bear it, would thus become a kind of living memorial. But in this operation the name, not the living person it described, would activate or vivify the "memorial" as a site of commemoration. In a similar way, names played a crucial role in constructing local monuments as substitute tombs, places where the bereaved could come to pray, to reflect, or simply to honor the memory of their dead. As the commune of Thenay, in the Loir-et-Cher, dedicated its monument in July 1922, the mayor declared that for those families who would never be able to visit their sons' graves in the local cemetery, "this is the place of meditation [*recueillement*]."[146] Monuments, and names themselves, as substitute tombs, on one level signified absence. Depending on one's perspective, names could either dignify an otherwise risible monument, by compelling the beholder to recall the dead, or seem abstract, remote, and desiccated in comparison to, say, an anthology of soldiers' writings. In either case the process is the same: names point to the absence of the dead, while something else—a memory, an image, a text, a prayer—is needed to summon their presence.[147]

The paramount French symbol of absence, loss, and whatever meaning one wished to attach to the war was of course the nameless body, the *soldat inconnu*, buried under the Arc de Triomphe on Armistice Day 1920.[148] In the fall of 1921 a brief but intense polemic broke out over a new proposal to inter an unidentified body from the Balkan theater as an "Unknown Soldier of the East [*Orient*]" in Marseille. The outrage of the veterans' community quickly led to the scrapping of this project and its replacement with a special monument, also in Marseille, to be built with the assistance of a large state contribution. As one veteran wrote in the conservative *La voix du combattant*, in response to the newspaper's informal poll of its readers, "To multiply him would be, it seems to me, to diminish his moral character; the Unknown is not a personality but an idealization."[149] Laqueur has written of the British unknown soldier in Westminster Abbey that "by being so intensely *a* body, it was *all* bodies."[150] But the unknown represented something more specific than simply all bodies: it was the ultimate missing body. The tomb of the unknown soldier (fig. 2.10) constituted, as one veterans' group leader, Henry de Jouvenel, put it in 1924, the heart of a "network of funeral monuments" that had replaced châteaus, churches, and schools as the signal feature of the French countryside. But the unknown also embodied what those local monuments desired but could not have, the bodies of the dead. As Victor Méric put it in the Communist daily *L'humanité*, for once in agreement with the right-wing *L'intransigeant*, if Marseille were to have its

FIGURE 2.10. Tomb of the Unknown Soldier, Paris. Photo: Author.

unknown soldier, Lyon would be next, and then Toulouse, and then every commune in France, including the prototypical French endsville, "Fouilly-les-Oies."[151]

Méric's rapid descent from Marseille to Fouilly-les-Oies obscures the specificity of the project in question. Although in this context the word *Orient* referred to a theater of battle, Marseille, one of France's leading colonial ports, had long cast itself as the country's gateway to the East; among other things it was the site of a monument, dedicated in 1923, to indigenous soldiers from Indochina who fought in the French army. Many of the French troops in the Dardanelles, the particular "Orient" to be commemorated, came from Senegal and the Caribbean; those who survived were later sent to Verdun, the Somme, and the Chemin des Dames.[152] A few monuments to the approximately 600,000 colonial troops who served in World War I, and the estimated 70,000 who died, exist in metropolitan France, notably in Fréjus (Var) and in the so-called Jardin tropical in Nogent-sur-Marne, where a half dozen monuments, including one in the form of a Vietnamese pagoda, are grouped together.[153] Too much recognition of colonial troops as a distinct category, however, risked raising uncomfortable questions about their subordinate status within the French empire; in this respect unitary narratives, such as those incarnated in the unknown soldier, clearly had their advantages.[154]

Yet this insistence on privileging a single unknown soldier, chosen from among eight caskets from different sectors of the front in a ceremony at the

Citadel of Verdun in November 1920, has its puzzling aspects. It cannot be explained simply in practical terms, for the number of unidentified bodies easily exceeded the total of French communes in the 1920s, approximately 38,000. Even in the highly unlikely event that Méric's ironic prediction had come true, and every French village had wanted "its" unknown soldier, in strictly practical terms the demand could have been met. Moreover, given the intensity of the dispute over burial, the enormous number of unidentified bodies, and the pervasive suspicion of military cemeteries and ossuaries, some sort of compromise, involving the transfer of a limited number of unknown bodies to towns willing to give them a decent burial, certainly seems conceivable. That such a possibility struck commentators in the immediate postwar period as the height of absurdity provides additional evidence of the potency of the body as social symbol.

For the body has a materiality, and a level of cultural signification, that even the name cannot match. Elaine Scarry has argued that "the body tends to be brought forward in its most extreme and absolute form only on behalf of a cultural artifact or symbolic fragment or made thing (a sentence) that is without any other basis in material reality: that is, it is only brought forward when there is a crisis of substantiation."[155] War is the "crisis of substantiation" par excellence; it uses bodies to connect "derealized and disembodied beliefs with the force and power of the material world."[156]

From this perspective, the unknown soldier offered, in the face of massive loss and profound grief, the reassurance that the war did have a purpose, a single or at least single set of knowable purposes that had brought the French nation together for four years and could, if rediscovered, do so again. The uniqueness of the memorial accorded to the unknown soldier both authorized the contestation over commemoration and provided a comforting set of limits to it. The unknown had something that could appeal to all sides. As a common soldier—veterans' groups always referred to the *poilu inconnu*—the unknown spoke to the universality of loss and privileged the efforts of troops rather than of commanders. Buried beneath the Arc de Triomphe, however, the unknown affirmed the continuing legitimacy of the nation-state in whose name he had died, and validated all narratives of the war that took the national polity as their basis, whatever their political perspective.[157]

At the same time, the uncertainty at the heart of this memorial site constituted the outer limit to the debate over commemoration, symbolically precluding any definitive resolution of the questions about the war that lay at its heart. Again as a function of its anonymity, the tomb of the unknown left knowledge of the war's purpose simply as a possibility, without ever identifying the means of securing it. Just as names assigned individuals a place in society, their specificity on monuments authorized the competing narratives to which commemoration gave rise. The consecration of anonymity as the center of commemoration stood for the unity of the French nation over and above struggles to interpret its history and define its identity. Nothing could have been more disturbing to those seeking to reorder their world on traditional lines than the prospect, however deeply buried in their unconscious, of thousands, tens of thousands of unknown bodies waiting for local communities to attach to them *their* particular understandings of the war. In this sense the tomb of the unknown soldier was what local monuments wanted to be but could not, as it harbored the body they desired but could not have: a form of signification at once collective and individual, a body that needed no name.

names not sufficient → Body

3

MAKING A SACRIFICE

In 1915 the Norman department of the Orne conducted a fund drive for war charities. A poster for the event (fig. 3.1) depicts a man and a woman in a generic village setting, signified by the church tower in the background. The woman, wearing a traditional headdress and *sabots*, holds a tin cup in her right hand and with her left appeals, ever so tentatively, for alms. The man's crutch, somewhat battered military greatcoat, and medals indicate his status as a wounded veteran. His right arm slipped under the woman's left, and his vacant eyes, in contrast with her direct gaze, convey his blindness. With rusticated lettering emphasizing its resolutely local character, the poster encapsulates in a vivid, highly personal image the day's purpose: "to benefit department war charities." That the woman, rather than the soldier, holds the cup emphasizes the way in which Orne day constitutes for civilians a duty akin to the soldier's, while constructing civilian charity as a form of gendered tribute.

The war years gave French civilians many such opportunities, welcome or not, to contribute to the national effort. Most of the posters examined in chapter 1 urged the purchase of war bonds. National *journées* held throughout the war benefited such causes as Belgian and Serbian refugees, the rebuilding of war-damaged departments, and the care of tubercular veterans. Local authorities asked for contributions in cash as well as in kind: gold for the war effort, linens and blankets for soldiers, clothing for refugees.[1] Private associations could demonstrate their patriotism by sponsoring their own causes, as the Touring-Club de France did with the Oeuvre des Pépinières Nationales, the national nursery charity, which undertook first to grow vegetables for the army, and eventually to replace destroyed fruit trees throughout the war zone.[2]

Appeals to support war charities normally fit comfortably within the boundaries of war discourse. Unlike female volunteer nursing, for example, the

FIGURE 3.1. Charles Léandre, "Journée de l'Orne." Poster Collection, FR 570, Hoover Institution Archives. © 1999 Artists Rights Society (ARS), New York/ADAGP Paris.

contribution of cash or goods involved no service, and thus little risk of being construed as in any way equivalent to soldiers' military service.[3] Nor does Charles Léandre's "Orne Day" poster in any way cross that line. Yet in its very naïveté this image seems to have violated an unspoken taboo. For the vast majority of posters depict, whether realistically or allegorically, the *object* of charity, rather than the act itself. The Orne image not only focuses on the act, it also couples solicitor and beneficiary in a way that at least hints at, if it in no way celebrates, the massive disruption of gendered power relations that the war had brought about. Moreover, it brings the viewer, the implied donor, into an uneasy triangle of potential equivalence with the wounded veteran and his supportive wife, sister, or female companion. Despite its insistent evocation of tradition—the church steeple, the costume, the gesture—the possibility of misreading lurks just beneath the surface of this image, which no doubt explains its rarity.

If commemoration depended on continuing the wartime economy and rhetoric of contribution, it also perpetuated the tension and ambiguity that lay at the heart of those practices. Indeed, one of the central terms of commemorative investment, "sacrifices," sums up that ambiguity. In the 1919 law, discussed in the previous chapter, that left local commemoration to the initiative of local government, the state offered to subsidize monument construction "in proportion to the effort and sacrifices [communes] will undertake to glorify the heroes who died for the fatherland."[4] The sponsor of the original bill, Louis Martin, wrote that the proposed subsidies were intended "to permit the construction of monuments more worthy of those whose memory they will recall"; by "more worthy," he specified in a subsequent debate, he meant—and the proposed subsidies meant— "more beautiful."[5]

The notion that the state should support local initiatives did not, of course, originate in the twentieth century, but the Great War cast that support in a new light. The word "sacrifices" enshrined in the law of October 1919 had a long history as a kind of official euphemism for public spending. Throughout the nineteenth century, for example, towns used the term to describe the expenditure of public funds on works of art for municipal museums: a town's sacrifice in this sense entitled it, the argument went, to state assistance in the same general domain.[6] Both in the law and in parliamentary discussions "sacrifice" appears as a synonym for "effort," while making clear that the latter term involves more than some vague coming together of the community in voluntary labor. But in the aftermath of a devastating conflict, an older use of "sacrifice" has taken on new prominence: as one senator, Magny, put it, "We feel infinite gratitude to our heroic soldiers, the greatest on earth, to whom we owe victory, and whose sacrifice will allow us to end our days in a reconstituted France."[7] Although the term applied to the experience of all soldiers who had fought in the war, it soon elided with the more explicit *sacrifice suprême*, death.

In both usages, of course, the word "sacrifice" functions as a metaphor. In the case of the soldier, the idea of sacrifice implicitly invokes a larger cause that justifies the taking of life. With regard to public works, the term eliminates money as the intermediary between the public will and its built expression. Precisely this evacuation of money, Marx's "general *confounding* and *compounding* of all things,"[8] from the discourse of public expenditure brings that discourse uncomfortably close to the rhetoric of military valor. No one, of course, ever claimed anything like an equivalence between the two types of sacrifice. But their implicit association provided a crucial alibi to those in charge of the commemorative enterprise. Whether construed as voluntary or imposed, soldiers' self-sacrifice benefited only the communities from which they came; the dead obviously derived no direct advantage from victory in the Great War. Those who invested in commemoration, however, individuals as well as collectivities, could enjoy benefits ranging from new open spaces to increased prestige within a community. The word "sacrifice" deflected attention from such benefits, nudging it toward the object of commemoration, the dead, and away from the commemorating subject.

The mechanics of commemoration, from fund-raising to expenditure, involved politics as well as economics. To qualify for a state subsidy, a monument had only to appear in a budget line (*crédit*) duly voted by the town council. Councils varied in size according to a commune's population; in villages and small towns members of the *conseil municipal* typically had fairly intimate relations with their constituents. But the construction of monuments also involved a range of structures and resources rooted in the community. Individuals and groups often organized fund drives or *souscriptions*, along the lines of wartime charities, to support monument construction. However informal, a fund drive often entailed the creation of a committee that took charge not only of raising funds but of building the monument, although the town council always had to approve at least a monument's site. The constitution of a committee, or simply the organization of a fund drive, gave a variety of groups—veterans, relatives of the dead, local notables, politicians, and ordinary citizens—the opportunity to express their views about commemoration. Though few of these groups challenged the basic pieties of commemorative tribute, notably the incommensurability of the soldier's experience, their views and interests did not always coincide. Veterans in particular found that their unique connection to the war "experience" did not automatically grant them uncontested authority over commemoration.

For the commemorative process involved its own set of rules and its own dynamics. Discursively constructed as a sacrifice in its own right, the expenditure of public and private funds on monuments gave the contributors of those funds a place at the commemorative table. Communities dealt with this most basic axiom in different ways, but all faced a common problem. Commemoration sought to inculcate, among other things, a sense of commonality; it represented a community as *united* in homage to the dead. To acknowledge, even at a practical level, that separable components of the community had different stakes in commemoration risked compromising that sense of common purpose, but then so did the failure to do so. Thus the structures of the commemorative enterprise had an importance beyond their effectiveness in securing resources. For these structures both embodied and elicited a number of deep-seated anxieties about commemoration that, along with more ostensible intentions, played a part in shaping the commemorative culture of interwar France.

Structures

In 1923 the prefect of the Var wrote to the mayors of his department, asking them to report on whether, under what circumstances, and on what authority[9] their commune had built a memorial to its citizens who had died in the Great War. Among other things, the questionnaire asked whether the municipal government or a "regularly constituted committee" was responsible for the construction of the monument.[10] Despite the either-or nature of the question, eighteen of the ninety-three communes that replied (an additional thirteen had not built memorials) indicated that some configuration of *conseil municipal* and committee or subscription had built the monument together.[11] Of the remainder, fourteen credited the city council with constructing the monument, while over three-fifths cited a committee. These figures come as no surprise in a precociously left-wing department steeped in the traditions of republican sociability. But that nearly 20 percent of the respondents referred to a "combination" not included among the recognized options points to the elasticity of the boundaries between elective bodies and private groups in this domain.

This overlap had a number of dimensions, beginning with the actual formation of committees. The mayor often played a crucial role in creating a committee: in some cases, the mayor, acting alone or in concert with the town council, actually selected the members of the committee himself.[12] In Chaumont-sur-Loire, in the Loir-et-Cher, the monument "committee" was simply a committee of the town council, chaired by the mayor.[13] In general, the smaller the town, the greater the chance that the town council could itself assume the role of a monument committee. Councillors in communes with populations of a few hundred or a thousand (Chaumont's pre-1914 population was 1,047) enjoyed both a certain prominence and easy familiarity with their constituents; they had no need of a special committee to take the pulse of the voters.

Yet the large proportion of communes in the Var with monument committees, more than four in five, suggests that mayors saw some benefit in a structured outlet for community participation. In order both to encourage such participation and to legitimate their control of it, committees, whatever the circumstances of their founding, sought to cast themselves as broadly representative of the community as a whole. One means of creating this impression, employed both in the Catholic Morbihan and in the socialist Var, involved forming the committee in a public meeting announced in advance and open to the whole population.[14] In one part of Toulon, where a number of neighborhoods (like some Paris *arrondissements*) put up their own monuments or plaques, such a meeting was held at a local café and organized by the establishment's owner.[15]

But whatever the circumstances of their founding, in order to establish their credibility committees needed a membership drawn from the various groups commonly understood to structure a community. This goal of inclusiveness sometimes resulted in lists of members that read like directories of local notables. The monument committee in Vannes, prefecture of the Morbihan, had no fewer than seventy-one members, including politicians, the heads of voluntary societies and veterans' groups, and three women active in local charities.[16] Committees in smaller towns also sought a varied membership. The common inclusion of both the curé and the teacher, traditionally an avatar of the secular Republic, aimed expressly to signal the persistence of the wartime *union sacrée* (sacred union) over and above the divisions of local politics. In Pignans, a small town in the Var, the curé and teacher at the girls' school were the committee's vice chairs; the boys' teacher served as treasurer; the committee secretary was a local landowner; and its chairman came from the cork trade, an important local industry.[17]

As these lists suggest, committees' notions of representation were generally limited to people perceived to be the leaders of a community, or in French terminology its *notables*. Certainly no notion of diversity, or of multiple voices, governed the formation of committees. Quite the contrary: on monument committees members of various associations were expected to represent not their own corporate interests but the overarching unity of the community that bound them together. The mayor of Ploërmel, a subprefecture in the Morbihan, wrote in calling an open meeting to constitute the committee that it "should be an emanation of the population itself, and it should be open broadly to all authorities and all talents."[18]

Of all the groups seeking a role in commemoration, only veterans could circumvent the problem of representation by simply taking on the task themselves. Indeed, their unique connection to the object of commemoration, their dead comrades (a term they used often), provided veterans a self-sufficient claim to a prominent, even preeminent role in the commemorative process. Bolstered, moreover, by veterans' presence in most conventional socioprofessional groups, such a claim could subsume most others, except possibly for those of the families of the dead. In some towns, veterans' associations—there were usually at least two, of different political stripes, and in some cities more—formed monument committees entirely from their own ranks, and took charge of the entire process. In Chauvigny-du-Perche, in the Loir-et-Cher, the veterans' initiative undoubtedly had to do with the fact that the municipality, despite years of discussion, had by 1936 failed to put up a monument.[19] But at a much earlier stage, in 1921, when the mayor of Cléguer (Morbihan) had to supply the prefect with the names of members of the monument committee, he simply sent a list of officers of the local chapter of the Union Nationale des Combattants (UNC), one of the major national veterans' organizations. All five members of the monument committee in St. Denis-sur-Loire (Loir-et-Cher) in 1920 were veterans, although four were also members of the town council.[20]

More commonly, committees simply made sure to include a substantial number of veterans in their ranks. In Gâvres, in the Morbihan, the town council chose five of its own members to form the committee along with five veterans, the curé, two teachers, and a "worker at La Falaise"; the committee's officers were carefully apportioned among these different constituencies.[21] Municipalities had to acknowledge veterans' claims to a voice, but most were unwilling to cede them the council's role as representative of the whole community. For veterans' insistence on their special moral authority could also, unsurprisingly, provoke suspicion or even resistance on the part of elected officials who feared a threat to their own legitimacy.

Although divided among numerous associations, the veterans movement numbered, according to the estimate of Antoine Prost, over three million in the mid-1930s.[22] Originating in the demands of wounded soldiers for a reform of pensions and survivor benefits, a number of veterans groups played, as we have seen, an important role in debates over burials, exhumations, and battlefield commemoration. Toward the end of the 1920s various groups came together in a successful campaign for a government-funded annuity for all veterans over the age of fifty. In the thirties, as depression-era cuts in public funding threatened these and other benefits, veterans' groups turned their energies to demanding fundamental political reforms.[23] Notwithstanding their differences, the major veterans' associations shared a number of common tendencies, including a refusal to engage in partisan politics, a republicanism they considered perfectly compatible with a sometimes bitter critique of parliamentarism, and an equally fervent pacifism. The two largest groups, the left-center Union Fédérale and the more right-wing Union Nationale des Combattants, drew their membership most heavily from the small-holding peasantry, shopkeepers and the petite bourgeoisie, and lower-level managers and civil servants. Indeed, Prost finds only a remote connection between the movement's ideology and "war experience," calling veterans' ideology more "a subterfuge or camouflage" employed by a lower-middle class reluctant to form its own pressure groups.[24] All the more reason for the movement to insist on its special role as guardian of the memory of the war, a role that formed the basis for its ever-expanding claims.

Veterans' sensitivities and high public profile made them at once difficult to work with and impossible to avoid. The mayor of Bordeaux neglected to name any veterans to a monument committee dominated by journalists, the art world, and local notables, but in response to the resulting protests appointed several veterans to the jury of the monument design competition.[25] In Levallois-Perret, a working-class suburb in the Paris red belt, Louis Rouquier, the independent communist mayor, was so determined to retain control over the town's monument that he eschewed even a subscription, let alone a committee. Rouquier too felt obliged to name several veterans to the competition jury, but this faction fiercely opposed the winning design, which they considered pacifist, and charged that the jury's decision was rigged. The local UNC newspaper waged a vicious campaign against the monument design, and when the monument, still under construction, was vandalized in November 1926, the mayor accused the veterans of responsibility.[26]

The outcomes of such disputes, of course, had much to do with the relative weight of the veterans' movement within a particular community. Indeed, the vandalism of the Levallois monument can in fact be regarded as a symptom of veterans' *lack* of influence there, a working-class town with little sympathy for their middle-class claims: with Rouquier still firmly in control, the slightly disfigured monument was simply repaired and dedicated with only a few months' delay. In Lorient (Morbihan), however, where in February 1927 UNC members unhappy with the winning monument design staged a demonstration that nearly turned violent, the socialist mayor had to resign from the committee. Dominated by veterans and naval officers, the committee eventually modified the design to its liking, replacing figures of a peasant and fisherman with a soldier and sailor.[27]

Though similar controversies sometimes arose in smaller towns as well, the weight of veterans' groups in local politics generally disposed mayors to conciliation rather than confrontation. Merely giving veterans more of a voice did not necessarily satisfy their demands, however: in Ligny-en-Barrois (Meuse) a group of dissident veterans won the right to raise funds for a new, more expensive site for the monument, but when their effort failed they resorted to a poster campaign attacking the mayor.[28] Mayors seeking another option besides antagonizing veterans or simply giving way to them thus sometimes turned to another constituency with unquestioned moral authority: the families of the dead, who of course could claim a place on committees even in the absence of any controversy. In Neuville-sur-Orne (Meuse), three members of the monument committee were elected officials, the remaining seven identified by the simple phrases *fils tué* or *frère tué*.[29] The characterization of relatives in such highly charged terms as *éprouvés*, connoting great suffering, closed off any possibility of criticism. Thus when a committee in Aups (Var) failed to raise sufficient funds for the monument, the mayor selected a new one consisting of, in addition to two technical experts, eight veterans and eight *éprouvés*, including two widows.[30]

The controversy that veterans generated had to do with the nature of their claims to authority in the commemorative process, for these claims rested on an assumption of moral superiority to which few politicians could afford to defer. The rhetoric of the veterans' movement, Prost has argued, deployed a fundamental contempt for party politics, politicians, and traditional process.[31] In the politics of commemoration, this attitude played on a structural tension between town councils and monument committees with any degree of autonomy. Although such tension often arose around the issue of the monument's location, the Var provides two revealing examples that did not, one from the resort town of Ste. Maxime, a second from its largest city, Toulon. In both places these tensions, principally over questions of money and authority, significantly delayed the monument project, and the delay itself then became the issue of dispute. At base, however, if in different ways, the disputes involved differing conceptions of the relationship commemoration entailed between private initiative and public investment.

When the members of the Ste. Maxime committee, after many requests, finally obtained a meeting with the town council to discuss the monument project, the mayor surprised them by insisting that they deposit the funds they had gathered from subscribers in the municipal treasury. Challenged by the committee chair, the mayor stated flatly that he did not trust the committee. After a delay of over a year, the prefect confirmed the committee's view that, duly constituted, it could undertake a monument project on its own, needing the municipality's approval only for the site.[32] The committee then proposed a course of reconciliation that would have enlisted relatives of the dead to supervise the project, along with two members each of the committee and of the town council.[33] Ignoring the prefect's urging, the mayor refused, citing vague administrative "formalities" the town would have to pay for.[34] It was not until three years later, when a new mayor worked with a reconstituted committee that included several town councillors, that Ste. Maxime actually got its monument.[35]

Founded in December 1918 from the ranks of a wartime volunteer group that helped organize soldiers' funerals, the Toulon monument committee was in many ways a model of correct relations between the public and private sectors. The city's mayor, Claude, invited to chair the committee, declined on the grounds that he considered it "preferable to leave [the project] to private initiative."[36] As though to confirm the extent of this initiative, a month later the provisional committee held a public meeting at a movie theater to establish itself definitively; over three hundred attended. The chairmanship fell to the meticulous and energetic Victor Castel, described in the committee's records only as a *propriétaire* (man of property).[37] The committee devoted most of its initial efforts to a public subscription, as well as to assembling the names it would inscribe on the monument. The results proved disappointing, perhaps because of competition from a number of other Toulon groups sponsoring commemorative projects after the war.[38] In the fall of 1920 a military officer on the committee found the sum of 65,000 francs raised so discouraging that he proposed turning over the project to the city. But a majority of committee members felt that they could not abandon their mission, and so the committee turned its attention to securing a substantial contribution from the left-dominated city council.[39]

In a meeting with a deputy mayor in November 1920, Castel said that the committee hoped it could count on a municipal contribution of 100,000 francs; his interlocutor replied only that the city hoped to make "a quite considerable effort."[40] After requests for meetings with city officials throughout 1921 went unanswered, the matter began to attract press attention. In January 1922 Castel, in a letter to the *Petit marseillais*, obliquely blamed the city for the delay, thus deflecting criticism away from the committee.[41] Only then did Mayor Claude agree to attend a committee meeting. Although he promised the city's support in principle, he refused to name a precise figure, citing budgetary difficulties. Even the *principle* of a subvention sparked controversy on the town council, where one member objected "to anything that can glorify war, and demanded that this sum [50,000 francs] be given rather to widows and orphans." The council did not approve the grant until December 1922.[42]

The further delay may have resulted from a short-lived but intense public controversy about the site of the monument. Castel's committee was deeply divided on the matter. Castel, for example, preferred a site at the city's old ramparts, and when his colleagues chose instead the Jardin Public in the city center, he promptly resigned, though he was quickly prevailed upon to change his mind.[43] When, following the committee's decision, a gateway at the ramparts that would have framed the monument was demolished, a letter to the *Petit marseillais* blamed the city, and charged that "the municipal government, being *socio-communiste*, is out of touch with the population."[44] But the mayor probably felt little pressure to support the project while the controversy, and the committee's own divisions, made it less a matter of "pious tribute"[45] than a political hot potato. Since a number of commemorative projects were competing for funds, Castel may have calculated that by agreeing to a site that the authorities as well as his colleagues favored, the Jardin Public, he would give his project a new claim on official support. This is in fact what happened: the council's vote followed the committee's decision by less than two weeks. Unlike his counterpart in Ste. Maxime, Mayor Claude did not seek to control the monument project, but he also had no intention of providing public funds to support an undertaking that might bring him more controversy than approval.

The case of Toulon makes clear how the perceived success or failure of a subscription, independent of municipal subsidies, could test a committee's claims to represent a community. Though discussions of subscriptions tended to focus on purely financial questions, subscriptions also served as a way of structuring a community's emotions, energies, and grief, channeling them into a form of collective representation. A fund drive might even *precede* the formation of a committee, as it did in Ploërmel beginning in 1917.[46] Such precocity points to the way commemoration sought to perpetuate the wartime gift economy. To bring memory and mourning into the public sphere, as a collective endeavor, entailed creating at least the appearance of spontaneity and genuine volition. For this reason the subscription campaign involved not simply raising money, but doing so in a way that visibly and publicly implicated the community as a whole.

But as the Orne Day poster suggests, if a fund drive appealed to a community in the abstract, its effectiveness depended on the ability both to harness concrete social relations within that community and, if necessary, to create new ones. To begin with, subscription organizers had to ensure that the basic distinction between donor and recipient did not compromise the impression of united effort they were trying to achieve. In a sense, of course, subscriptions were intended to benefit two collective "recipients": one abstract—the community as a whole—and one absent—the dead commemorated on the monument. But committees or municipalities often used door-to-door solicitations, or *quêtes*, to raise funds, and though the collectors usually made donations themselves, they were also acting as agents for the community and the dead. This was, in part, a strategic decision: fund-raising campaigns typically choose solicitors whom the solicited have difficulty refusing. Though records are scanty, they do point to several categories of people judged particularly suitable for this role.

Veterans, naturally, sometimes undertook subscriptions on their own: this was the case in Gueltas, a village in the Morbihan with about 900 residents, where a subscription of just over 1,000 francs seems to have spurred the town council to action.[47] In Oucques, in the Loir-et-Cher, the town council itself organized the subscription; in Gourin (Morbihan), each *quête* paired a member of the town council and "a poilu" as collectors.[48] We might also note the frequency with which the names of the collectors echo those on the lists of the community's dead. Most of the evidence here comes from the Morbihan: in Guern, seven of the twelve collectors share names with the dead; in Guénin, where six of the eighteen collectors were members of the town council, ten had relatives among the dead.[49]

These patterns, to the extent they parallel the composition of committees, are hardly surprising. It is possible, however, to posit another group favored for fund-raising that featured far less prominently on committees: women. Although in many cases the lists of collectors do not specify gender, town councillors were obviously male, and in Guénin we know that other collectors were as well. But in Kerfourn, another small town in the Morbihan, all twenty-two collectors were women, ten of them widows. All except one of their names also appear on the list of the dead.[50] When the committee in Vannes, a much larger city, concluded that the amount of money it was seeking necessitated door-to-door solicitations, it decided to organize "a committee of ladies," or *Dames quêteuses*.[51] The list of subscribers in Brovès (Var) uses the same term, though it does not name the collectors.[52]

Obviously, the widows and mothers of dead soldiers enjoyed an inherent prestige that made their requests for funds difficult to refuse. But fund-raising fit easily into the set of activities judged appropriate for women, particularly as it could be deemed a continuation of war charity work. In Étain, a cantonal seat in the Meuse, the women members of the committee (which, exceptionally, was chaired by a woman, the mayor's wife) not only undertook a *quête*, they ran a charity sale to benefit the monument. In the neighboring canton of Damvillers, a group of *demoiselles d'honneur* collected money for the monument at an agricultural fair; in Ploërmel, ladies were asked to contribute "works of art or of the needle" for sale at a *kermesse*, or village fair, to benefit the monument.[53]

But choosing women to collect monument subscriptions did another kind of cultural work: it reinforced the way in which the *quêtes* themselves sought to reproduce a primary structure of the community, its land. "Let us not forget," declared the mayor of Caro (Morbihan) at the dedication of that community's war memorial, "that if it was the business of men to save the *Patrie* and Civilization, it was the business of women to save the home and the land; and you, women and children of Caro, you have saved the *pays* through your devotion, your valiance, and your resolution."[54] *Pays* here serves as a mediating term between *patrie* and *terre*, the land; although it can mean the country as a whole, it also refers to the region, the more intimate "country" where one feels oneself at home. As men went off to defend the *patrie*, women, in this view, stayed home to protect the "land." In the aftermath of a war that had subverted many distinctions, this one especially needed reassertion.

But what has this to do with subscriptions? Whether conducted by men, by women, or by both, *quêtes* had, for the sake of efficiency, to divide up a commune by area. In La Trinité-sur-Mer, in the Morbihan, the town council divided the commune into two simple categories for purposes of the *quête: le bourg,* the center of the village, and *la campagne,* its rural dependencies. In Kerfourn, the areas for which each team of collectors was responsible were designated by what the French call their *lieux-dits*, common names or, in large metropolitan areas, subdivisions.[55] *Lieux-dits* differ from the names of communes, of which they form a part, in one crucial sense: they have no legal status. The mayor of every commune in France, no matter how small, has the right to wear a tricolor sash indicating his authority as an officer of the Republic. The *commune* is a legal entity, the place where its citizens' births and deaths are officially recorded. But as a microcosm of the state, a commune, like the state, can incorporate a great deal of territory, of highly varied character; as with a nation, it can take a certain amount of imagination to constitute a commune as a community. *Lieux-dits*, however, used in many Morbihan communes, indicate a greater degree of complexity, and perhaps a lingering attachment to a traditional geography not sanctioned by the state. Newspaper lists of subscribers in St. Gonnery, a village with a pre-1914 population of 907, named no fewer than twenty-eight *lieux-dits*; Kergrist, only slightly larger, had twenty. The average contributions differed markedly by *lieu-dit* within Bieuzy, moreover, pointing to the kinds of socioeconomic variations that demarcate communities.[56]

To build, as Le Castellet in the Var did, multiple monuments within a single commune, one in each of four *lieux-dits*, suggests a kind of resistance to state-imposed categories in a department where communes often include vast amounts of sparsely settled territory. (Even here, however, the monument in the center of Le Castellet had clear primacy, and the names of all the dead were inscribed on it.)[57] More commonly, subscribers divided communes into the familiar *lieux-dits* simply as a matter of convenience. At the same time, the association of that division with the *quête*, an activity considered especially suitable for women, had a significant consequence. In this mode of thinking, traditional quotidian geography—the home, the land, the *pays*—belonged to the realm of women. As such, while meriting praise, it remained clearly subordinate to the more formal, more abstract categories—the nation, law, civilization—that men and men alone had fought to preserve.

In larger towns and cities, the *quête* with its neighborhood orientation formed part of an array of fund-raising activities that at once represented and constructed a sense of communal solidarity. This is not to say that fund drives in small towns limited themselves to door-to-door solicitations, only that the range of other means—fairs, charity sales, recreational events—increased with the size of the community. One typical method, employed in various parts of the country, involved taking up collections at special events, including family celebrations like weddings. "Our best wishes for happiness to the new couples," wrote a local newspaper after two wedding subscriptions in Brignoles (Var), "and our congratulations on the fine gesture they have made toward the memory of our war dead."[58] Military personnel also offered a good prospect, whether recent draftees in the Var or a battalion at Metz.[59]

Some communities came up with more inventive strategies. A justice of the peace in Étain (Meuse) persuaded two men to settle a legal dispute by making a contribution to the subscription.[60] A group raising money for a monument to the dead of the Sologne in Romorantin (Loir-et-Cher) sold insignia, presumably of patriotic emblems, to be worn on the lapel. In several villages in the Var, vine growers contributed a small percentage of the value of their production to the subscription: twenty centimes per hundred liters in La Londe, for example; a franc per hundred liters in Bormes.[61] In these ways subscription organizers sought to tap the economic pulse of the community, and at the same time to make contributing simple. Wine production was recorded at the point of sale, and in La Londe the rural gendarme, or *garde champêtre*, was supposed to collect the relevant sums. The economic lifeblood of a community thus became part of the capital invested in memorializing those who died in the name of France.

But another type of fund-raising activity relied on an inducement more practical than moral, offering donors entertainment, or even something tangible, in exchange for their contributions. Such activities could be modest in scale:

an *adjoint* or deputy mayor in the village of Baudonvilliers (Meuse) "organized, with the help of the youth of the village, recreational evenings exclusively for this Monument," probably meaning games, singing, and refreshments.[62] Some towns held benefit concerts or showed films, usually relying on donated space or services to help defray expenses.[63] In Toulon, the committee spent 3,500 francs to purchase prizes for a raffle: the grand prize was a dining room or bedroom set, and other lots included a bronze statuette of *Victory* and a dress. The lottery netted a profit of 6,300 francs.[64]

Although such raffles seemed to have passed without controversy, more elaborate entertainments could provoke criticism. The *kermesse* or fair in Ploërmel, according to *Le ploërmelais*, was to include shooting, gymnastics, a fishing contest, *guignol,* circus acts, a café concert, and "numerous and brilliant" booths selling flowers, pastry, confectionery, and tobacco. Perhaps to fend off any possible criticism, the staunchly Catholic weekly characterized the fair as "a patriotic effort [*oeuvre*]" and described the preparations for it in these terms:

Already in ladies' salons and in working women's little rooms people are working feverishly to prepare marvelous items for the booths; already imaginations are on the move and striving to come up with the sensational attraction that will monopolize attention, attract crowds . . . and make huge profits. It is a noble competition. . . . For is it not, in the end, a matter of glorifying [the town's] Heroes, its dear, great Poilus, its sublime Children! This will be a festival, no doubt, but a festival stamped with a certain seriousness, a degree of reflection, as in the vicinity of a temple where the spirit of the Departed will hover, present but invisible at *their* Kermesse.[65]

Visitors, the paper added, should respect the feelings of the families of the dead: "so no jarring cries, no too noisy enthusiasm, no rowdy behavior, no provocative dress or eccentric hats!" Summarizing the results of the *kermesse* a few weeks later, the paper, noting that the subprefect, the mayor, and the curé—representatives of the secular state and the church—had been seen mingling, called it "a fine demonstration of *Union sacrée*," and said that "politics, at least so we think, did not show its ugly face."[66] This raising of an issue only to deny its importance suggests a kind of anticipatory displacement, an attempt to make harmony and common effort the figure for an event that also, plainly, involved diversion, competition, and pleasure.

Such pleasures as the Ploërmel fair had to offer seem mild in comparison to the galas organized to benefit monuments in larger towns. A festival in the Var resort town of St. Raphaël included, in addition to the usual sports, a parade, performances by Senegalese and Malagasy dancers, a concert with dramatic readings, and a ball. Perhaps because it was sponsored by veterans and families of the dead and took place at the height of the summer season, the festival seems to have been entirely uncontroversial.[67] In Verdun, a gala concert, attended by the subprefect and the general commanding the local garrison, included both amateur and professional musicians and choral groups donating their services. A newspaper account reported that "a happy innovation" enlivened the evening: at intermission, a jazz band in the lobby encouraged many couples to dance.[68] Even as late as 1927, when this event took place, an entire evening of jazz or dancing would probably have provoked too much controversy to work effectively as a benefit.

Specific community standards obviously played a part in shaping attitudes toward benefit events, but these views also bear traces of stricter wartime notions of sobriety. At Hyères, in the Var, the view that "one should not organize *fêtes* for a war charity" stopped a series of concerts to benefit the monument; a local newspaper called this attitude "respectable, but highly debatable."[69] In Vannes in 1922, a city councillor defended the use of *kermesses*, plays, lectures, films, and concerts, all under the general rubric of *fêtes* or festivals, simply by saying that the committee had never had any intention of sponsoring "dances (*bals*)," which he said would be "supremely unsuitable."[70] In another conservative city, Bar-le-Duc, however, a 1925 gala concert, which seems not to have involved dancing, prompted grumbling apparently because of the impression of opulence it produced. A newspaper defending the organizers noted that the suppliers of flowers and refreshments did so at cost, attacked the critics for their lack of civic spirit and "initiative," and reported that the concert had netted 1,500 francs for the subscription.[71] But it was less the effectiveness than the whole principle of spending money in order to raise more—of speculative investment for the purposes of commemoration—that seems to have been at issue. Speculation in general had a bad name in postwar France, and in the context of commemoration might too easily feed the notion, only partly mythical, of fortunes made by capitalists in war industries.[72]

Fairs and concerts suffered from a paradox: the publicity they attracted for the commemorative enterprise ultimately worked against them. In order to succeed, a fund-raising campaign had to cast itself as uniting a community in a common, altruistic cause. Special events did literally bring people together, rather than simply conjoin them in the artificial category of "subscriber." Yet fairs drew people in the first instance not as donors but as pleasure-seekers. The end, commemoration, may have justified the means, some form of paid diversion, but those means did not constitute an adequate *representation* of the end. If the term "sacrifice" had to be used with care, it nonetheless had a vital role to play in distancing donations from the idea of exchange. The strain of connecting a band concert or a three-legged race to a notion of sacrifice clearly played its part in privileging more direct means of collecting money, especially the face-to-face solicitation or *quête*.

Newspaper commentary on fund drives makes clear the connection between this preference and the notion of a collective effort composed of individual *sacrifices*. Structurally, door-to-door solicitations spared those of modest means the embarrassment of entering the businesses, usually banks and newspaper offices, that centralized collection efforts in towns of some size, such as Bar-le-Duc.[73] But the *quête* remained a public activity, albeit one carried out at the physical threshold of the private sphere, and as such lent itself to a publicity wholly focused on the linked concepts of generosity, sacrifice, and community. This publicity habitually took a form, the publication of donors' names, that on its own signified (as we saw in chapter 2) both individual sacrifice and a larger cause.

A common, indeed pervasive, practice of rural journalism in the interwar period, the serial publication of monument subscription lists sought to spur *émulation* or competition in two arenas: both within a community and between one community and its counterparts. In Commercy, where the monument campaign was lagging, the *Républicain de l'est* editorialized that "publicizing the donations already gathered would surely serve as a useful encouragement to subscribers who have not yet said their last word"; a week later, it published a letter observing that a newspaper in Pamiers, in the southwestern department of the Ariège, had just published its twentieth list, and that it had already raised a third more than Commercy.[74] Yet donor lists did not simply act as a spur: they also, when coupled with figures, facilitated a kind of ritual shaming with deep roots in the social imaginary of postwar France.

All too often subscriptions failed to produce the desired results. After public opinion forced a cancellation of benefit concerts in Hyères, the *Petit Var* wrote pointedly, "The music stopped, but wallets did not open."[75] Sometimes, as in Toulon or Auray (Morbihan), disputes or uncertainty over a monument's design or site could cripple a fund drive; usually, however, the subscription took place before a committee even considered such questions.[76] For the most part, then, explanations for poor subscription results came down to a simple lack of generosity, but such an argument usually had an accusatory tone, and a specific target.

"It is a great pity," wrote the *Réveil de la Meuse* about the Bar subscription, "that it should always be the less fortunate [*les humbles*] who keep up the effort to gather the money needed to commemorate so many heroes in a worthy fashion."[77] A few months later the paper went farther:

There are in Bar-le-Duc some fine large fortunes that the Poilus of the Great War defended valiantly; there are others, even more considerable, which were built up rapidly behind the wall of men that rose between Verdun and Bar-le-Duc. Gratitude of the most elementary sort would prompt the holders of these fortunes to make a larger gesture.[78]

The rhetoric in this traditionally nationalist center differs hardly at all from that employed in the left-dominated port city of Lorient: although *Ouest républicain* urged the poor to contribute their pittance, it declared that "the rich must remember even more that what they have, if they had it before the war, was preserved by those whose names will be inscribed in stone or bronze, and if they acquired it during or after the war, they nonetheless owe it to the glorious dead."[79] A city councillor in Vannes, Pleyben, expected that for this kind of effort "it would occur to the rich to pay for the poor," but found "some ridiculously paltry sums" on the lists of subscribers, "notably with regard to the names of people enriched by the war. One will find a contribution of 5 francs in the name of some merchant enriched by the war, next to the figure of 20 francs given by an aged spinster whose only resource is a daily salary of 4 francs."[80]

The resurrection of the widely hated figure of the war profiteer operates in the same mode as the publication of names: it aims, through comparison, to shame the dilatory or begrudging into making a contribution. The choice of this image can hardly be regarded as coincidental.[81] Such references served to place the enterprise of commemoration within a conceptual framework that the war had made not only familiar, but the surest agent of sacralization within secular Republican politics. Potential donors were meant, indeed were confidently expected, not simply to recoil from the implied comparison with the profiteer, but to identify with the term in opposition to him: the self-sacrificing poilu. When the committee in Brignoles began a second subscription after the first one had run into difficulties, it appealed to the memory of "the heroes of Brignoles who did not hesitate to make the supreme sacrifice, not only to preserve our France intact, but to make it greater and more generous."[82] To make a contribution, itself a "sacrifice" of one's resources, would, in other words, align the donor with a group whose own merits appeared in other respects incomparable. The initial appeal for contributions in Vannes makes clear what is at stake: "At the very least the importance of the monument we are to build must be in proportion to their sacrifice."[83]

Lists of subscribers had more than a generic connection to lists of the dead. We had occasion to note, in the previous chapter, the care with which most communes established the lists to be engraved on their memorials. The controversy over the awarding of the designation *mort pour la France*, as well as the inevitability of occasional bureaucratic errors, gave committees and municipalities good reason to worry about the accuracy and completeness of their lists of names. Nonetheless, that newspapers frequently printed such lists, and appeals to families to verify them, at the same time that they launched or renewed subscription drives, reminds us of the way names functioned as a kind of currency that fueled commemorative investment. On the completion of house-to-house solicitations in Ligny, the *Réveil* urged those who wished to be included on the list of contributors, shortly to be published, to come to the town hall to subscribe; at the same time, families were "invited" to visit the same place to make sure that their sons' names were included on the list of dead. In Toulon, a reminder to families to visit the committee's offices ran immediately after the twenty-first published subscription list.[84] Both types of list play on the same basic emotion, the fear of being forgotten. In the columns of local newspapers that often circulated among natives of a region who had moved away, lists also invoked the traditional ties between families and the *pays*, the particular land of their roots. Hence the responses of the baker of Morée and the postal worker from St. Maurice, which were far from unusual: published subscription lists often included a category of contributions from outside the department.[85]

But whatever its functional efficacy, the publication of lists belongs to the realm of representation. And the lists represent above all an act of inscription, a performative gesture that paralleled that of the monument itself. As they made their contributions, that is, donors put their names to a register of contributors.[86] This signature both signified their gratitude and entitled them to another kind of gratitude, more diffuse perhaps but no less constitutive of the desired sense of community. For only the act of signing one's name, especially to a list but also to a letter or check, could fully enact the link that subscriptions sought to effect between the sacrifice of the living and the sacrifice of the dead. How many investments, after all, can aspire to be their own memorial?

Resources

In 1936 the mayor of La Versanne, in the Loire, explained at the dedication of the communal war memorial why it had taken the village so long to build one. The dead knew, he said, that their loved ones had not forgotten them, that only poverty had held them back. He continued:

> Thanks to generous donors and patiently, *sou* by *sou*, we had to gather the necessary sum [of money]; people may regard this sum as minimal, but our farmers had to wrest it from the soil with the sweat of their brow; it represents an abundance of small deprivations, a giving up not only of luxuries but sometimes of necessities as well.[87]

Constructed entirely around images of labor and of privation, this classic account of sacrifice avoids the generic word for money, *argent*, though it does make use of a popular, and antiquated, term for a small coin. The state's term, "resources," had the same metaphorical value: to remove commemoration one step from the cash economy. In the dryly technical domain of memorial finance, as in so many others, we will discover that a great many things go unmentioned.

In May 1920 the minister of the interior sent a circular to prefects setting out the documentation needed for official approval of monuments. Under a Restoration ordinance, all such monuments, as testimonies of *hommage public*, required the authorization of the sovereign, now the president of the Republic.

Communes seeking such decrees had to submit a sketch of the monument, specify its location, and provide not only a detailed budget but an accounting of the *ressources* that would cover it. "In general," the circular stated, "they come from three sources: a) an item in the municipal budget; b) a public subscription; c) a state subvention, as provided for in the law of 25 October 1919."[88] We will return to the state's role in financing monuments, but for the moment this simple breakdown establishes the basic rules and categories of monument finance. Although in theory a monument could be built either entirely by subscription or entirely with public funds, in practice financing a monument involved a delicate balancing act between the three "elements."

What does the amassing, distribution, and expenditure of these monies tell us about commemoration? The *Annales* school's preoccupation with the analysis of "series" still exercises considerable influence on historical practice in France; thus French scholars typically use the financing of monuments as one of several statistical indices of the political valence of commemoration in particular regions.[89] Although quantitative analyses have their uses, I want to argue for a more nuanced approach that avoids assigning political meaning to simple frequencies or correlations. Though opposition to the war or hostility to commemoration could explain why, for example, one commune raised a much smaller subscription than another of equivalent size, so might a host of other reasons. A town council with a budget surplus and a desire to monumentalize itself might allocate so much for a monument as to make the subscription results almost irrelevant. Or the absence of a suitable site for an imposing monument might lead a commune to decide on a more modest one in a cemetery. And in poor communities, even a relatively modest per capita contribution could represent a major investment for many. The median contribution to monument subscriptions in the Vaucluse (see table 1) represents more than twice the hourly wage for a provincial printer or plumber in 1921; even the much lower figure for the Morbihan amounts to nearly three-quarters of an hour's salary for the mason who might end up building it.[90] Rather than one determining the other in some dependable or unproblematic way, the relationship between finance and commemorative ambition involved a complex imbrication, a continuum of norms and practices, and a constant construction and reconstruction in discourse. As in any such construction, no single term used in financial discussions, whether "economy" or "generosity," "simplicity" or "decoration," can be taken unproblematically as a sign for something else.

Let us look first at subscriptions, already familiar as one of the structures of local commemorative investment. Table 1 illustrates both the interest and the limitations of statistical evidence in the study of monument finance. Can we conclude that the Morbihannais were less patriotic as individuals than residents of the Loir-et-Cher because they gave less per person, or more patriotic as a group because more of their communities held subscriptions? Were residents of

TABLE I. MONUMENT FINANCE

Department	Loir-et-Cher	Morbihan	Vaucluse
Number of cases	99[a]	146	109
Median subscription per capita (francs)	3.20	1.68	5.38
Median percentage of total cost covered by subscription	32	35	—
Communes with no subscription	26 (26.2%)	20 (13.7%)	—
Average cost of monuments (francs)	11,353	15,432	12,001

[a]For average cost, information was available for only ninety-seven communes in the Loir-et-Cher.

SOURCES: Calculated from archival data in the Loir-et-Cher and Morbihan and, for the Vaucluse, from Giroud, Michel, and Michel, *Les monuments aux morts*, annexes IV–V, pp. 141–48.

the Vaucluse more generous as individuals than their counterparts elsewhere, or did their subscriptions benefit from an unusual number of very large contributions (say, in comparison to the norm, a hundred francs or more)? What do higher levels of public funding, as opposed to subscriptions, really indicate about popular attitudes toward commemoration? Attempts to correlate these figures to additional variables generally do not yield clear patterns. Of the variables that three local historians tested in the Vaucluse, for example, including percentage of the population lost in the war and electoral behavior, only the most obvious, wealth, has any neat predictive value: per capita contributions to monument subscriptions tended to be higher in more prosperous parts of the department, broadly speaking the valleys.[91]

As the various explanations of "disappointing" subscription results make clear, the expectations for such campaigns were elastic, the determination of success subjective. But even when framed in comparative terms, perceptions of the success or failure of a fund-raising drive depended not on statistical criteria but on a highly contingent sense of what kind of monument a particular commune should be able to build to honor its dead. A glance at a few stories behind the numbers will make clear why the variable relationship of subscriptions to overall resources so resists global explanation.

Take the case of Savigny-sur-Braye, a cantonal seat with a prewar population of 2,832 and one of the more distinctive monuments in the Loir-et-Cher. The per capita contribution, 5.65 francs, ranks in the top quartile of the department, and the subscription covered 38 percent of the hefty 38,000-franc cost of the monument, also above the median. A closer look at the documentation, however, reveals that the entirety of the recorded subscription came from a *single* gift of 16,000 francs. The mayor, Dr. Hurault, who as a member of the departmental general council had occasion to see a good many memorials, clearly wanted a major monument, and he solicited an artist of Armenian extraction with Salon experience to design it (fig. 3.2). One may suspect that the mayor's

FIGURE 3.2. War monument, Savigny-sur-Braye (Loir-et-Cher). Photo: Author.

ambitions exceeded those of his compatriots. Besides the anonymous gift, he secured a short-term loan on favorable terms from a private citizen, a way of avoiding even a temporary increase in taxes; he probably did not want to press his constituents too hard.[92]

An apparently similar example in the Morbihan reveals a rather different dynamic. The town of Pont-Scorff, a cantonal seat in the west of the department with a prewar population of just under 2,000, spent around 13,000 francs on its monument, somewhat below the department average. The subscription, however, paid for 60 percent of the total cost, in the top 10 percent of the department, and represented a per capita contribution of 4 francs, more than three times the median. Once again, however, the lion's share of the subscription, 6,880 francs out of a total of 7,880, came from a single contribution. In contrast to Savigny, the donor was not anonymous: she was the Princesse de Polignac, widow of a mayor of Pont-Scorff killed during the war, and bearer of one of the most prestigious names in the French armorial. The monument (fig. 3.3), designed to resemble a traditional Breton calvary group, features a medallion depicting the late mayor.[93] Moreover, that the remainder of this subscription comes to exactly 1,000 francs suggests a few round-sum contributions from other local notables rather than any kind of sustained fund-raising campaign. Rather than ambition and local pride, as in Savigny, both the financing of the Pont-Scorff monument and its ultimate appearance convey an aura of noblesse oblige.

What links these two cases is the relative independence of commemorative ambition from the subscription as presumed or effective index of the vox populi. For Hurault the goal of endowing his town with a distinctive monument mattered more than any measurement of opinion beyond the town council he controlled. Although the documentary record for Pont-Scorff is scanty, it suggests the outlook of a benevolent patriarchy, accustomed to both responsibility and deference, for whom the distinction between the community and its leaders had little meaning. This does not mean that the subscription has no significance as an index of public opinion, only that it does not always have the revelatory value that quantitative analysis assumes.

In normal circumstances, town councils awaited at least the organization and sometimes the results of a subscription to decide on the amount of their own contribution, thus making a show of following public opinion. In practice, however, as Pont-Scorff and Savigny-sur-Braye suggest, commemorative ambition sometimes crystallized not in the subscription per se but in the attitudes that mayors and town councils took toward it. Although discursively cast as a response to the results of popular effort, this attitude could also, depending on both the state of the public purse and subjective judgments of the popular mood, involve considerable initiative. In Ploërmel, a committee came into being late in 1918 at an open meeting of interested townspeople, ostensibly the contributors to a wartime subscription; the mayor served as chairman. The

FIGURE 3.3. War monument, Pont-Scorff (Morbihan). Photo: Author.

committee had continued to raise money, notably through a *kermesse*, while also drawing up plans for the monument itself. In November 1920 the town council approved a grant of 4,000 francs, plus 2,400 francs for renovation of the designated site, but when the committee received an estimate two months later it realized that it had a 7,000-franc shortfall. Rather than scale back the monument design, the committee decided to undertake a new subscription.[94] Only after this second campaign, launched with an editorial in *Le ploërmelais* accusing some noncontributors of unrestrained "opulence," produced additional funds (how much is not exactly clear) did the council vote an additional 3,000-franc grant.[95] Here the relatively high per capita contribution, and the high percentage of the cost borne by the subscription, 3.35 francs and 54 percent respectively, represent hard work coordinated by the mayor to tap as much private wealth as possible.

By contrast, in Pontivy, another subprefecture in the Morbihan, commemorative ambition took a very different form. The municipality had no hesitation in responding favorably to a nascent committee's request for a 10,000-franc grant, even though, with the subscription having yet to begin and no definite plans for the monument, one councillor wondered if they were not about to *mettre la charrue avant les boeufs* (put the cart before the horse).[96] At the conclusion of the subscription, in June 1920, the committee voted to build the monument in the cemetery, notwithstanding many contributors' preference for a site in the center of town, on the grounds that "the funds gathered do not allow us to construct a monument in town worthy of our dead." Indeed, the committee's secretary proposed that they organize a *fête* to increase the available funds, "which are not even enough to build anything decent in the cemetery."[97] But when the artist presented his design a few months later, the committee had still amassed only about half of the estimated 40–45,000-franc cost. In May 1921 the council had to agree to an additional grant of 15,000 francs, bringing the total to 25,000, or more than twice the subscription.[98]

Although two successive mayors sat on the committee, neither seems to have had a particular vision of the monument or its place in the city. The city did have standards: the monument itself, commissioned from a Paris-based sculptor with local connections, cost so much because it included bas-reliefs and plaques in bronze.[99] The town government was prepared to spend what it had to in order to provide Pontivy with a monument suitable to the town's importance, but it clearly had no interest in rallying public opinion to build something grander. Ironically, whereas broad public support in Ploërmel made possible the economy of public funds there, the freer fiscal policies of Pontivy reflected an altogether more circumscribed moral investment.[100]

With a population less than half that of Pontivy, the town of Port-Louis, near Lorient, spent almost as much, 43,440 francs as opposed to 44,000, on its monument. A subscription that amounted to only 14.3 percent of the cost points to a significant contribution, and probably initiative, on the part of the Port-Louis town council. In 1921, a year after voting 2,000 francs toward the monument's construction, the town council approved the principal of taking out a loan to cover the cost. Though a loan might appear to be a way of putting off the problem of financial "sacrifice," in fact the mayor rightly warned of the burdens it would impose on the population.[101] The council left the amount of the loan open until learning the size of the subsidies it could expect from the department and the state; ultimately it needed to borrow 27,000 francs, over 60 percent of the total cost. In accordance with customary procedures, the prefect approved the loan only on condition that the town council approve an additional municipal tax to cover its annual payment obligations for the thirty-year term.[102] Port-Louis clearly conceived of its commemorative responsibilities in an expansive frame that conjoined the signifiers of bodies and names. At the same meeting that it approved the loan, the council decided to include a crypt for the remains of dead soldiers in the monument, which was to be built in the cemetery, thus adding to the monument's cost by nearly a third. The council also sought to contract with a supplier "who will offer the most favorable terms without lowering the quality of the construction materials."[103]

The concrete financial burden imposed by loans probably explains why relatively few communes contracted them to pay for monuments. In addition, the state, which had to approve all financial transactions undertaken by communes and was perennially concerned with their solvency, actively discouraged borrowing. The prefect of the Loir-et-Cher at first resisted the plans of the village of St. Léonard to borrow 4,000 francs, saying that the sum seemed excessive in view of the modest cost of the monument and the resources available from both a subscription and a municipal grant of 3,000 francs. The mayor replied, however, that the contractor's estimate for the monument left out any *imprévus* or unexpected costs, as well as the additional cost of a fence, and the loan was approved.[104] Moreover, although in the abstract borrowing imposed an equal burden on all members of a community, it sometimes provided a means of tapping unusual, highly particular resources. In La Trinité-Porhoët (Morbihan), the town council borrowed 10,000 francs in anticipation of a promised gift of that amount from an anonymous lady, to be paid on her death. "Given her advanced age," the council minutes reported, "this sum will become available quite soon."[105] Also in the Morbihan, the town of Rohan passed up a loan from the Crédit Foncier in favor of the more advantageous terms offered by a private citizen.[106] The records do not make clear whether the town held a subscription and if so how much it produced, but the town's population of 686 could hardly have come close to the 20,745-franc cost of this ambitious monument. Unusual for a cantonal seat, albeit one that shares a name with one of the premier noble families of Brittany, the monument, which cost an extraordinary 30 francs per inhabitant (compared to 10.76 in Port-Louis, for example, or 6.2 in Ploërmel), stands out even today (fig. 3.4).

The recourse to private lenders emerges, in this context, as one of a number of expedients for communes whose commemorative reach exceeded their grasp. Some of these expedients even had the effect of expanding the definition of "resources" to encompass not simply financial wherewithal but in-kind

FIGURE 3.4. War monument, Rohan (Morbihan). Photo: Author.

in-kind contributions

contributions to monument construction. No matter how small, such contributions represented a real investment, and like fairs, *quêtes*, or percentages of wine sales, linked the monument project to the everyday life of the community. The Ploërmel committee, for example, not only thanked local farmers for their loan of carts to transport construction materials but placed a concrete value on this service, estimated at a thousand francs by completion.[107] Usually, however, in-kind contributions consisted of labor, either free or at rates below those commanded by skilled construction workers or artists' assistants. Perhaps to emphasize that despite its recourse to a loan (which it contracted from a bank) the village of Grand-Champ still had an eye for economy, its preliminary estimate (*cahier des charges*) for the project divided the construction work into multiple lots, "in order to permit the use of local labor for part of it" while using technically qualified labor for the rest.[108]

"Confronted with the constant rise in the cost of materials and labor," wrote the deputy mayor in Carnac to a prefect suspicious of an apparently inadequate budget, "our commune has every interest in having this work done by workers from the area, without the assistance of a contractor, especially since the materials are being given to us free by local residents."[109] A celebrated site of prehistoric monuments, the menhirs that inspired war memorials in neighboring communities, Carnac contented itself with a fairly modest stela in the cemetery (fig. 3.5) at a cost of less than three francs per inhabitant. In more

FIGURE 3.5.
War monument,
Carnac (Morbihan).
Photo: Author.

ambitious towns, commercial monument suppliers, to be discussed in a subsequent chapter, made possible the use of local labor. Pourcieux, in the Var, ordered perhaps the most recognizable statue of a poilu, as well as one of the cheapest, from the Jacomet firm in the Vaucluse; it entrusted the actual construction to a local stonecutter, whose individual "labor" may have been responsible for the initial paint job on the statue.[110] By the time Hévilliers (Meuse) undertook to build a monument in 1928 the use of local labor was as standard as undertaking a *quête* on the tenth of November, and the monument committee adopted both measures in its first meeting. It eventually ordered the statue of a poilu and the base from different suppliers, and put the two together with local labor.[111]

On this wide range of local practices state subsidies, the last major category of funding, sought without great success to impose a certain uniformity. The budget law of 1920 established a formula for determining the amount of the state's subvention, calculated as a percentage of municipal appropriations for the monument. The formula added together two figures, each determined by a sliding scale, or *barême:* first, the percentage of the 1914 population killed during the war, a proportional scale; and second, the value of the communal tax base, an inverse scale. The total grant could thus range from 5 to 26 percent of the direct municipal expenditure.[112] The exclusion of subscriptions from the calculation was not a foregone conclusion. In the Senate discussion of the second version of the law on commemoration, the reporter, Louis Martin, said in answer to a question that he assumed that subsidies would be calculated in relation to "the effort made by all the inhabitants of the commune, not just that of the municipality": this "effort," in other words, would include money raised by subscription.[113] The actual text of the law, however, limits the grant to a percentage of the *crédits inscrits au budget,* the direct municipal appropriation. The difficulty of verifying subscriptions, concerns that the subsidy program might become a drain on the budget, and a tendency among bureaucrats to discount private activity could all explain this otherwise puzzling narrowness.

Some members of the Chamber of Deputies objected that the twin scales, which originated in the Senate, were too complicated, and urged a simpler method of calculating state support. Certain *conseils généraux,* the departmental elected assemblies, also chose to subsidize communal monuments, and they used much simpler formulas: the Morbihan offered ten francs per dead soldier, but no more than 25 percent of the total cost; the Vaucluse a flat 5 percent of the total.[114] The state formula seems to have survived the legislative process only because the budget committee of the Chamber offered no alternative.[115] Though no one mentioned this at the time, the complexity of the scales in some ways harkened back to the debate over the original law on commemoration of October 1919, in which the Chamber had at one point tried to restrict subsidies to towns with fewer than 5,000 inhabitants. In insisting on the Senate's provision, which had no such restriction, Martin accused the other house of thinking too much in terms of "municipal expenditure" and not enough of tribute to the dead.[116] Restricting support to less populous communes amounted to a crude version of the second scale, since it assumed that larger communes would have the resources to build monuments on their own; the bill ultimately enacted retained the criterion of need but applied it to large and small communes alike.

Although prefects sent circulars to mayors setting out the required procedures,[117] the state subvention program sometimes caused confusion. The monument committee in Ligny-en-Barrois, on learning of the program from the mayor, decided to deposit the proceeds of the subscription in the municipal treasury in order to "obtain a higher percentage" in the state grant.[118] After hearing from the prefect of the Morbihan that he could reduce the municipal appropriation by 18 percent, the amount of the state subvention, the perplexed mayor of Trédion wrote to ask, "On what amount should these eighteen percent be calculated to obtain the 285 francs and more that would permit us to lower our appropriation of 3,000 francs?"[119] Though technically separate from the subsidy program, and mandatory rather than optional, the decree of *hommage public* resulted from a review of the same documents required for a subvention, first by a prefectoral review board, which evaluated the design, then by the Ministry of the Interior or, after 1922, the prefect. And, as prefects had occasion to inform towns that had not bothered to seek official approval, the state would not subsidize unauthorized monuments; the minister of public instruction and fine arts had said as much in one of the Senate debates on the commemoration bill.[120]

This link between subsidies and aesthetic standards recalls Martin's assertion that the subsidy program was intended less to defray local expenses than to make monuments more beautiful. Legislators must have realized that by leaving the initiative to localities, the state could hope only to encourage, not to compel, the construction of monuments that met its artistic criteria—criteria that were in any case, as we will see, never well defined. Though on the one hand a kind of return on their investment, subventions seem also to have connoted, for local officials, bureaucracy and delay, and they provided too little in the way of concrete resources to make up for this inconvenience. The town council in Morée (Loiret-Cher) drew the logical consequences: "Since the construction work should be carried out with as little delay as possible, the council, in view of the resources available to the commune, believes that there is no reason to ask for a subvention from the state."[121] Prefects sometimes went to extraordinary lengths to assist communes in applying for grants: the prefect of the Var himself initiated the official review of an already completed monument in Belgentier, hoping eventually to obtain a subvention for the commune.[122]

This is not to say, of course, that state and departmental subsidies had no effect at all on monument financing. It would be difficult to determine whether the program had the specific impact on design that Martin hoped for: even ignoring the discourse of aesthetic disparagement that sprang up virtually simultaneously with the first monument, most local officials did not, in conceiving their monuments, break down their anticipated expenses so minutely. Some communes did, however, seek to find out how much assistance they could expect from subventions before finalizing their budgets. Even the nine-month delay in issuing the subvention tables must have frustrated many; as early as October 1919, according to Senator Martin, mayors had written to say that "we do not yet know the amount of [the subsidies], and consequently the extent to which we can honor our heroes."[123] Though after the issuance of the tables communes could in theory have made the calculations themselves, the complexity of the process led many to seek official information. This was the case both in a large city like Toulon, where the committee chairman wrote directly to the interior minister before establishing a design budget, and in the rural Morbihan communes of Taupont and Pluméliau.[124]

In a few towns the announcement of the subsidy program, or some years later of its impending expiration, seems to have been the principal catalyst to monument construction. The mayor of Binas (Loir-et-Cher) assembled his town council on Christmas Day 1920 to read the prefectoral circular on the availability of subventions, and the council voted to request one before doing anything else. In the fall of 1924, prefects informed mayors that the government was discontinuing the subsidy program and that requests for subsidies received after December 1924 would not be honored. These circulars clearly provoked villages like Contrisson, in the Meuse, and Avaray, in the Loir-et-Cher, finally to give substance to long-dormant monument projects.[125] Such cases remained the exception, however. Far more numerous were, on the one hand, towns that requested subventions to supplement local funds raised or appropriated well before publication of the *barèmes*. On the other hand, towns that first had to be rebuilt after heavy war damage often did not build monuments until the late twenties, when they served as a kind of symbolic conclusion to reconstruction; for them the expiration of the subsidy program years before could hardly have been a major concern.[126]

State subventions, and parallel programs in certain departments, seem to have had the greatest impact in providing financial assistance to needy communes. Evidence for this comes, paradoxically, from the desperation that delays in receiving subsidies sometimes occasioned. As with any kind of program involving the state bureaucracy, delays were routine. In 1921 Selles-sur-Cher, a cantonal seat in the Loir-et-Cher (and the source of a very fine *chèvre*), enlisted a senator in its attempt to speed up the administrative formalities; in response, the prefect proposed to keep a running list of subvention requests, though it is not clear how this would have helped.[127] The town of Gourin (Morbihan) obtained official approval for its monument in June 1922, a month before its inauguration. That November, the mayor wrote the prefect to inquire about the state subsidy payment, saying that he found it painful not to be able to pay the contractor "because he carried out his work with great care." Nine months later, having paid off the contractor with available funds, the mayor needed money to pay the water bill; the prefect replied that he had as yet received no answer from the ministry.[128]

Béganne and Plumelin, much smaller communes in the same department, seem to have made a different kind of calculation: that they could build monuments without undertaking a subscription at all, instead using subventions to supplement their own appropriations. Rather than the elaborate stone figure in Gourin, a cantonal seat, both chose commercial monuments, Béganne's a fairly simple one. Citing the relevant passage in the minutes of the *conseil général*, the mayor of Béganne told the prefect he needed to know urgently how much the state and department subventions would amount to, since the contractors were warning him of imminent price increases. Unfortunately it was only August 1919, and the prefect could not give him precise information, but the two grants eventually would cover more than a quarter of the cost. The town did not actually contract for the monument project until the summer of 1921; hardly had construction begun than a shortage of funds brought it to a halt. On receiving the departmental subsidy in January 1922, the mayor wrote the prefect that work could now resume, "but we still do not have the amount necessary to finish the project"; he found it intensely disagreeable to have to tell contractors, "'Wait, I have no money.'"[129] In a similar situation, the mayor of Plumelin wrote that the town would be subject to a lawsuit if it did not soon pay its contractors.[130]

Surprisingly, given the traditional paradigms of French history, relatively few communes were so dependent on higher authority for their commemorative efforts: although frequent, delays in state funding almost never brought a project to a halt. Also relatively rare is rhetoric like the following, the beginning of a subvention request in the Loir-et-Cher: "Considering that the commune, which was sorely tried [*éprouvée*] during the war, has taken out a loan of 9,000 francs to build a monument to its dead. . . ."[131] Whatever difficulties they had with the details, most communes understood the subsidy program for what it was: a gesture on the part of the state, a short-term entitlement based on numbers, not words. The state's subsidy program, because it recognized only officially appropriated funds, operated at a dryly bureaucratic level far removed from the emotion and purposiveness that marked local fund-raising. For the resources that each commune assembled, sometimes slowly and painfully, to commemorate its dead conveyed a sense that the end not so much transcended but transformed the means. State subsidies could be important, but they were, ultimately, only money. Subscriptions, loans, public funds, and local labor used to build monuments were something more: an investment not only financial but emotional, a share in identifying a community with its memory of the dead.

The Broken Plaque

One of the fundamental dynamics of commemoration interweaves memory and forgetting, privileging some aspects of experience, consigning others to a lesser place, perhaps to oblivion. On the fence surrounding the modest war memorial in Gueltas (Morbihan, fig. 3.6) one finds a plaque (fig. 3.7) dedicated

FIGURE 3.6. War monument, Gueltas (Morbihan). Photo: Author.

FIGURE 3.7. War monument, Gueltas: detail of plaque. Photo: Author.

to "Olivier Brient, mayor of Gueltas, victim of an accident during the construction of this monument: in grateful memory, 1921." In a letter to the minister of the interior requesting authorization to put up the plaque, the mayor's widow, who along with a group of friends had paid for this unusual tribute, explained that her husband had died "after four days of horrible suffering" caused when a surplus missile being installed as part of a fence around the monument rolled over and crushed him.[132] Plaques like this one supplement the standard dedication and list of names, adding another layer to the memories monuments enshrine, a kind of recursive memory that calls attention to the commemorative process itself. The two layers must, at some level, fit together: the mayor of Gueltas got a special plaque because his death could emblematize the commemorative spirit of the wider community. But the overall effect is to particularize. Slightly unexpectedly, like the palm trees on either side of it, the now regilded plaque offers the outsider a glimpse into the special weight of memory in Gueltas.

In contrast, the basic markers that virtually all monuments share, dedications and lists of names, emphasize the aspects of memory that communities hold in common. The dedication at Gueltas is on the flowery end of the conventional spectrum: "A la Glorieuse Mémoire des Enfants de Gueltas morts pour la France, 1914–1918." Together with the names of the dead, these inscriptions play a crucial role in a signifying process that seeks to collapse the distinction between signifier and signified—or, more accurately, to represent that distinction as having already collapsed. The monument, in these semiotics, *is* both dedicator, the commune, and dedicatee, its dead; the names, before the war only an arbitrary signifier of human lives, now constitute the irreducible essence of what remains of them. A monument so inscribed presents commemoration as a closed system, virtually self-sufficient: what more, it seems to ask the stranger, could you possibly want to know? In contrast, additional markers like the Gueltas plaque actively point to the investment that produces monuments, serving as claims of authorship akin to the more frequent but far less conspicuous artists' signatures or casting marks.

The frequency of supplemental markers varies from department to department, but nowhere do they exist on more than a relatively small proportion of monuments. Most typically, they record the simple facts of a monument's creation: "Monument érigé en 1921 par souscription publique," reads the plaque in Pourcieux. Monuments in the Var, perhaps because of its deeply rooted Republican tradition, were twice as likely as in the other sample departments to contain such an inscription. In the Morbihan, supplementary inscriptions sometimes give only the names of the mayor and the curé, a veiled sign of the reconciliation with the state that many Catholics hoped would come about in the aftermath of the war.[133] Occasionally, the additional plaques provide details that form a kind of snapshot of the monument's founding moment: "This monument," reads the plaque in Hyères, "was inaugurated on 3 January 1926, by the minister of justice [*Garde des Sceaux*], René Renoult, under the municipal administration of Paul Gensollen." A plaque in Selles-sur-Cher gives even more detail.

Only those with a discernible stake in the commemorative process have a right to such a marker. That is the difference between the mayor of Gueltas and a Turkish worker killed by an unexploded missile while preparing the site of the future Douaumont Ossuary. The worker earned no in situ tribute; one learns of his fate only through reading an obscure local newspaper.[134] Another type of supplementary marker evokes the tribute of specific groups, most commonly veterans but also, occasionally, new conscripts and even local firemen, to the dead. Though more easily assimilable than plaques to the semiotics of the basic inscriptions, these bronze palms or wreaths on one level serve a distancing function with respect to the commemorative act. By calling attention, that is, to distinct *components* of the community, they disrupt the seamless continuity between the community, construed as a single entity, and the dedicator, and at least pose the question of authorship that basic inscriptions leave unspoken.

The necessary concision of supplementary plaques could, of course, confer a kind of retrospective harmony on the often contentious process of monument construction. A small plaque to one side of the Toulon monument, for example, describes it as "constructed by public subscription, with the financial assistance of the City, and on the initiative of a committee chaired by M. Victor Castel." But inasmuch as they tended to emphasize, even glorify, the ostensibly mundane, supplementary markers had an inherent disadvantage: they brought to the forefront a signifying process that wanted to remain, as it proclaimed itself, invisible. Though such inscriptions might seem unexceptionable, their very rarity makes them stand out and invites questions about the process they sum up. If not redacted as carefully as in Toulon, supplemental markers could themselves become objects of controversy. In Aups, the site of a particularly bitter dispute between the mayor and the monument committee, a plaque "describing the inauguration ceremonies" clearly sought to signify above all the municipality's *control* of the completed monument, on the principle that a monument's dedication brought the committee's role to an end. The committee, which still controlled the subscription proceeds, smashed the mayor's plaque and replaced it with another, and the dispute between the two continued for several more months.[135] Today the supplementary inscription reveals only what was not in dispute: "Dedicated on 25 September 1922."

This was an unusual event, but nonetheless central to the cultural work of commemoration. A similar incident occurs in Maurice Genevoix's novel *La joie*. The mayor, a prototypical small-town politician in an ostentatiously generic (if fictional) department, the "Loire-Moyenne," uses the war memorial to construct memory in his own image. For Genevoix's hero, a disillusioned veteran, "the mayor maneuvered cleverly to reach his goal, the only one that really, passionately, interested him: to engrave his name in the granite base, to take advantage of this unique opportunity to make the memory of his glorious administration eternal." At the monument's dedication, the veteran cannot take his eyes off this plaque: "This Monument was constructed by public subscription, during the mayoralty of OCTAVE THOMASSIER." But on the night after the ceremony, "persons unknown" defaced the mayor's name, breaking the plaque with a chisel and covering the name with a layer of minium, red lead.[136]

For Genevoix, the mayor's crime and punishment stem from a cynical inversion of the commemorative process. The monument here points so insistently to its own conditions of production that its ostensible object becomes lost. Though this incident serves its own purpose within the narrative of *La joie*, where it stands for the inevitable inadequacy of collective forms of remembrance, it also points to a risk that all supplementary plaques ran, the risk of casting investment as the purpose of commemoration rather than simply as means to that end. Given the enormous effort that went into the building of monuments, the financial burden so often lionized in the press, it may seem curious that more monuments do not commemorate their own construction, do not offer at least a hint of the investment that produced them. That this type of self-reflexive commemoration is, relatively speaking, so rare reflects, on the contrary, what it really put at risk: nothing less than the unique sacredness of the war dead.

We can best understand this dynamic by returning to Gueltas and the mayor's widow. In a second letter to the minister, Madame Brient, not having received a response to her first, evidently felt the need to establish in even greater detail her husband's merits, including the fact that he had borrowed money personally to hasten the monument's construction. Faced with having to pay the interest on the loan herself, as well as over 300 francs in unreimbursed fees, the widow wrote of her discouragement: "Having spared neither our time nor our money during the war—we closed our business and both devoted ourselves entirely to the commune—to see that now I'm reduced to wondering how to survive, well, that is pretty hard."[137] Both letters refer to the mayor's death in the line of duty, but in the second the monument becomes, powerfully if ungrammatically, the site of their connection: "I would be sorry if I could not put his name on this monument where his so cruel death took him by surprise while he was doing his duty."[138]

Duty, death, the name, inscription: the dynamics are familiar, and they create an eerie parallel with the dead whom monuments normally commemorate. Except in the war zone, and even there in fairly limited measure, there could not have been many communal monuments that were themselves sites of death or fatal injury. Madame Brient, in short, had an impeccable claim, and its outcome, as a surprised official wrote after receiving her second letter, was not in doubt. But her portrait of selfless devotion to the common good melds a little too easily with the prevailing discourse of combatant experience, making clear why commemorating commemorative investment as such touched so many nerves. For disillusioned veterans like Genevoix's hero, and undoubtedly for bereaved families as well, financial investment in monuments, whether public or private, should have no goal other than paying tribute to the dead. No other *sacrifice*, in this view, could possibly match that of their sons, husbands, and comrades, and any comparison to it bordered on the obscene.

The dual connotations of "sacrifice," and the moral value ascribed to financial sacrifice both during and after the war, sometimes in the specific context of monument subscriptions, sowed ambiguity at the heart of the commemorative enterprise. This ambiguity, the possibility that the merit of participating in commemoration not only could, but was intended to, overwhelm, even erase, the valor of the honorees, in a sense reproduced one of the fundamental ambiguities of commemoration itself. On one level, the discourse of mourning in the interwar period insisted on the unique merits of the war dead, implying that survivors could never equal them, that they could only remain faithful to their memory. Yet one of the objectives of mourning, indeed, according to Freud, what distinguishes it from the pathology of melancholia, is the transfer of libido from the lost love object to a new one.[139] Commemoration inevitably seeks to mask, even to deny, this transference, but to the extent it does so successfully, it can be said to facilitate it.

Because it involved money, because it could, under certain circumstances, appear to turn the act of tribute into a mere transaction, financial investment risked laying bare the ambiguities, the essential dichotomy of commemoration. The broken plaque stood for the boundary line that commemoration dared not cross in signaling its reliance on a kind of "sacrifice." The possibility that contributing to a monument campaign could profit an individual in any material way, even, say, by providing a newly landscaped park around a monument, never entered the discussion at all. At this literal level, the idea of a return on the commemorative investment was simply beyond the pale. Rather, that troubling notion hovers around the apparently innocuous tribute paid to donors' very generosity and self-sacrifice. For after all, what had the dead received for their "supreme sacrifice" but gratitude and glory? Their survivors might, in exchange for their generosity, bask in the reflection of that glory, but only if it were thoroughly circumscribed and, preferably, impermanent. The mayor of La Versanne could pay tribute to the sweat of the farmer's brow, to the privations of his fellow citizens, in a dedication speech, but no supplementary plaque could go so far. In order to efface and naturalize the work of transference they accomplish, monuments had little choice but to conceal the financial as well as the emotional investment that fueled them, calling as little attention as possible to the circumstances of their production.

4

SEEING THE SIGNIFIED

In 1939 the son of a former governor of the Invalides, General Niox, wrote to prefects all over France seeking assistance in locating noteworthy war memorials in their departments. Niox's father had written a book on Great War memorial sites, and was hoping to illustrate it with photographs of monuments of particular artistic distinction. In reply, the prefect of the Loir-et-Cher wrote that most of the monuments in his department were "modest pyramids or commemorative stelae, or statues of banal appearance." Only two seemed to him of artistic note: the Blois memorial, designed by the prominent sculptor Sicard, and the *borne sobre* (austere stone) in the small town of Trôo, "which is marked by the originality of its creator [*auteur*], the master Bourdelle."[1]

The prefect's dismissiveness has become a commonplace, a trope for the late twentieth-century's relationship to the public art of the past. A few monuments may be of interest because we can attach the name of a famous artist to them; a few more might strike us only because in their scale or complexity they so obviously aspire to the status of "art." Most, we would agree with the prefect, are too "modest" or "banal" to have any aesthetic claim on our attention. Such an attitude and its logical extension, the view that commemoration involves a complex of beliefs and practices operating independently of the aesthetic realm, underlies the first and still most influential scholarly study of French war memorials. In his analysis of the "semiology and typology of war monuments," Antoine Prost excludes artist-designed monuments in major cities on the grounds that "the intentions of the community are too often concealed by aesthetic preoccupations."[2] But simply to ignore the "aesthetic" leaves out one of the crucial terms that gave shape to commemorative discourse and practice in the interwar period. We cannot hope to understand commemoration historically if we take the conventional distinction between art and commemoration as a given. For that dichotomy itself has a history, one that played an integral part in the larger history at stake here.

As a way of interrogating the art/commemoration dichotomy, it is helpful to conceive of both monuments and commemoration as forms of cultural "production." Increasingly in cultural studies, the notion of the artist as sole and solitary "creator" has given way to a conception of the work of art, or of any object with an identifiable maker, as "the complex product of economic, social, and ideological factors, mediated through the formal structures of the text (literary or other), and owing its existence to the particular practice of the located individual."[3] This sense of the term needs to be recovered and foregrounded in a study of works we are all too willing to see as "produced," even mass produced, rather than "created." For "production" does not apply only to a making: in common usage, the term has a double meaning, involving both a process and its end result, for example a theatrical production.[4] The latter sense refers to an object or presentation that seeks to intervene as signification in a world distinct from the circumstances of its making. When we see an advertising poster, for instance, normally we attend first to what it means—thus invoking a world of signification—and only secondarily, if at all, to the human, mechanical, and economic processes that brought it about. A set of discourses and practices mediates between these two senses of the term, which can also be understood as two phases of cultural production. These discourses frame our beliefs and assumptions about two social worlds: the world that produced the object, and the world that activates its cultural meaning.

Far from a stable, unchanging entity, discourse itself undergoes continual shifts in both its terms and its syntax, that is, in the relationship it posits between those terms. At issue here are the ways in which discourses of various kinds produce meanings within, and understandings of, commemorative culture. The prefect's reverent allusion to the *marque* of *maître Bourdelle, auteur* of the modest monument in Trôo, for example, recalls Michel Foucault's insight that "in our culture, the name of an author is a variable that accompanies only certain texts to the exclusion of others . . . In this sense, the function of an author is to characterize the existence, circulation, and operation of certain discourses within a society."[5] Looking at this block of stone in a quiet churchyard (fig. 4.1), we would be hard put to distinguish it from the many monuments whose modesty condemns them to obscurity; so the discourse of authorship, in this case independent of any signifying marks other than that of "style," performs the distinction for us.[6] The name of the author or artist, Foucault has suggested, lies in the gap or breach between different kinds of texts, which he conceives as sites where "new groups of discourse and their singular mode of existence" arise.[7] The parallel existence of authored and "nonauthored" monuments points to just this sort of breach and to the crucial role played by artistic discourse in

monument production. For in the gaps and fissures of that discourse, in its organization and manipulation of the signs of art, and in its connection to other discourses of cultural status, another discourse, commemoration, was emerging.

The production of monuments before 1914 involved two sectors that for contemporaries appeared largely distinct. Major works, such as Jules Dalou's *Triumph of the Republic* and Alexandre Falguière's *Monument to Pasteur*, both erected in Paris around the turn of the century, were the works of recognized, trained artists, chiefly sculptors and architects who received artistic training and exhibited at the Paris Salon.[8] That their output involved the collaboration of others outside their studios, from foundries to construction workers, did not diminish the prestige attached to their work. In contrast, the commercial enterprises that produced altogether more modest pieces for both the private (tombstones and funerary monuments) and the public (statues of the Republic, monuments to the 1870 war dead) spheres seemed to be operating in an essentially nonartistic realm.[9] Of course the two sectors did overlap, notably at the high end of funerary monument production,[10] but not in a way that could undermine long-standing distinctions between high art and popular culture. After the war, the massive demand for public monuments had the effect of making the underlying continuities in monument production both inescapable and, discursively at least, intolerable.

A number of factors combined to facilitate this shift in the production of monuments and of commemorative discourse. The war and its aftermath brought about a profound transformation in the cultural climate in France, extending, as Kenneth Silver has shown, to the highest reaches of the avant-garde. A new embrace of tradition, discipline, and austerity, as well as the rejection of recent experimentation, such as cubism, as frivolous and decadent, brought a renewed prestige and legitimacy to the forms and ideals of classicism, notably its restraint and highly conventional stylistic vocabulary. "Individualism," with its overtones of unbridled creative originality, became suspect; collective endeavor, the model for judging the artistic enterprise and its contribution to the reconstruction of France.[11] At the same time, the need for certain sectors of the French art world, notably the decorative arts, to embrace modern techniques of mass production to remain economically competitive provoked considerable debate, as it had for some years before the war. Such debates, particularly over whether artist or manufacturer would control the rights to a design, must have resonated with the professionals most involved in monument production, sculptors and architects. For their trades, although they shared the academic pedigree and critical apparatus of painting and literature, had been included in the realm of high culture protected by the Revolutionary law on copyright, or *droit d'auteur*, only since 1902.[12]

The transformation of artistic discourse thus had an economic as well as an ideological dimension. The new demand for monuments did not radically alter the structures of monument production, which remained, as we will see, predominantly local and hybrid, involving various combinations of producers and suppliers. But this demand effectively accorded a few large national firms a monopoly over certain *types* of monuments, and these types, particularly the poilu, soon occupied a privileged position in both popular and critical notions of what constituted a monument. Professional artists had no choice but to respond with similar types, but they faced a related problem. The capital and resources of large commercial firms gave them the means to appropriate and deploy artistic discourse on behalf of their own production. In these circumstances the discourse of art became, for its traditional purveyors in the world of high art, no longer a weapon but a strategy for survival. The condemnation of the bulk of monument production as "modest" or "banal" served at once as a modus vivendi, a sealing off, and, ironically, a kind of consecration. For out of this struggle over the artistic status of monuments something unintended had emerged: a sense of commemoration as involving standards and criteria proper to itself, a discursive system with its own signs, intersecting with those of art, but autonomous from it.

If the commercial appropriation of artistic discourse makes clear the stakes of this contestation, on the critics' side the target remained veiled and elusive. The debate over the artistic status of monuments, moreover, was not confined to critics and commercial suppliers. In each department, advisory panels consisting of officials, notables, and design professionals reviewed monument projects and passed judgment on them. Though they had only limited powers to compel towns to modify their plans, the prefectoral review boards played a vital role in diffusing artistic discourse to the provinces. They did not, however, work in a vacuum. Deploying a powerful sense of memory as rooted in the visual, the local officials and committees who made up the clientele for war memorials did not hesitate to assign them their own set of meanings and their own notion of what constituted "art." Local appropriations of both artistic and commemorative discourse may no longer resonate for us in the way that proto-modernist criticism does, but we should not underestimate their importance. It was, after all, the unprecedented demand of a vast new market that so dramatically transformed the production both of monuments and of the discourses that inserted them into a network of social practices. As a result of that transformation, we have come to see monuments as, in Prost's terms, "a system of signs that reinforce or respond to each other."[13] But to the extent that that system still preserves some traces of the circumstances of its emergence, we need to examine them in all their complexity, material as well as discursive.

"A Kind of Anguished Terror": Salons, Critics, and Artists

The discourse of high art circulated with considerable energy through the multiple levels of French culture, occasionally altering in shape, purpose, and strategies as it encountered unfamiliar objects, like mass-produced monuments, or streamed through newly created channels. It would be futile to try to identify a particular space, institution, or profession as the "source" of this or any other discourse; we can, however, locate the milieu regarded, then and now, as its privileged seat: the world of the Paris exhibitions and critics. Beginning our exploration of monument production with the evaluative framework in which it took place, it makes sense to look first at that world, dedicated, by its own lights and by common consent, to critical judgment and the setting of standards.[14]

Wartime subjects, most of them either explicitly or implicitly commemorative, dominated the sculpture sections of the various annual art exhibitions known as Salons for several years after the end of the war. In contrast to painting, where war-related themes dropped off dramatically after 1920 and had practically disappeared by 1924,[15] the ongoing importance of monuments through the mid-twenties reflected, on one level, the slowness of sculptural production: some sculptors even displayed the same work in subsequent years, a plaster one year, a bronze the next.[16] This drawn-out process also gave critics repeated opportunities to expound on the impact of commemoration on the art of sculpture. It did not take long for a general critical line on monuments to establish itself. In general, critics echoed Jean Ajalbert's fear of a "hideous repetition of monuments" cited in chapter 2. Commenting on the Salon of 1919, Robert de la Sizeranne hoped that most of the monuments on display would long remain in their current state, that is as unbuilt projects.[17] A year later, in the establishment daily *Le temps*, the critic Thiébault-Sisson exclaimed at the number of "monuments, distressingly mediocre, which evoke the war's mourning." That year's *salonnier* in the *Gazette des beaux-arts*, Etienne Bricot, proclaimed his verdict as though confirming his worst predictions: "We knew well—we knew it from the day it was declared—that the war would stimulate the imagination of sculptors as well as their tools, and that it would do so, as alas it must in any invasion of the crowd, with disorder and mediocrity."[18] Though each critic had compliments to dispense, none had much good to say about the overall quality of the projects on view.

This attitude had, as Ajalbert's earlier comments indicate, a prehistory, a frustration with the existing tradition of monumental sculpture that reached something of an apogee in a 1921 article by the critic Frantz Jourdain. The article, which appeared in a new magazine with a fairly progressive profile, *L'amour de l'art*,[19] is worth citing at some length:

The more or less commemorative or triumphalist monuments with which modern France is infested cause me a kind of anguished terror. Nothing has been able to conquer, nor even to attenuate, this plague, of which the École des Beaux-Arts carried the seed, a plague that seems to increase from day to day and that is breaking out anew with a truly demonic intensity.

Turning to the work he was actually reviewing, a new Reformation monument in Geneva, Jourdain expressed his relief at the absence of the

mythological bric-a-brac, banal symbolism, [and] pedantic declamation [*clamicisme*] with which we are saturated to the point of vomiting. No more topless models representing Force or Justice or Abundance or Constitutional Revision or God knows what, no more [classical] orders, no more pediments, corbels, scrolls, or escutcheons, no more academic memories as disgusting as dishwater, no more pages of stupidly impersonal lettering, no more ornamental salads pilfered from all over, no more provincial tables d'hôte.[20]

His unusual ferocity notwithstanding, Jourdain here sets out, in the formal language of his professional colleagues, a kind of visual catalogue of everything critics objected to in the public art of the past half century. Although he does not directly mention sculpture related to the war, the clause "qui prend recrudescence d'[une] intensité véritablement démoniaque" almost certainly refers to it implicitly. The entire article, moreover, manifests a critical outlook that condemned the lion's share of monument production before it had even begun. For precisely the classical elements that Jourdain decries—the pediments, scrolls, corbels, and so on—formed the vocabulary that commercial suppliers and others outside the Paris art world would seize on in their efforts to market their products as both monumental and artistic.

By the early 1920s projects for war memorials had become the dominant motif of the sculpture salons, their mediocrity a critical commonplace. Jeanne Dion, the *Gazette des beaux-arts'* Salon critic for 1922, called the monuments generally *manqués* (off, failed), declaring that they were conceived "without life, without poetry, without reflection." Admitting the thanklessness of the genre, Dion wrote that so far artists' efforts had produced only "bombast, stiffness, convention, and improbability."[21] Writing in early 1921, another critic, Edouard André, condemned the "banality" and "vulgar declamation" of most monuments, suggesting that the difficulties Dion perceived might be insuperable: "How difficult it is, after so many masterpieces of the past, to imagine a funerary monument worthy both of the epic we have lived through and of the conscience and ambition of a talented artist!"[22] Commenting on the Salon of 1922, Arsène Alexandre also perceived the great monuments of the past, notably François Rude's celebrated sculpture on the Arc de Triomphe (fig. 4.2), familiarly known as *La Marseillaise*, as an obstacle to contemporary representation: "We will, of course, refrain from mentioning all the figures with outstretched arms and open mouths that innocently plagiarize the *Victory* [*sic*] of Rude."[23]

In evoking the difficulty that the representation of the war posed to *any* conventional form, these critics articulate a theme that has become familiar in the history of modernism. In the context of art criticism, however, this theme served a primarily rhetorical function, clearing a space in which, notwithstanding, an ideal monumental sculpture to the war dead could be sketched out. Obviously this conception differed from critic to critic. But over and above their disagreements about particular projects, and whether they wrote for mainstream or more avant-garde publications, the critics converged on a core group

FIGURE 4.2. François Rude, *La marseillaise*, Arc de Triomphe, Paris. Photo: Author.

of characteristics they considered essential for a successful modern monument. Together these characteristics describe a monument that, unsurprisingly, broke sharply with the traditional mold.

From the earliest exhibition of monument projects in 1919, the critics consistently praised projects in terms of sobriety, simplicity, and plainness. Many admired the sculptor Bartholomé's bas-reliefs for a memorial in Montbrison: Arsène Alexandre, writing in *Le Figaro*, called them "polished and pure, carefully considered."[24] Perrault-Harry's monument to aviators killed in the line of duty, *La mort de l'aigle*, attracted praise in similar terms. But in the *Revue des deux mondes* de la Sizeranne, while endorsing the use of animals in commemorative sculpture, recognized that "in sculpture, every symbol requires an explanation."[25] The appeal of what he called monuments "freighted [*embarrassée*] with the accoutrements of modern life," that is details of the military uniform, lay precisely in their transcending this requirement. More signs than symbols, the poilu's helmet or canteen needed no explanation. Beyond their professed dislike of excess ornament, critics may have distrusted signs that so clearly, as we will see later in this chapter, enabled interpretation to operate outside traditional critical channels.

The figural monuments receiving critical approval simply added another class to the larger category of simplicity. Praising Henri Bouchard's project for a monument in the Pantheon exhibited in the Salon of 1920, Alexandre wrote, "There is nothing more strongly conceived than these two simple figures . . . nothing more sober or more striking than the base decorated with a narrow bas-relief." Female as well as male figures could meet the critical standards for a suitable commemorative monument. But through descriptions of these monuments a particular set of limits emerges, pertaining less to monuments' formal characteristics than to their suitability for certain discursive constructions. Bricot's favorite monument at the Salon of 1920 was Maxime Réal del Sarte's *Terre de France* (Earth of France, fig. 4.3), which he described as follows: "Alone, dressed with a simplicity that Millet would have liked, a peasant woman, primitive and healthy in her youthfulness, gathers the sheaves that have sprouted more beautiful in the Earth around the tomb of the soldier who died for her."[26] This figure is not France or some abstract quality. Dressed simply, she is a recognizable contemporary type, even a slice of life: a young rural widow paying tribute to the dead by continuing their work.[27]

If Bricot's interpretation of this statue seems far from self-evident, that is the point: it seeks to close off other plausible characterizations, notably a reading of the monument, and its title, as allegorical. Other critics echo this hesitation or skepticism about allegory. In late 1921, the inauguration of the war memorial in the town of Menin, in Belgium (fig. 4.4), brought a certain amount of attention, most of it favorable, to its designer, the Franco-Belgian sculptor Yvonne Sérruys. Edouard André mused in *L'art et les artistes* on the difficulty of creating a war memorial at once contemporary and artistic, and though he lauded the artist's conscientious attention to site and theme, this was clearly not his favorite of her works. "The allegory," he sighed, "is, alas, an allegory!"[28] In the *Gazette des beaux-arts* L. Dumont-Wilden justified the sculptor's choice of allegory in terms of "the grandeur of the subject, the concern for architecture [which] led her quite naturally to a classical simplification." Yet "these two

don't like allegory

FIGURE 4.3. Maxime Réal del Sarte, *Terre de France*, 1920. *GBA*, ser. 5, 2 (January-June 1920): 21.

allegorical figures are two living bodies, whose muscles move, whose physiognomies and poses are expressive." Far from the lifeless allegorical figures of nineteenth-century monumental sculpture, the critic saw them as at once modest, "gracious," and familiar, the weeping woman "symbolizing so well the mothers and widows afflicted with the great sorrow of the war."[29] We are, in other words, closer to Réal del Sarte's peasant woman than we might have realized.

Allegory, then, could find its place among critically accepted monuments to the war dead only within a tightly constructed discourse of simplicity. Similar constraints applied to work in a more realist mode. Thiébault-Sisson had announced the acceptability of such monuments by deeming Gaston Broquet's

Dans les boues de la Somme the only truly noteworthy monument at the Salon of 1920. The critic called the piece less a monument than "an episodic group depicting two poilus who carry the corpse of one of their comrades in a sheet of canvas hung over a heavy rod"; he found it "moving in its brutal realism."[30] But if signs of life and vitality could save sculpture from the crushing boredom of over-elaborate allegory, the same signs taken to excess—excessive movement, a profusion of detail, exaggerated expressions—could condemn a realistic monument to the category of the "anecdotal" or "banal." In his review of the Salons of 1923, Waldemar George called Réal del Sarte's project for a monument to the armies of Champagne, featuring three infantrymen, "a banal group," and declared that Fernand Dubois's *Tu ne tueras point* "incarnates the anecdotal, commercial, and outdated mode of a number of official sculptors."[31]

The ideal of simplicity that by the early 1920s dominated the critical discourse about commemorative sculpture had consequences beyond the aesthetic realm. As a trope it tended to disadvantage the best-known sculptors, those experienced teachers and practitioners, exempt from jury selection at the Salons

FIGURE 4.4. Yvonne Sérruys, war monument for Menin (Belgium), 1921. *GBA*, ser. 5, 4 (July-December 1921): 351.

FIGURE 4.5. Paul Landowski, *Les fantômes*, 1923. *GBA*, ser. 5, 7 (January-June 1923): 288. © 1999 Artists Rights Society (ARS), New York/ADAGP Paris.

(*hors concours*), who received the most elaborate and costly commissions. Consider Thiébault-Sisson's reaction to Paul Gasq's *La mobilisation 1914*, a high relief, exhibited in 1923, destined to serve as part of the war memorial in Dijon. Attacking the monument's "shockingly realist stance [*parti pris*]," the critic described the now familiar signs of excess—gesticulating arms, wide-open mouths—and dismissed the work's obvious reference to Rude: "Rude's *Marseillaise* is to Gasq's *Mobilisation* what the dramas of Corneille are to the cinema." Thiébault-Sisson may have had a particular antipathy to Gasq—in 1920 the critic described one of the artist's submissions as "bearing an unfortunate resemblance to Italian cemetery monuments"[32]—but no well-known artist could entirely escape such invective. That same year George called Paul Landowski's *Fantômes* (fig. 4.5), which won the medal of honor in 1923 and lavish praise from other critics, "a betrayal of bronze, which it transforms into something limp, impure, and cottony."[33]

That major artists who regularly submitted works to the Salons garnered less than universal praise should in no way surprise us. Each of the comments just cited has its own genealogy, involving, among other factors, the critic's personal taste, the cultural politics of the periodical for which he or she wrote, and the career trajectory of the artist under review. But critics occasionally pondered the reasons for the general mediocrity they perceived, or for more surprising trends, such as the greater success of little-known artists in making "austere" and "simple" monuments. Though nominally focused on individual artists and works, their reflections encompass a number of more general issues within the art world, thus pointing to the larger stakes of the debate over the aesthetics of commemoration.

Criticism of monuments both relied on and reinforced an assumed distinction between "high" or enlightened and "popular" taste. This distinction forms a kind of leitmotif for Thiébault-Sisson, with the popular coded as *la foule* (the crowd), but it also crops up in the writings of other critics. Only the exceptional work, such as, in Thiébault-Sisson's view, Landowski's *Fantômes*, had the gift of appealing to both "the crowd and connoisseurs"; the critic praised the "intelligence" of the monument's conception as well as the care and restraint of its execution.[34] More often, however, an artist's appeal to the crowd summed up all his defects: thus the Gasq project for Dijon "has all the necessary qualities to strike the crowd in just the right spot."[35] In 1929 de la Sizeranne found Gaston Broquet's *La patrouille* less elemental than his previous work, but said, "It will nonetheless touch the hearts of the crowd, because it makes palpable to all eyes what veterans are trying, awkwardly, to express, on those rare occasions when they break their silence: Misery and Glory."[36] The critic employs one of the gendered tropes of the discourse of war experience, the soldier's and veteran's silence, to pay subtle, indeed slightly ambiguous, tribute to the prowess of a male artist.

Critical discourse here displays all its adaptability: by the late 1920s the appeal to the crowd has become so common in commemorative sculpture that the critics have developed criteria for evaluating it. Such judgment, of course, only accentuates the dichotomy between the crowd and connoisseurs, even as it provides artists with a way of saving face. The sculptors, the critics are telling us, know better, but they have no choice. De la Sizeranne urged readers not to be put off by "the crowd's" affection for two works by Broquet at the 1926 Salon, *La relève*, for Châlons-sur-Marne, and *Sur le sol lorrain*, for Étain (Meuse, fig. 4.6): "It is to these two works that the crowd goes first, before them that it stays the longest, quiet and reflective, to them that it returns." The crowd's favor was not a sign of genius, he declared, but neither was it a disgrace: "This is assuredly not Olympian, monumental sculpture: it is realistic and anecdotal modeling. . . . The art is not epic, but the subject is and so is the feeling behind it."[37] Here, in effect, the critic summons both meritorious artists and art aficionados to help him build a wall between art and commemoration. At the same time, the

FIGURE 4.6. Gaston Broquet, *Sur le sol lorrain*, for the war monument in Étain (Meuse), 1926. Photo: Author.

high/popular dichotomy provides the critics with a ready-made explanation of the general mediocrity of monument production, one that conveniently evokes another familiar binary opposition, between Paris and *la France profonde*.

This opposition between center and periphery appears in both avant-garde and mainstream criticism, unfiltered by their differing attitudes toward "official" sculpture. Thus this unsigned note in *L'art et les artistes* in 1923:

[War memorials] are as innumerable as the glorious tombs they had to commemorate. This was fatal. Most are unworthy of their purpose, and the generally deplorable municipal taste that led to their fabrication has revealed itself so often that one wonders where the invasion of our beautiful France by all this lamentable sculpture will end. In a few more years the traveler will be unable to pass through our cities, our villages, our countryside without covering his eyes.[38]

This lament recalls the general characterizations with which we began, but note its construction: the traveler, presumably a Parisian, is fated to suffer because of the lapses of "municipal," which is to say provincial, taste. The "fatal" error lay in deeming monument construction an act of commemoration and leaving it to local authorities rather than to anyone knowledgeable about art.

Discussing monument production at some length in his Salon reviews for 1922 and 1923, Thiébault-Sisson, writing in *Le temps*, also made use of the Paris-provinces dichotomy, but to somewhat more subtle effect. In 1922 the critic praised the younger sculptors who were receiving the bulk of local commissions for war memorials. Their local roots and lack of an established reputation made them cheaper than the acknowledged masters, but they were also more dedicated, and the results were beginning to pay off: "Their monuments have a totally new appearance and tone. Of course one will still find far too many of those isolated figures of poilus with mouths agape and violent gestures that horrify people of taste and that the crowd so eagerly devours. But one sees other things as well."[39] At the same time that the critic demonstrates, in time-honored fashion, his openness to new talent, he also reinforces his own authority. The next year, following his tirade against Gasq, Thiébault-Sisson's tone remains negative, though he makes essentially the same point. Most vulgar, excessively violent monuments, he declared,

are commissioned by ignorant municipalities or committees, with only a rudimentary artistic sense, and those seeking the commissions, having so often witnessed the elimination of projects of far higher artistic quality than that of the winner, are unwilling to deprive themselves of sustenance. They work in the manner of which they know juries approve. From that results the snapshot character [*d'instantané photographique*] that shocks us, and which, in all likelihood, they will give up when they work no longer for the multitude, but for themselves and the refined [*les délicats*].

There are exceptions, and those exceptions tend to be less monuments in cities than those of very humble villages. The man of the fields is less pretentious than urban man; his natural taste is not falsified by the half-education and the self-importance of the latter; he lacks the city-dweller's horror of simple things.[40]

The critical voice has a number of familiar elements. Thiébault-Sisson dislikes modern technologies of reproduction: for him the cinema cannot compare to Corneille, and the *instantané photographique* obviously represents a mode of representation inferior to older media. Both cinema and the snapshot, moreover, invoke the vulgar masses, the former as audience, the latter, even more troublingly, as practitioners. In contrast, in a second familiar theme, the passage insists on the good taste of artists. But a new timbre comes in the attempt to carve a space between "the crowd" and *les délicats* and to insert in that space the nebulous "man of the fields." The untutored taste of this generic character is apparently superior not only to that of the crowd, but to that of most city-dwellers. Indeed, this construction restores some specificity to the notion of "the crowd," aligning Thiébault-Sisson with the conservative tendency, widespread in the twenties, to romanticize the rural world.[41] Like the very notion of monumental "simplicity," the allusion to the "man of the fields" grounds Thiébault-Sisson's distinction in the simplicity of an imaginary past, in which true artists went about their work without having to compete with popular culture or cater to an untutored crowd.

Thiébault-Sisson's general comments usually served to introduce a work he considered especially noteworthy—in 1922 one he called "the most beautiful of all those stimulated by the war," Gabriel Forestier's war memorial for the town of Eymet, in the Dordogne (fig. 4.7).[42] *L'art et les artistes* also praised the Dordogne sculptor, noting that "some works of moving simplicity or of noble appearance . . . emerge from the throng of cumbersome banalities." The journal published a full-page illustration of the work and in its next issue reported with satisfaction that the state had, as it had urged, awarded the artist one of the much-coveted travel grants given out at the end of each Salon.[43] Although its praise was not very specific, the obvious skill of the modeling, the harmonious combination of classical forms (the fretwork and the grave marker) and modern, almost art deco detailing (the hair and robe of the female figure), as well as the subtle allure of the gendered tribute, all help account for the general admiration. Both *Le temps* and *L'art et les artistes* followed Forestier's career in subsequent years, dispensing judicious compliments—"the figure's sober simplicity has character"—with the air of proud parents trying to retain some semblance of objectivity.[44] Finding bright spots in the general gloom was, after all, critics' business, and in the context of their work as a whole commemorative monuments came off no worse than anything else.

Indeed, the mediocrity of war memorials often functions in critical writing as a microcosm for what many critics considered a larger crisis of French sculpture in the postwar period. Although critics defined this crisis variously, depending on their cultural politics, most agreed that the absence of great masters, the inimitable, and thus dangerous, example of Rodin (who had died in 1917), and the fruitless search for parallels in sculpture to the techniques of avant-garde painting had thrown sculpture into disarray.[45] Added to the early and pervasive skepticism within critical discourse about the possibility of representing the war at all, this sense of crisis made it virtually impossible for monument producers to achieve success in traditional art-critical terms alone. The

mourning own war dead?

FIGURE 4.7. Gabriel Forestier, war monument for Eymet (Dordogne), 1922: detail of figure. Photo: Author.

problem for the critics, however, lay in the dramatically expanded market for monuments that the war had created. As Thiébault-Sisson's description of provincial clients suggests, in this market, catering to high-art standards might not have been in sculptors' best interest. Since the prospects for *critical* success were always uncertain, small wonder that many sculptors opted to cast their lot with the new channels of evaluation that had arisen alongside the new market.

"An Artistic Character": Prefectoral Review Boards and Provincial Standards

High-art discourse had its provincial relays, but the process of transmission often altered the message in subtle ways. The provincial press, for example, offered a distinctive version of the prevailing critical discourse, one emphasizing local talent and blurring the distinction between educated taste and the vox populi. In 1922 the weekly newspaper in Commercy (Meuse), the *Républicain de l'est*, received a number of letters criticizing a jury's choice of Gaston Broquet to execute the town's monument. In defense of the artist, the newspaper ran several reports on the project's favorable reception in Paris, although it omitted another reference, in a basically favorable Thiébault-Sisson review, to the artist's "brutal realism."[46] The *Républicain de l'est* clearly endorsed the traditional view of the Salon, and of Paris in general, as a proving ground for artists, although it took a kinder view of overall monument production than did the art press. A front-page note nearly a year earlier had declared that the thirty or so monument projects on view at the 1921 Salon "are noteworthy for their artistic interest, and at the same time provide favorable evidence on the state of French sculpture." The paper urged members of local monument committees to visit the Paris studios of Broquet and another sculptor from the Meuse, Léo Roussel, and provided their addresses.[47]

The newspaper's embrace of the Salon was strategic: it portrays the Paris art world, with its studios, public and private exhibitions, and critics, as a mysterious, coherent entity, which only experts could unravel and decode. Such a construct lent credence to the position (which the *Républicain* was tacitly to endorse in the controversy over Broquet's project a few months later) that local "experts" should essentially have carte blanche in choosing monument projects. The *Républicain* had, however, no choice but to provide a forum for the expression of the contrary view, which crystallized around the notion that a popular referendum would have been a more appropriate means of selecting a project than the juried competition the town had held. As one letter to the editor put it, "Good taste is not the prerogative of a single class, and sometimes modest workers may be true connoisseurs."[48] "Modest workers" and, perhaps, men of the fields?

In this and similar texts the local inflection of artistic discourse shows less interest in questions of taste than in the criteria for evaluating the making of monuments. An artist's local roots and connection to the *pays* take on an importance as great as the qualities of taste and skill. At the dedication of the war memorial in Vaucouleurs (Meuse) in 1922, the president of the all-veteran monument committee, Rauber, explained its decision to entrust the project to a local, albeit nationally known, foundry, the Union Internationale Artistique:

"We thought that a sepulchral column like this one should spring from the heart and not from a chisel, that any mechanical or indifferent gesture in its execution would amount to a sacrilege, and that, since it is designed to honor Valcolorois, none could glorify their memory better than Valcolorois."[49]

The theme of simplicity, the central element of the art-critical discourse on commemoration, lent itself less problematically to local appropriation than did notions of expertise or technical mastery. Indeed, the discourse of simplicity and sobriety also had a provincial wellspring, a site that combined the symbolics of centralized power with the distinctive contours of local culture: the prefectoral commissions appointed specifically to review monument designs. While the local press occasionally provided a forum for the expression of public opinion about monuments, at the design stage its attention generally encompassed only a few monuments in large towns. The prefectoral review boards, on the other hand, had administrative authority over all monuments built in their departments; after 1920, no monument could receive official approval without their endorsement. Like any bureaucratic procedure, the review process provided the occasion for a continual and intensive production of discourse. But if the rhetoric of the review boards bore a distinct resemblance to the Paris criticism with which we are now familiar, in practice they also had to confront its local variants, with sometimes unpredictable results.

The prefectoral review boards grew out of the government's desire to ensure some basic aesthetic standards for commemorative monuments, while shielding the state from unwanted cost or embarrassment. In the year or so Parliament was debating the appropriate role for the state in honoring the dead, the Ministry of Fine Arts received a number of requests from mayors and deputies for standard artistic models or sketches of monuments that even small communes could afford. A discarded draft reply reflects the preoccupations of an agency that historically had seen working artists as its primary constituency: "Models, even those of great artistic merit, would, as a consequence of their distribution, fall into the realm of the banal. Sculptors, moreover, would not fail to reproach my office for making the exercise of their profession more difficult after a long war."[50] The standard reply the Fine Arts Ministry had devised by the summer of 1919 carefully avoids a term as qualitative as "banal": "the ministry has abstained from intervening in the choice of artists in order to leave towns and committees the greatest scope for initiative."[51] But not long thereafter, Fine Arts officials had to respond to reports from the Interior Ministry of what amounted to consumer fraud in the booming monument business. The letter bringing the issue to the attention of the minister of fine arts cited verbatim from an advertisement for a "Genius of France glorifying the bravery of her children," available in ten sizes with custom inscriptions. The project was apparently the brainchild of a mayor in the Haute-Garonne "whose morals are reputed to be poor." The two agencies quickly agreed on the need for some kind of review process that would combine the expertise of the Fine Arts Ministry with the police authority of the Interior.[52]

In a circular of May 1920, the minister of the interior instructed prefects to appoint a commission in each department "to advise and guide municipalities" on the aesthetic aspects of monument construction. The circular specified only that the prefect himself should chair the commission and that it should consist of "a small number of members, notably the departmental architect and some other persons, either [individuals] active in decorative arts instruction or artists willing to participate."[53] In the Morbihan the commission had only three members besides the prefect: the departmental architect, a drawing professor at the Collège de Vannes, and an artist. Elsewhere, commissions were somewhat larger and included politicians as well as art professionals: twelve members in the Var, including the prefect and the mayors of Draguignan and Toulon; nine members in the Loire-Atlantique.[54] In the Var, at least, the art professionals, including two architects, a museum curator, and the director of a Toulon commercial art school, had the dominant voice, and the evidence suggests that the commissions, more or less as the minister intended, conceived of their task principally in aesthetic terms.

The review boards did not take long to formulate their own conclusions concerning the overwhelming mediocrity of monument production. In a circular to mayors announcing the creation of his department's commission, the prefect of the Loir-et-Cher wrote that in its first meeting the commission "was struck by the aesthetic lack of most of the projects presented." In a report on its first meeting in October 1920, the Var commission observed that "although municipalities are anxious to commemorate the sacrifice of their children who died for France, they show no concern for glorifying this memory with monuments of an artistic character equal to the spirit that guides their construction."[55] In its initial review of the monument projects submitted before its creation, the Morbihan review board rejected four as totally without "artistic character," adding of one that it "in no way recalls the purpose for which it is intended," and asked another commune to resubmit a proposal in a "more aesthetic" vein.[56]

Both in the critiques of individual proposals that formed the bulk of their work and in the general comments they occasionally circulated to mayors, commissioners evinced an attitude closely attuned to that of the Paris critics. Many of the commissioners' comments involved fairly minor technical matters, such as the proportions of shaft to base, the shape or extent of decorative molding or a vital measurement omitted from a sketch. Such comments at once established the expertise and authority of those issuing them and, often, called into question the competence and training of local monument designers.[57] But whatever their reactions to specific monuments, commissions all over the country provided a regional site for the now familiar critical discourse of simplicity and restraint. Excess ornament, exaggerated gestures, and fuzzy allegory thus risked the same condemnation in local projects they faced in the Salons.

The general guidelines circulated to municipalities, texts that began with the criticisms cited above, make this orientation very clear. The commission, wrote the prefect of the Loir-et-Cher, "believes—and I completely share its opinion—that the country's gratitude is not to be measured in terms of the financial sacrifice it entails, and that it is possible to honor the dead in worthy fashion by works in a simple, sober, but tasteful style." The Var commission made the same point even more explicitly:

Communities, particularly those whose resources are limited, should not lose sight of the fact that if the profusion of details, ornaments, or attributes invariably has the effect of increasing costs, it generally detracts from a monument's beauty. A commemorative monument will, because of the sublime sentiments it should celebrate, be all the more beautiful if its character comes from a noble simplicity emphasized [*mise en valeur*] by harmonious lines and irreproachable proportions. In this sense a carefully planned stela [or] a simple marble plaque with artistically engraved inscriptions will always be more eloquent than over-decorated productions of a purely commercial character [*des productions surchargées dans un but purement commercial*].⁵⁸

The review boards' insistence on simplicity had a number of implications. The Loir-et-Cher circular too contains a derogatory reference to commercial monuments; as the next section will make clear, serial production was a major preoccupation both of the state and of its representatives at the local level. Dominated by art professionals, the review boards left no doubt of where their allegiances lay. The advisory circulars urged towns in all cases to consult a trained expert or, failing that, the board itself about their monument plans. More subtly, the language of reports on individual monuments signaled that artists who used the appropriate formulas could count on commissioners' support. Whereas the town council of Lestiou, in the Loir-et-Cher, protested in 1923 that the commission's suggestions "simplify the monument too much," an architect working for another commune felt free to complain to the prefect of the mayor's attachment to excessive ornamentation. "I had to be very forceful," the architect wrote, "to make him understand that the budget he had given me would not permit the construction of a monument as imposing (I was going to say pretentious) as the one that seems to be desired."⁵⁹

Review boards could tap into the prevailing artistic discourse in other ways; reports on projects in the Var, notably, read like a virtual compendium of Paris Salon criticism. One report recommended approval of the project in Mazauges, but expressed misgivings about a "contorted and grimacing" poilu and hoped that the actual statue would be "more calm, more reflective, more smilingly victorious" than the sketch. Another deplored the "signs of a dated [*périmée*] symbolism" in the plans for a monument in Aups.[60] On the other hand, one commission member's own design for the monument in Brignoles (fig. 4.8) received the praise of another for its evocation of "a classic motif, astutely [*sagement*] modernized."[61] Thus the notion of a kind of modernist classicism, a *juste milieu* that avoided the excesses of both modernism and classicism, found an echo in the provinces. So did the Parisian vogue for *taille directe* or carving directly in stone, which may explain the otherwise perplexing enthusiasm of Jules Roustan, architect of the Brignoles project, for the monument in Cotignac (fig. 4.9).[62]

The patency of commissions' preferences and the repetitiveness of their vocabulary offered a golden opportunity for astute artists or for town councils briefed by them. Commissioners were supposed to make their evaluations on the basis of sketches, but they also had access to verbal descriptions. Usually fairly perfunctory, such descriptions occasionally sought to establish a discursive commonality between the monument's progenitors and its evaluators. In its resolution approving the mayor's project, the town council in Guénin (Morbihan, fig. 4.10) noted that "in drawing up the plan for the monument it has sought only the greatest simplicity, without, however, any vulgarity."[63] The town of Trôo appended a statement ostensibly by Bourdelle to the materials it submitted concerning its monument project (fig. 4.1). In it the artist expressed his preference that the stones used for the monument not be polished: "Each stone would then be alive, personal, giving the ensemble an animated quality. . . . A great end by modest means [*Grand effet par petits moyens*]."[64] Such might almost have been the slogan of the review boards.

An ambiguity at the heart of the review boards' charge, as well as the lack of any means to enforce their recommendations beyond withholding the state's minimal financial support, seriously hindered their efforts. The ministerial instructions of May 1920 told prefects to establish commissions in order to ensure artistic standards for all monuments. But in a letter to the minister of fine arts enclosing the circular, the interior minister, Théodore Steeg, added a practical note:

> Because of the limited resources available to most communes, there can be no question of requiring them [the communes] to present projects that constitute true works of art, but rather to guide them in this domain by, above all, warning them against monuments produced "serially" by manufacturers alien to all aesthetic concerns.[65]

The circular itself does not use the word "artist" except in relation to potential commission members. In the provinces, the term that review boards used most frequently in urging communes to consult a competent professional was *homme*

FIGURE 4.8. War monument, Brignoles (Var). Photo: Author.

FIGURE 4.9. War monument, Cotignac (Var). Photo: Author.

de l'art.[66] As a phrase *homme de l'art* means simply an expert or specialist; it could apply as well to a plumber as to a sculptor, and in modern usage, without further context, tends to refer to doctors.[67] In relation to local monument production, the term proved surprisingly broad. In 1924 the prefect of the Morbihan replied to a request from the town of St. Nicolas-du-Tertre for standard monument models, "I have no such models, and I can only advise you to consult an *homme de l'art* (architect, contractor, monument-maker) to establish one."[68] The last two words in parentheses, "contractor" (*entrepreneur*) and "monument-maker" (*marbrier*), suggest that at least by 1924 the notion of *homme de l'art* encompassed a wide range of expertise; the term *marbrier* bears roughly the same relationship to *sculpteur* or *statuaire* as the English "house-painter" does to a "painter" exercising an artistic vocation.

From the earliest years of monument construction the term *homme de l'art* could be signified simply by a competent technical drawing. The review board in the Morbihan approved a professional-looking project in Etel (fig. 4.11) "from an artistic point of view," even though the design, by a local contractor, included a mass-produced sculpture.[69] But technical drawing had a problematic artistic status. The *droit d'auteur* instituted during the Revolution did not apply to technical drawing, which formally appertained to the realm of industry rather than culture. Technical drawing was not art because it had a practical purpose beyond expressing the artist's creativity or genius. Industrial design enjoyed its own regime of legal protections, but this was distinct from the laws protecting the creative artist or *auteur*.[70] Within the phrase *homme de l'art*, in other words, "art" has two different connotations: both expertise and "art" in the sense of creative work. Where the first connotation dominates over the second, it could be found, as the Morbihan prefect's gloss on the term suggests, in a wide variety of professional settings. It was, for instance, undoubtedly for their technical drawing skills as well as their accessibility that some towns asked the local *agent-voyer* or road inspector to draw up or review designs for simple monuments. By no stretch of the imagination could such inspectors be considered members of the art world. Indeed, at one point the prefect of the Morbihan expressed concern that the *agents-voyer* were moonlighting in an area beyond their competence; the head of the Morbihan roads department replied simply that mayors of isolated rural communes had virtually no other access to expertise of any kind.[71]

A surprising number of communes nonetheless proved willing to contest the review boards' judgment, some of them even venturing their own opinion of what constituted an *homme de l'art*. To the suggestion that the town consult such a person, the mayor of Lestiou (Loir-et-Cher), whose resistance to the "simplifying" mandate of the commission we have already had occasion to re-

FIGURE 4.10.
Sketch for the war monument in Guénin (Morbihan). Archives Départementales du Morbihan, 2 O 74/259.

FIGURE 4.11. War monument, Etel (Morbihan). Photo: Author.

mark, replied in lofty terms. Since, he wrote, the monument's designer, listed elsewhere as an *entrepreneur*, "was for some years employed as a clerk (*commis*) in an architect's office in Paris, he may be presumed to have some familiarity (*quelques connaissances*) with the subject."[72] Often, however, communes forthrightly proposed their own criteria for judging monuments, suggesting that other than artistic standards might apply. The mayor of Les Salles, in the Var, defended his contractor against a commissioner's criticism of the molding, saying the man was much better at carving than at drawing. But he also noted that "the contractor has already done those [monuments] of Aiguines and Baudinard, and surely during your recent visit to those two places you were able to take note of their perfect conception."[73] It did not seem to occur to the mayor that the very similarity of this design to others might, from the commission's perspective, actually count against it.

As we will see in the next chapter, the design and construction of monuments could involve a wide range of practitioners, often working in formal or informal partnerships: architects with sculptors or commercial suppliers, contractors with sculptors, and so on. Even for an artist-designed project, the actual fabrication of a monument involved contractors, who, depending on the nature and scale of their business, might describe themselves as anything from *entrepreneur de monuments funèbres* to the more modest *marbrier* or *tailleur de pierre* (stonecutter). By referring the mayor of St. Nicolas to contractors as well as to architects, the prefect of the Morbihan was acknowledging what the state and the design commissions had at first been reluctant to recognize: that local craftsmen had sufficient expertise to serve not simply as auxiliaries but as the *primary* producers of monuments. Resources more than anything guided an individual commune in its selection from the various types of practitioners available, but artistic criteria certainly figured among the factors used in selecting one. At the top of the hierarchy, larger towns, from prefectures to wealthy cantonal seats, could call on practicing artists by holding design competitions. But whatever their merits, such competitions could not be relied on to secure a consensus even on the artistic worth of the winning proposal. Indeed, the controversy that design competitions tended to generate often spilled over from the actual submissions to the very principle on which competitions were based, the superiority of "expert" judgment in artistic matters.

Like all such procedures, design competitions invoked a consistent set of standards and principles that were thought to unify the art world and perpetuate its goals, broadly speaking to produce monuments of real artistic distinction. Competition programs, publicized in the local press as well as in national art magazines, set out the qualifications required of competitors, often that they be sculptors or architects born or resident in the department or region in question. In Blois and Vannes, however, the committee made no such stipulation, and in Verdun the competition was open to artists who had fought at Verdun as well as to natives or residents of the Meuse.[74] The program usually asked for a model and a budget not to exceed a specified amount—50,000 francs in Commercy, 60,000 in Blois, 80,000 in Vannes, 120,000 in Toulon—and offered some limited guidance on the type of monument desired. Projects, with their authors identified only in sealed envelopes, were judged by juries consisting, like the review boards, of artists and politicians in varying proportions. To increase the appearance of impartiality, committees sometimes brought in an artist from outside the department as a member of the jury.[75]

If educated opinion acknowledged that towns of a certain importance had little alternative to a juried competition in choosing a monument design, the link that such competitions constructed between commemoration and the world of art remained controversial. Only within the reach of critical artistic discourse did the competition signify impartiality, quality, excellence.[76] Elsewhere it as often betokened snobbishness, a distressing appropriation of the commemorative process by those whose "expertise" did not necessarily extend to the loss that communities were seeking to represent. In Levallois-Perret and Lorient political opponents even charged mayors with stacking the jury, or the jury itself of allowing political bias to outweigh professional "expertise."[77] In Commercy, where the winning design by Broquet attracted little outright opposition but not much enthusiasm, the competition produced the defense of popular as opposed to expert or "elite" taste cited above. In Verdun, the exhibition of the project selected and the runners-up enabled one newspaper, the *Bulletin meusien*, to solicit the opinion of the public; the letters it ran were massively unfavorable to the winning design (the public preferred the third-place project, ironically enough by Broquet). In one article the newspaper's editor, Henri Frémont, created a parodic spokesman for the jurors, who declared, "Including the suburbs, you are 12,000 good, ignorant people versus eleven technical experts, eleven professionals, eleven leading lights! Your judgment, then, no matter how solid it seems, doesn't count for much next to ours."[78]

In this context a number of towns preferred to canvass artists informally, usually behind closed doors. In Vendôme, a subprefecture of the Loir-et-Cher, the town received ten sketches from which to choose. Following some of the procedures of a competition, three council committees considered the submissions on an anonymous basis, with two outside experts "reputed for their artistic knowledge" present to offer advice. The design selected was by a "well-known Vendôme artist," Fernand Hamar, the sculptor of an existing monument to Rochambeau; in these intimate conditions, he readily agreed to modify the design and to lower his price from 30,000 to 18,000 francs.[79] In Rochefort-en-Terre (Morbihan) the mayor, having presented a variety of plans to the council, invited the Lorient sculptor Gouzien, who had executed a number of monuments in the department, to a council meeting. The appearance of an artist already praised in the press for the monument at Baud (fig. 4.49) so impressed the council that it decided to break off discussions with a commercial supplier and award the commission to Gouzien.[80]

But even at this level of commitment to "artistic" standards, the choice of a monument design remained shadowed by commerce. Deluged by advertising material and letters from entrepreneurs, the Vannes committee included in its competition program the provision that it would not consider "serial monuments." The initial proposal in Vendôme involved contacting only makers of funeral monuments, and in Rochefort Gouzien triumphed over a commercial supplier not only because of the "aesthetic" superiority of his project, but because he apparently offered better terms. Serial producers could afford to aim high on occasion, knowing that their real clientele lay among smaller communes that could not afford to commission a monument from a professional sculptor.

In any case, monument suppliers by no means accepted an absolute distinction between "art" and "commerce." The structures of monument production, moreover, facilitated a certain blurring of the distinction. Artistic discourse itself became a kind of market commodity, and as such may have emboldened small-town officials and journalists to develop their own "artistic" standards for evaluating monument production. This is not to say that entrepreneurs were offering words for sale, except in the form of monument inscriptions.[81] But the monument industry had so carefully melded a discourse of artistic standards to their product line that in the end even the "experts," the prefectoral review boards, found it virtually impossible to disentangle them.

"All My Designs Are Approved": The Business of Commemoration

Members of prefectoral commissions were, for the most part, local art professionals who shared both the interests and the outlook of their Paris counterparts. In contrast, commercial enterprises appropriated the language of art precisely in order to disguise their very different aims. Whether national companies or local contractors, monument suppliers were concerned with selling a product, not with preserving artistic standards. Many of their clients, moreover, like the Lestiou town council, framed their desires in terms of untrained or "popular" notions of commemorative art. Yet monument firms also had to satisfy the critical demands of the prefectoral commissions, and to do so they had to speak the commissions' language. Suppliers generally responded to this exigency by elevating artistic standards to a scarcely credible primacy in their own rhetoric, conveniently displacing their commercial aims. The contradictions of such an enterprise, and the ambiguity of the whole business of serial monument production, account for some of the strains visible in the commercial version of artistic discourse. What resulted was, if not an entirely new discourse, a new variant, a kind of *patois*.[82]

The preoccupation of monument suppliers with the prefectoral commissions had, of course, a practical dimension, one that emerges in a flyer for Jacomet, a Vaucluse firm whose product line emphasized a single monument type, a poilu catering to the middle and bottom of the market. Its design, Jacomet claimed, "could not be criticized by any of the artistic commissions so judiciously created, at the behest of the ministry of fine arts, in each prefecture to prevent the disfigurement [*enlaidissement*] of our communes and to protect their material interests."[83] In a price list dated January 1923 offering a number

of commemorative motifs in a wide variety of sizes and combinations, the Nord supplier Rombaux-Roland made an even bolder claim: "All my designs are approved without difficulty by the *departmental supervisory commissions created in the prefectures by the ministry of fine arts for the beautification of cities and the preservation of sites.*" Thus, he went on, towns and committees "can be sure that their plans, dossiers, and forms will be accepted by the administrative authorities, without having to fear the usual annoyances that arise when the drawings submitted are not irreproachably composed."[84] Here practicality shades into a subtle claim about standards, expertise, and professional skills.

The Jacomet poilu (fig. 4.12) had the advantage of being, as its publicity immodestly but not without reason claimed, "the only subject that truly corresponds to the idea that has been developed of a Monument to the Dead of the Great War."[85] In fact the simple stela or obelisk, with perhaps a *croix de guerre* or entwined palm and laurel as adornments, was by far the most common monument type throughout the country, probably because of its low cost.[86] But among figural monuments the *poilu* had a privileged place, and Jacomet's version fit in well with the prevailing notion of simplicity: "Whether built in a public square, a park or a cemetery, its aura is imposing in its very simplicity." But for firms with a more elaborate line catering specifically to the notorious municipal taste for ornament, simplicity may not have seemed a promising sales pitch. Like Rombaux-Roland, such companies instead highlighted other aspects of their work that lent it "artistic" status. These aspects tended to be qualities that remained implicit, or, occasionally, were even dismissed as insufficient, in high-art discourse: technical skill, solidity, and taste. Even at the risk of seeming to protest too much, companies needed these characteristics as a way of distinguishing their output from the banal norm of monument production so frequently decried by art critics.

In a printed circular addressed to mayors and chairmen of monument committees, a Paris architect called Clermont vaunted his experience but above all his credentials: "one of our best architects, a graduate of a state art school [diplomé du gouvernement] and a prize winner at the Paris Salon and in various competitions." The circular, quoting the prefect of the Deux-Sèvres, urged potential clients to "avoid those art sharks [mercantis de l'art] who are going to offer you serially produced figures that have nothing in common with true sculpture."[87] The director of the Marbreries Générales in Paris, Gourdon, made a similar point even more emphatically. In a thinly veiled allusion to the inexperience of some of his competitors, Gourdon noted in a printed circular dated October 1920 that the company "was not organized for this circumstance alone" but had been in existence for over a century, had built a number of monuments to the dead of the Franco-Prussian War, and controlled fourteen quarries "of the most beautiful granite in France."[88]

Gourdon even confronted the prevailing press criticism, noting sarcastically that "the impartiality of some cannot be doubted." A new circular the following month went further:

A partisan campaign is being conducted by some anonymous man full of hatred and jealousy, who, in the guise of a newspaper speaking in the name of Art, publishes a prospectus distributed free everywhere, where he treats Foundries and Marble-Works in existence for over a century as incompetent sharks. . . . All that leads up (still for the love of Art) to an advertisement for a single sculptor to whom he ascribes a monopoly of taste and talent, and also to the sale (on a non-profit basis, naturally) in the greatest possible number of a few works by this sculptor, serially cast and executed.[89]

Gourdon's description fits in most respects a monthly (occasionally bimonthly) newspaper called L'art funéraire et commémoratif, which ran from May 1919 till at least the end of 1924. His reference to an anonyme haineux et jaloux is puzzling, however, since many of the newspaper's substantive articles and editorials bear the signature of its editor, one Lucien Marie. Gourdon may, however, have been alluding to some shadowy interest behind the paper.

In L'art funéraire et commémoratif the discursive strategies that Gourdon himself so adeptly employed reach something of an apogee. In its first incarnation the newspaper had two avowed purposes: to provide information and advocacy for those seeking to recover the bodies of their loved ones from the front, and to promote suitable commemoration of the dead by upholding artistic standards for monuments.[90] As we saw in chapter 2, the paper espoused the cause of home-town burial in the most extreme rhetoric of the day. But after the law on state-funded reburials was passed in the summer of 1920, *L'art funéraire* increasingly narrowed its focus to the problem of artistic standards. Yet this did not substantially change the character of the newspaper. The editorial content always reads like so much filler, and it simply served to mask and legitimate the publication's primary function, as a promotional vehicle for the commercial interests behind the Salon sculptor and monument specialist Charles-Henri Pourquet. Beginning with the catalog essay for an exhibition by Pourquet, reprinted in the first issue, *L'art funéraire* teemed with references to the sculptor, both in articles and in photo spreads that can only be considered, though they were never so labeled, advertising. The newspaper covered many other topics, its features including articles on burial practices through the ages, Salon reviews, and notes on recent monument dedications, but Pourquet was the only artist, indeed the only topic of any kind, to receive both editorial coverage and advertising.

To this extent Gourdon presents an accurate reading of *L'art funéraire*, and his vehemence about the newspaper makes clear that he did not consider its tactics fair play. But the interest of *L'art funéraire* lies precisely in those tactics, for the persuasiveness of its publicity for Pourquet depended on its ability to establish its own artistic expertise. However transparent to its competitors, *L'art funéraire* perfectly exemplifies the hybrid discourse in which advertisers were engaged. The critical articles in *L'art funéraire* form a kind of compendium of prevailing ideas about commemorative art, ideas already familiar to us from criticism in the mainstream art periodicals. In 1921 the paper's editor, Lucien Marie, endorsed the generally harsh criticism of Salon sculpture in other publications, but assigned himself the task of identifying and encouraging "sincere" artists. That these included Pourquet goes without saying, but like the artists they dignify—Bouchard, Boucher, Broquet, Yvonne Sérruys—Marie's adjectives hew to a canonical path: "serious [*grave*]," "lively [*vivant*]," "bold [*hardie*]," as do the comparisons to antique sculpture.[91] It would be too much to say that such articles served only to legitimate *L'art funéraire*'s relentless praise of Pourquet, though doubtless they were intended to have that effect; for the most part, though, that praise operated without any adornment. In 1924, for example, Marie described the artist's *La France pleurant ses morts* as "one of the finest figures the war has inspired."[92] Undoubtedly, however, the incorporation of references to Pourquet in a larger critical framework served to blur the distinction between criticism, with its aura of ostensible disinterest, and advertising.

Advertisements for Pourquet's work informed readers that *L'art funéraire* could provide prices and terms for the pictured monument in bronze, stone, or, occasionally, "any material at all."[93] Less explicit but more revealing, other texts

FIGURE 4.13. War monument in Broussey-en-Woëvre (Meuse: *La résistance* type). Photo: Author.

clearly aimed to convert the reader's gaze into desire, a desire that only consumption, purchase, could satisfy. Yet the similarity of the descriptions to the language of criticism clearly sought to occlude the commercial nature of the transaction they were promoting. In 1922 *La résistance* (fig. 4.13), one of Pourquet's most popular figures, is described as

one of the most admirable statues that the commemoration of the war has brought us. The rough stance of this "Poilu," whose face and posture express the indomitable stiffening of the will, epitomizes the fierce resistance of the French soldier. Look at the virile resolution of this form, the tightening of the hands on the gun placed vertically [*sic*] to make the enemy understand that he will go no farther. This statue by Pourquet seems to cry out, "Halt! No passage!" and it must be considered one of the works that most aptly and most movingly symbolize the character of this frightful war.[94]

This text, technically a photo caption, urges the reader only to "look" (*regardez*); it assumes the voice of the connoisseur or critic, pointing out the work's technical merit as well as its larger significance, constructed in terms of familiar tropes of the war experience (*On ne passe pas!*). The commercial motive, while clear, remains at the level of implication; only in the following, and the preceding, issues could readers find an advertisement featuring a much smaller photograph and the message that *L'art funéraire* could provide information on reproducing the work.

But *L'art funéraire* also confronted the issue of reproduction head-on. In doing so, it tacitly acknowledged the low status of commercial monuments, but attributed it to the methods and purposes of commerce rather than to the processes of mass production. "In commemoration," it wrote in November 1919, "the affliction [*plaie*, literally wound] comes from middlemen. *L'art funéraire* takes it upon itself to place municipalities and private citizens in direct contact with artists, either architects or sculptors."[95] In the fall of 1919 *L'art funéraire* began a series called "Les horreurs de l'après-guerre," and asked readers to send their own favorite examples of awkward or disfiguring monuments. The article introducing the series, besides expanding on the title's connection to the "horrors of war," made clear the intended targets: "If industrial commemorative firms, created with capital from war profiteers, succeed in their designs, thanks to a noisy advertising campaign, the picturesque beauty and charm of our country will be finished."[96] Although the newspaper occasionally reprinted its appeal, it published only a few responses.[97] Five years later, however, it was still harping on the same theme, reprinting an article from *Le journal* in which Clément Vautel excoriated "those factories where commemorative war monuments are serially produced according to the system of Taylorism."[98]

L'art funéraire's denunciation of middlemen, *intermédiaires*, or less politely *mercantis*, of course reflects a certain disingenuousness. The newspaper's own editorial practice subtly shadowed its blurring of the distinction between art and reproduction, thus serving its fundamentally commercial interests. Throughout each issue of *L'art funéraire*, brief maxims or aphorisms summarized the editorial perspective, providing gentle but insistent guidance to potential monument builders. "You want, do you not," ran one such aphorism in December 1920, "to erect a commemorative monument that is a work of art? The first condition [for doing so] is to call on an artist." Many of these sidebars were longer, and some were more pointed, for example referring to commercial monument suppliers as "ignorant pieceworkers, philistine imbeciles."[99] But their primary interest lies in their generic indeterminacy: unsigned editorials?

subtle advertisements (but for what)? words of wisdom (but by whom)? A few of the aphorisms come with attributions, ironically enough to German writers, Goethe and Grimm. Most do not, however, for the simple reason that they represent *fragments* of articles published earlier in *L'art funéraire* itself.[100] The repeated publication of identical fragments over several issues, usually nonconsecutive, belongs as a tactic to the realm of advertising, and as such totally elides any remaining distinction between the newspaper's editorial and commercial ends. But the maxims continue to occupy a space of their own in *L'art funéraire*, a space distinct from advertising, and so stand for an ostensible independence, the sine qua non of the art critical discourse the newspaper was always invoking.

The rigidity of *L'art funéraire*'s distinction between art and commerce thus emerges as both consequence and sign of the essential strain of its enterprise. That same rigidity, however, clearly differentiates *L'art funéraire* not only from its commercial competitors but also from the critical discourse upon which it drew so lavishly. The radicalism of the newspaper's position lay in its willingness to assert that an inferior work of art could never be a fitting commemorative monument. An editorial had even alluded to a group of "young artists, veterans familiar with explosives," who were contemplating "taking into their own hands some of those monuments that call themselves Victory Monuments and are nothing but Symbols of Stupidity, Mediocrity, and Platitude."[101] Although acts of vandalism directed against monuments did occur, such incidents were rare, and virtually never claimed as their basis the artistic character of the monument. True, *L'art funéraire* declined any responsibility for such acts, but of those who contemplated them it asked rhetorically, "Is their indignation so blameworthy?" No mainstream critic could ever have taken such a position, which represents less an extreme than a parody of the critical discourse of Great War commemoration.

Most advertising for commercial concerns lacked the hard edge of *L'art funéraire:* firms simply offered their clients a product line that met their needs, including those of an aesthetic order. Local officials had no hesitation in accepting the suppliers' artistic claims. The monument project in St. Thuriau (Morbihan, fig. 4.14), for example, attracted the review board's attention only for some minor matters of scale. Returning a corrected plan to the prefect, the mayor announced with palpable pride that "the statue 'the Poilu,' which will top the monument, has already arrived. . . . It is a work of art from the Jacomet firm of Villedieu (Vaucluse)."[102]

At a life-sized but hardly heroic 1.6 meters (approximately five-foot-three), in "chiseled and heat-bronzed cast iron," St. Thuriau's figure of the Jacomet poilu hardly fit the elite definition of art. The mayor was clearly following different standards, to which Jacomet's advertising provides some clues. "This is,"

FIGURE 4.14. War monument, St. Thuriau (Morbihan). Photo: Author.

one flyer stated flatly, "not a personal conception—so many of them are in dubious taste, lacking in any aesthetic sense—it is the TRUE POILU, modeled from life, the POILU transformed into bronze to immortalize himself."[103] Unlike the Loir-et-Cher review board, which regretted that the town of Marchenoir, in choosing the Déchin *Dying poilu* marketed by Rombaux-Roland (fig. 4.15), had not given its monument "a more personal character,"[104] Jacomet's use of the reflexive, *devenu bronze pour s'immortaliser,* suggests that art lies in a kind of metarealism, in which the personality of the artist disappears behind the sweep of the mimetic gesture. The description of the Jacomet poilu evacuates the

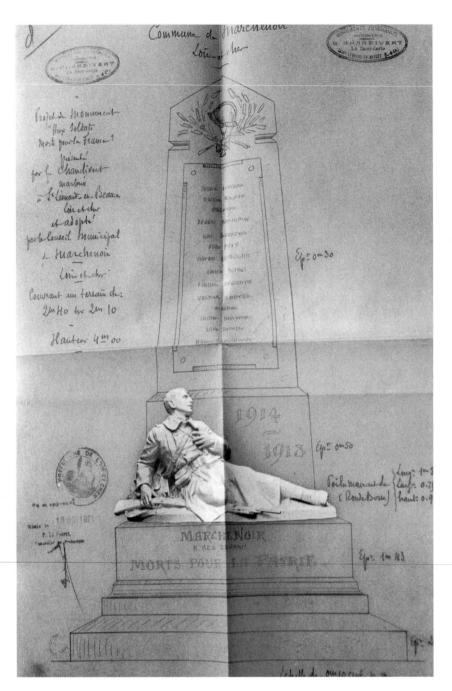

FIGURE 4.15. Sketch for the war monument in Marchenoir (Loir-et-Cher: *Dying poilu* type). Archives Départementales de Loir-et-Cher, 127 O⁶9.

personality of the artist from the notion of art, which thus emerges simply as an order of representation with a special ability to communicate meaning. Against the background of the serial production at the heart of the Jacomet enterprise, though never mentioned in its advertising, this claim has almost a modernist flavor.

Another Jacomet broadsheet continues even more strikingly in this vein: "In its simplicity, this monument represents exactly what one wants it to represent."[105] The suggestion of semiotic flexibility is no doubt unintentional; rather, the idea of "the TRUE POILU" casts the desired signification (*ce que l'on veut qu'il représente*) as universal. Whether deliberately or not, however, the ad offers potential consumers like St. Thuriau the essential characteristics of the work of art as defined in critical discourse: simplicity and signifying power, but with an important difference. Whereas criticism aims to bolster and secure the aesthetic as a quality in its own right, with its contingent meanings secondary, the status of the Jacomet poilu as a work of art simply establishes its ability to carry meaning outside the aesthetic realm. The artistic and the commemorative remain linked, but with the former clearly in the service of the latter.

Art critics could not, of course, have accepted a formulation that both downgraded the importance of the aesthetic and implicitly challenged their sole claim to define it. The *L'art funéraire* position, tainted by the marketplace and too extreme in its sotto voce contemplation of vandalism, did not offer a viable alternative. Yet the critics could not simply ignore the way in which the monument boom had changed the terms of sculptural production in France, for its artifacts loomed too large. From this dilemma emerged a third alternative: effectively a divorce between art and commemoration. This divorce began with a certain grudging recognition that in the realm of commemoration public sanction made professional criticism irrelevant. In certain passages, some ironic, some evidently heartfelt, the critic virtually performs his own self-effacement. Arsène Alexandre, for example, wrote of the plethora of war memorials in the 1922 Salons, "It is not I who will consider these testimonies in an ironic vein. Monuments to such beloved beings, even should they be mean [*mesquin*] or even downright poor art, touch me. I no longer see the sign, but the thing signified, and there could be very poor ones that bring tears to my eyes."[106] In the more sardonic tone he favored, Robert de la Sizeranne made a similar point a few years later, describing monuments with popular appeal but little artistic interest as "signs and emblems rather than aesthetic organisms living by and for themselves." He continued,

The faithful who for forty-three years passed respectfully by a certain statue in the place de la Concorde were hardly thinking of its plastic beauty, and Courbet, for all the artist he was and notwithstanding his own version of the story, was no more concerned about the problems of perspective of a certain column when he undertook to blow it up. One thinks of something completely different [when standing] before such tongue-tied witnesses, and the revival of grand memories submerges and represses, sometimes fortunately, all other impressions.[107]

This is the critical (in both senses of the word) moment at which "the commemorative" takes leave of "art" and emerges as a quality in its own right. Usually only an undertone to critical discourse, occasionally this development bursts to the surface. Like Antoine Prost a half century later, both Alexandre and de la Sizeranne treat commemorative sculptures primarily as signs, and the contrast the latter draws between signs and living "aesthetic organisms" makes clear why. A sign or emblem, in this view, is a part incapable of becoming a whole. The sign communicates an obvious message—witness Alexandre's ability as it were to see *through* the signifier to the *chose signifiée*—and that message or meaning may form an integral part of the work. But in the world of art, it has no independent existence, it animates nothing, and, crucially for the critic, it has no inherent connection to the work's formal properties. Critics might, like other French citizens, find such a sign moving, but they could hardly regard interpreting it as a task worthy of their professional attention. At the local level, however, assigning meaning to monuments was an essential task, one that made use of artistic discourse, but in which its critical arbiters were hardly missed.

"So Superior to Panegyrics": Monuments and Meanings

The journalist Léon Florentin begins his long account of the dedication of the war memorial in Commercy (Meuse) with a glowing description, perhaps intending to dispel recollections of the controversy the monument had generated (fig. 4.16). Situating the reader among the crowd of onlookers, he reports on his efforts to gauge public reactions to the monument.

Artists spoke to me as artists; enthusiasts went on at length. And I would have certainly left without what I was looking for when, finding myself surrounded in the crowd, I heard a fine woman [*une brave femme*] say, "I can tell it's beautiful, I see that well, but I can't say why!" A simple judgment that does the greatest honor to the artist! For was not this good woman conveying the common opinion [*le sentiment populaire*], so superior to panegyrics and to the reflections of art critics? The Commercy monument is beautiful because it speaks to the heart and because the sight of it recalls something terrifying: the war, sublime in all its horror.[108]

Florentin did not take artistic attainment lightly; his description recalls the prize Broquet won when he exhibited the monument at the 1921 Salon. But for his purposes public opinion, voiced by a woman who all but admits her ignorance

FIGURE 4.16. War monument, Commercy (Meuse). Photo: Author.

of artistic matters, counts for more than critical expertise. The voice testifies to the monument's power to move, to signify, and to prompt memory, thus bolstering the journalist's own effort to assign it meaning.

To some extent Florentin's construction of the local vox populi recalls Thiébault-Sisson's discerning "man of the fields." But if Thiébault-Sisson had, in 1920, found Broquet's work "moving in its brutal realism," a phrase he also applied to the Commercy project, he had never called it beautiful. Thiébault-Sisson employs, moreover, the same distinction between emotion and artistic sense that some of his colleagues articulated. For the critic's paean to the man of the fields—published, coincidentally, just a week after the Commercy dedication—also included a condemnation of the "ignorance" of local officials. Thiébault-Sisson began, moreover, by denouncing the sculptors of overwrought, wildly gesticulating figures: "I don't want to aggrieve the creators [*auteurs*] of monuments or monument projects conceived in that spirit of violent, gross, and excessive truth by naming them and calling attention to the vulgarity of their inspiration."[109] The gap between these two views lies in the word *vulgarité*, from the Latin *vulgus*, the common people. For Florentin the monument's "beauty" lay in its ability to convey, to the common people, "the war in all its reality";[110] for the critic that same effectiveness inevitably tainted the work's status as art.

But what "vulgarity of inspiration" did Thiébault-Sisson have in mind? The vast visual culture of the Great War extended, as we saw in chapter 1, from photographs to cartoons to illustrated posters. The latter two genres could be incorporated in the high-art category of engraving, and as such attracted the attention of two *Gazette des beaux-arts* critics: Clément-Janin surveyed "Les estampes et la guerre" in three articles published in the journal in 1917, and André Blum added an essay, "La caricature de guerre en France," in 1921. These articles perform much of the standard work of art criticism: defining genres, dispensing plaudits and demerits, naming masters, encouraging talented newcomers.[111] Yet the critics make clear the particularity of the works they are discussing: cartoonists, Blum writes, are interested "not in creating a unique work of art, composed with care and reflection, but in making a few pencil marks that will, printed in many copies, spread the idea for which they are fighting."[112]

Many artists, according to Clément-Janin, turned to poster-making for the first time during the war, attracted by the scope it offered the imagination and decorative ingenuity, by the chance to manipulate "popular imagery," but also by the opportunity to promote good causes.[113] If the poster as a genre bore some relation to the fresco, in that both covered walls, it also resembled an illustration, because it depended on a text. Indeed, Clément-Janin asserts, "what is important in a poster is not the image but the text. The image should only reenforce the idea, capture attention, fix a memory: it is the text that defines, that details, that has the primary role."[114] The medium, in other words, was a message. Critics in the high-art arena did not object to the message per se, or even necessarily to its dominance, but to the way it came from outside the artist's mind and thus dictated his creative process. The subordination of the artist's vision and talent to some external purpose, however admirable, in its very obviousness subverts the notion of the autonomy of artistic creation from which critical discourse draws its lifeblood.

The conception of an art form rooted in popular imagery, and aimed above all at conveying a message, links cartoons and prints not only to the critical view of most war memorials, but also to claims such as Jacomet's "[It] represents exactly what one wants it to represent." In its emphasis on what the work conveys rather than on its formal qualities this conception also evokes the construction of memory in, say, *Ceux de 14:* for Genevoix the image that prompts memory matters less than the associations to which it leads. Because of the discursive connection between memory and experience, with all its political ramifications, the perceived authenticity of the memorial image also counts. Florentin, for example, wrote of the Commercy memorial, "One has the impression that he who conceived this group saw [the war] from close up, and that he knows all about the misery of the trenches."[115]

But what constitutes authenticity in the visual field of commemoration? For those who had not shared the poilus' "experience," only a close correspondence between a monument motif and an image familiar from the war years could confer the stamp of truth. This recourse to a common fund of visual imagery had a number of consequences. The power of familiarity explains why monument clients were not concerned with authorship, that is with the visible traces of an artist's personality. Such traces formed the common currency of artistic judgment, enabling critics to consider works of art as the product of discernible temperaments. This currency clearly held good in towns large enough to hold a design competition for their monument. Yet the bold claim by Jacomet that its poilu was "not a personal conception" but a universal type suggests that, for most clients, the personal threatened to obstruct rather than enhance the monument's commemorative and signifying functions. The desire for familiar types that dominated the lower and middle ranges of the monument market left little room for artistic originality. As they deplored this phenomenon, critics, ignoring practical considerations like cost as beneath them, might attribute it either to "ignorance" on the clients' part or to "vulgarity" on the artist's, but the two obviously went together.

The critics maintained that they had no *generic* objection to the most familiar of the monument sculpture types, the poilu; of course any suggestion to the contrary would have branded them as unpatriotic. De la Sizeranne, for instance, wrote somewhat grudgingly that "the poilu . . . offers no *counterindication* to sculpture. The helmet, as simple as its ancient counterpart, the almost monastic cape, the puttees that mold the ankle so precisely, offer solid and ample lines, without constraint or artificiality." But, the critic warned, sculptors had the responsibility to represent this figure as a hero, avoiding, "under the pretext of realism or of 'character,' a gross or vulgar appearance, blemishes or deformities."[116] The telltale use of the word "vulgar" clearly implies that sculptors should avoid modeling their work on existing images. It also suggests that the critical disdain for the bulk of commemorative sculpture has to do with precisely the quality that made it marketable: its visible relationship to existing popular images, and to genres in which the aesthetic took second place to words or ideas.

This is not to say that commercial designers took direct inspiration from individual posters or cartoons, only that they strove to tap into poses, attitudes, and emblems on which the graphic arts had already conferred an aura of authenticity. The Jacomet poilu, for instance (fig. 4.12), may appear so generic as to be unmediated, or, as the company claimed, "the TRUE POILU, modeled from life." This standard-issue figure nonetheless adopts a type constructed by a specific set of visual images at a particular moment. In the first year or so of the war, French soldiers wore soft caps or *képis*, not the metal helmet that the Jacomet poilu and most of his brethren wear. Considerable publicity attended the introduction, in July 1915, of the protective helmet, or *casque Adrian*, the name of its designer. With photographs of the helmet viewed from the front and the side, *L'illustration* reassured traditionalists that the helmet "will in no way

FIGURE 4.17.
Anonymous, "Nos fantassins de la deuxième
année de guerre." *L'illustration*, 23 October
1915, 421.

dethrone the *képi*," that it would be used only at the front, not when the soldier
returned home on leave. But a few months later, the magazine reported that
wounded soldiers had worn their helmets home; it anticipated that the wide
popularity of the helmets, as well as other changes in the original French uniform, "is going to bring us, beginning with the battles currently engaged, images of the war rather different from the ones we have seen up to now."[117]
Within weeks the magazine published its first cover photo of poilus in the new
helmet (fig. 4.17). Decked out in kit, canteen, and puttees, the two figures, one
holding his rifle in front of him, the other, a grenadier, with a grenade in his left
hand, offer a virtual prototype for the poilu. Indeed, the Jacomet poilu seems to
combine the stance of the marksman with the features and resolute stare of the
grenadier.

It is worth noting that the helmet itself had a career ahead of it as a monument emblem, usually but not invariably in a supporting role. At the end of October 1915, a week after the cover just cited, *L'illustration* published an article on
the success of the *casque Adrian* in preventing head injuries at the battles of
Champagne and Artois. Complete with six photographs of helmets dented in
various places but still intact, the article amounted to an account of the heroic
deeds of a character named Adrian. "We have become so accustomed to his

simple forms," the magazine gushed, "that it is likely he will survive the war, even at parades."[118] A quick glance at the posters reproduced in chapter 1 will confirm the presence of the helmet in virtually all images of poilus made after 1915. After the war, the helmet became a frequent symbol for the poilu, in both high-art and commercial monuments. It serves as the emblem of the lost father in Chaillon (Meuse, fig. 4.18); in Villerbon (Loir-et-Cher), it tops the *croix de guerre*, the decoration introduced during the war, and, framed by a laurel wreath, a symbol of victory, is the monument's dominant sign (fig. 4.19). In the high-art arena, Paul Moreau-Vauthier designed a *borne*, a small milestone topped by a helmet, to be placed at strategic points along the former front; the project was funded by a subscription organized by the Touring-Club de France.[119] Similar *bornes* can be found marking each of the fifty-two kilometers of the Voie Sacrée between Bar-le-Duc and Verdun (fig. 4.20).

In its occasional use as a stand-alone emblem the helmet parallels the figure of the Gallic cock or rooster, a traditional symbol of French courage and aggressiveness.[120] The *coq gallois* appeared in one of the first illustrated war

FIGURE 4.18.
War monument, Chaillon (Meuse).
Photo: Author.

FIGURE 4.19.
War monument, Villerbon
(Loir-et-Cher). Photo:
Author.

FIGURE 4.20.
Borne (kilometer marker),
Voie Sacrée (Meuse). Photo:
Author.

FIGURE 4.21.
Abel Faivre, "Pour la France, versez votre or." Poster Collection, FR 647, Hoover Institution Archives. © 1999 Artists Rights Society (ARS), New York / ADAGP Paris.

posters (fig. 4.21), the image of a rooster emerging from a gold coin to attack an intimidated German soldier (recognizable by *his* distinctive pointed helmet); a group of art patrons commissioned the poster from the well-known cartoonist Abel Faivre to encourage the surrender of gold bullion to the treasury.[121] The rooster crops up in other posters during the war, in suppliers' catalogs, and in monuments, atop either simple stelae (Ronvaux, fig. 4.22) or figural monuments. The coq has the effect of displacing violence and aggression from the individual soldier to what the symbol stands for, the nation itself. As a conventional symbol, the coq also ties the remainder of the monument, a shaft and a list of names, to a more abstract order of representation than the "experience" of warfare. The helmet works in a different way, pointing to the concrete rather than to the abstract. One may speculate that it became a privileged symbol of the poilu because soldiers wore it as a badge of honor, a token of the harshness and brutality of their war. In both cases, however, the motif derives its resonance from its prevalence in wartime visual imagery.

Not all monumental poilus display the still attentiveness of the Jacomet type. Yet the relaxed, bored, even jocular figures depicted in some war posters

FIGURE 4.22. War monument, Ronvaux (Meuse). Photo: Author.

(fig. 1.16) and in many cartoons do not appear on monuments. Although the poilu, and by extension his experience, retained the privileged position in commemorative culture that soldiers' and veterans' exclusionary claims had won for them, that triumph has its paradoxical side. The Jacomet poilu and related types are as tidy and well scrubbed as the figures in the *L'illustration* photograph they resemble; we see none of the dirt or mud that soldiers so lament in their writings. Nor do the boredom, the endless waiting, the anxiety, or the homosocial bonding register in the monuments; even in the rare, costly monuments that depict soldier groups, such as the municipal monument in Verdun itself (fig. 4.23), the soldiers generally do not even look at each other.[122]

Several familiar monument types immortalize a moment that for soldiers occurred only rarely, and which they often had difficulty remembering: the as-

FIGURE 4.23. War monument, Verdun (Meuse). Photo: Author.

monument types

sault or attack. The graphic arts provided many images of this moment. Per-haps the most celebrated war poster (fig. 4.24), Faivre's *On les aura!* ("We'll get 'em!" from a communication by Pétain to his troops in 1916), shows an en-thusiastic poilu, his head turned back to encourage his mates as he charges, one arm outstretched, a gun in the other. This celebrated figure finds an echo in a type known as the *Victorious poilu* (fig. 4.25), the work of the sculptor Eugène Benet marketed by both Rombaux-Roland and the Durenne firm in Paris.[123] Alexandre probably had this type in mind when he condemned figures with "outstretched arms and open mouths" as plagiarisms of Rude's *Marseillaise*. Although the wreath in the right hand and the slightly less insistent diagonals distinguish the monument from the poster, the sculptor nonetheless probably owes more to Faivre than to Rude. A poster for war bonds captures a grenadier at the moment he launches the grenade (fig. 4.26); so does a monument avail-able from the Durenne foundry and a number of artist-designed variants, like the monument in Cléguérec (Morbihan, fig. 4.27). In a poster much praised by Clément-Janin, the soldier-artist Jean Droit, who also contributed drawings to *L'illustration*, uses the poilu's bent knee, alert attitude, and tensed muscles to signify preparation for an attack (fig. 4.28).[124] The pose, particularly the bent knee, carries over to the monument in Selles-sur-Cher (fig. 4.29), by the Paris sculptor Camille Ravot.

One popular monument type had few direct precedents in wartime visual culture: the dying or dead poilu. Artists seeking inspiration may have turned to

FIGURE 4.24. (top)
Abel Faivre, "On les aura!" Poster
Collection, FR 793A, Hoover Institution
Archives. © 1999 Artists Rights Society
(ARS), New York/ADAGP Paris.

FIGURE 4.25. (bottom, left)
War monument, Salbris (Loir-et-Cher:
Victorious poilu type). Photo: Author.

FIGURE 4.26. (bottom, right)
Lucien Jonas, "Souscrivez pour la victoire
et pour le triomphe de la liberté." Poster
Collection, FR 189, Hoover Institution
Archives.

FIGURE 4.27. (top)
War monument, Cléguérec (Morbihan).
Photo: Author.

FIGURE 4.28. (bottom, left)
Jean Droit, "4ᵉ emprunt national." Poster
Collection, FR 644, Hoover Institution
Archives.

FIGURE 4.29. (bottom, right)
War monument, Selles-sur-Cher (Loir-
et-Cher). Photo: Author.

FIGURE 4.30. (left)
War monument, Troyon
(Meuse). Photo: Author.

FIGURE 4.31. (right)
War monument, Carcès
(Var). Photo: Author.

traditional *gisants*, or tomb figures, clearly the inspiration for Broquet's monument in Ligny-en-Barrois (Meuse, fig. 5.2). We can identify two main types. Rombaux-Roland advertised a recumbent figure, bareheaded and clutching his chest (fig. 4.30), which some towns paired with the *Victorious poilu*, but which many used alone.[125] Gourdon offered a somewhat maudlin poilu defending the flag; the figure is standing but sways backward, suggesting he has just been hit (fig. 4.31). The flag appears in a number of war posters, including the improbable seminude warrior fighting the imperial eagle (fig. 1.13) and an odd war-bond poster (fig. 4.32) in which a poilu carries the female allegory of the Republic and an enormous tricolor. Durenne distributed a variation of the Gourdon soldier defending the flag (fig. 4.33), a monument by Charles Breton in which the poilu may be making a last stand but does not appear to be dying.[126]

The critical distaste for these conventional monument types, I have suggested, involved their connection to an art form aimed primarily at conveying a message external to the artist's imagination. In posters and illustrations, the dominance of words, whether a caption or an exhortation, epitomized the rela-

tionship between artist and external message that critics found so troubling. Monuments did not, of course, bear quite the same relationship to words as did posters and cartoons. Some suppliers did give their sculptures titles, thus subtly invoking high-art practice as well as a set of verbal-visual pairings that dated from the war. Examples include *On les aura!* and another military slogan, *On ne passe pas!* ("They shall not pass"), which led to both a poster (fig. 4.34) and to a number of monument types, including one by Pourquet, *La résistance* (fig. 4.13). Some commercial monuments also came adorned with patriotic inscriptions, such as "Pro Patria."[127] Yet, except perhaps for monuments consisting chiefly of walls with inscribed names, texts hardly dominate images as *visibly* in monuments as they do in posters.

To associate monuments with an (inferior) art of words or ideas, then, itself involves assumption and argument, including visual association. Describing a monument or explaining its meaning thus became a sensitive task, at least in terms of its artistic status. For the critics, who condemned the connection between monumental sculpture and the "popular" largely by reference, such

FIGURE 4.32. (left) William Malherbe, "Souscrivez à l'emprunt de la libération." Poster Collection, FR 446, Hoover Institution Archives.

FIGURE 4.33. (right) War monument, Bracieux (Loir-et-Cher). Photo: Author.

SEEING
THE SIGNIFIED

193

FIGURE 4.34.
Maurice Neumont,
"On ne passe pas!" Poster
Collection, FR 669A,
Hoover Institution
Archives.

associations remained largely unconscious. But both in commercial discourse and at the local level extensive verbal construction was involved in identifying monuments as particular types and in articulating their meanings and status. And the processes and contexts that linked monuments to words—descriptions, narratives, speeches—reveal a great deal about the intersection of their construction as aesthetic objects and as signifiers. Monuments prompted verbal explanations on numerous occasions: in advertising and in artists' statements, in correspondence between the review boards and local officials, in the press, and in speeches at the monument's dedication, as we saw in Commercy. We will examine dedication ceremonies more closely in chapter 6, but they command attention here both as the delta into which descriptive language flowed and as self-consciously public occasions on which authorities sought to fix certain ideas and images in memory.

Whether in the accounts of journalists like Léon Florentin or in actual speeches reprinted in the press, descriptions of completed monuments usually involved three elements. An affirmation of the monument's beauty, with thanks to the artist or *homme de l'art* responsible, came first, followed by a formal description, often very concise. The description led, finally, into an explanation of the monument's meaning and of the values it incarnated. Although the combination of the elements varied, the type of monument—commercial or commissioned, simple or elaborate, figural or not—had little bearing on the terms used to describe and explain it, suggesting that issues beyond the monument's provenance and appearance were at stake.

Salbris, with its standard-issue *Victorious poilu* (fig. 4.25), offers a fairly typical example. At the dedication ceremony the mayor thanked the "distinguished artist who conceived the fine monument we all are admiring," an Orléans contractor called Pijoury, as well as his daughter, an art student. After evoking various historic events, which he called memories, from the town's past, Mayor Durand declared that "this statue, so artistic and so moving, will incarnate, in its expression full of élan and bravura, the unswerving devotion of these men to France." Future generations, he continued, would recall in passing the monument not only the suffering and death of the war, but also that the dead "had avenged the right, preserved the principles on which civilization rests, and saved their country's freedom and its future."[128]

Why, first of all, did the mayor insist on the "artistic" character of the monument and its producer? When Florentin extolled the work of Broquet in Commercy, he was vaunting the prestige that the town acquired in choosing a recognized artist and, perhaps, responding by implication to critics of the design. But Pijoury, whose letterhead offered "All Kinds of Cemetery Work, Vaults and Monuments, Modern Equipment and Saw-Yard," had no such pretensions, and the contract for the monument clearly identifies Benet as its producer.[129] Durand's claims have less in common with Florentin's than with a newspaper's characterization of a Jacomet poilu in Beignon (Morbihan) as "of a fine [*belle*] artistic appearance" or with a description of a stela in Euville (Meuse, fig. 4.35) as "in good taste."[130] These phrases remind us of St. Thuriau's description of the Jacomet poilu as a "work of art," and suggest that in this context "art" says more about the client than about the producer. At a time when the state had secured a near monopoly over the training of artisans, the artistic quality and taste of a monument testified to a community's place, political as well as cultural, among the tastemakers rather than the craftsmen who simply followed directions.[131] The actual quality of the monument, in other words, mattered less than the ability to recognize it.

Many local officials and journalists, moreover, displayed a considerable ability to appropriate art-critical discourse to their own ends. A journalist attending the dedication of the monument in La Gacilly (Morbihan) had clearly read his Salon reviews. He called the monument "a simple and beautiful stela of classic lines," and congratulated its designer for having "resisted the temptation

FIGURE 4.35.
War monument, Euville
(Meuse). Photo: Author.

of poilus cutting an eagle's throat, which so quickly grow stale." In Montiers-sur-Saulx (Meuse), with yet another Benet poilu on a pedestal, the mayor, Albert Thomas, declared that "we eliminated all architectural motifs, capitals or Roman molding, for it seemed to us that the sculptural lines of this monument expressed in a simpler, more natural and purer way the idea of noble beauty that alone had guided us."[132] Even the imposing allegorical figure in Vannes, prefecture of the Morbihan, earned this description in *Ouest républicain*: "Thanks to the well-known talent of M. Ladmiral, the Paris architect, it rises cleanly and without unnecessary embellishments."[133] Especially in Euville, where the *Républicain de l'est* called the stela "simple like the lives of those it commemorates," and in Montiers artistic judgment takes on a moral tone that implicitly trumps any attempt to contest it on purely aesthetic grounds.

FIGURE 4.36.
War monument, St.
Caradec-Trégomel
(Morbihan). Photo: Author.

Turning to the second element in Mayor Durand's speech, we find that he offers a brief, not very specific description of the Salbris poilu, attending only to the figure's expression. He does not evoke the monument's title, explain its symbolism, or even mention the "victory" to which it alludes. On one level, the words *élan* and *bravoure* with which he characterizes the figure do much of the work a more elaborate description could perform. Summary descriptions of this kind sought simply to verbalize the connection onlookers would have made to already familiar soldier-types. The *Journal de Pontivy* described the monument in St. Caradec-Trégomel (fig. 4.36) as "a Verdun poilu at his post, blocking the enemy's passage." The newspaper called the monument in Cléguérec (fig. 4.27), also artist-designed but a familiar type, "a poilu, energetic in attitude, who emerges from a trench with the motion of a grenade launcher."[134]

These few words sketch out a general type and, at the same time, allow members of the public to conjure up their own specific memories corresponding to it. Both the general and the particular would then be available for assimilation into the third part of the discursive operation, the establishment of meaning.

Yet one type of monument made concise description very difficult, as it almost demanded detailed explanation. Consider this newspaper report on the monument in Bar-le-Duc (fig. 4.37), then nearing completion:

The group of poilus, whom the sculptor has captured in the midst of battle, justly elicits the admiration of passers-by; it is full of life, full of expression, and indeed, in our humble opinion, the base plus this group of life-size soldiers would have been more than adequate for a monument. Unfortunately, this magnificent work can only be weakened by the woman [figure] with whom it is supposed to be capped; too tall for the block that it will top, this graceless female statue, the allegorical meaning of which is far from apparent, will only bring to the monument a note of banality as regrettable as it is unnecessary.[135]

The writer's unease involves both allegory and femininity, for in both commercial and commissioned monuments the two tended to go together.

Gourdon and Rombaux-Roland both offered several types of female figure, either alone or in combination with poilus. A figure with a flag, and sometimes a helmet, represented France (fig. 4.40); a winged woman stood for Victory. Rombaux-Roland also offered a female mourner in high relief, in the act of carving an inscription on a stela (fig. 4.38). The first two of these types had many precedents in both high and vernacular sculpture and in posters (figs. 4.32, 4.39), and female figures had long allegorized grief in funerary monuments.[136] Of the Gourdon type representing France chosen for the monument in Tanneron (Var, fig. 4.40), Poupé wrote that "it does not have the character of an original work," but he found in it "nothing shocking from an aesthetic point of view."[137] The *République de Loir-et-Cher* called the commissioned monument in Chouzy-sur-Cisse (fig. 4.41) "very attractive" and described it as "a fine figure of a woman who personifies victorious France distributing wreaths to those of her children who gave their lives for her."[138] None of this seems to pose any serious conceptual difficulty. Why, then, should the figure in Bar-le-Duc have provoked such unease?

The key word concerning the Chouzy monument is "personifies." For as "a manner of speech endowing things or abstractions with life," personification introduces a median term between signifier and signified and calls attention to the interpretation that representation entails. In monumental form such figures generally demand a full narrative explanation, just as, in poetics, interpretation "begins with the fact that allegory is a structural element in narrative."[139] It is precisely because allegory summons interpretation that the traditional gendering of visual allegory as feminine had such troubling implications in postwar

FIGURE 4.37. War monument, Bar-le-Duc (Meuse). Photo: Author.

France. The sculptor and the authorities in Bar-le-Duc dismissed both their critics and what they regarded as inaccurate interpretations of the monument: for them the female figure unambiguously represented memory paying tribute to the dead.[140] Such an assertion may have sought to put to rest another interpretation to which female allegories lend themselves: that women themselves have some political identity linked to the nation directly, rather than through

FIGURE 4.38. (top)
War monument, St. Maximin (Var). Photo: Author.

FIGURE 4.39. (bottom)
Albert Besnard, "Souscrivez pour hâter la paix par la
victoire." Poster Collection, FR 660, Hoover Institution
Archives. © 1999 Artists Rights Society (ARS),
New York / ADAGP Paris.

subordination to men. As France engaged in a divisive debate about whether to grant women the vote, an interpretation of this kind could not but have made men uncomfortable.[141]

The notion of female tribute to male sacrifice thus emerged as a way of neutralizing the potentially subversive connotations of female allegories. In some instances, for example at Sommedieue (Meuse, fig. 4.42), the allegory hardly needs any elucidation. Nonetheless, a speaker at the dedication, the councillor general Noel, offered this description: "France brings a laurel wreath to the glorious and generous soldier."[142] Yet discourse insisted on the tributary nature of the gesture even in monuments with *only* a female figure. One newspaper compared the unusual mosaic motif in the Lamotte-Beuvron monument (fig. 4.43) to "an icon," and saw in it "the Angel of victory, wings spread, [who] offers palm-leaves and wreaths to the heroes."[143] The praise of monuments' aesthetic qualities—Noel contrasted the Sommedieue monument favorably with the aggressive soldiers of other works, including the Rude *Marseillaise*—assists in the articulation of this interpretation and the foreclosing of others. For the appreciation of art, and the ability to speak its language ("icon," "proportions"), testifies to a speaker's taste and knowledge, and confers on description an authority to which mere interpretation cannot aspire.

FIGURE 4.40. (left) War monument, Tanneron (Var). Photo: Author.

FIGURE 4.41. (right) War monument, Chouzy-sur-Cisse (Loir-et-Cher). Photo: Author.

The evocation of "children" in relation to the Chouzy monument suggests another frame of reference that sought to circumscribe the interpretation of allegorical monuments. Likening female figures to mothers served twin purposes: it domesticated the abstract forces represented, notably the nation, and implicitly cast as normative the domestic and gender relations that the war had disrupted. When the reconstructed village of St. Rémy-la-Calonne dedicated its monument in 1932 (fig. 4.44), the *Bulletin meusien* lauded its "expressive and simple beauty," and described it as "representing France, our mother, holding up one of her wounded sons."[144] The construction of the nation as a "mother," of course, personalizes the authority that led the commemorated to their deaths, and lends plausibility to the unspoken assumption underlying the term "sacrifice," that soldiers had given their lives willingly. The maternal image also subtly defuses the potentially troubling implications of a female figure "holding up [*soutenant*]" a man. For a woman to be supporting a grown man casts the circumstances of war, in which women's new roles had provoked much anxiety, as extraordinary, even unnatural.[145] But a reading of that woman as "mother" promises that, just as mothers' physical strength in relation to their children fades with time, the disruption will be temporary, provided that

FIGURE 4.44.
War monument, St. Rémy-la-Calonne
(Meuse). Photo: Author.

women in the postwar period emulate the qualities of loyalty, tenderness, and devotion traditionally associated with the maternal role. The figure of the mother had such resonance that it often appears as a central term in the discursive construction of commemoration itself, so that the building of monuments becomes the act of a "grateful mother."[146]

Any description of a monument, then, aims to promote and secure a particular interpretation, while at the same time blocking or erasing potentially contestatory readings. Although all images can prompt multiple readings, those employing a realist mode make an implicit claim about the transparency of their representation that allows the reader or onlooker to defer interpretation, at least as a conscious act. Allegory provides no such reassurance; to the contrary, it foregrounds the interpretive act as a prerequisite for understanding meaning. The longer and more elaborate the explanation, the greater the risk that it will expose the contradictions, paradoxes, and anxieties that any culture with normative ambitions, like commemoration, seeks to repress as part of its own self-definition. In the French culture of commemoration after World War I, the gendering of allegory as feminine and of realism as masculine had to do not only with the prevalence of allegorical women as opposed to realist poilus. It also, and more significantly, flowed from the way gender served as a figure for the discursive distinction at the heart of commemoration, between soldiers' and civilians' "experiences" of the war.

Descriptions of allegorical groups thus offer a fitting introduction to the question of the meanings that discourse draws out of monuments. In Salbris, the mayor's concise formal description quickly linked the poilu's expression, his *élan* and bravura, to certain themes: soldiers' devotion to duty, their suffering, their defense of civilization. In contrast to the more elaborate explanation an allegory would have required, the conventional "realism" of the Benet statue facilitated that concision, which in turn associates both the speaker and the monument with a masculine "experience" that language cannot adequately convey.[147] Other descriptions, equally concise, affirm the same values in more explicitly gendered terms. A newspaper called the poilu in Noyal-Pontivy "as masculine in his features as [he is] heroic in expression"; the mayor of Séglien, also in the Morbihan, spoke of "the virile figure of the Breton poilu" atop its monument.[148] In St. Mihiel, the monument by the sculptor Peynot, also responsible for the Bar-le-Duc memorial, includes scenes of the trenches and of the German occupation of the town, but the chair of the monument committee emphasized its "principal motif," "a poilu with a virile and energetic expression whom Victory is crowning [with laurel]." Another account noted the contrast between the relief figure of Victory and the nearly three-dimensional poilu, saying that the Victory "fades away [*s'estompe*]" behind him.[149] Perhaps Peynot had learned his lesson from Bar-le-Duc.

The word *mâle,* which I have translated as both "masculine" and "virile," clearly genders the meanings that journalists and speakers construct around monuments. So do *énergique* and *crâne* (bold, brave), which a newspaper used to describe a poilu in Quistinic (Morbihan).[150] Men are active, heroic, resourceful. One press account offered this description of the monument in Rohan (Morbihan, fig 3.4): "This soldier, who has burned his last cartridge, holds his rifle by the barrel, ready to use it as a club. His face is expressive; his physiognomy reflects the fierce nobility of his character, ready to make the ultimate sacrifice."[151] War tests men to the limits, and by following the values of courage, bravura, and boldness to the death, soldiers prove not only their own worth, but that of the code of masculinity that governed their actions. Thus in Bracieux (Loir-et-Cher, fig. 4.33), the monument "represents a poilu, bent over, embracing with supreme effort the folds of the tricolor flag."[152] The meaning could not be clearer: the survival of the nation depended, and still depends, on the kind of devotion of which only men are capable.

Sexual difference, then, plays a fundamental signifying role in the language of description. For the meanings that explanatory texts "find" in monuments rest on the potent notion of the incommensurability of the soldier's "experience" of war. Adjectives like *crâne, farouche* (fierce), and, obviously, *mâle* did not apply to women in interwar France. To fit into the masculinist order, women had to be grieving, suffering, emotional: the mayor of Vendôme, Robert Barillet, described the female figure on the monument there (fig. 4.45) as moved by "a feeling of grief and of maternal pity." The woman, an allegory of the city, is awarding a wreath of gratitude and memory to a poilu and a

FIGURE 4.45. War monument, Vendôme (Loir-et-Cher). Photo: Author.

British aviator, an allusion to the allied air station nearby.[153] Even the virtues of courage, stoicism, and devotion, which seem so patent on many female figures, cannot be ascribed to women without some circumlocution that points to feminine weakness. In postwar discourse, women's wartime devotion—to their families, to newfound responsibilities, to the nation—so effortlessly becomes a devotion to men that it excludes the possibility it was ever anything else.

Two months after the dedication in Bracieux, with its poilu's "supreme effort," the same newspaper, the *République de Loir-et-Cher*, reported on a dedication in the nearby town of Mont-près-Chambord. The monument (fig. 4.46) consisted of "a high four-sided pyramid bearing the names of the 74 heroes to whose glory it was built. A woman steps out of the stone and, in a motion of superb ascent [*envolée*], brings the 'Children of Mont who died for France' the hero's palm."[154] A *superbe envolée* recalls, if it does not quite match, the soldier's "supreme effort." Although *envolée* has some of the overtones of *élan*, in its primary meaning it applies to birds, not people; in this context it suggests a momentary rise to a higher level. It is, in any case, the grandest gesture of which women are capable in commemorative culture: a gesture of tribute to men.

Monuments of this kind thus become a central term in a process of gendering, extending from the use of women as collectors of funds (chapter 3) to the discursive construction of commemorative ritual (chapter 6), which casts commemoration as a tribute from women to men. Why should women in particular bear this responsibility? We saw in chapter 1 how women became the privileged sign of the civilian, of the France that soldiers gave their lives to protect, but also resented. It was a small step from gender as a figure for incommensurable experience to the view that women stood for all civilians, and as such owed veterans a debt they could never repay. The anxiety and unease that such a debt could provoke underlies councillor general Hérault's description of the female figure of "Glory" in the Sologne monument in Romorantin (fig. 4.47):

Neither rigid nor austere, she is humane and compassionate toward the suffering. See how she leans over to succor him. This is the Glory of France, who suffers herself to ask so much of her children, to impose so much sacrifice upon them, even that of their life. The

FIGURE 4.47.
Monument to the dead of the Sologne, Romorantin (Loir-et-Cher). Photo: Author.

adolescent dying at her feet is her blood son; her heart is rent at the sight of this youth with no morrow.[155]

The religious overtones of this passage, which constructs the monument as a kind of secular pietà, do not vitiate its contemporaneity. The women of France, Hérault suggests, did not ask lightly for men's sacrifice: veterans have only to look at the suffering of mothers and widows to find the recognition and tribute they demand.

Taken together, these highly political texts can almost efface the monuments they describe. They seem, like Alexandre, to read *through* the signifier to the "thing signified," thus inserting monuments in their own "system of signs," wholly independent of the world of art. Yet almost all of these texts not only contain but link together the three elements of praise for the monument as work of art, formal description, and explication. Hérault, for example, said of the Romorantin monument that "M. Bristol, the very distinguished sculptor who created it, has realized a work admirable not only for its sculptural beauty but also for the feelings and the emotion that it inspires. None of his works will do him greater honor, because he devoted to it all his talent as an artist, and all of his soldier's heart."[156] As was so often the case, the same text that inserted the monument in a system of signs also situated it firmly within the world of art.

Such praise often went along with claims to originality. At the dedication of the monument in Creuë in 1926, *La Meuse* described it as "diverging completely from serial models," despite its clear resemblance to the Rombaux-Roland type built in Stenay three years earlier; it was even closer to the Rombaux-Roland monument that St. Rémy-la-Calonne chose in 1932 (fig. 4.44).[157] When the Loir-et-Cher review board, echoing its comments on Marchenoir (fig. 4.15), expressed its regret that Bracieux (fig. 4.33) had chosen a "serial figure rather than . . . the personal work of an artist," the mayor responded by noting the Salon credentials of the sculptor, Charles Breton, and the artistic reputation of the supplier, Val d'Osne. He described the monument as "of remarkable beauty," and said that to his knowledge it resembled no other in the department.[158] He may have been correct at the time, but a similar monument in Sambin, a Rombaux-Roland type rather than Val d'Osne, was dedicated a week before Bracieux's.[159]

What did it mean for local officials to defend the artistic status of their monuments? In some cases, as in Bracieux, their position was defensive. Yet the prefectoral review boards, despite their expressed antipathy to mass-produced monuments, had no consistent rule against them. Three monuments in the Morbihan with virtually identical sculptures from the Chapal foundry, though with different designers of record, all won quick approval from the review board.[160] In a far more egregious example, Beignon actually sent the prefect Jacomet advertising copy to describe its monument; commissioners approved the project apparently without a second thought.[161] Ultimately the review boards fell back on the belief, rooted in the very workings of the art world, that one could not demand artistic production in places so foreign to artistic standards. When Poupé faced yet another Jacomet sketch for the monument in Pourcieux (Var), he identified its source and wrote that it could not "be considered an original work. It will undoubtedly appear in other communes and will evoke the idea of commerce more than of art." But finding "nothing truly disgraceful" in the project, he recommended that, "to recognize the meritorious efforts of a community of about 350 inhabitants that is spending more than 7,500 francs to glorify its dead," the review board approve the project.[162]

So some monument clients might have used the language of art strategically, because they thought the state expected it. But towns defending the originality of their monuments would not have accepted Poupé's condescension as the last word: recall, for example, St. Thuriau's pride in acquiring "a work of art" from Jacomet. I have also suggested that the language of art conferred a certain status on the local officials who used it, aligning them with the wealthy and powerful, those who throughout history have controlled the making of art. To speak of monuments as "art" in this sense authorizes the many attempts to assign them meaning. Finally, a third reason motivated local claims for monuments' artistic status. Beyond the first or strategic order of claims, a kind of practical relativism ("to us it's art" or "there's nothing like it for miles around"), beyond the second order, a kind of Bourdelian distinction ("I've read the art criticism too, so we're on the same level"), the notion of "art" stands for what makes commemoration a public, collective activity. It stands, in other words, for representation. All these strands can be traced to particular sources: the idea that a monument should *be* a work of art to the review boards, the artistic status of even a commercial monument to commercial discourse, the prestige of art, along with the trope of simplicity, to both art criticism and the state. In the end, the confluence of these artistic, commercial, and administrative discourses produced at the local level a profound, if largely unconscious, sense of how commemoration works to construct meaning.

To grasp how this understanding came about, let us return briefly to the gendered dichotomy between realist and allegorical monuments. Before admitting that the figure of the poilu offered "no counterindication to sculpture," Robert de la Sizeranne had referred disparagingly to the unfortunate consequences of "vestmental realism" in earlier monumental sculpture.[163] But the details of the poilu's uniform in both serially produced and commissioned works played a key role in defining, and gendering, the kind of representation in which they were engaged. The helmet, puttees, kit, canteen, and greatcoat perpetuated a level of detail long familiar from wartime imagery. At the same time they made a monument "realist," they also made it "masculine." No one could have confused *sculptural* detail with the real thing: it was representation, or, more simply, art. But as representation it enjoyed a privileged link to what it represented, a link resting on the conventional claims of mimesis.

Much of the privileged status of realist monuments had to do with the way they seemed to make explanation, indeed language itself, unnecessary. Despite the enormous body of soldiers' writing the war had produced, in its aftermath veterans' silence—their inability to communicate what they had experienced— became one of the principal signs of the uniqueness of that experience.[164] Silence, signified in various ways at dedication ceremonies (refusals to speak, breaking down in the middle of a speech), betokened authenticity in ways that speech could not.[165] Realist detail, while acknowledging its own status as representation, or "art," offered secure passage to a set of preexisting, consensual meanings, and thus enabled representation to take place virtually automatically, and in silence. In this way realism offered a means of cloaking and bypassing the allegorical aspect of *all* monuments, their reference to a moral or political meaning larger than the visual sign they offer. A statue of a poilu, for example, represents not just one soldier, but all soldiers, as well as the qualities that have earned them the nation's gratitude. Allegorical monuments, as we have seen, foreground the interpretive act essential to deciphering their meaning. Their gendering as "feminine" involved not only the traditional association of female figures with allegory, but also the new opposition of "speech" about the war to soldiers' and veterans' silence. The explanatory speech an allegorical monument entailed automatically linked it to the civilian side of the soldier/civilian dichotomy, the term gendered as feminine.

Inasmuch as gender rests on social and cultural convention, alternatives did present themselves. Certain monuments, without challenging the notion of commemoration as a tribute paid by women to men, represented that tribute in "realist" detail. The monument in Chaillon (fig. 4.18), where the helmet stands in for the absent father, depicts a mother, in recognizably modern dress, instructing her son in the values that the monument offers. Examples can be found all over the country: a woman pointing to the word "Reconnaissance" in St. Maximin (Var, fig. 4.38), probably a Rombaux-Roland model; mothers showing their little sons the names of the dead in Guémené-sur-Scorff (Morbihan, fig. 2.7) and Bapaume (Pas-de-Calais, fig. 4.48); parents with heads bowed before a helmet at their feet in Baud (Morbihan, fig. 4.49), the mother holding a wreath of tribute.[166] In Hattonchâtel, a small town near Les Éparges that had served as a German observation post, an American benefactor, Belle Skinner, financed most of the reconstruction, including the war memorial (fig. 4.50). The figure needed no more, in *Le républicain de l'est*, than this concise description: "an old woman of the Lorraine soil who prays for the heroes who fell on

FIGURE 4.48. War monument, Bapaume (Pas-de-Calais): detail of figures. Photo: Author.

FIGURE 4.49. (left)
War monument,
Baud (Morbihan).
Photo: Author.

FIGURE 4.50. (right)
War monument,
Hattonchâtel
(Meuse). Photo:
Author.

the field of honor."[167] Because a masculine mode of representation circumscribes the female figure, we may gather that the monument signified as unambiguously as did any poilu.

A 1921 letter defending a monument project in the Morbihan offers a fitting coda to a chapter that began with a search for monuments of distinction in the provinces. The writer, a local notable and member of the departmental council named du Halgouët, cautions the prefect that "the beautiful is a question of standards and of perspective; it differs by time and place. It is, it seems to me, very delicate to maintain that a monument that avoids the grotesque and the ridiculous is unaesthetic. Furthermore, it is also very delicate to tell people highly sensitive as to their principles and their sense of things that their taste is off [*n'est pas juste*]." Du Halgouët was protesting the review board's rejection of a plan to convert an existing memorial calvary in the cemetery of La Croix-Helléan into a war memorial; eventually the decision was reversed.[168]

Du Halgouët's argument rests on two elements: the lack of any timeless, universal definition of "the beautiful" and the importance, in the commemorative arena, of distinctly local perspectives. As an educated man, he retained his faith in the standards that underlie critical discourse; he may well have condemned as "grotesque" many monuments that others called works of art. The proposed calvary, he noted, imitated a popular Breton type "of unpolished [*fruste*] appearance" that would, "with the patina of time, take on the allure of archaism." But the key to his defense lies in the connection he effected between the subjectivity of aesthetics and local commemoration. The communities that put up monuments, he suggested, were representing their *conception des choses* in a manner they deemed artistic. One could not challenge the latter claim without calling the whole commemorative operation into question. No one, from critics to the state to its local representatives, was willing to go so far.

The defense of a monument straddling a number of categories—art, commemoration, religion, local traditions—reminds us that a monument's meanings encompassed far more than the understandings of war, sacrifice, tribute, and memory that speakers could attach to it. In a provincial cemetery or town square, so full of "historical memories," as the mayor of Salbris put it,[169] a monument's "signified" would almost certainly differ from those a critic could discern within the confines of a Paris exhibition hall. We will turn in the next chapter to the ways in which the local context, from the monument's site to religious attitudes to building materials, inflected its signifying role. In doing so, however, we should note that the success of local communities in constructing monuments as uniquely their own has had the effect of reinforcing a distinction between art and commemoration that first emerged in critical discourse. On both sides, the distinction serves particular interests: those of the art world in its own autonomy, those of communities (and their historians) in a notion of their organic coherence. But the familiarity of the distinction should not be allowed to obscure the historical circumstances in which it emerged.

For in some ways the dichotomization of art and commemoration arose out of, and in reaction to, a profoundly different notion that characterized the postwar world, that of a fundamental *connection* between art and commemoration as forms of representation. Because the terms of "art" offered local communities their principal means of thinking about visual representation, they attributed the signifying power of commemorative monuments in large part to their status as works of art. If, in other words, in the aftermath of the war French women and men could, from the depths of their grief, see beyond a monument to its signification, they believed they owed that facility to the skill of the artist, loosely defined, who had made it. That expansive notion of signifying power, moreover, authorized a discursive construction that would prove crucial to the whole commemorative process. For art, in the common (and critical) conception, says as much about its maker as about its ostensible purpose; nothing less than art, then, could make monuments signifiers not only of a set of ideas and values, but also of the communities that espoused them.

CONTESTED SPACES

"Places," Michel de Certeau has written, "are fragmentary and withdrawn histories, pasts others have robbed of legibility, accumulated times that can be unfolded but which are present much more as stories in waiting, remaining like rebuses. . . ."[1] De Certeau admirably captures the partial and often frustrating ways memories become rooted in particular settings. Places contain the promise of meaning, of coherent narratives (*histoires*), but these narratives remain either fragmentary or *en attente:* the locale prompts a visual image, or perhaps a set of images, but does not supply the thread that ties them together. Perhaps an intervening event, an encounter one would sooner forget, blocks access to the desired story, hence pasts "others have robbed of legibility [*des passés volés à la lisibilité par autrui*]." Perhaps the memory remains only as an affect, a dull ache or a smile of pleasure that comes, unbidden and unexplained, when one crosses a once-familiar spot. Prompting memories as discrete images, but depriving us of the narrative fabric we weave in our own lives,[2] places stand for both the continuity and the disjunction between past and present.

But de Certeau's text also evokes our tendency to assign particular places their *own* stories, thus transforming them into "spaces" with defined purposes and meanings. Large public spaces, from the Grand' Place in Brussels to the Mall in Washington, often sport signs, Dean MacCannell's "markers," that point to or summarize such narratives: plaques, dates, tour guides with umbrellas, and of course statues. Thus the sense that such places, which may bear the official designation "historic sites" or landmarks, contain or, for de Certeau, actually *are* (*sont*) the stories that have become attached to them. But Henri Lefebvre reminds us that the meanings spaces harbor result from contestation, as different "groups or classes [seek] to appropriate the space in question."[3] The stories we seek in places remain fragmentary and inaccessible, not only because of lapses of memory, but because the definition of particular spaces works to obscure the social and political conflicts that constructed them.

It is salutary to keep this element of conflict in mind when considering Maurice Halbwachs's influential notion that "every collective memory unfolds within a spatial framework." For Halbwachs, "Space is a reality that endures: since our impressions rush by, one after another, and leave nothing behind in the mind, we can understand how we recapture the past only by understanding how it is, in effect, preserved by our physical surroundings."[4] Halbwachs himself pointed to the complexity of this link, for in his view memories of space do not limit themselves to objects and forms but encompass people and habitual activities. Equally vital in all sectors of social life, collective memories focus on different kinds of spaces as a function of the groups or institutions from which both groups and memories emerge. Financiers and economists conceive of space in terms of markets, which, even when they operate across spatial boundaries, still may employ geographical monikers (Wall Street) as distinguishing signs; clerics place special emphasis on the contrast between sacred and profane spaces.[5] As a member of several groups, each individual collects memories within a number of distinct spatial frameworks, some of which may intersect.

The spatial metaphor of intersection leads back to Halbwachs's conception of the relationship between individual and collective memories. Memory as a collective phenomenon inheres in a group, but "it is individuals as group members who remember"; thus "each memory is a viewpoint on the collective memory" and changes along with the individual's membership in various groups.[6] Still, his emphasis remains resolutely on the collective element: "There is no universal memory. Every collective memory requires the support of a group delimited in space and time."[7] The particularity of individual memories, then, results from the ways different groups intersect. For Halbwachs this is a natural, even mysterious process. He takes little interest in the contestation over collective memory that results from groups' conflicting interests and objectives. Yet such contestation often involves the very spaces in which groups seek to enshrine their memories.

Between de Certeau's "places" as fragmentary histories and Lefebvre's "spaces" as sites of appropriation lies the whole range of social and political activities that animate sites and cast them as repositories of meaning, of narratives both apparent and tantalizingly concealed. Public spaces have long served to symbolize power, but since the eighteenth century, European planners have seen in the fabric of the city a way of inculcating norms, regulations, and behaviors in the citizens who occupy its spaces. By the turn of the twentieth century, urban theorists "demanded that places and monuments transfer meaning and knowledge across generations, indeed that these artifacts actually generate memory and inscribe civic conduct."[8] Lefebvre reminds us, then, that "a spatial code is not simply a means of reading or interpreting space: rather it is a means of living in that space, of understanding it, and of producing it. As such it brings together verbal signs (words and sentences, along with the meaning invested in them by a signifying process) and nonverbal signs (music, sounds, evocations, architectural constructions)."[9]

Since the same place may serve as a stage for activities and signifying processes pertaining to a variety of group affiliations, the construction of commemorative spaces in interwar France involved elements that tied individuals to an array of groups, abstract and concrete. The nation as historical entity presented both a need and the occasion for commemoration, while its markets and media furnished much of the verbal and visual imagery that commemoration employed. Regional units like the department provided materials, workers, and proximate examples through which various commemorative practices could spread. Localities contained both the physical sites that would become commemorative spaces and, more abstractly, the memories that commemoration sought to enshrine, memories of individuals who had special ties to those places. Local communities also were home to the veterans, families, and ordinary citizens who raised money, organized committees, and elected, petitioned, and sometimes browbeat the officials who had the last word on monument projects.

Each commemorative site thus represented a confluence of national, regional, and local elements. But making a monument a local artifact, and a particular site a commemorative space, also involved an act of will, a series of manipulations. This process involved two forms of signification. In one, communities chose signs that represented their sense of themselves, of what distinguished them from others. A municipal coat of arms, a distinctive local stone, or inscribed names proclaiming the specificity of a community's loss framed and accompanied the signs that linked it to larger groups, such as the nation, veterans, the bereaved. On a second level, the sites chosen for monuments established a concrete set of relationships between commemoration and the life of the community. Each of these choices sought to delimit, in Halbwachs's terms, a group, the community constituted as mourners. But each also had the potential to provoke contestation.

We saw in the previous chapter that localities, while employing discourses that had a national reach, often had to defend their own notion of commemorative art against those of regulatory authorities and critics. The choice of symbols could also bring a community into conflict with the state. A traditional local form might lack legibility as a commemorative symbol, while the cross, ostensibly chosen to signal nothing more than local piety, often overflowed the boundaries of the local, reviving memories of the church-state conflict that had riven the nation a generation earlier. Arbitration of these disputes touched on a community's deepest sense of itself, and, by identifying the source and nature of its sacrality, played a decisive role in framing its commemorative culture.

Yet within a community, few issues proved more divisive than the simple physical definition of commemorative space. Many controversies pitted those who desired a secluded, contemplative spot for the monument, typically the cemetery, against those who wanted to erect a monument in a prominent public place. In a cemetery, the bereaved could mourn in peace; on a public square a monument stood more emphatically for the community's will to commemorate. Such debates raised emotional questions about the primary constituency of commemoration, the bereaved or the entire community. Thus did the paradox of commemoration present itself in its starkest form: the displacement and appropriation of individual mourning by collective tribute. Monument sites prompted strong reactions, moreover, because they entailed a kind of geographical superposition of memories: memories of individuals had to share mental space with the memories attached and attributed to places.

At the same time the fashioning of commemorative space almost inevitably touched off or rekindled debates about the nature of the community itself. As Hubert Pérès has pointed out, the local framework for interwar commemoration, the commune, belongs to the realm of administrative abstraction.[10] Many communes incorporate distinct urban neighborhoods or rural settlements, some discrete enough, as we have seen, that they wished to build their own monuments. (Fearing a threat to the unitary French polity, the prefect of the Morbihan expressed his strong opposition to this trend in 1923.)[11] For Pérès, "a fund of knowledge organized as a basis for a feeling of common belonging" enables the commune to become, in Lefebvre's terms, not merely a "representation of space" but also a "representational space," that is to say "a space lived through [à travers] the images and symbols that accompany it." Debates over commemoration thus go to the heart of the process through which people in communities imagine them as spaces they hold in common.[12]

The commune in France is not only a unit of local government: it is the basic building block of the national polity. The institutions and rituals of local life followed the rhythms and employed the discourses of national politics, and the commune thereby served as the privileged terrain for the construction of a national community. In exchange for inculcating in citizens the values of nationhood, for following procedures and regulations that protected these values, and for the regular loan of their young men, communities received not only a voice in the affairs of the nation, but certain concrete benefits: schools, infrastructure, expertise. This was the fundamental bargain of the Third Republic. War, however, exposed the terrible cost of that bargain: not simply that citizens could be compelled to give their lives for the state, for that is true in most political systems, but that localities had a crucial place in constructing the abstraction, the nation, for which they died. Beyond its psychological burden, of subsuming individual into collective memories, the political burden of postwar commemoration lay in the way the "local" itself became both obligatory and constrained. For from the point of view of the state, communities had to represent their loss as voluntary, indeed as virtually automatic, thus displacing onto the citizen the tremendous power of the modern nation-state.

Communities generally bore this burden without complaint, at some level understanding it as the price of democracy. But the weight of the burden made itself felt in the tensions and strains that marked the elaboration of commemorative culture and its focal point, the construction of monuments. In this sense the price of democracy was politics, the struggle of competing interests that war ostensibly transcends, but that emerged in its wake as a kind of return of the repressed. Whatever the issue at hand—the location of a monument, a religious emblem or procession, the use of local materials, the progress of physical construction—the stakes of the debate went deeper. In the insistence of some that commemoration could work only in certain kinds of spaces, in the contestation of state restrictions, in the desire for distinctly local forms, we can sense a clinging to the local and personal memories that commemoration seeks to displace. And if the thread tying communities to the state became somewhat frayed between the wars, it may in part be because so much energy had to be devoted not only to "imagining" the nation, but to reimagining the local as a space with memories of its own.[13]

Sites of Commemoration

In July 1920 a group of petitioners from the village of Mons wrote the prefect of the Var to protest the site chosen for the war memorial there. "The families of the victims," they declared,

cannot bear the thought of seeing the monument built in the Place Saint-Sébastien, the square where all holiday celebrations take place and where everyone gambols and frolics. Has it ever occurred to anyone that the pleasures of some will be a great sorrow for others?

We ask that this monument, which is above all funerary in character, be erected in a place of contemplation and respect, not of joy. The cemetery would satisfy us; there, where the memory of our forebears lies, we could evoke the memory of our beloved dead.[14]

Queried by the prefect, the mayor of Mons rejected both the petitioners' characterization of the site and their larger claims. The town council and the monument committee had together decided that "since the monument is in no way of a funerary type, it was appropriate to build it in one of the most visible places in the region [*pays*]." In his reply to the lead petitioner, a former deputy mayor named Porre, the prefect expanded on the mayor's language:

The monument to be built is thus not solely a funerary monument; it is above the passions and sentiments of the moment and belongs to posterity. . . . the committee should be praised for having chosen a site in a busy spot where the entire population will have forever in view the names of those who, through their sacrifice, contributed mightily to saving the world from barbarism.[15]

Spaces of commemoration, then, draw their character not only from the monument they frame but from the structures and signs that frame them. Notwithstanding the two sides' insistence that the monument had an *inherent* character, in broad terms funerary or pedagogical, clearly the same monument could have very different valences in different sites. By objecting not to the monument's design but to its location, the petitioners suggested that what imbued a monument with a "funerary" character was above all its setting, a "place of contemplation." In the views of the mayor and prefect, however, such a location would have compromised the demonstrative or exemplary purpose the monument was intended to serve.

The positions of the two sides in Mons echo the concurrent national debate about the burial of the dead; both arguments turn on who has the ultimate authority over commemoration, the bereaved or the community as a whole. But the contours of this debate did not follow entirely predictable lines. A few months after the Mons petition, the monument committee and the town council in Brignoles, a subprefecture of the Var, were planning a monument in the cemetery when they received a petition from the families of the dead calling for a more public site. A month later, after consulting with the petitioners, the committee's president reported that in deference to the families the monument would be built in a public square.

A local newspaper agreed with the committee that "the cemetery was the most worthy site for the monument to be erected in gratitude to our glorious dead; but because the majority of the relatives of these beloved *disparus* has decided differently, we can only yield to their determination."[16] Practical matters clearly influenced the debate: the committee had to organize a new subscription to cover the greater cost of a more prominently situated monument. Nonetheless, in Brignoles the families of the dead were seeking not "a place of contemplation" for their own grief but the rather different consolation of public tribute. Unlike their counterparts in Mons, they also had the moral suasion to get their way. The monument (fig. 4.8) remains at the edge of one of Brignoles's busiest thoroughfares to this day.

Both the similarities and the differences between these two cases from the Var illuminate the complexities of commemorative space in interwar France. The recourse to the petition in both communities highlights the sensitivity of monument siting as a political issue. The mayor of Mons suggested that the leader of the petition drive had political motives, though he carefully exempted the bulk of the signatories, "the afflicted," from this charge. In commemorative culture, the notion of the "political" tainted anyone who came in contact with it, which meant that political debates had to be conducted without acknowledging the interests behind them. The differing objectives of the petitioners help explain this attempt to cast commemoration as being above politics. For commemoration encompassed a number of purposes that were not always compatible: comforting the bereaved, restoring a disrupted political and social order, paying tribute to the dead, and writing a new chapter in the narrative of French history. To discuss aspects of commemorative culture in the terms of contemporary political debate did more than "politicize" a domain that demanded unity, the ostensible reason for avoiding politics. Beyond this, the incursion of the political threatened to expose the contradictions of the commemorative project itself, an exposure all the more shocking in that it took place on, and in a sense over, the home ground of the commemorated dead.

Scholarly attempts to analyze monument sites statistically have not really broken this taboo. Inasmuch as they characterize the site as a choice with clear political ramifications, they cast the "political" as something that unifies localities, distinguishes among them, and marks their place in the national polity. Thus, regional differences in monument location often seem to confirm well-known patterns of political and religious belief: the percentage of monuments located in cemeteries, for example, is considerably higher in regions of traditionally high Catholic observance than elsewhere.[17] Yet such analyses, as many of their authors readily acknowledge, fall far short of establishing some kind of transparent relationship between monument locations and national politics. "The choice of site," caution the historians of Vaucluse monuments, "certainly is not a function of political orientations alone"; local traditions, and the wishes of victims' families and other groups, also played their part.[18] And Yves Pilven le Sevellec, after an extraordinarily exhaustive analysis of monument sites in the Loire-Atlantique, could not find a single factor or combination of factors that reliably predicted the monument's location.[19]

Part of the problem with statistical analyses has to do with the categorization of spaces in French towns. Debates over monument sites often pitted a "secluded" spot, usually the cemetery, against a "public" one. In general, scholars have suggested, conservative Catholic communities preferred the cemetery or, failing that, a site adjacent to the church, whereas more left-leaning towns opted for a more open site, if possible close to the town hall. But local space, particularly in the smallest towns, does not always come so clearly demarcated: there might be only one *place* or public square, with the church and town hall at either end of it.[20] Another ambiguity arises with respect to the distinctly Breton space that communes called "the former cemetery." This term referred to a plot of land next to the church, left empty after graves were transferred to a new site, generally on the edge of town. A common phenomenon in Brittany in the early decades of this century, the creation of new cemeteries grew out of both hygienic and aesthetic concerns,[21] but it also tacitly acknowledged that churchyards in the middle of towns were not always places of contemplation. Although the former cemetery surely retained, in shared memories, traces of the sacred, it was usually deconsecrated. Without the graves to instill silence, and exposed to the comings and goings of daily life, former cemeteries could thus easily become public space.

The figures in table 2 convey something of this ambiguity. Adding together, for the Morbihan, monuments in the current or former cemetery or in proximity to the church, we arrive at 67 percent, comparable to Florence Regourd's figure for the Vendée, which she takes as testimony to that department's traditional conservatism.[22] But considerable evidence suggests that the communes themselves did not regard current and former cemeteries as comparable sites. In 1921 the mayor of Neulliac asked the town council to choose between two sites, the former cemetery and the new one, "without debate, by secret ballot and by majority vote," provisions that suggest some previous controversy. Seven councillors voted for the disused cemetery next to the church, four for the new one.[23] By doing so the council was not making a self-consciously antireligious decision, since the approved design included a cross; it was simply choosing the more central, and more public, of two alternative sites. The category of former cemeteries could easily, and with as much justification, be added to that of public squares, just under a third of the Morbihan sample, as to that of cemeteries.

The relatively small number of monuments built near churches in the Loir-et-Cher, less than half the percentage in the Morbihan, at first glance sets up a familiar dichotomy between a largely secularized, center-left department on the one hand and Catholic Brittany on the other. But if a slightly higher proportion of communes in the Loir-et-Cher sample built their monuments on public roads and squares, a slightly higher percentage did so in cemeteries as well, and the building of monuments *outside* the cemetery walls strongly suggests an effort at compromise. The chief difference that these figures establish between the two departments may well involve real estate rather than politics or religion. Between a quarter and a third of the communes in both departments placed their monuments in the relative seclusion of the cemetery. The rest chose, for reasons we will examine, sites more visible and more accessible to the public. Many communes in the Morbihan probably chose the former cemetery as a site because it was that rare commodity, open public land in the center of town. In the rest of the country, where the transfer of cemeteries had occurred a generation or more earlier, the space next to the church was less likely to be vacant, and towns in search of a central or public site for their monuments usually had to look elsewhere.

TABLE 2. MONUMENT SITES IN TWO DEPARTMENTS

Department	Loir-et-Cher	Morbihan
Number of cases	103	150
Cemetery (no./%)	33/32%	39/26%
Next to church; former cemetery	10/9.7%	55/36.7%
In front of church, "place de l'Englise"	9/8.7%	7/4.7%
In front of town hall	6/5.8%	12/8%
"Place"	25/24.3%	37/24.6%
Outside cemetery	9/8.7%	—
Other public site[a]	11/10.7%	—

NOTE: Percentages may not total 100 because of rounding.

[a]A roadside, entrance to the village, or near the school.

SOURCES: Prefectoral dossiers in ADM and ADL, series O.

If monument sites resist generalization, we can, by looking at different types of sites, attempt to understand the factors that led to particular choices in individual communities. These types form four large groups: cemeteries, public squares or parks, roadsides or entrances to towns, and spaces next to or within public buildings. They overlap in a number of ways, the most obvious being that towns generally chose to build their monuments on public land. Few communes had the resources to acquire privately owned land, and fewer wanted to undertake the often drawn-out process of expropriation required for certain types of purchase. "The formalities involved in any expropriation are long and complicated," one prefect wrote.[24] In addition, the public hearings involved in expropriating private land gave opponents of a particular site the chance to voice their disagreement, and perhaps to foment further opposition. The *enquête* into a nonexpropriative sale of a parcel of land in Montlivault (Loir-et-Cher) produced no fewer than twenty-one critical comments, including a number from families of the dead insisting that the monument be built inside the cemetery (the proposed site was outside it). Since legally the hearing concerned only the price of the land, these complaints did not block the purchase, but the incident created hard feelings that even came to the attention of the local deputy.[25]

The topography of commemoration divided potential sites into two principal types: the secluded and the frequented, with some sites, such as parks, quiet squares or churchyards, and cemetery entrances, serving as median terms between the two main types. Partisans of public sites, particularly squares in the center of town, generally saw monuments both as the focuses for public *acts* of remembrance and as spurs to individual memory for generations to come. We may recall from chapter 4 that, at the dedication of the monument in Salbris (Loir-et-Cher) in 1922, the mayor described the square where it stood as a sacred center of the community. Having witnessed many historic events in the past, "this place where the great, the holy patriotic idea has blazed so many times" already functioned as a space of commemoration. The square was also "the busiest, the most visible site, in the center of the city and the only large square that could accommodate such a fine large audience."[26]

Most of those favoring central locations would probably not have gone as far as the mayor of Vannes, Marin, who declared that "in our conception, the monument is not a funerary monument but much more a triumphal monument glorifying our heroes." They would, however, have agreed that "the passer-by must stop for a pious moment before these glorious inscriptions; the monument must remain, for future generations, the magnificent witness to the glories of the past."[27] A veteran in Lorient, Eugène Jéhanno, expressed a similar view: "It is the city of Lorient that is paying tribute to its dead, and everyone, whether from Lorient or not, must be able to admire this tribute by having the monument always in sight without any effort." For Jéhanno, a monument built "to glorify our compatriots who died in the war must endure for all time, and therefore is not designed to allow people today to kneel down and pray before it."[28]

In this concern for posterity, children naturally loomed large, making clear that the schoolyard, wherever physically located, constituted a public site par excellence. The town council in Le Lavandou (Var) approved the mayor's choice of the school garden, calling the site "particularly appropriate as much for its situation at the edge of the principal road in Le Lavandou as for its proximity to our school building, which means that our monument will be in sight of everyone arriving in Le Lavandou, as of all the children attending our school."[29] A newspaper reporting on the dedication of the monument in Ouzouer-le-Marché (Loir-et-Cher, fig. 5.1) described its site, the place des Écoles, as "felicitous," and wrote: "Our beloved little schoolchildren, hope of our victorious France, will thus forever have nearby the image of the sacrifice of their elders, those who wanted to preserve their freedom in the sweet fatherland."[30] The desire for visibility could lead a particularly remote village to situate its monument not in the center of the *bourg* but at the periphery, where farmers heading for the fields, or travelers from other villages, could see it.[31]

Monuments in public places also attracted opposition, however, much of it along the lines of the petition in Mons. Although not all opponents of frequented sites were relatives of the dead, they shared a conception of commemorative space that privileged mourning and reflection. One resident of Commercy expressed the view that "it would have been difficult to find a site less

FIGURE 5.1. War monument, Ouzouer-le-Marché (Loir-et-Cher). Photo: Author.

suitable" than the town's central square. "The noisy and lively market-day crowds," he continued,

who give the square such a picturesque aspect, would be shocking in the vicinity of the monument. I really don't see a family in mourning coming to lay a palm or a wreath there, between a fair stall and a hawker, amidst the noise of the market, the dust of the main road, the comings-and-goings of carriages and automobiles. It should, therefore, be built in a calm and silent place that evokes ideas of respect, of reflection, and of memory tinged with emotion.[32]

This was the standard argument; on rare occasions it came with a slightly different emphasis. A city councillor contesting a proposal to build the Vendôme monument on a busy square noted that "fairs take place nearby, and it would not be very cheerful [*gai*] to see a monument with two dead soldiers on it placed in the midst of the festivities."[33]

Moving from the general to the specific, from the idea of a central, visible, or frequented site to an actual location, could also pose problems. In larger towns and cities, the monument project often became caught up in plans and debates concerning future urban expansion. The initial city council decision in Lorient (Morbihan) would have placed the monument at the edge of a new residential neighborhood to the west of the city center.[34] Continuing controversy over the monument, and a change in the city administration, reopened debate on the site, but a preoccupation with the urban fabric persisted. With a final site decision pending, an architect foresaw that a square leading to a planned new district not only would provide a fitting setting for the monument, "a Place de la Victoire, on the scale of the Idea the monument represents," but would ensure a consistent aesthetic standard for the buildings to be erected around it. In contrast, an assistant mayor hoped that a monument "in a central spot, on a corner of a great, broad boulevard, would symbolize, to some degree, the future of greater Lorient."[35] Discussions of possible sites for various commemorative structures in Toulon raised issues both of the rehabilitation of disused military buildings and of the place of an old gateway in the city's new circulation plan.[36] Even in smaller centers, debates over the monument site often touched on issues of town planning. In Haudainville, a village just south of Verdun, the town council, as it voted 20,000 francs for the monument, opened a special subscription to "permit the construction in the center of the village of a square worthy of this symbol of gratitude and of memory."[37]

Major towns often faced another problem: the ideal site might already be taken. In Toulon, Lorient, and Bar-le-Duc the squares many preferred already housed monuments, in Lorient a statue of Jules Simon, in the other two cities a memorial to the dead of 1870. Some argued that the existing monument should simply be moved: in Bar-le-Duc the committee found the 1870 monument, then barely twenty years old, "leaving much to be desired aesthetically," and a letter to a Toulon newspaper described the 1870 monument there as "in a deplorable state of decay; the monument that concerns us could easily be built there, for we would in so doing unite the first victims of the Boche with their glorious avengers."[38] But the Toulon monument committee hesitated to request the removal of "a symbolic work that has, so to speak, acquired rights."[39] In Lorient practical considerations, as well as the existing statue, led to the choice of a square quieter than the central place Clemenceau, formerly known as the place du Morbihan. As one wag wrote, putting the war memorial in that traffic-clogged square would make it necessary "to anticipate a second monument, in memory of those foolhardy enough to have tried to pay tribute to our glorious dead"[40] simply by crossing the street.

Bar-le-Duc, Toulon, and Lorient all found alternative public squares for their monuments; so, after a long debate, did Vannes, although its choice, a park on a hill above the old town, struck many as too remote.[41] In smaller towns, however, practical difficulties could lead in the same direction as ideological opposition, to the cemetery. In the overwhelming majority of cases, partisans of a place of reflection wanted to see the monument in the communal cemetery; in most towns the cemetery also represented the cheapest and most practical solution to the siting dilemma. A member of the prefectoral design commission in the Var even indicated that "we are much less exacting toward a monument in a cemetery than toward one in a public place";[42] recall that in Brignoles the decision to move the monument from the cemetery to a public site forced a second fund-raising campaign, to make the now more visible monument more imposing. In Limerzel, in the Morbihan, the town council chose the cemetery as a way of putting up the monument "as quickly as possible."[43]

Beyond these practical considerations, situating a monument in a cemetery identified mourners, rather than the community as a whole, as the group with the best claim to control commemorative space. Such a "funerary monument" acknowledged and sought to facilitate individual and particular expressions of grief and to cast official commemoration as a collective form of mourning. For some, the choice of the cemetery emerged as the logical outgrowth of the dynamic of bodies and names. The town of Béganne (Morbihan) chose the cemetery in anticipation of burying around the monument veterans who would die of war injuries; by the summer of 1919 two had already succumbed to effects of poison gas.[44] A former school principal in Cléguérec, also in the Morbihan, for his part emphasized the needs of the families of the dead:

If the public square is indeed suitable for markets, fairs, public celebrations and dances, it is not suitable for the reflection that is owed the memory of those who died for their country. The parents, widows, and orphans will go to the cemetery to call forth the memory of those they loved so much; all of us will go to the cemetery to bear the tribute of our gratitude to these brave children of Cléguérec who fell on the field of honor.[45]

Thus the secluded site conjoins public tribute and private mourning in a manner that clearly privileges the latter. By placing the monument in a context that emphasizes its funerary character, the cemetery diminishes its availability, if not its utility, to more overtly political discourses.

But the immunization that cemeteries offered from politics amounted to little more than a discursive sleight of hand, for wherever they stood monuments participated in the cultural work of commemoration. The political valence even of funerary monuments, moreover, varied from place to place. As we will see, the cemetery offered the only sure way, under one reading of the 1905 separation of church and state, to imbue a monument with a clearly Christian significance. But the choice of the cemetery did not necessarily indicate a religious purpose, still less the conservative politics that usually accompanied Catholic devotion. Indeed, the cemetery could offer a sanctuary from *any* movement that local politics rendered oppositional. The communist town of Levallois-Perret, in the suburban Paris "red belt," built its highly controversial war memorial (fig. 2.5) in the municipal cemetery, where it remains visible from suburban trains entering and leaving the Gare St. Lazare. The right-wing veterans who decried the monument design as a pacifist travesty also accused the mayor of sequestering the monument to prevent its use in patriotic, by which they meant nationalist, demonstrations.[46] At the dedication of the monument in Vallières (Loir-et-Cher), the socialist mayor of the town, Barrat, declared that in placing the monument in the cemetery, the town avoided "glorifying the horrible butchery." Addressing the dead, the mayor did not hesitate to employ terminology increasingly popular on the left: "Sleep in peace, children of Vallières, innocent victims of the most terrible war that history has ever known; your memory and that of the sacrifice you made will remain forever engraved in our hearts."[47] The language, the imagery, the gestures certainly bespeak a familiarity with religious discourse, but Barrat was participating in the construction of a new kind of observance, the *culte du souvenir*, or religion of memory.

The same sort of transformation, an appropriation of existing discourse for the purposes of a distinctive new practice, can be found in a text from a traditionally Catholic area, the subprefecture of Pontivy in the Morbihan. Reporting on the debate over the monument site in the spring of 1919, the local newspaper noted that

those who are asking for the cemetery say that the monument to be built is the monument of the dead [*des morts*]: it is a pious tribute to those who fell for France's salvation; its place, therefore, is in the cemetery, shaded by cypresses and in a place completely given over to reflection. It is, they go on, the only suitable setting under the circumstances, for it is there that the families of the dead, of those whose last remains could not be found, will come to kneel down.[48]

Those advocating a more prominent site, on the other hand, while admitting that a monument so located would not be suitable for individual acts of mourning, argued that this *public* location "in the shadow of the church" would preserve the "pious character" of the monument.[49] Yet even if derived from a space sacralized by the church, this "piety" is directed toward the dead. Just as the kneeling may be for prayer or simply for "reflection" (*recueillement*), the monument records the "salvation" of France as a secular event, even if it implicitly recalls the sacrifice of Christ. In the course of this discursive shift, the names of the dead have acquired sacred status. When families objected to the prospect of seeing those names in a square occasionally disturbed by "street organs [and] . . . noisy political demonstrations," proponents of a public site replied that the names would not be inscribed there, but on a plaque in city hall. Commemoration, then, could draw equally and indifferently on the sacrality conferred by antagonistic systems of belief, secular republicanism and Catholicism.

system of beliefs

In Pontivy "the shadow of the church" represented a compromise not so much between the sacred and the profane, but between private mourning and public commemoration. Elsewhere too, sites close to the church, whether a *place* or a disused cemetery, represented a kind of middle ground. At the dedication of the monument in Montrichard (Loir-et-Cher), the mayor, Michard, described the monument, at the entrance to the old cemetery next to the church, as follows:

> In the shadow of the old church, in this cemetery where generations have kneeled down, in this Nantolium that was the cradle of Montrichard, it will be the place where parents and friends come to reflect and to commune with their beloved dead, those who sleep in the Argonne, in Flanders, in the Vosges, often in a place known only to God.
>
> At the intersection of the roads that lead to our city, it will be the first thing that passers-by and tourists see, and they will thereby naturally be inclined to meditate for a moment and address a devoted thought to our Dead.[50]

Note how even in its public, commemorative role, as a sign to travelers arriving in town, the monument promotes quiet *méditation*, although the mayor avoids the word "prayer." As opposed to those who consider that any public space irretrievably compromises the monument's funerary character, the mayor insists on the monument's larger role in shaping the space around it.

A judicious letter from a resident of Locminé (Morbihan) summarized the range of opinions concerning the monument site and offered the square in front of the church as a compromise. Having himself lost a family member in the war, the anonymous letter-writer understood the desire to build the monument in the cemetery, which would bring "at least the names of your sons" into the customary domain of private grief. He noted, however, that these names were already inscribed on family vaults and plaques, and he worried that the songs accompanying the patriotic ceremonies that would take place around the monument would create some awkwardness in the cemetery. Of the church square he wrote,

> Does this not offer the possibility of bringing everyone together? The monument might not be religious in style, perhaps, but it would be built in the shadow of the church, under the protection of the old bell tower; patriotic and commemorative ceremonies, which would be somewhat out of place in a cemetery, could easily take place around it, and the

children playing near the Pyramid would read there the names of their elders and relatives and would never forget them.[51]

An indelible, almost hackneyed sign of the local, the *clocher natal* also played a part in a considerably more secular reading of the monument site in Souesmes (Loir-et-Cher), the former cemetery adjoining the church. Here the *clocher* articulates the connection, in shared memory, between the commune and the nation: "this bell-tower, from which, on the second of August 1914, came the sounds of the tocsin calling an entire people to arms, fateful sounds of the alarm bell that stirred us to the depths of our hearts and opened, in the eyes of mothers, wives, and children a stream of tears that for many has not yet dried up."[52] In this construction the "shadow of the church" becomes a space as much of civic as of religious memories.

The letter-writer in Locminé took care not to claim any special insight into the siting issue. Yet by mentioning with deceptive casualness that, "like almost all families," his had lost a loved one in the war, the writer stakes his claim to the unique authority of the bereaved in the politics of commemoration. As a group only veterans approached the prestige of the families of the dead, and families were the first to be consulted, their grievances the most likely to be redressed. No matter how great their moral authority, nonetheless, families had to contend with other groups who implicitly (rarely explicitly) contested their right to speak on behalf of the whole community.

Legally, whether the commune or a private committee actually built it, and whatever the extent of its financial contribution to the project, in all cases the town council had the final say on the monument's location. As chairmen of their town councils, mayors often claimed to have discovered their constituents' preferences, sometimes very precisely, without saying exactly how.[53] In practice, however, councils had various means of surveying the views of their constituents. In larger towns, as we have seen in the cases of Commercy, Pontivy, and Lorient, the local press often provided a forum for the expression of public opinion, but such *enquêtes* rarely arrived at any consensus. Elsewhere, communities held various kinds of referenda, ranging from informal polls of contributors to more formal registries in the town hall, in the hope, not always realized, of arriving at a decision that all parties could respect.

Surveys or referenda almost always represented a response to some kind of dispute, to a situation in which no one site commanded enough support to convince the partisans of others. In Le Palais, on the island of Belle-Isle (Morbihan), the city council called a referendum when it could not itself agree on a site.[54] The *Journal de Pontivy*'s survey in Pontivy began at the request of collectors to whom contributors had expressed doubt or surprise about the committee's chosen site.[55] The newspaper solicited opinions only from contributors, although anyone could have written in. The newspaper dutifully reported, too, that some of its correspondents felt that families rather than contributors should be choosing the site.[56] Les Monthairons, in the Meuse, held a more tightly regulated referendum, asking each subscriber, presumably at the moment of making a pledge, to indicate in a register his or her choice between two sites, the station plaza and the town hall.[57] Like the survey of bereaved families in Brignoles, the Monthairons referendum produced an unambiguous result—the town hall in Les Monthairons, a public square in Brignoles—that the authorities were willing to accept. Not all surveys had such a happy outcome.

surveys

In his letter about the monument in Cléguérec, the former school principal Huet rejected the referendum organized to measure support for a public site:

> A register has been started by God knows who at the town hall for the signatures of those in favor of a monument to be built on the square. There are about 200 signatories. But this figure cannot mean that public opinion has shifted. A number of people did not sign; others signed because they had been told that the cemetery monument would have cost 1,000 francs more.
>
> Public opinion will not take these divisive maneuvers seriously, and the monument will be built in the cemetery, following promises that were made, following above all the feelings of virtually the entire population.[58]

Contrary to Huet's prediction, the town proceeded to build its monument on the public square, as decided by the town council.

In Ligny-en-Barrois (Meuse), a semiofficial committee, chaired by the mayor and including members of the town council as well as private citizens, asked the families of the dead for their preferences among four options for the monument site. Their unanimous choice of the place Notre-Dame, in front of the church, which the committee duly recommended to the town council, did not prevent a controversy so heated that it spilled over to electoral politics.[59] In the first instance, when the city council approved not only the site but a commercial design that the mayor, Husson, considered "unworthy of the dead,"[60] he and two of his colleagues resigned, then were reelected in a special election. One local newspaper denounced the use of the site issue as a "dishonest maneuver" against the mayor, but it also imagined that the dead, "in the glorious shade where they rest, must be saying to themselves, 'We did not give our lives, and we did not get rid of the Boches, so that the survivors, those whom we saved from German tyranny and oppression, could fight over our corpses.'"[61]

Less than two years later, in February 1923, the choice of a new site, a park a few blocks from the town center, prompted a poster campaign by the local chapter of the right-wing veterans' association, the Union Nationale des Combattants.[62] Although the veterans had failed, in a special subscription carried out with the town's approval, to raise the additional funds needed for the site they preferred, the poster cast the issue as one of principle: "Without any thought to politics, they rise in solemn protest against a decision that profoundly wounds their deepest feelings." Yet the fact that veterans *had* been consulted and had worked with the town made it difficult for them to occupy the moral high ground. The poster bespeaks the weakness of the UNC's position: it appropriates various familiar tropes, oblivious to their contradictions. The park, they charged, was both near "noisy festivities" and "poorly frequented at night"; one of their alternative proposals, rejected by the town because of poor accessibility, they called a "contemplative site, in the middle of town," a characterization that could also apply to the designated site.[63]

In March the *Républicain de l'est* reported that the debate had turned Ligny "topsy-turvy, or at least so one would think from all the posters covering its walls. We're not in the midst of a campaign—simply discussing the site of the war memorial." Published in Commercy, a little less than fifteen miles from Ligny, the *Républicain* used its position as outsider to issue both parties a mild reproof, concluding, "The memory of the dead demands a bit less noise."[64] Unlike an election campaign, it declared, a "purely local matter" like the monument site should not involve such ostensible political contestation. The veterans themselves had disclaimed any political motive, but in the wake of the mayor's earlier resignation, this was a difficult position to sustain. The press attention, in any case, put the town on notice that its peculiar mix of commemorative politics was making it look ridiculous. Mayor Husson undoubtedly used this notoriety to rally support on the council, and in October 1923 the monument was dedicated in the city park.

The actual politics of the siting decision took place at a level quite distinct, if not wholly disconnected, from the drama of electoral and poster campaigns. Although a minority on the council still opposed him, the mayor played his cards shrewdly, portraying himself as the reasonable and prudent spokesman for the town's interests. In the meeting of 10 February 1923 that decided the site, Husson gave a detailed summary of the veterans' abortive efforts to raise money for their preferred site. To choose among the remaining sites, he sought the views of the monument's designers, the ubiquitous Gaston Broquet and his architect partner, Hardelay. For the 1921 project the city had negotiated with Gourdon's Marbreries Générales, one of the leading marketers of mass-produced monuments, but now, for 55,000 francs instead of 40,000, the mayor had the prestige of an artist, and a "unique" work of art, on his side (fig. 5.2).[65]

Unsurprisingly, Broquet and Hardelay sided with their client, the mayor, and recommended the park as marginally but clearly the preferable site. Yet in the commemorative process this counted as neutral, expert opinion: no one could accuse two art professionals, both outsiders, of having political motives.[66]

FIGURE 5.2. War monument, Ligny-en-Barrois (Meuse). Photo: Author.

Meanwhile, the city government continued to act as the official guardian of the town's dead. At the end of February, virtually the same time the UNC posters went up, the town posted a list of the names to be inscribed on the monument, and asked families to send any additions or corrections by the end of March.[67] The implicit message was unmistakable: the city government had a monument in view, a genuine tribute to the dead; the veterans, only obstruction.

The appearance of the list of names at this time may only have been a co-incidence: the town had, just a month before, signed a contract for the monument (a contract for landscaping followed in July), and it had to supply the artist with the names to inscribe. Unwittingly or not, however, the list brought before the public, at a moment of some controversy, what remained for many the most powerful symbol of the whole commemorative enterprise. If anything the publication of names testifies to the mayor's confidence, for in controversial cases elsewhere partisans of particular sites were not above holding the names of their loved ones hostage to their goals.

In August 1920 the mayor of Sanary submitted to the prefect of the Var a letter from a father who requested that his son's name not appear on the monument, although he did not oppose its inscription on a plaque "in any other place." The mayor explained that the monument's site had not won unanimous support, "and it is to protest the majority's decision that the Dougnon family has sent me the enclosed letter." The mayor defended the site on the familiar grounds that it would keep the monument "constantly in view" and would enable it to serve as a reminder for "successive generations" of the commune's sacrifice.[68] Forwarding the dossier to the prefect, the subprefect of Toulon fully supported the mayor's view that individual opinions, "however worthy of respect they may be," could not take precedence over collective acts of commemoration. His reasoning echoed Viviani's rationale for legislation on the transmission of names, though in even more categorical terms: "The names of residents who were killed for their country belong to the country, and in a matter of such high importance, the personal opinions of private citizens, even those of the forebears of a war hero, cannot be taken into account." The prefect agreed, but suggested that M. Dougnon at least deserved an explanation for the choice of this site. He enclosed a letter of his own to Dougnon, repeating the language he had used just over a month before to the petitioner in Mons.[69]

In their letters, the subprefect and prefect used the word *étroit*, narrow, to describe M. Dougnon's motivation for withholding his son's name from the Sanary monument; the mayor called his reasoning *peu sérieux*, not serious. But the bereaved families who channeled their grief into protest hardly regarded the issue of monument siting as of little importance. Dougnon's letter to the mayor of Sanary is dry, formal, and correct: he pleaded only *convenance personnelle*, or simple propriety. We can only guess at the feelings that prompted his determination, but it could hardly have been easy for him to contemplate his son's absence from the communal tribute. This rejection bespeaks the anguish of those unable to reconcile the memory of an individual with the memories attached to places, but it goes further. It was not so much that memories of places, filled with the noise, conviviality, and hurly-burly of daily life, could contaminate Dougnon's memory of his son, as that for him those personal memories made external commemoration irrelevant, even repugnant.

Representatives of the state, as we have seen, usually sided with local officials in debates over monument sites, accepting their judgment as long as they had followed accepted procedures. Since such disputes often challenged the collectivity's basic competence to shape commemorative space, the state had little choice. Prefects valued harmony, of course, and thus often addressed disgruntled citizens in moderate language they hoped would appease them. But to question the authority of elected local councils over the communal space would have undermined the very principle of republican government, as well as the potential of commemorative culture to bolster it. Like all matters of local competence, however, that authority existed within tightly circumscribed limits, and when it came to another potentially divisive matter, religion, prefects often found themselves in the role not of mayors' supporters but of their adversaries. Moreover, the desire of some towns to put crosses on their monuments brought into play difficult issues of local self-definition. What was intended as consolation became a form of self-assertion, summoning up memories of division and marking the limits to, rather than perpetuating, the war's reintegration of observant Catholics into the national community.

For God and Country?

The religious aspects of commemorative culture make it particularly difficult to distinguish the local from the nonlocal, the community from the nation. Like issues of design and siting, efforts to endow monuments with a discernibly Christian character involved local as well as national concerns, and their dynamics, notably conflicts with prefects, took shape in the discursive space where those concerns intersected. The plaques with names of the parish war dead that can be found inside most village churches occupied their own space in commemorative culture, staking the church's claim to memory quietly, on the margins of more overtly political debates.[70] But a project for a monument topped by a cross, whatever the local factors from which it emerged, had a political significance immediately recognizable on the national stage in a way that one or another site did not. Moreover, although local officials often claimed that the vast majority of their constituents wanted crosses on monuments, religious symbols had an enormous potential to inflame preexisting local divisions. Those who, within a local community, took a vocal position on religious matters were usually appealing to a *portion* of their fellow citizens, not to all of them. Given the pejorative connotations of the word "politics" within commemorative culture, a debate over religion might seem less objectionable, since it at least touched on core beliefs about death, sacrifice, and eternal recompense. Thus we may suspect that, when they reached the level of public debate, conflicts over the religious versus secular dimensions of commemoration generally involved something else besides.

The role that signs of local religious devotion could play in national politics emerged in an article published in November 1920 in the Catholic newspaper *La croix*. According to the writer, Jean Guiraud,

These multiple crosses that mark, with almost total unanimity, the graves of all the cemeteries in France demonstrate that the entire nation wanted to see the cross on war monuments. A tiny minority of sectarians has sought to prevent this, and in order to proscribe the sacred sign has invoked the article of the law of Separation that prohibits its presence on public land. "Secular" [*laïques*] these monuments must be, that the country's gratitude might be "secular," that the tears of widows and orphans be "secular," that nothingness might replace immortality.[71]

The article came, however, not to criticize the government but to praise it. Guiraud reported that since the legislative elections of a year before, which had returned one of the largest right-wing majorities in the history of the Third

Republic, the minister of the interior had interpreted the law of separation more loosely, understanding that "[war] monuments being funerary, the ban on adding crosses to them is illegal." Guiraud urged prefects to adapt to the "new spirit" of the age, while telling the newspaper's readers that "the time has come to reconquer lost freedoms."

Yet although the new minister of the interior, Théodore Steeg, had indicated some flexibility in the matter, he never formally altered the policy that his predecessor, Jules Pams, had spelled out. In a circular to prefects of April 1919, which Guiraud roundly criticized, Pams interpreted the 1905 law of separation as permitting crosses on monuments in cemeteries, but not on public roads. The law banned religious emblems on "public monuments," with the exception of buildings serving religious functions, cemeteries, "funerary monuments" and museums.[72] Pams's instructions thus took a conservative approach to the question of whether war memorials could in fact be called "funerary," but that approach continued to guide prefects throughout the early twenties. The prefect of the Morbihan ordered crosses removed from monument designs in Néant in 1921 and Guer in 1922; both were planned for sites other than cemeteries.[73]

Observant Catholics cherished the fond hope that the wartime *union sacrée*, a supposed burial of political and religious differences in the interests of the war effort, could provide the basis for their reintegration into the national community after the war's end.[74] We will examine the discursive politics of the term in the next chapter; for now we may note that it remained popular on the right as a reminder of Catholics' participation in the war effort and in the right's triumph in the 1919 elections. Thus Guiraud's article, if not exactly the victory statement it appears to be, amounts to more than wishful thinking: it was in fact a call to battle. Some historians have criticized the short-lived leftist government that came to power in 1924 for reviving "a rather old-fashioned, dogmatic anti-clericalism" as a diversion from its other inadequacies.[75] Four years earlier, however, the Catholic right was already preparing an explicitly political, albeit modest, campaign of religious self-assertion. To have waited any longer would have risked the disappearance of the memories of the war on which the campaign was based.

The provisions of the law of separation had the effect of tightly interweaving the issue of religious emblems on monuments with that of location. Mayors were aware of this, and aware from the local press, which syndicated national titles like *La croix* and also carried news from surrounding communes, that a town could easily top its monument with a cross simply by building it in the cemetery. Prefects did not go looking for trouble: though his phrasing has a formulaic quality, the prefect of the Morbihan was summing up his policy with reasonable accuracy when he wrote the mayor of Guer, "Whatever my desire not to interfere with the intentions of the Guer town council, you will understand that my administration could not approve a project that contravenes the requirements of the law."[76]

When, on the other hand, the site conformed to the law, prefects did not interfere. In August 1920 residents of the village of St. Denis-sur-Loire, not far from Blois, sent a petition to the prefect protesting the town council's recent decision to build the monument in the cemetery, with a cross on top (fig. 5.3). The petitioners complained that they had contributed to the monument on the basis

FIGURE 5.3. War monument, St. Denis-sur-Loire (Loir-et-Cher). Photo: Author.

of a plan approved in May "that bore no religious emblem"; the council's more recent decision, they claimed, "violates freedom of conscience as well as the very conditions of the subscription in which we participated."[77] Asked to explain the situation, the mayor of St. Denis did not contest the petitioners' account, but said they represented only a small minority of subscribers (23 of 150); all the families of the dead approved of the cross. Since the remains of some of St. Denis's soldiers would eventually be buried in the cemetery, "the cross surmounting [the monument] will simply replace the thousands of crosses that mark the tombs of the front." The prefect refused to intervene, noting that the decision did not violate the law of separation.[78]

Thus the wish to top a monument with a cross did not in itself suffice to bring a town into conflict with the state. For that to happen the town had *in addition* to desire a public location for the monument, thus calling into question its "funerary" character. Disused cemeteries next to churches raised particular problems of definition: public or private? secular or religious? This is one area in which the ministerial interpretation of the law of separation does seem to have changed after 1920. To the mayor of Réguiny's query, in 1919, as to whether the former cemetery, "surrounded by walls, planted with shrubs, and to which either steps or gates will give access," constituted a public thoroughfare, the prefect of the Morbihan, Pierre Guillemaut, replied that the site "doubtless forms part of the commune's public domain." Thus he could not authorize a cross on the monument.[79] The town then decided to build the monument in the cemetery, but found space there lacking and returned, two years later, to the site next to the church. In a letter to the prefect the mayor said that the designer had changed the Catholic cross to a military decoration, the *croix de guerre*, but that the population still desired a confessional cross.[80] In another letter he claimed that the proposed site was

not strictly speaking a public square. Forming a terrace around the church, approximately 1.8 meters from the roads that surround it, it has no practical use. No fair or merchant has ever been installed there, no celebration is held there, and the people of the town, out of respect for the former cemetery, out of habit, and because of problems of access, spend no time there, except to pass through part of it in entering and leaving the church.

Like his counterpart in St. Denis, the mayor insisted on the importance of a cross to the townspeople, "especially the families of the dead, who, instead of distant graves, will find a religious emblem on the monument that will replace them."[81] Eventually the project was approved.

In a letter to another mayor a few weeks earlier, Prefect Guillemaut summarized the ministry's new interpretation of the law of separation. The law, the policy now held, did not prevent the placement of a religious emblem on a monument "in a disused cemetery or on private or public land, but visible and located near a public road, on the condition that the site of the monument be located *outside* the public thoroughfare, that is to say the streets, squares, or roads of the commune."[82] Hence the need, here in Ploërdut as in Réguiny, for a precise map, so that the prefect could decide whether the site conformed to the modified regulations; he found that it did. The complicated and somewhat legalistic instructions handed down from Paris actually had the effect of giving prefects more latitude, for it was they who had to determine a site's relation to the street. At least in the Morbihan, however, the prefect showed no inclination to use this authority for anticlerical purposes. Guillemaut himself went to inspect the planned site in Plouay, where the mayor, well-informed through the press about ministerial declarations, declared that the cross, "which the families of our dead insist on, was the determining factor." The commune got its way; the prefect characterized the Plouay monument, a calvary with poilus instead of saints (fig. 5.4) as a regional type and the site as an extension of the church.[83] Today it tends to be surrounded by parked cars.

Preserving order and tranquillity constituted every prefect's primary goal, for whatever its political views and objectives, no government wanted to act against a background of rural discontent. The case of Locminé, where we read such a sober discussion of site possibilities, provides an illuminating example of why prefects, especially in traditionally observant regions like Brittany, treated the issue with care. Locminé had some difficulty assembling the funds necessary for an elaborate Gourdon monument (fig. 5.5) and experienced the usual bureaucratic delays, but the voluminous prefectoral archives on the Locminé monument contain no trace of any dispute about a religious emblem.[84] The monument was erected, as our anonymous correspondent had proposed, in the place de l'Eglise. But the night before its dedication, in December 1921, unknown vandals, in the words of one press account, "amused themselves by profaning the memorial to the glory of our heroic Poilus, drawing a crude cross on one of its sides with a layer of paint. This infamous act aroused the indignation of the entire population, which was able to show its scorn to those responsible."[85] The incident acquired a certain notoriety. Over a year later, when Prefect Guillemaut informed the town of Allaire that the planned site of the monument there ruled out a cross, the mayor replied that the change might provoke resentment, and asked, "Are you not afraid that the Locminé incident might be repeated in Allaire?"[86]

What actually happened in Locminé? Again, however "heated" the initial discussion of the monument's site in 1918, it had not come to the prefect's attention prior to its dedication three years later.[87] Presumably, some members of the community, like the vandals in Genevoix's novel and their real-life counterparts in Levallois-Perret, wished to signal their opposition to a municipal decision. The article from the *Progrès du Morbihan* cited above concluded by saluting "the Republican municipality of Locminé" for its "most worthy tribute" to the dead. Any mayor in the Morbihan with clearly secular ("Republican") lean-

FIGURE 5.4. War monument, Plouay (Morbihan). Photo: Author.

ings would certainly have had some opponents, which may be why the paper referred to "vandals" in the plural.[88] The more right-wing *Journal de Pontivy*, on the other hand, treated the vandal as a single individual and emphasized that his identity was unknown. Even more significantly, the *Journal* did not describe the graffiti, saying only that the "imbecile" had "profaned the monument by scribbling over one of its sides." Although it agreed that "the *auteur* of this unspeakable act merits only the scorn of the public," it did not indicate that any-

FIGURE 5.5. War monument, Locminé (Morbihan). Photo: Author.

one had "shown" such scorn to those responsible.[89] This lack of specificity suggests that the *Journal de Pontivy* was resolutely avoiding the *Progrès*'s suggestion that the incident originated in a combination of confessional and local politics.

The *Journal*'s effort to conceal the central piece of information about
Locminé was obviously futile: Allaire is almost as far from Pontivy as it could
be within the confines of a single French department, and yet officials there had

clearly heard about the Locminé incident. The reminder from the mayor of Allaire, to which Guillemaut did not deign to reply, has a menacing undertone: look at what happens, he says, when the heavy hand of the state opposes local expressions of religious feeling. Yet all the evidence suggests that the contestation in Locminé did not involve the state at all but rather opposing factions within *local* politics, one of which simply appropriated the cross as an emblem. That the *Journal de Pontivy* avoided the religious implications of the incident, rather than seize on them for polemical purposes, suggests its awareness that the scrawl on the Locminé monument did not serve the Catholic cause. For, imbecile or not, the incident made clear that the cross could be a sign of division and not invariably of unity.

Descriptions of the cross as a universal symbol of mourning, or as a reminder of graves at the front, may or may not have been sincere, but they had a certain plausibility. As we saw in chapter 1, the wooden grave markers or *croix de bois* had become a common and resonant image of the battlefront well before Roland Dorgelès's popular novel of that name was published in 1919. When Vendôme decided to build its monument (fig. 4.45) not in the cemetery, as first planned, but on a public square, the mayor pointed out that the design included "the reproduction of a tomb at the front, that is to say a small wooden cross topped by a helmet." The prefect, however, agreed with him that such an image "does not constitute what one would call a religious emblem."[90] But when religion moved from the level of symbol to that of ritual, its significance as a political gesture became less ambiguous, less easy to conceal with commemorative rhetoric, and thus inevitably more provocative.

Just as the vast majority of communes and prefects sought to avoid outright conflict in the matter of monument emblems and locations, most also planned ceremonies to be as inclusive and uncontroversial as possible. In their most typical form, which we will examine in detail in the next chapter, ceremonies generally achieved the desired harmony. But the organization of some ceremonies did give rise to controversy. The usual arrangement placed a mass or religious service *before* the official ceremony, so that prefects and other dignitaries could plead scheduling as an excuse for skipping them. When mayors or curés violated this protocol, newspapers aligned with the center-left did not hesitate to take them to task. A report on the 1919 victory celebrations in Chissay (Loir-et-Cher), signed by "a horrified free-thinker," described his indignant refusal of the mayor's summons to a memorial mass. In Thenay the lay contingent—several councillors, the schoolteachers, and others—joined the procession to the cemetery as it left the church; at the cemetery, "a sacred but undisciplined union reigned during the ceremony."[91]

A particularly vicious conflict erupted over the observance of Armistice Day in Étain, a cantonal seat east of Verdun, in 1924. The volunteer marching band, "La Stainoise," refused to participate in the procession on the grounds that the president of the local veterans' association was organizing the ceremony as a religious, and hence political, "demonstration." The ceremony took place nonetheless, but lacked the customary "animation." In the cemetery the veterans' president, Webanck, accused the musicians of "cowardice" and called the mayor, who supported them, a hypocrite. The affair soon degenerated into bitter name-calling in the pages of the local newspaper. One letter from the musicians, noting that many of them were veterans, hints at a familiar difference of opinion transformed into political dispute: "We musicians wanted to make of November 11th a celebration of victory and not a festival of sadness and mourning. We will never begrudge our support in paying tribute to all our comrades who died for France, as long as it involves a disinterested demonstration."[92] Webanck of course denied any political intent.

In the Meuse, at least, musicians seem to have had something of a vocation as Republican troublemakers. Two years later, the left-leaning *Avenir de la Meuse* gave this account of the dedication of the monument in Béthelainville:

In the morning a mass was celebrated. Tendentious sermon by the curé, which prompted the words "Ta g..." [*Ta gueule*, or shut up] from one of the musicians. Obviously, this was hardly polite. But on such a solemn occasion, the dead of all beliefs who fell for the salvation of the same country should be respected, which means not offending the convictions of those in attendance.

In the afternoon, the same tendentious words from M. Schleiter [the conservative deputy and mayor of Verdun], which were hardly suitable coming from him. Forget it. Let's return to the pious tribute of the population to their dead.[93]

Although the sources do not record these "tendentious words," clearly someone discerned an attempt to attach a confessional character to a secular occasion, and, by extension, to the monument as well.

Their sketchiness notwithstanding, these descriptions allow us some insight into the stakes and dynamics of religious controversy in commemorative culture. First, a dispute over one aspect of commemoration almost inevitably opens up other issues, often displacing the initial focus of debate. In Étain the discussion quickly turned to the nature of commemoration itself and to the always volatile question of the legitimacy of the interlocutors. The musicians took particular umbrage at the word "cowardice" (*lâcheté*) as applied to them, and insisted on defending their war records. The phrase "hardly suitable coming from him" (*fort mal placées dans sa bouche*) in relation to Schleiter also seems to hint at a disputed war record, which calls into question the speaker's right to intervene in the commemorative process.

The contestation of both Schleiter's and Webanck's claims to speak on behalf of the community takes place at the point where local and national become inextricably linked. Schleiter represented Béthelainville in Parliament, but in the village, only a few miles from Verdun, a false step could easily cast him as an outsider. In Étain, Webanck was also a member of the town council, so in attacking the mayor he was perhaps playing out some long-standing political antagonism. In both places, however, the newspaper endorsed an identification of "politics" with external, disruptive forces that would disturb the presumed unity and concord of the "local." But claims to authority within the local community often, and in the postwar period more than ever before, rested on claimants' ties to groups outside it. Religious beliefs, political affiliations, and military service records converged within commemorative culture, the highly sensitive arena in which both existing and emergent political groups sought a new legitimacy in the articulation of memories of the war.

The very sensitivity of religion explains why prefects tried so hard to keep it out of their regulation of commemoration. Although committed secularists may have expected their support, both the administrative temperament and the nature of their duties inclined prefects to conciliation rather than confrontation. Lacking prefects' direct contact with local problems and public opinion, the central administration may have been less inclined to compromise on principle, but channels did exist through which local conflicts could have an effect on national policy. One of the most prominent was (and remains) the Conseil d'État or Council of State, the highest tribunal for resolving disputes of a primarily administrative nature. In 1922, after prolonged resistance and a ruling from the minister of the interior himself, the town council in Plumelec had bowed to regulations and replaced a cross planned for the monument with a carved urn and eternal flame. Three years later the prefect of the Morbihan received a letter from Plumelec's lay teacher complaining that, although the monument still stood across from the town hall, in a very public *place*, a cross had replaced the urn. In reply, the prefect informed him that in a ruling of 4 July 1924, the Conseil d'État had determined that *all* war monuments should be considered "funerary" in character, and thus could be decorated with crosses whatever their location.[94]

Both religious conflicts and the state's changing attitude toward them lend themselves to a variety of interpretations. Following Annette Becker's conception of commemoration as both part and continuation of a wartime religious revival,[95] we might well view the early controversies and the state's pre-1924 interpretation of the law of separation simply as vestiges of old conflicts that the war had essentially appeased. If prefects, with their more comprehensive local knowledge, responded to the new situation more quickly than did their superiors in Paris, eventually the state had no choice but to acknowledge the religious character of much postwar commemoration. Yet the church's presence on the national stage after the war owed as much to the astute tactics of its leaders as to the devotion of its followers. We saw in chapter 2 that finding financial support for the church's grandest contribution to the commemorative landscape, the major ossuaries, required a discursive flexibility extending well beyond the tropes of traditional Catholic piety.[96] To the extent that the war appeased secular-religious tensions, as it undoubtedly did, disputes over matters like crosses on monuments no longer seemed likely to threaten public order, the integrity of the Republic, or the separation of church and state.

The prefectoral attitude ultimately adopted as official policy represented a political calculation as much as a graceful adaptation to the spirit of the age. The war and its aftermath had made leniency more effective than stringent enforcement in avoiding public disputes over religion. But the war had not "miraculously" transformed religion from a divisive to a unifying force. Whether within communities or in the relations between localities and the state, French Catholicism had long been the focus and source of contention as well as of devotion. Its role as both local and universal sign epitomized the complexity of the relationship in postwar commemoration between local and national, the bereaved and the general public, veterans and noncombatants. But whatever the wishes of the community, in postwar France the cross and the mass always stood for more than simply local practices.

Making It Local

Communities that sought to imbed purely local signification in their monuments confronted a number of obstacles, not least, as we have seen, the controversial nature of some of the available symbols. Religious emblems and ceremonies, even if they commanded unanimity within a community, risked unfavorable attention from the state. Local artifacts without such a charge, however, posed another kind of problem: the possibility that state regulators might be unable to discern in them any commemorative significance at all.

In 1921 the town council of La Trinité-sur-Mer (Morbihan) approved a project for a monument supplied gratis by a long-time summer resident, the Paris sculptor Charles Rivaud. The monument (fig. 5.6) consisted of a menhir, a Neolithic stone marker typical of the region, on a base of carved blue Breton granite. Misreading the plan submitted to it, the review board rejected the design, finding that the monument "lacked harmony and, in addition, that it did not seem a good idea to put a megalith on a masonry base."[97] In his long and indignant defense of his project, Rivaud adduced not only his professional expertise, but also his long association with La Trinité, on the basis of which "I believe I have understood the feelings of the people of the area [*pays*] enough to be able to pay tribute to their dear departed." Rivaud had even made a special trip "in the middle of winter, to try to gather impressions at a moment

FIGURE 5.6. War monument, La Trinité-sur-Mer (Morbihan). Photo: Author.

when, in the absence of summer visitors [*baigneurs*] the area retains its true character."[98]

From his discussions with people "of the most diverse backgrounds," the artist had concluded that

The spirit of our dear departed could not fail to coincide with everything that our ancestors have left us, the old ones who with unflagging tenacity wrested fertile fields out of the granitic heath, built houses, protected from wind and rain, that appear to clutch the earth like the plants whose forms, for an artist observer, are so distinct and appropriate. We are here in the land of the menhirs—for me they are like an escutcheon that personifies the rock-like resistance of all our heroes; thus I grasped that it would be fitting to enshrine a menhir, to display it like a symbolic jewel and so to convey their imperishable presence in the memory of the generations to come.

For the same reason, Rivaud continued, he had selected a native material for the base, one that he and his son, a veteran, anticipated carving and polishing themselves. "To my knowledge," he added, "there will be very few monuments in France that will be executed from beginning to end with the same artistic attention [*souci*]."[99]

If Rivaud's letter thus concludes with art, he stakes his claim for the monument on a kind of organic—indeed, at the level of the "granitic," even preorganic—connection to the Breton *pays*. The monument embodies knowledge of two different kinds, professional and local, but given that neither Rivaud nor his son accepted any payment for the project, in this text the local predominates. Nor was Rivaud alone in emphasizing, as he did in a letter to the prefect not long before the commission's reconsideration of the project, the signifying value of native materials.[100] In an article in the newspaper *Ouest républicain* one Émile Gilles, vice president of the departmental committee on applied art, wrote of his pleasure that "this Breton stone, which has been too little used in the last few years, will soon receive more recognition." Among the works in granite cited in the article Gilles described the monument in Le Sourn (fig. 5.7) as "representing a menhir; on this megalith, lightly sketched in relief, will be a Poilu tossing a grenade; it's original, and it will be a departure from those mausoleums fabricated serially in certain Paris establishments, such as can be found in the four corners of France."[101] The Rivaud project for La Trinité duly won the commission's approval on its second submission. The project in Le Sourn, however, was approved without comment on the commission's first pass.[102]

Notwithstanding this adroit coupling of two distinct dichotomies, original/serial and local/national, the monument in Le Sourn had much in common with mass-produced "mausoleums." The designer of record, the local road inspector Allias, in requesting permission from his superiors to undertake this and another monument project described them as "undemanding [*peu importants*]." The blueprint for the sculpture is literally unauthored: it contains no signature and probably came either from a commercial supplier or from the contractor acting as a middleman.[103] Like so many other monuments, this one emerged from the capacity of an experienced local contractor—Vernery, mentioned in the *Ouest républicain* article—to weave elements of varying provenance into a coherent whole. Yet its use of local materials gave it the cachet of originality, which in this formulation is coterminous with its regional character.

Like Rivaud's understanding of local feelings and traditions, Vernery's expertise with local materials gave him an important advantage in securing

FIGURE 5.7. War monument, Le Sourn (Morbihan). Photo: Author.

monument commissions. Contractors like Vernery could endow a monument with two valued attributes at the same time: the artistic and the local. But the stage of the monument's life at which people like Vernery intervened, its physical construction, has left relatively few traces in the documentary record. Archival sources, so rich in documenting disputes surrounding a monument's conception, tend to break off at the signing of a contract, sometimes (not always) resuming at completion and the settling of accounts.[104] Yet those details that have survived, as well as the rare controversies that arose at this stage,[105] can tell us a great deal about the relationship between monuments' physical construction and the discursive construction of local spaces of commemoration.

As with any public works project, an unseemly delay could become a cause célèbre, even if it usually resulted from administrative wrangling beyond the control of a mayor or committee. In Six-Fours, in the Var, criticism over delays caused the entire monument committee to resign, leaving negotiations with the contractor to its successor, formed for the purpose.[106] Gourdon was so concerned about the slowness of bureaucratic procedures that one of his flyers offered advice to potential clients on how to work around them:

Many communes lose precious time waiting for a subsidy from the State, an additional subscription, and so on; this is a bad calculation, because to have at most 20% more, they must wait several months, during which time the prices go up by more than the sum they save.

Municipalities that do not wish to experience these delays must show some initiative: as soon as the choice is made and the contract written up, they should make an initial payment to lock in the contract. This payment can be made with the money gathered from a subscription (if it has not been deposited with the collector, for in such cases he will often refuse to release it until all the formalities are completed) or with any other available money; if funds are lacking a few people, whether or not members of a monument committee, could make the necessary advance. Then, with a definitive contract in hand, the contractor can work in all security while the formalities are being carried out.[107]

Payment in installments was standard for contracted projects of this kind, and indeed remains so—typically a third at the signing of a contract, a third on completion of a specified portion of the work, and the remainder on final acceptance.[108] But Gourdon's "advice" of course amounted to a way of ensuring prompt payment regardless of bureaucratic procedures, for which he did not hide his scorn.

Towns that followed such advice could find themselves in a bind. All communal expenditures required prefectoral approval, and when formalities dragged on, a town might be unable to make the second or third payments, in which case the contractor could halt work or refuse delivery. In August 1921 this happened to Locminé, which had made an unauthorized initial payment to Gourdon a year and a half earlier. As the mayor told the prefect, "The materials, the statue and the emblems were delivered to Locminé four months ago. There is only the installation to be done, but M. Gourdon will not carry it out because he has not been paid the last installment of 7,500 [francs]."[109] Fundamentally, of course, the problem involved finance, not the actual building of the monument. Indeed, by choosing a commercial supplier who used his own workers the town essentially ruled out both the benefits and the problems attendant on the use of local contractors. The mayor's reference to *les matériaux, la statue et les emblêmes* suggests a kind of quick-assemble approach, one familiar to Ikea customers today, except that the "materials" needed special equipment to manipulate. The sight of the components of a monument, just a few days' labor from completion but visibly not yet a monument, might well have embarrassed the municipality and fueled some of the discontent that exploded at the dedication. But one might also note that the people of Locminé did not actually witness the building of their monument: they saw only its assemblage, from parts shaped in the anonymity of a distant quarry.

Towns that made use of local artists or contractors, in contrast, encountered a spectrum of issues that had a bearing both on monuments' status and on their insertion into the community. The issue might be nothing more—or less—serious than the inability of an exacting stone-carver to find blocks of stone that fit his specifications. So, at least, Allias explained the four-year wait for the monument in Malguénac (Morbihan, fig. 5.8), the work of a sculptor-contractor team, Tardivel and the celebrated Vernery. Like any builder with a strong reputation and client base, Vernery apparently followed his own timetable, and Allias had not wished to pressure him.[110] More frequently, a town might have to deal with discontent over the way in which it awarded the monument contract. These issues had in common an unpredictable mix of personal quirks, standard procedures and notions of fairness, and claims about the character and durability of various materials: a mix, in other words, of quintessentially local knowledges refracted through a monument project.

Depending on the nature and cost of the project, the awarding of contracts for public works entailed one of three different procedures: *adjudication,* or competitive bidding; a contract *de gré à gré,* by mutual agreement; or direct control by the town, known as *en régie* construction. In principle, a 1918 law required a town to contract, through bidding or by mutual agreement, for all expenditures greater than 600 francs, but the "artistic" character of a monument project dispensed towns from seeking bids even when the size of the contract would normally have required them to do so.[111] After the prefectoral commission urged the commune of Méhers (Loir-et-Cher) to consult an *homme de l'art* about its monument, a Blois architect named Grenouillot agreed to prepare plans for a simple stela, but in a letter to the prefect he expressed his hope that the monument would "be treated as a work of art" and not put out for bids. The prefect replied that a *gré à gré* contract, the contractor to be chosen on the basis of competence without competitive bidding, could easily apply to the Méhers project.[112]

In a few towns in the Loir-et-Cher the lack of public bidding created discontent among contractors who felt deprived of potential work. A locksmith who had sought the contract for a fence surrounding the monument in Châtillon-sur-Cher claimed, for example, that the winning bidder had had access to privileged information. A similar protest came from a mason regarding the monu-

FIGURE 5.8. War monument, Malguénac (Morbihan). Photo: Author.

ment project in Molineuf. In both cases the prefect informed the petitioners that
the municipality had every right to forgo public bidding, and approved the contracts in question.[113] The fence at issue in Châtillon owed its exemption from
bidding not to any "artistic" status, which no one claimed for it, but to an estimated cost below the threshold at which the law required adjudication. Although often not built until some time after the monument's completion, fences
played an essential role in demarcating the space around a monument. They

served not to keep people out (I have yet to find an enclosure that locks) but to prevent, or at least make more difficult, certain kinds of defilement: "the barrier on either side of the monument," reads a note on the project in Langoëlan (Morbihan), "will keep the tombs from violation and will prevent animals from entering the cemetery."[114] In addition, some suppliers with a sense of the market offered a product line intended specifically for monuments, incorporating *croix de guerre*, laurel wreaths, and the like, and surviving fences show that they found a clientele. Towns could also adorn their fences with disarmed shell casings available from army surplus, thus lending them a certain symbolic weight.[115] Still, most probably followed the course of Châtillon's mayor, consulting a number of suppliers to find the best price.

Ensuring a certain professional standard in the construction of monuments themselves, however, was more problematic, and gave rise to a number of strategies. Subdividing the contract into a number of components, all of them, except perhaps the central element of the monument itself, costing less than 3,000 francs, allowed a town to avoid bidding and choose contractors it trusted. The town of Vignot, in the Meuse, signed three contracts for the construction of its fairly simple monument (fig. 5.9): for the stone and construction of the foundations steps, for the "pyramid" constituting the monument proper, and for a fence; only the monument itself exceeded 3,000 francs.[116] Such a method usually implied fairly minimal "design," of a mix-and-match variety. Alternatively, an extremely precise working drawing and specifications (*cahier des charges*) from an architect provided a measure of security for a community that, in the presence of several experienced contractors, felt obliged to seek competitive bids. The Blois architect Amiot supplied detailed renderings and estimates for his monument designs, but in 1921 a project of his in Contres evaluated at more than 20,000 francs attracted only one bidder. Two years later, however, an Amiot design for Couddes totaling just under 9,700 francs produced spirited bidding, and the town awarded contracts at discounts ranging from 2 to 16 percent under the estimates.[117]

In some communities competitive bidding had the air of a public ritual, a way of implanting a monument, whatever its origins, in its local setting, while also signaling its difference from ordinary public works projects. In Bubry (Morbihan) the adjudication of a complicated sculptural and architectural project (fig. 5.10) evaluated at over 26,000 francs attracted no bids at all, at which point the mayor sought the prefect's authorization to contract directly. With the cost estimate increased by over a third, the project went to the architect's habitual sculptor, Gaston Schweitzer, and to one of his usual contractors.[118] In light of the five-month delay it caused, the procedure seems pointless, but the mayor may have wished to make a show of his impartiality and willingness to employ local workers, and to establish publicly that the monument's status as a work of

FIGURE 5.9. War monument, Vignot (Meuse). Photo: Author.

art justified special procedures. Obviously the town had no choice but to meet the sculptor's price, since no one else could possibly have made the monument.

Schweitzer had reason to be grateful that Bubry divided its project into several contracts, leaving him with responsibility only for the actual sculpture. Elsewhere, particularly in major towns that chose monument designs by competition, the winning artist assumed the direction of the entire project and, with it, the burden of paying workers and assuring the timely completion of the

FIGURE 5.10. War monument, Bubry (Morbihan). Photo: Author.

monument. The contract between the seaside town of Hyères (Var) and a well-known Paris sculptor, Eric de Nussy, gave him a year to execute his design for the sum, fixed in the competition, of 65,000 francs. The contract imposed precise materials for the foundation, base, statue (Carrara marble), and fence, the use of local workers to union scale, all of them insured for workman's compensation by an approved company, and a rigorous standard of workmanship. After an initial payment of 15,000 francs, the artist was to receive nine monthly payments of 3,500 francs, subject to continual progress, with the balance to be paid on completion. De Nussy would be penalized at the rate of 500 francs per week for any delay.[119]

Emmanuel Ladmiral, the self-described *architecte-statuaire* who won the Vannes monument competition, found similar contract provisions unacceptable. The city was offering only 5 percent of the total contract, or 4,000 francs, as an initial payment, but Ladmiral, not being a contractor, had to pay substantial deposits to the quarry and bronze foundry as guarantees. He requested 12,000 francs and as a compromise received 8,000, with the promise that the city would pay the foundry directly once casting began.[120] The artist's relationship with the city never really improved. The mayor of Vannes, Charles Marin, anxious to dedicate the monument, repeatedly pressed Ladmiral to commit himself to a schedule, reproached him for delays the city found inexplicable, and on three occasions threatened to take legal action to compel him to begin or resume construction.[121] Ladmiral, for his part, blamed the delays on uncooperative contractors and unreasonable demands from the city, often pleading ill health and the city's rainy and chilly climate to excuse his failure to appear in Vannes on schedule.[122] Although the mayor had hoped for completion by Bastille Day 1923, on-site construction did not begin until the spring of 1924, and the monument was not dedicated until November 1925.

Many of Ladmiral's comments about contractors evince the helplessness of the outsider, and his lack of local knowledge clearly lay at the heart of his troubles with the Vannes project. This was, in a sense, the price of the prestige conferred by an open design competition, which Vannes had not limited, as many cities did, to artists born or residing in the department. But Ladmiral's discussions with the city focused on the linked issues of labor and materials that everywhere structured a monument's insertion into the community. Contractors did not simply carve the stone, they also supplied it, from quarries they owned or controlled. Ladmiral's problem, as he reported it, lay in finding a contractor with enough of the required stone to supply. The contract called for all parts of the monument, other than the bronze figure, the panels for the inscriptions of names, and the sidewalks, to be erected in Kersanton granite, a typically Breton material, known for its solidity, but expensive and in short supply. At one point Ladmiral wrote the mayor that the city would simply have to find another material, adding in exasperation, "For centuries many monuments have been built in France in stones other than granite, and I am not aware that they have shown premature signs of age or disrepair, even near the sea."[123] Having at length resolved the supply problem, the architect had difficulty finding a contractor who would carve the stone for the budgeted sum. After sacking his original, Paris-based contractor for dishonesty, Ladmiral quickly turned to one recommended by his contacts in Vannes, presumably a source of the reliable local workers he needed.[124]

The requirement in the Hyères contract that the artist use local labor reflects the sensitivities of local workers with regard even to minor construction projects. In Melrand (Morbihan), a *gré à gré* contract represented a way not so much of ensuring artistic quality but of protecting local labor. By introducing competition (*la concurrence*), the mayor told the town council, adjudication has the effect of "depriving local contractors and workers of the chance to do the work." In La Trinité, the mayor tried hard to maintain good feelings about the monument. Having persuaded a few citizens to donate small parcels of land to round out the monument site, the mayor wrote the prefect that he wanted to start construction right away, "because there is a bit of unemployment at the moment that this work will somewhat alleviate."[125]

For mayors and town councils recourse to their own workers mattered less for its performative dimension or the individual memories it would meld into commemoration than for its practical value. Mayors were politicians, on however small a scale, and if many aspects of monument construction risked controversy of the sort politicians dread, the use of local workers could only redound to their credit. Still, and notwithstanding its own practical tenor, it would be hard to miss the deeper signification of this statement from an assistant mayor of Carnac: "Faced with the constant increase in the cost of materials and labor, it is in the interest of our commune to carry out this project on its own, with workers from the area [pays], without the assistance of a contractor, and all the more so since local residents are making the materials available to us free of charge."[126] Through such methods Carnac managed to build a quite respectable monument (fig. 3.5) for a relatively modest 10,000 francs, but it did more than that. The image of townspeople digging up blocks of stone from their back gardens and carting them to the cemetery for use in a monument may seem improbable, but in Carnac, the premier megalithic site in France, it could have some basis in fact. With the abundant resources available to it, Carnac could give literal substance to the notion, represented symbolically by the menhirs used as monuments in La Trinité and Quiberon, of a monument emerging from the local soil. For a project so deeply embedded in regional tradition local labor represented less a convenience than an imperative.

Much of the detail about materials that runs through contracts had to do with the issue of solidity and durability. Towns in their role as clients wanted to make sure their monuments would last. The specifications for the monument in Montrichard (Loir-et-Cher) ran for two pages and included the following clause: "All materials will be of the first quality and will be used following the rules of art. The Monument will be in grainy Lavoux stone of first quality, free of any defect."[127] The contractor responsible for the monument in the nearby town of Chissay-en-Touraine assured the town that the industrial composite he used, "granilith granité," was guaranteed "against all weather conditions and frost" and did not deteriorate.[128] De Nussy's contract for the Hyères monument required *pierre de taille*, or ashlar, for the base and fence pilasters, and specified that it "come from the best beds of the Tourris quarries; it should respond to hammer blows with a very light sound, and should be free of any defect."[129]

Yet for many communities stone had a significance that went beyond the merely practical. The city of Vannes's reluctance to contemplate any material other than Kersanton (blue) granite recalls Gilles's article in *Ouest républicain* extolling its use in monuments. "We had here," the article said simply, "a local resource to use and to develop."[130] Towns did not need encouragement: from just after the war through the mid-twenties, many Breton contracts specified Kersanton granite.[131] Some communities were even prepared to contemplate nonstandard construction methods to permit the use of local materials. The estimate for the monument in Limerzel, in the southern part of the Morbihan, included this provision: "So that all this stone may be taken from local [*du pays*] quarries, according to the wishes of the town council, the contractor is authorized to build the body of the monument proper in two parts; the joint should be visible only on the sides, the front panel remaining in a single piece."[132] A monument in local stone would blend in with a commune's existing architecture and landscape, thus ensuring that the space of commemoration would be distinctly and recognizably local. At the same time, local materials almost inevitably required local craftsmen to work them, thus indelibly linking the monument, its environment, and regional traditions. For, as Gilles pointed out, and as the reputations of contractors like Vernery makes clear, each distinct type of stone required particular carving techniques. Thus the continued use of local granite helped renew specialized artisanal instruction.

The attachment to local materials was not, of course, limited to Brittany. The rules for the design competition in Commercy (Meuse) stated that, though it did not insist on any particular material, "the committee would be pleased to see artists using the marble-like Euville stone for all or part of the Monument." Naturally, all the designs submitted, including the winning project by Broquet, did use this local stone to some degree.[133] In a brief article in 1922 entitled simply "La pierre d'Euville," the editor of a local newspaper argued that the stone had an international reputation, noting its use in the place Stanislas in Nancy and the Belgian royal palace at Laeken. "And now, after the war," the article continued, "this fine Euville stone—which lasts forever—symbolizes the gratitude of the living toward the dead. A large number of monuments are being built all over, and all over the 'Meusian marble' can hold its own, in its beauty and durability, with the most sumptuous granites."[134] The monument in the Meuse town of Euville (fig. 4.35) stands, appropriately enough, as a particularly proud example of the stone-carver's art.

Requiem for an Elm Tree

In the end, of course, we can hope to recover only a small portion of those "fragmentary and withdrawn histories" that the spaces of commemoration seem to harbor. But an unusually detailed account of the construction of a Breton monument conveys something of the complex and multilayered process through which monuments became local artifacts. Part of *Ouest républicain*'s full

FIGURE 5.11. War monument, Cléguer (Morbihan). Photo: Author.

report on the dedication of the monument in Cléguer (fig. 5.11) in June 1922, the narrative records the impressions of the town secretary, a veteran called Vincent Gragnic. The Cléguer monument draws together many of the themes of this chapter: it was built by local labor, of Kersanton granite, and stands next to the church in a deconsecrated cemetery. Let Gragnic take up the tale:

The first cart was brought in on 22 March. On 24 March, the site was marked out by M. Kergaravat [a teacher and president of a local veterans' group]. Excavations began on Monday 27 March. On the 28th, a coffin was brought in to hold the large number of relics found in this corner of the former cemetery; they were immediately transported to the new cemetery. On Monday 3 April, M. Chenadec, a mason from Calan, arrived to begin work, and on Tuesday 4 April, the foundation cornerstone was laid in the presence of the rector, M. Kergaravat . . . [others], and Gragnic, secretary at the town hall. On Wednesday 5 April, eleven cars from the Bas Pont-Scorff neighborhood went to Gestel to take delivery of the monument, which reached the station by the 10:54 train. M. Adol, mayor of Cléguer, was present for the loading of the various parts of the monument, which was accomplished without incident, as was their transport into town. The cornerstone of the monument proper was laid on Thursday 6 April, and by sunset on Friday the 17th, all was in place. The fine elm next to which the monument was built was cut down on 8 April, and finally, on Monday 10 April, the fence at the entrance to the old cemetery, which had stood until that time, was demolished. The masons needed five days of hard work to carry out this project, for which seventeen cartloads of quarry stone were brought in.[135]

The monument, it becomes clear from this extraordinarily detailed account, conjoined several sets of memories and traditions. The bones of unknown ancestors, elevated to the status of "relics," remain, despite their transfer to the new communal cemetery, fixed to the site of their original interment. For those townspeople, now long gone, who grew up with the old cemetery, the monument's figure of a recumbent soldier might summon up memories not only of the war dead, but of earlier bearers of the names inscribed on the monument. A "fine elm tree," perhaps beloved, as many trees are, to people whose private memories it sheltered, gives way to an official representation of collective grief. The modest rituals that attend the process of construction, rehearsals for the highly organized solemnity of dedication, summon their own witnesses, undoubtedly including some casual passers-by.

What purpose, we may wonder, does such an account itself serve? Although highly unusual in its level of detail, this narrative contains little that could have been peculiar to Cléguer: the discovery of bones in a former cemetery, the mayor's anxious supervision of a monument's transport, the sudden transformation of a familiar site. In the four weeks of construction, moreover, few residents of this small town could have failed to observe its progress, so the article would hardly have been news to them. Only their memories make this distinctly Cléguer's story, and they are irretrievable except to our imaginations: the sweat pouring off the faces of the masons, the mud left by a sudden spring rainstorm, curious schoolchildren looking on, the half-smothered sighs of those who secretly felt that even in the familiar local granite, a monument represented a poor exchange for an elm tree.

Of course *Ouest républicain*, which described itself as the "newspaper of the agricultural and maritime populations of the Morbihan," in other words most of the department's inhabitants, had a readership much larger than the people of Cléguer. The issue of the newspaper in which this story appears also contains, on the front page, an account of the monument dedication on Groix, an island in the Golfe du Morbihan. The newspaper apparently assumed that all such ceremonies would interest the entire department. Dedication ceremonies, as we will see in the next chapter, encapsulated the moment at which local communities registered their memories as part of a larger history; press accounts, often drawn up by particular members of those communities, played a crucial role in that historical construction. But first the community had to put its collection of memories, and the monument that represented them, into its *own* history. The literal framing of the Cléguer account by an even more detailed, but much more familiar, narrative of the dedication, including a description of the "very fine monument" itself,[136] suggests that a monument's physical construction occupied a central place, both spatially and temporally, in this local history.

Every aspect of the construction of a monument, from its location to its materials to the workers who built it, attracted attention, often controversy, because the period of construction confronted members of a community for the first time with an actual object and space baldly claiming to represent their memories. Those responsible for building monuments contended, of course, that these memories concerned above all the dead to whom a town wished to pay tribute, as well as their surviving comrades and families. But no memory exists in isolation. Whether or not we accept Halbwachs's notion that only memories captured within a particular space survive, the process of building monuments makes clear that the representation of one set of memories always summons up other discourses and relationships. What one member of a community, perhaps even most, regarded as deserving local labor, familiar local stone, a cherished symbol, or the only possible site, might, as we have seen, strike another, with a different set of memories, as painfully unsuitable. Construction, therefore, meant negotiation at a number of levels, as different kinds of memories struggled to find a space in which they could coexist, and commemorative discourse began to displace the private memories that first gave it life. Both the singular moment of dedication, and the regular rituals to which the inaugural ceremony gave rise, sought to conceal the contestatory elements of that displacement by, in effect, celebrating it as a harmonious and, indeed, natural process. We already know, from Locminé and from the broken plaques in chapter 3, that they did not always succeed, for such struggles are never entirely resolved. In this sense the construction of a monument put into history a fragile, complex, and sometimes volatile mixture of memory and forgetting, a legacy that, beneath the sameness of its forms, ritual would only perpetuate.

6

DEDICATION

At the heart of arguably the most famous speech in American history lies a paradox: "But in a larger sense, we can not dedicate—we can not consecrate—we can not hallow—this ground. The brave men, living and dead, who struggled here, have consecrated it, far above our poor power to add or detract. The world will little note, nor long remember what we say here, but it can never forget what they did here." The opposition between speech and action in the Gettysburg Address recalls, as Garry Wills has observed, one of the basic dichotomies that have structured the funeral oration in the West from the moment of its invention in ancient Athens. Memory, Lincoln suggests, does not depend on words but flows spontaneously from actions that in themselves merit remembrance.[1] Indeed, writing of Pericles's funeral oration as rendered by Thucydides, Nicole Loraux notes that "the most famous of the speeches uses the logos against itself, disavowing it or at least declaring it to be superfluous from the outset."[2]

In Greek funeral orations, Loraux argues, the contrast between *logos* (speech) and *ergon* (action, deeds) sets up a structural dilemma that can be resolved only by recourse to the city itself, and the democratic system it embodies, as "the single, universal source of all logos."[3] Neither false modesty nor a simple rhetorical device, the logos/ergon dichotomy at once inscribes commemoration within a larger political purpose and casts the orator as simply a vehicle for reasserting its value. Yet the trope of reassertion may actually conceal considerable innovation, substantive as well as rhetorical. For Lincoln, the larger purpose of commemoration, "the great task remaining before us," was not victory but democratic self-government on the basis of absolute equality: less a reassertion, as Wills observes, than a reinterpretation of the founding principles of the United States.[4] The opposition between speech and action

memory as action

displaces this interpretive act onto the actions of the dead, naturalizing Lincoln's rereading of the Constitution as an inherent meaning sanctified by the soldiers of Gettysburg.

In postwar France, the trope of the inadequacy of speech perfectly suited the ceremonies that both summed up the process of monument construction and announced its completion. Speaking at a dedication ceremony in May 1923, André Maginot, who as both a celebrated war veteran and a prominent politician was often called upon to give such addresses, declared that "faced with the greatness of their [soldiers'] sacrifice speeches amount to little, and it is perhaps the silence of reflective hearts that would, in circumstances like these, constitute the most splendid and most moving tribute."[5] As, in a sense, representations of representations, dedication ceremonies (in French, *inaugurations*) played out all the ambivalence *about* representation that characterized commemoration from the beginning. This ambivalence took the form of "classic" dichotomies evoking not only the tradition of commemorating the dead but the orations that had always been a part of it. Casting doubt on the efficacy of speech authorized the orator's own intervention by situating it within the classical tradition of which the French had long claimed to be the inheritors.[6] On another level, the dichotomy between speech and action implicitly acknowledged the discourse of war experience, and in particular soldiers' and veterans' insistence that only their accounts of the war had any value.

As events involving various forms of stylized behavior—for the most part highly ordered but with some room for spontaneity—dedication ceremonies exhibit many of the features that social scientists have studied under two linked but separate rubrics, rituals and festivals. Anthropologists generally understand rituals as "formulaic patterns of symbolic action" that regulate situations of disorder, indeterminacy, or transition, whether arising in the normal course of the life cycle or brought on by a community's confrontation with external risk or change.[7] Rituals establish order and reassert tradition through a morphology that typically includes staging, repetition, role-playing, stylization, and the manipulation of symbols. In this sense, as the sociologist Frederick Bird has observed, "rituals are culturally transmitted codes and not particular patterns of behavior." Whereas ritual acts or processes consist of particular forms of behavior, the rituals they constitute are collective representations that operate at the level of culture.[8] Although individuals can exhibit ritualized behavior, in traditional societies rituals respond both to an authoritative designation and a collective belief in their efficacy. The expected outcome of a ritual, however, is usually complex and may not always be clearly stated.[9]

The sense that rituals tend to operate in situations of uncertainty or transition owes much to Arnold van Gennep's influential 1908 study *Les rites de passage*. Van Gennep argued that all such rituals involve, though not necessarily in equal measure, three phases: rites of separation, rites of transition—the famous liminal phase—and rites of incorporation or reaggregation.[10] Starting from van Gennep's schema, Victor Turner emphasized the creative, spontaneous character of the liminal phase, its tendency to generate an egalitarian *communitas* among ritual participants. This ritual bonding temporarily subverts the confining bonds of social structure in order to revitalize them, thus reaffirming their value.[11] Avner Ben-Amos and others believe that one can legitimately speak of funerary festivals, noting that funerals effect a kind of slippage between the sadness of mourning and the restoration of the social fabric.[12] The notion of a funerary festival coincides with van Gennep's understanding of both funerals and mourning in general as rites of passage: mourning, he writes, "is a transitional period for the survivors, and they enter it through rites of separation and emerge from it through rites of reintegration into society (rites of the lifting of mourning)."[13]

Ben-Amos has argued that the state funerals of the Third Republic "were both rites of passage and civic festivals,"[14] and dedication ceremonies also exemplify this combination. Lacking one of the crucial elements of the funeral, the body of the deceased, dedications emphasized even more than ordinary funeral rites the transition that survivors and the community as a whole must undergo.[15] This same absence also heightened the symbolic element of the ritual through a transfer of sacrality and, in theory at least, of emotion from bodies to the monument itself.[16] The very term *inauguration* calls attention to the initiatory aspects of the occasion, which in theory marks not only an end to a period of loss but the start of an era of both commemoration and reconstruction. The self-referentiality of the ceremonies also reminds the community that it is inventing a new ritual, one it has an obligation to repeat at regular intervals. Van Gennep observed that traditional societies attach special resonance to the first iteration of a new ritual; this may be because ritual depends so heavily on "tradition" that implanting new ones requires a strong level of acceptance from a particular community.[17] That this consecration involves festive rejoicing as well as ritual solemnity emerges from the concerts, fireworks, gymnastics displays, games, and races that followed many dedication ceremonies, as well as the de rigueur banquet.[18]

Like the process of funding, design, and construction they conclude, dedication ceremonies entail various kinds of politics they for the most part seek to mask or deny. At Gettysburg, for example, Lincoln not only cloaked a new reading of the Constitution in a rhetoric of tribute, he cast that sense of "government of the people, by the people, for the people" as the ultimate purpose of Union soldiers' deaths. Even apart from the specific political tenor of some speeches, the order of the ceremonies embodies a traditional ritual notion of reintegration and renewal. Ritual embraces the past as a source not only of

politics !

solace but of wisdom, as desirable in its own right, and suggests that if a return to the past is unattainable, communities should nonetheless seek to emulate the disrupted "order" that rituals themselves enact. To assert, as Jay Winter has done, that recourse to traditional forms in postwar monuments and commemoration has no political significance, that it results simply from the ability of such forms to "mediate bereavement," misses the way in which ritual *itself* is a political project.[19] For ritual implies, as it structurally analogizes the ideal society it seeks to restore, the "permanence and legitimacy of what are actually evanescent cultural constructs."[20]

In this respect the speeches that local and national politicians delivered at dedication ceremonies played a central, not a parenthetical, role in the commemorative process. Speeches usually closed the official program, giving orators the last word on the occasion's meaning and purpose. To the extent that monument dedications symbolically knit together a community sundered by war, officially initiating a new era, speakers had the opportunity to propose the terms on which that reaggregation would take place. Support for, or, more rarely, criticism of, the government of the day as carrying on (or not) the "work" of the dead had its place in these speeches, as topoi or formulas that varied only within certain limited parameters.[21] Yet even the most ostensibly apolitical speech often made manifest assumptions, latent within the ritual structure itself, about the proper relationships between local and national, individuals and communities, veterans and noncombatants, men and women.[22]

Commemorative rituals, then, can most fruitfully be studied as representations. Like monuments themselves, ceremonies convey meaning in many different ways, but they function most notably as idealizing representations of the communities they seek to shape. Ceremonies, that is, present the community to itself as unified and harmonious, hoping thereby to instill, at least at a subconscious level, allegiance to the social and political arrangements that have produced such harmony.[23] Rituals' invocation of tradition offers a ground for the memories they transform into commemoration, but in its public, collective dimension this process diverges sharply from personal grief. For in making certain positive values the basis for commemoration, rituals screen out ideas and images that might disrupt the process of reintegration, and thus promote forgetting. To the extent that they displace the personal with the abstract and general, commemorative rituals contain within them the seeds of irrelevance, of an eventual metamorphosis into what sociologists call "ritualism," or ritual forms emptied of emotional resonance.[24] If this is, as Lincoln implies ("the world will little note"), in some sense the expected outcome of ritual, it is not because of any "natural" process of fading memory.[25] For dedications and the rituals they inaugurate, the *11 novembre* or Armistice Day observances, depend for their vitality on the existence of memories they seek simultaneously to master and to purge. The dynamic of any commemorative ritual involves a constant tension between creating, preserving, and destroying memories: a ritual that endures for any length of time is more surprising, in other words, than one that simply disappears.

Patterns of Ceremony

Dedication ceremonies, and the annual Armistice Day rites to which they gave rise, had a number of sources, including earlier ceremonies and a number devised over the course of the war. In late October 1918, the *Journal de Pontivy* reminded its readers that in a few days, on the second of November,[26] people all over France would carry out their "annual pilgrimage" to the local cemetery, to remember not only deceased family members, "but above all our great war dead." At this point in the war very few soldiers, chiefly those who had died of their wounds in civilian hospitals, lay buried in their hometowns, and the paper mused on the large number who had no tombs at all. "No matter, beloved and glorious dead," the article concluded, "so vital to our national life, we will celebrate your immortal spirit, we will bring you our hopes and our regrets."[27] A few weeks after the All Souls' observance, which featured a speech in the cemetery by an officer from the local garrison, the same newspaper reported that a group of veterans was organizing a procession to the Pontivy cemetery at the conclusion of a Te Deum celebrating the armistice. The civil and military authorities, veterans of the Franco-Prussian War, Red Cross volunteers, and active soldiers in the area would march in honor of the dead, and anyone who wished could participate. Held on 17 November, the procession gathered an estimated 7,000 people, stopped at a monument to the Fédérés of 1790, where a chorus of the "Marseillaise" was sung, and concluded with speeches in honor of the dead by the mayor, a representative of the veterans, and the garrison commander. The mayor made a solemn vow to build a monument to the dead as soon as practicable.[28]

All Souls' visits to cemeteries did not, of course, originate during the Great War; they marked the annual peak of family visits to the cemetery that had become popular over the course of the nineteenth century.[29] To the symbolic practice of laying flowers at a loved one's grave, the war added a more abstract element, the remembrance of absent dead, and institutionalized it as a responsibility of the entire community. The wartime cemetery visit thus became a model for ceremonies honoring the dead, and its major components—the procession of officials, associations, and private mourners; music; and speeches— carried over into many postwar observances. On the eve of the *14 juillet* 1919, celebrated across the country as a festival of victory, with a triumphal parade in Paris, the town of Brignoles, in the Var, held a procession to the cemetery, where a veteran and the subprefect gave speeches. Reporting on this ceremony, the local newspaper declared that "from the largest to the smallest towns, every one, no matter how humble or obscure, has wanted to mark on this day its gratitude to the heroes of the great war."[30]

Yet the combination of festivity and commemoration did not always go smoothly. Brignoles itself may have chosen the thirteenth of July, which in 1919 conveniently fell on a Sunday, in order not to overshadow with memorial observances the festivities planned for the fourteenth: a *boules* contest, foot and bicycle races, a dance, and fireworks.[31] In one village in the Loir-et-Cher, official plans for the Fête de la Victoire omitted any tribute to the dead, so private citizens, including one father whose son was buried in the Somme, visited the cemetery on their own to lay flowers at the provisional war memorial. In nearby Vendôme, however, the city organized a procession to the cemetery, where British as well as French soldiers were buried, and a ceremony with a number of speeches in honor of the dead. A leftist newspaper reporting on these events criticized the village of St. Georges for ignoring its dead, excoriated the Clemenceau government for providing fireworks when the country needed coal, and questioned the sincerity of "reactionaries" in Vendôme who displayed the tricolor flag on the fourteenth.[32]

Communities seeking to dedicate their monuments in harmony had an additional model, however: the ceremonies marking the return of dead soldiers for burial in their hometowns. In April 1921, a delegation consisting of the mayor, city council, prefect, local prosecutors, schoolchildren, veterans, and others waited at the train station for the first such convoy to arrive in Draguignan, prefecture of the Var. A procession accompanied the three coffins first to the town hall, where a civil ceremony was held, then to the cathedral for a funeral mass, then to the cemetery for burial.[33] Although the ceremonies tended to focus on the lives and accomplishments of the dead being honored, civic leaders lost no opportunity to emphasize and to promote the collective aspect of the tribute.[34]

In 1922 the city of Draguignan arranged a single funeral for six soldiers whose remains had arrived separately; the mayor noted that "since collective grief always seems more intense than the grief of individuals, we are even more deeply moved before these six young heroes returning together to take their last rest among us."[35] Yet the public character of these funerals could cause strains that threatened to take on political dimensions. A newspaper in the Morbihan criticized both the town council (the mayor had recently died) and the local chapter of the Union Nationale des Combattants for not sending representatives to a funeral in a small town.[36] Perhaps to avoid such controversies, and lower the expectations of politicians, funerals in Brignoles normally took place without any speech-making at all.[37]

Occasions like All Souls' processions and soldiers' funerals offered more than simply formal precedents for monument inaugurations: they developed within the same conceptual framework and cast themselves as part of the same enterprise. On All Souls' Day 1920, the mayor of Brignoles, taking note of the many monuments going up all over the country, apologized for the delay in building the town's own monument, but expressed the hope that it would be completed soon.[38] In Draguignan in 1920 and 1921 a cenotaph was placed in the middle of the cemetery, surrounded by torches that the mayor referred to as "this flame of memory." Besides serving as the focus for All Souls' observances, the temporary monument, like monuments to the 1870 dead in larger towns and calvaries in Brittany, became the offering point for flowers and wreaths in memory of the dead.[39]

As the town of Ploërmel (Morbihan) buried four of its soldiers in July 1922, the mayor, Senator Guillois, also reflected on the connection between funerals and dedication ceremonies (the implicit referent of the word "Sunday," when most dedications were held):

Every Sunday, in large cities and humble *bourgades*, granite shafts, simple or grand, are erected on which the blessed names of the heroes fallen on fields of honor are inscribed against forgetfulness. We bring these valiant soldiers the greeting of France, testimony to our inalterable veneration, a pious duty toward the saviors of the world that we happily carry out. How much more moving in its simplicity is this ceremony, in which we celebrate as a family the return of four of our young friends to their native soil.[40]

The previous October, at Ploërmel's dedication of its own monument, Guillois had called attention to the participation of a number of invited guests in the ceremony: "It is because we must magnify our Martyrs that so many important people have come: your elected officials, your leaders, and your friends."[41] In the gap between these "important people" and the more familial funeral service lies one of the features that distinguished dedications from other kinds of ceremonies: quite simply, the presence of outsiders.

Towns that could look back on past dedications would have found many traces of politicians and other notables from outside the community. Indeed, few aspects of commemorative ceremonies attracted so much controversy as the invitation of dignitaries. At the 1900 dedication of Bar-le-Duc's monument to its 1870 war dead General André, the Dreyfusard minister of war, was greeted with derisive cries from the staunchly nationalist crowd. A right-wing newspaper reporting on the occasion characterized André's peroration, in which he declared that "patriotism is not the appanage of a few, but the innate virtue of all," as "threatening and hateful," and dismissed such applause as he received as the work of "a few dozen masons" organized by Raymond Poincaré, then an ambitious local deputy with progovernment leanings. Much of the

Écho de l'est's report on the occasion consisted of an unflattering description of André's physical appearance and career.[42]

The dedication of the 1870 monument in Blois nine years later seems to have passed more smoothly, the crowd cheering for, not against, the featured speaker, the minister of finance Georges Cochery. But one newspaper commented acidly that the presence of the minister and his "partisan volubility" had politicized "a day that should have remained above all a festival of memory and of patriotism." In any case, the newspaper wrote, "it wasn't a civvy (*un pékin*), it was a soldier who should have presided over the celebration"; for good measure it published a toast that an officer veteran of the Franco-Prussian War had not had the opportunity to deliver at the dedication.[43]

The Blois dedication contained most of the elements that would make up similar ceremonies a decade later: a memorial mass, the reception of a distinguished visitor at the station, a parade of local veterans groups and private associations, local and national politicians assembled on a dais, speeches, a reception at the Hôtel de Ville, and a banquet. It also featured one principal diversion, a shooting competition, that would have been unthinkable after the war.[44] But one additional aspect of the Blois dedication calls for consideration before we turn to the ceremonies themselves: the disparity between two newspapers' versions of the event. *L'avenir*, quoted above, described itself as a "political, Catholic, agrarian and commercial" daily; the words "Catholic" and "political" together convey the paper's conservatism, whereas the weekly *République de Loir-et-Cher* signaled its political allegiances in its title. Although *La République*, like *L'avenir*, commented unfavorably on the lack of any veterans' representative among the speakers, it muted its criticism by noting that veterans could at least take comfort in the crowd's respect for the flag. It called Cochery's language "noble" and his speech "moving," and characterized the day as "profoundly comforting."[45]

Both *L'avenir* and *La République* published full transcripts of Cochery's speech, and even the *Écho de l'est* had printed the remarks of the despised General André. After the war, however, newspapers, especially local weeklies with limited space, tended to become more selective, reprinting only speeches by their political allies.[46] In effect, newspapers thus reenacted politicians' use of the occasion to legitimate, and to cast as nonpartisan, the contingent political messages they were delivering. But the inevitable partiality of newspaper stories, the major source on dedication ceremonies, should be regarded not as a handicap but as a reminder that all such narratives are personal, subjective, and situated. Print and the masthead make obvious the kinds of expectations and resistances that shape any version of such an event.

Newspapers simply add another layer to the complex imbrication of the social and the political that make up commemorative rituals. City leaders simultaneously tried to cast their dedications as apolitical, viewed outsiders as representatives of "the political," and wanted such dignitaries present. These contradictory desires rested on the belief that ritual could contain "the political," and on the assumption that ritual's fundamental investment in continuity and tradition had no political implications. Much of the work that went into the organization, the unfolding, and the later narration of commemorative ceremonies was aimed at keeping the political duly confined.[47] At every step, however, the potential for contestation loomed.

Virtually all newspaper stories of any length commented on two aspects of the dedication day: the weather and the decorations put up for the occasion. In December 1921 one newspaper issued a gentle protest to the towns planning to dedicate monuments in the coming weeks, despite the cold and damp: "It is all very well to honor the dead, but we should not compromise the health of the living." In October 1925 the prefect of the Meuse sent a letter to all mayors asking them not to hold any dedications between 11 November and spring.[48] Most frequently the problem was rain, over which authorities obviously had little control. Even downpours like the one that greeted Raymond Poincaré in Neuvilly-en-Argonne in May 1926 did not stop ceremonies from taking place, although after a lightning strike in Plumelec (Morbihan) in April 1923 the dedication was moved indoors.[49] In general newspapers tried to put a positive spin on bad weather, noting the large size or good spirits of the crowd despite the rain, or commenting on its appropriateness, as in St. Rémy-la-Calonne (Meuse): "It was truly a day of mourning: the mourning of the gray sky, mourning of the rain, mourning as well, and above all, in our hearts." In Romorantin (Loir-et-Cher) the rain "hardly bothered anyone; it harmonized too well with the melancholy of the moment"; in Vins (Var) the dedication took place "in weather appropriate to the circumstance, that is to say a little sad."[50]

Decorations, however, had a greater significance, because they offered a point of comparison to other towns and reflected on the care and attention the community had devoted to planning the ceremony. Towns impressed visitors by metaphorically putting on their best; the French expression is *faire sa toilette*.[51] Typically, decorations consisted of greenery, bunting, streamers, and flags; the goal was both magnificence and "harmony." A newspaper reported that in Droué (Loir-et-Cher) the "harmonious ensemble testifies to the good taste of the inhabitants and the industry of the Comité des fêtes." Floral decorations were common as well, especially around the monument itself.[52] Some towns also put up temporary triumphal arches along the procession route; in Clermont-en-Argonne, they were fashioned from leaves. In Mauron, a cantonal seat in the Morbihan, one arch was topped with a ship representing the merchant marine and another with a "perfectly realized airplane," later echoed in a flyover by an air force officer whose brother had been killed in the war.[53]

When a junior minister arrived by ship at the island of Groix (Morbihan), he was greeted by tuna boats with tricolor bunting; in another port, on a slightly different note, ships flew their flags at half-staff.[54]

That communities intended decorations as a display of civic pride emerges most clearly in the banners that a number of Meuse communities displayed in the early twenties. Some featured patriotic texts, such as *Gloire à nos morts* and *Honneur à nos disparus*, but many simply welcomed either visitors in general (*Soyez les bienvenus*) or the guest of honor (*Gloire au sergent Maginot*).[55] It is difficult to believe that, beyond the odd incident of vandalism—in Josselin (Morbihan) poles with tricolor streamers were thrown into a canal—the simple matter of decorations could provoke controversy, but one monument committee chair found it necessary to defend them against possible criticism. Speaking at the dedication of the monument in Vaucouleurs (Meuse), M. Rauber mused, "Perhaps we will be reproached for having tarnished the purity of this commemoration by decorating our city with pennants and bunting; perhaps people will think that raising posts and hanging streamers will offend the families in mourning for their beloved dead. But is this ceremony of memory not also a festival of national pride?"[56] The key word here is *parer*, to decorate, with its feminizing connotations of makeup and ornament. When the town of Auray (Morbihan) dedicated its monument in the fall of 1925, a newspaper found that it had taken on its *parure des grandes fêtes*. Perhaps to mitigate this connotation, an account of the dedication in Demange-aux-Eaux (Meuse) paid tribute not only to the "admirable" floral decoration but to the "pious devotion" of the woman responsible, mother of two soldiers killed in the war.[57]

Decorations received so much press attention, then, because they both set the scene for the ceremony and provided a ready index to the work that had gone into organizing it. Except in major cities, dedications rarely involved much long-term planning: the uncertainties of construction schedules often prevented communities from dedicating their monuments at the symbolic moments, like the *14 juillet* and the *11 novembre*, that many desired.[58] By 1925 dedication ceremonies had become less frequent, especially in areas far from the war zone, but in the heyday of monument construction, roughly 1920–1922, towns had to be flexible if they wished to secure the participation of dignitaries. Neuville-sur-Ornain put off its dedication for nearly six weeks to accommodate the busy schedule of André Maginot, whose combination of a local parliamentary seat, ministerial rank, and a celebrated war record made him much in demand in the Meuse, perhaps even more than his patron, Poincaré. A veterans' leader in another Meuse village welcomed Maginot with an apology for the presumption of their invitation, but said, "Excuse us! For the Poilus of this district you alone seemed qualified to preside over this fête!"[59] Even on the date he suggested to Neuville, Maginot had another ceremony to attend; politicians and prefects frequently attended two in one day, and in August 1924 Poincaré attended four on a single Sunday.[60]

By the summer of 1922, when Ploërmel's mayor drew his comparison between dedications and funerals, the notion of the regularity of dedication ceremonies had itself become a trope. "Since every commune," wrote one Morbihan newspaper, "builds a monument in the heartfelt desire to demonstrate its gratitude to its valiant children who died on the field of honor, hardly a Sunday goes by in which a fine ceremony is not held to dedicate these imposing testimonies to public devotion."[61] By the late twenties, the form of the ritual held such currency that newspapers could abbreviate their accounts by referring to the "habitual rite" or the "habitual program."[62] Repetition is, of course, one of the standard attributes of ritual, but in the case of dedication ceremonies it served to magnify the event and to emphasize the shared purposes of the commemorative process. In building a monument, the subprefect of Commercy declared, the people of Houdelaincourt sought to perpetuate the memory of their own dead. "But you also realized that you were marking the place of your small city in the collective endeavor. You knew that your monument formed part of a splendid mosaic of the thousands and thousands of monuments through which the Nation communes in its love of those who sacrificed themselves for her."[63]

Of what, though, did this common ritual consist? A concise answer comes in a letter sent to the mayor of St. Maurice-sous-les-Côtes (Meuse) three days before the dedication of its monument in October 1921. Having spoken to the subprefect of Commercy, Toucas-Massillon, the monument's contractor passed along his advice. The band and the gymnastic society enlisted for the ceremony would meet the subprefect and other official guests at the entrance to the commune and lead them in procession to the monument, where the mayor would greet them. After the playing of the "Marseillaise," the mayor would open the series of speeches with "greetings—memories of the dead heroes and a word on each of the civilian victims—etc. etc.," and would then officially entrust the monument to the town. Visiting politicians would speak next, culminating in the major address by Toucas-Massillon. Music from the band would precede the awarding of posthumous medals, which would lead into songs by schoolchildren. The formal program complete, the band would lead the participants back to the town hall, where a reception would be held, followed by a banquet concluding with brief toasts.[64] To judge from the account in the *Républicain de l'est*, the actual ceremony closely followed this script, but it also included two elements omitted from the letter, one classic—the roll call of the town's dead—the other more unusual, a speech by the mayor's son in the name of the youth of St. Maurice. The newspaper also noted the village's "very festive atmosphere that contrasted with its ruins"; St. Maurice had not yet fully repaired the damage from wartime bombardment.[65]

The "habitual rite," of course, encompassed a range of variations, depending on the size of the commune, the number and schedule of invited guests, the location of the monument, and so on. Yet to enumerate all the possible permutations of the dedication ritual would risk obscuring the elements that most ceremonies had in common, and their larger meaning. Let us, then, follow the course of one ceremony, a composite drawn from large and small towns alike. The principal features of the St. Maurice ceremony—formal greetings, music, a procession, the role of schoolchildren, the reading of names, and speeches—provide a fitting starting point. But several elements missing from St. Maurice, notably veterans' groups and religious observances, also had their place in the standard ritual.[66]

In major towns, the ritual often began on the eve of the dedication itself, with a *veillée* around the monument. Long a part of French funerary ritual, the *veillée* or wake traditionally brought together the deceased's family and friends to watch over the soul's initial passage to the afterlife. In our town, the watchers might be veterans, recalling "the troubling reality of an evening's troop rotation, as the canons fell silent." Some soldiers from the local garrison might also participate, or a troop of boy scouts demonstrating their manliness and their patriotism.[67] Thomas Kselman observes that the folk *veillée* "renewed the solidarity of relatives and neighbors in the face of their loss,"[68] and it undoubtedly served this purpose around monuments as well. At the same time the *veillée* marked the monument not only as a site of mourning but as substitute tomb, imbuing it with the sacrality of the dead. Such *veillées* tended to be held around monuments in public squares; on the consecrated ground of cemeteries they would have been superfluous.

On Sunday morning, as villagers hang the last streamers or bits of greenery from their houses, visitors from the surrounding communes, perhaps including the band or gymnastic society from the cantonal seat, arrive by car, bus, or even special train.[69] In towns, police put up barriers blocking off the procession route and the area around the monument, where workers might be hammering in a few extra supports on the speakers' platform, anxious to prevent an embarrassing collapse.[70] Some communities, replicating an old festive custom, distribute bread or the wartime equivalent, bread coupons, to the poor.[71] It being Sunday, the crowd heads first to church, where the curé or a visiting cleric, usually a veteran, celebrates a mass in memory of the dead. If we are in Brittany, the mayor and other local officials will first have greeted the visiting dignitaries, then accompanied them to church. Elsewhere, the church service precedes the formal welcome, though the resemblance of the ceremony to a funeral rather than to Sunday mass swells the congregation to capacity.[72] At the conclusion of the service, the crowd proceeds to the monument, where the curé blesses it with a brief prayer. Perhaps, if the monument is in town, the procession will continue on to the cemetery. In larger towns in some parts of the country, we would have our choice among Catholic, Protestant, and Jewish services, followed by an ecumenical blessing by all three clergymen in succession.[73] As in St. Maurice, however, the ceremony may be entirely secular.

As we saw in the previous chapter, the admixture of religion and politics could prove volatile in the commemorative process. The scheduling of religious ceremonies reflected the desire of all parties to avoid offending sensibilities. Public officials could attend religious services if they wished, either out of respect for the convictions of their constituents or out of genuine faith, but keeping the religious and civic ceremonies separate spared officials the strain of an unwelcome obligation. Obviously practices differed greatly from department to department. Alphonse Rio, as undersecretary for the merchant marine the only Morbihan politician in the cabinet, and most Morbihan deputies routinely attended religious as well as secular portions of the ceremony. At mass they heard priests like the abbé Le Trionnaire, in Brech, celebrate the monument as a symbol of "union," the cross as fitting "because every single man whose memory [the monument] recalls lived under its sign." Significantly, a newspaper report on the ceremony in Brech called it "a day of *Union sacrée*."[74]

The church knew that it had nothing to gain from belligerency. Even as staunchly Catholic a newspaper as *Le ploërmelais* was happy to paint a picture of "Religion and the Fatherland giving each other a hand to spread their charms, their prayers, and their smiles."[75] In the Var, a far less observant department, a curé who blessed the official ceremony was clearly appealing to his secularist listeners when he extolled "in moving terms those who died for the victory of right."[76] A dedication offered Catholic clergy a chance to conflate the church's own version of the sacred with that of the Republic: readily verifiable claims about the piety of a select group of soldiers, or banalities on the theme "They loved God and Country!" were more likely to secure that connection than incendiary anti-republican homilies.[77] But in conceding to *la Patrie* its own sacrality, the implication of distinct religious and secular ceremonies, the church and its adherents effectively acknowledged that the battle of the separation could not be refought. Catholics seem to have grasped that, as Sally Moore and Barbara Myerhoff put it, "if sacred is understood in the sense of 'unquestionable' and traditionalizing, then something may be sacred, yet not religious."[78] Sharing the war dead with the Republic was the best Catholics could hope for, yet the possibility of appropriating that particular sacrality, if skillfully handled, made earlier struggles irrelevant.

Let us return, then, to our dedication ceremony. It is now late morning, and with the religious services ended, the community now prepares to welcome the most important dignitaries. In a larger town, this may mean proceeding to the train station; elsewhere, the mayor, town council, and others await the arrival of an automobile, still something of an event in rural France in the early twenties. Whatever the actual site of this meeting, the wording of the contractor's memo to the mayor of St. Maurice specifies its conceptual location: "The subprefect and the external authorities [*étrangères à la Commune*] will gather at the edge of the communal territory [*à l'entrée du Pays*], on the Billy road."[79] Symbolically, the encounter with distinguished guests takes place at a point of demarcation, a boundary—statutory or imagined. At this boundary the community's "social space," to use Henri Lefebvre's term, begins, and with it "the relationships established by boundaries."[80]

The greeting ceremony both asserts the authority of local officials within their territory and acknowledges the higher authority, circumscribing their own, that the guests represent. In an echo of the customary gendered tribute to masculine authority, an official, particularly one as distinguished as Poincaré, the prime minister and former president of France, may receive a bouquet of flowers from a young girl.[81] Implicitly associating the visitor with the floral decorations visible on the procession route, the work of the feminine art of *parure*, the bouquet effects a kind of domestication, initiating the guest into the village community. At the same time the gesture recalls tributes paid in literature and memory to victorious or simply valiant soldiers. Yet if the minister or other official represents the nation that gives value to soldiers' deaths, that nation would not exist without the latter's sacrifice, which the flowers gracefully, if not entirely accurately, construe as free and voluntary.

What happens now depends in part on the schedule of the newly welcomed official, the one invited to serve as *president* of the dedication, although this is an honorific title generally bestowed on the person we might call the keynote speaker. If he has another ceremony to attend later, or if he arrived earlier and attended the religious service, we might now proceed directly to the dedication. A more elaborately arranged program, however, may take advantage of the prefect's or minister's presence to stage a kind of ancillary ritual in the hour or so before lunch. The minister might confer an official flag on a veterans' group, award medals to recently discharged soldiers or survivors, or give out certificates honoring mothers of large families.[82] In the Meuse in the mid-twenties, where the construction of a monument often marked the last stage in the reconstruction of a bombarded village, the guest might tour, and perhaps open, the rebuilt town hall and school.[83]

These activities remind us, and the rest of those in attendance, that the aims and functions of commemorative rituals go beyond comforting the bereaved and remembering the dead: like all rituals, they also celebrate continuity, reaffirm values cast as "traditional," and look to the future. The *médaille de la famille française*, for example, awarded in several categories to mothers who had produced five or more children, drew not only on fears of demographic decline that the war had accentuated, but also on the wide cultural resonance of reproduction and domesticity as norms for women after the war.[84] Rather than recognize women who had taken on unusual roles during the war, the state honored those exemplifying values of continuity, occluding the very real social upheaval of wartime and, at least symbolically, neutralizing its potentially subversive implications. To link such medals to the commemoration of the dead not only reciprocally transferred prestige between the categories of soldier and mother, it also reenergized the discursive basis for the link, the notion of "sacrifice" for one's country. On another level, to award military decorations on the day of a dedication constructs as "natural" a connection between remembrance and a code of military values—obedience, patriotism, unreasoning courage—that had provoked considerable hostility among soldiers and veterans during and after the war.[85]

At midday, if we have heeded the notices in the local press and obtained tickets in advance, we can follow the dignitaries, veterans, and other subscribers to a café, hotel, or school common room for a banquet. In most towns the veterans took charge of organizing the banquet, at a cost of perhaps ten francs per person, though the town would be expected to pick up the tab for invited guests.[86] One newspaper described the luncheon in La Trinité-sur-Mer (Morbihan) as "a copious and succulent menu"; the banquet in Montiers-sur-Saulx (Meuse) included "saumon sauce verte, poulet Marengo, flageolets maître d'hôtel, gigot d'agneau," as well as hors d'oeuvres, salad, and dessert.[87] The toasts at the end of the banquet provide one of the few sanctioned moments on the commemorative program for unabashedly political discourse. The mayor and other local officials bring up the improvement projects (sewage, electrification, street paving) they have postponed while completing the monument, and request government assistance; members of Parliament laud the commune's efforts; the prefect or minister present promises his support, then moves on to praise the government's current policies in warmer terms than he could use in front of a monument.

The banquet's combination of conviviality and politics had a precedent in the local commemorative banquet of the Third Republic, a pause in a day of solemnity and distraction in which like-minded citizens came together to celebrate the virtues of a political system they had helped to establish. Such gatherings often took place on commemorative holidays like the *14 juillet*, and the form itself memorialized the oppositional gathering of the July Monarchy and Second Empire. But the banquet always teetered uneasily between the poles of civic ritual and political meeting and, after the turn of the century, tended more toward the latter.[88]

In 1925 a dissident veterans' group in Bar-le-Duc issued a poster that, while attacking the whole dedication, focused on the banquet, which it called "the inheritors' funeral meal!" and "the feast of the profiteers of glory." The poster reproduced the entire elaborate menu and asked sarcastically, "To celebrate the dead, must the living die of hunger?"[89] Recognizing that the provocative aspect of the occasion had to do as much with politics as with cuisine, some banquet organizers banned toasts. Anxious not to cause offense, Laheycourt (Meuse) included members of bereaved families in its banquet; Poincaré asked that the meals to which he was invited not be called "banquets" at all.[90] Yet if the banquet's hybrid character resulted from not only its own past but current sensibilities, it also embodied the structural duality of the dedication itself, part commemorative ritual, part festival.

As lunch concludes, officials and members of the community assemble for the procession that will begin the dedication proper.[91] Except in very small towns, the order of the procession required more attention and planning than any other aspect of the ceremony, for the risk of inadvertent omissions and consequent hurt feelings ran high. Some towns published an order of procession in the local press, but private correspondence and face-to-face meetings were probably more effective in avoiding misunderstandings.[92]

The order of the procession varies from place to place. Like any parade, it may well begin with the local band. Then come the children from the communal schools, veterans' groups, local associations, the families of the dead, and the town council accompanying the visiting dignitaries and other officials.[93] The families of the dead may have a special place in the procession; in any case, they usually find special seating awaiting them on or near the platform. Groups carry flags or wear distinctive dress or emblems to identify themselves; notably, the procession usually allocates distinct positions to the different veterans' associations.[94] Almost everywhere, the population at large joins the rear of the procession.

Certain aspects of the procession stand out. First, the lack of prominence of the official party: the mayor, town council, and distinguished guests sometimes come last (until the crowd joins the procession), almost never come first, and usually end up in the middle. Second, the importance of children: schoolchildren, and sometimes offspring of the dead (*pupilles de la nation*) usually come directly behind the band, or else they bring the procession to a close.[95] Third, the "impressive spectacle" of groups whose association with the war seems tenuous at best: the Union Sportive in Pignans, the Cercle le Reveil Social in St. Maximin, both in the Var, firemen in St. Julien-le-Chédon (Loir-et-Cher), gymnasts almost everywhere. The mayor of Rilly-sur-Loire even invited a band and a gymnasts' group from a neighboring town, "to give the ceremony more *éclat* in a commune that has no associations of its own."[96]

The procession, then, emphasizes horizontal affiliations, whether of age or of affinity, rather than vertical hierarchies, picturing the community not as a set of authority relations, nor even of professional connections, but as a network of willed sociality. The various components of the procession thus form a living, mobile summary of the kinds of activities that transform, in Lefebvre's terms, the passively diagrammatic "representations of space" into a "representational space," one "directly *lived* through its associated images and symbols." The procession, in its multigenerational character, also stands for the community's continuity over time; Lefebvre observes that time and space can be grasped as social realities only in terms of each other.[97] We cannot forget, of course, the special purpose of this procession. The band may be playing Chopin's funeral march; the flags are fringed in black; the somber families and the mutualists recall an era when mutual aid meant care for the sick and the provision of a decent burial, before commercial funeral directors began their slow incursion into the countryside.[98] On this level, and with the reception of guests at the symbolic "boundary" of the commune, the procession claims kinship with traditional rites of passage, which according to van Gennep have their roots in ancient threshold rituals and thus often enact a passage through space.[99]

Yet if the procession represents a community in mourning, it represents first of all a community, one looking simultaneously to the past and to the future. Thus the importance of children, the community's future, for the ceremony seeks above all to shape their memories, and thereby to incorporate this occasion into the community's conception of itself. But the ceremony also reaffirms the link between a community and the larger polity as the basis of its fundamental allegiances. For the children, the respect accorded the bewhiskered guests wearing decorations and sashes drives home this connection much more concretely than the abstract notion of dying for one's country. Their floral tributes cast man-made political bonds as a kind of inherence, as natural as the generational succession the children themselves represent. The power of the state underlies the whole proceeding, yet the procession plays down the state's role in shaping social categories, referring to it only obliquely, for example in the division of children according to the type of school, public or religious, they attend.[100] Thus authority presents itself in the midst of society, a benign configuration eminently suited to a democracy. Like the state funerals of the Third Republic, these processions elide the distinction between participants and onlookers, and as the crowd, often so called in contemporary accounts, joins the dedication procession, that distinction, for the time of the ceremony at least, functionally disappears.[101]

As the procession arrives at the monument, the officials, dignitaries, and, sometimes, the families of the dead take their seats on the platform; in larger towns, the various groups may have assigned places in which to stand, and the crowd disposes itself as close to the monument as possible.[102] The ceremony usually begins with music, perhaps a dirge played by the band, perhaps the

past + future

"Marseillaise," although just as frequently the national anthem comes at the end.[103] The mayor, or the chairman of the monument committee, offers a few words of welcome, and then entrusts the new monument to the community. If we are looking for the moment of dedication, this comes close: newspaper accounts record few actual unveilings of monuments, and those that do occur do not always have much ritual significance. In Mont-près-Chambord (Loir-et-Cher) the unveiling takes place almost casually, as the procession arrives at the monument.[104] In any case, the ritual center of the ceremony involves the monument not directly but by reference: the calling of the names of the dead.

Not a simple enumeration, the reading of the names inscribed on the monument has a staged quality, involving at least two people, often more. The first, usually the mayor, but sometimes a veteran or a teacher, reads out the names; in response to each name, a veteran, a schoolchild, or even the crowd as a whole calls out "Mort pour la France." In certain communities the staging is even more elaborate: in Ville-en-Woëvre (Meuse), schoolchildren as a group answer "Mort pour la France" to each of the twenty-four names, and at each one, a child steps forward and places a bouquet of flowers at the foot of the monument.[105] The personalization of this ritual moment, especially when it involves children, attenuates the coercive bond between the state and the soldier by displacing it onto the more familiar and "natural" relations among members of a face-to-face community. This is especially significant given that the phrase "Mort pour la France," in addition to its ritual function, had an intensely practical one as well. Bounded by the dates of the conflict (extended through October 1919) and certified by official service records, the designation "Mort pour la France" was required for eligible survivors to obtain pensions and other benefits from the state.

In some cities, the reading takes considerable time—800 names in Vannes, 530 in Verdun—but even in smaller communities, this moment by common consent distills the essence of the ceremony. The crowd remains bareheaded throughout, silent but for the muffled sobs of mothers, widows, sisters, and perhaps sons and brothers as well.[106] For the *appel des morts* combines the emotive power of the name with the power of ritual repetition: the names change—although newspapers sometimes single out families who lost several brothers—but the response remains the same. The *appel* conjoins in a single ritual procedure van Gennep's three stages of the rite of passage: separation, transition, and reaggregation. It is at once a personal farewell (separation), a passage (transition) from individual memories to collective remembrance, and an affirmation of the continuity (reaggregation) inherent in a community's shared responsibility to remember. The community "inaugurates" not simply a monument but a set of practices centering on it, and "dedicates" itself to their perpetuation.

The *appel des morts* gives way to tributes from the living: often, schoolchildren recite patriotic poems or sing hymns.[107] This may also be the moment for the laying of wreaths or flowers, again by schoolchildren or by some of the groups who marched in the procession.[108] These gestures of tribute confirm the transfer of sacrality from the dead to their new avatar, the monument. Children's participation, of course, points to the pedagogical function of ritual and of the monument itself. But at the same time children's performance also offers both an image and a promise of timelessness. The continuing reproduction of memory and of traditional values thus becomes as "natural" as children's own presence in the community.[109]

symbol of child

Songs and readings provide a buffer between the solemnity and emotion of the *appel* and the more stylized formulas of political speeches, which come next. Speakers may include representatives of local veterans' groups, but most come from the ranks of invited guests, the order of their remarks usually following an ascending hierarchy of elected office: first the local member of the departmental general council, then a deputy or senator, then the prefect, and finally a minister.[110] We will consider these speeches in detail in subsequent sections; for the moment it suffices to note that the lengthy oratorical portion of the ceremony continues the transfer of sacrality operating throughout. In "monumental space," as Lefebvre has put it, the sacred and the political symbolically "exchange . . . the attributes of power; in this way the authority of the sacred and the sacred aspect of authority are transferred back and forth, mutually reinforcing one another in the process."[111]

After the last speech, the ceremony concludes with a wreath-laying, the playing of the "Marseillaise," or a simple word from the mayor. Yet the crowd may wish to take one last opportunity to insert itself in the ritual. At the end of the ceremony, children, members of other groups, and the general public disperse by way of the monument, perhaps laying flowers. In Salbris (Loir-et-Cher), "the crowd files slowly past the monument, casting a long look at this poilu, moving symbol of the sufferings the soldiers of the Great War endured, symbol of the horrible death that pitilessly mowed down so many young lives." In Mont-près-Chambord "the crowd, under a radiant sun, files past the monument and there lays flowers of memory"; the tone is different but the process the same.[112] The townspeople are taking a last look at the monument at the moment of its dedication, fixing in their own memories the various meanings it contains and the varied functions that it serves—tribute, lesson, reminder.

The mayor may now lead veterans, bereaved families, and perhaps other groups and the population as a whole, to the town hall for a brief reception, or *vin d'honneur*. In a few communities, mainly but not exclusively in Brittany, the town presents survivors with engraved certificates bearing the names of their loved ones, personal counterparts to a monument inscription.[113] The reception may bring the ritual to a close, but for some towns the festive aspects of the day are just beginning. Festivities range from the relatively sober band concert, torch-lit parade, and "illumination" of the principal streets, to gymnastics exhibitions, foot and bicycle races, fireworks, and dancing. The program of festivities tends to be more elaborate and more joyous in the Morbihan, where memories of folk traditions may be stronger and ties to the lay, civic culture that frowns on them weaker.[114] We would not, of course, expect to find dancing and rejoicing in the communes of the Meuse, many still bearing the physical scars of war, all of them close to the battlefields where the commemorated lost their lives. Although often combining the monument dedication with a true celebration, that of the village's own reconstruction, these communes limit themselves to music and to gymnastics.[115] The latter demonstrates a degree of physical skill that, in its seriousness of purpose and patriotic readiness, connects contemporary youth to the forebears they have just commemorated.

Even in Brittany, the melding of commemoration and festivity could provoke unease. One prefect of the Morbihan seems to have disliked such combinations to the point of refusing to attend them.[116] In Pontivy a veterans' group protested the coincidence of the dedication with an agricultural festival, declaring that the honored dead deserved a day of their own.[117] A newspaper praised the city of Vannes for deciding not to hold a banquet in connection with the dedication: "Such a day," it editorialized, "should not be sullied by the playful thoughts that the 'communicative gaiety of banquets' suggest."[118] *Le ploërmelais* reported that in Loyat, "the fête took place amidst the reflection and the seriousness appropriate to the circumstances, a reflection and seriousness that did not, however, exclude a certain external éclat, since it was also a festival of all that is most intimate and touching in patriotism." Yet Loyat had nothing more to explain, or excuse, than a gymnastics festival and a concert.[119]

The difficulty, and the ambiguity, lies in the juxtaposition of the word *fête* with the discourses of memory, mourning, and commemoration. Although France had since 1881 had a commemorative festival, the *14 juillet*, the immediacy and the magnitude of what the country now had to commemorate placed such festivities in an unfamiliar light. The town council of Port-Louis (Morbihan) seemed to stumble over the very concept when it resolved that it would hold a *fête du souvenir* annually on the *14 juillet:* "This festival, or rather this commemoration," would consist of a wreath-laying at the war memorial.[120] In a sense, however, the problem lay as much with the second part of the term, *souvenir*, as with the first.

According to speakers and reporters, ceremonies consoled families, offered a final farewell to those who did not otherwise receive one, and paid tribute to the dead and their survivors. But they had another purpose as well: to create their own set of memories.[121] "The population of Kerfourn," declared the *Journal de Pontivy*, "will forever remember this day of gratitude toward the best of its children, who are no more." The mayor of Montiers-sur-Saulx (Meuse) had a similar if rather more expansive vision: "The solemn moments we have just experienced will leave in the hearts of those who attended an imperishable memory that will be perpetuated from generation to generation. Old men will tell their grandchildren that together we all communed in a common feeling of gratitude to those who saved the Fatherland and civilization."[122] His remarks make palpable the extent to which commemoration entails a passage or succession construed as "natural," even as the ritual itself becomes a cultural artifact to be remembered.

The dead, the object of commemoration, remain paramount here, as the discursive norms demand, but the primary object of the anticipated recollection (in Kerfourn) or of narrative memory (in Montiers) has become the commemoration itself. And the dedication ceremony, by common consent, has had as its own object not only the dead, but other things as well. If the observances in Ménil-sur-Saulx, not far from Montiers, were, according to one account, "worthy of the brave boys who shed their blood unsparingly for France and who died for us," they were also "a fine festival of pure patriotism, of gratitude toward the dead, of the concord and union of the Meuse."[123] A few years later André Maginot told the people of Varennes that "a ceremony like this one, which, at the same time as it commemorates the sacrifice of our heroic fellow citizens consecrates the resurrection of your homes, cannot but move Frenchmen attached to their fatherland, reinforcing their faith in its destiny, and offering them as well the opportunity for some useful reflection."[124]

Like monuments themselves, and like most rituals, dedication ceremonies aim to mean, to achieve, to communicate far more than they can openly admit. At the same time, as Maginot's "cannot but [*ne peut que*]" suggests, rituals also work to constrain and to shut down interpretation by providing an authoritative meaning or set of meanings for the commemorated deaths. In so doing, commemoration promotes forgetting as an integral part of public memory, just as Lincoln in the Gettysburg Address sought to obliterate those aspects of America's founding that quite explicitly countered "the proposition that all men are created equal."[125] In this respect the self-consciousness with which we began emerges as a kind of ruse. Contrary to what their self-presentation suggests, commemorative rituals do not simply transmit self-evident meanings: they construct, shape, and frame them in a context so eminently adapted to a particular set of social arrangements as to discredit any possible alternative.

silencing

The Dead and the Living

Accounts of dedication ceremonies specialize in recording emotion, from the "poignant emotion" produced by the appearance of two orphans bearing wreaths in a procession, to the "intense emotion" as a ceremony got under way, to the "sincere emotion" of a speaker and "the greatest emotion" with which the audience responded.[126] Of all these moments, the calling of the names of the dead emerges as consistently the most moving, perhaps because names have a special connection to memory. "At that moment," observed one newspaper, "how many memories each of these names conjured up in our hearts!"[127] The remarks of an official in Sivry-sur-Meuse offer a clue to the power of this ritual: "The names of those who died for their country will be called as if they were still alive. Their names will echo painfully in the hearts of those who loved them, the words will fall like drops of blood."[128] The theme of the presence of the dead resurfaces frequently in postwar commemoration, intimately bound up with the memories of the living. For in most conceptions of the sacred, as Victor Turner has observed, "the dead have *influence over* the living and are reciprocally *influenced by* their thoughts, words, and deeds."[129]

It may be useful to retrace, step by step, the complex series of mediations developed here. The reading of a list of names, a staged event involving at least two voices, produces a set of memories that differ according to the individuals named and those remembering. These memories constitute images of the dead that may foster a belief in their presence, whether symbolic or in some way efficacious. Then, various textual interventions—spoken at the time, written afterward, or both—articulate the meaning of these memories by situating them within the context that the ritual constructs. As integral components of the ritual process, such texts profess to convey the genuine emotion of the speaker or writer, and sometimes undoubtedly they do, but they also mediate between individual memories and the larger social, cultural, and political discourses that frame them and give them meaning. Indeed, one of the primary functions of commemorative ritual is to institute and secure a concrete framework of meaning for its constituent elements. The texts that secure these meanings do so through a series of elisions: between speaker and mourners, between the commemorated and the ostensible purpose of their deaths, between the polity as a human construct and social bonds so familiar as to seem "natural." Summed up in the self-conscious effacement of speech before the actions it commemorates, these elisions seek to mask above all an act of appropriation central to commemoration: the construction of a Barthesian myth around the dead, a myth woven from the fabric of their names.[130]

One could argue that the multiplicity of meanings attached to names in the course of monument dedications effectively vitiates the attempt to make them signifiers, that for all intents and purposes they remained, as Thomas Laqueur would have it, a kind of hypertrophied signified.[131] For Toucas-Massillon, subprefect of Commercy and a voluble participant in many dedication ceremonies, names were a "ransom of glory," their inscription in stone "a cry of patriotic faith and a call to toil." For Georges Diard, mayor of Onzain (Loir-et-Cher), names signified heroism and martyrdom, constituting "a page of glory and sorrow written in blood."[132] For a member of the Morbihan general council, names constituted "a symbol of the union in which these heroes fought and in which they died," whereas André Maginot emphasized "the inscription's consecration of their individual heroism."[133] For Louis Taton-Vassal, a deputy and mayor of St. Mihiel, the reading of names "will summon up for us painful hours lived on the battlefield or in our besieged city; as well, they will bring together, for our pride as Lorrainers and our national pride, everything that is purest in the French character." The mayor also warned that the *appel des morts* "will, for each family, revive all the cruelty of their mourning." Less than two years later, however, at a ceremony Taton-Vassal also attended, the mayor of Spada, Devin, declared that "all those who mourn a loved one must have the supreme consolation of seeing his name inscribed in marble."[134]

Ransom of glory or individual tribute? Cruel reminder or eternal consolation? Names clearly offer a capacious channel to other discourses, but the functions assigned to names tend to cohere around two poles of the memory process: familiarity and transmission. In Taton-Vassal's speech, names could recreate the feeling of bereavement because they "recall to us the beloved and familiar faces of our streets," those "we knew as children and youths, who became men and citizens." For Mayor Devin, the inscription not only served as a consolation, but ensured that "future generations know their glorious names." Commemorative discourse seeks not only to occupy the field these two poles generate, but to secure and control a continuous passage between them.

In the dedication speech of Deroche, mayor of Noyers (Loir-et-Cher), the notions of familiarity and transmission stand in apposition: "The names engraved in this inalterable granite will show future generations that the children of Noyers did their duty, all their duty. All these names are familiar to us. Each of you will find here a son, a husband, a father, a big brother whose memory will remain forever engraved in your hearts."[135] Deroche's reversal of what might seem the logical order, the recollection of loved ones first, then the transmission of memory to future generations, suggests some unease with the underlying dynamic of commemoration, in which a collective, impersonal tribute comes to supplant personal memories. Lionel Huette, mayor of Auray (Morbihan), tried to attenuate the pain of this transition by personalizing the theme of generational transition. Noting that the monument stood on the path to the communal schools, Huette declared that "If some schoolchildren can, with deep emotion, read on it the name of their father or of a close relative, [schoolchildren] of the future will be proud to find there the glorious name of a forebear [*un ancien*] whom the entire population of Auray honored on the 11th of November 1925."[136]

In a sense, then, the emphasis on names in dedication ceremonies may represent a technique of evasion, a way to mask the difference of commemoration from personal memories. The crux of the idea of familiarity is spontaneity, the involuntary summoning of memories in response to the trigger of names, whereas names on monuments serve as the focal point for a collective *obligation* to remember.[137] By making names crucial to both processes, the "spontaneous" recollection of loved ones as well as the transmission of their memory to future generations, authorities could suggest some kind of natural flow between the two. This was no doubt easier than acknowledging that the dedication ceremony, in instituting an official commemorative rite, signals the community's long-term alignment with transmission, with memory as obligation rather than as spontaneous act. Comforting the bereaved of course plays a part in the ceremony, but their personal memories clearly represent the past, not the future.

Several aspects of dedication ceremonies lend weight to this hypothesis. The notion of familiarity is adduced chiefly in connection with the *appel des morts*, that is, with an ephemeral act of public declamation, and only secondarily as an effect of the permanent record the inscribed names provide. At the dedication of a monument at the École Normale in Commercy, according to a newspaper report, the call of names was long, "but how comforting it was as well. For did not each name recall a comrade, a friend, a relative? So we conjured up their memory, and we saw them again strong, vigorous, full of ardor and courage. . . . And today, hearing the names of these dead, we cannot conquer the emotion that wrings our hearts."[138] Some, like a teacher speaking at the dedication in Jouy (Meuse) in 1922, anticipated the same involuntary recollection, the same play of emotion, on future *readings* of the monument's names. But the teacher, M. Lalfert, went on to draw a specific contrast between his generation, which had no need of monuments in order to remember the dead, and future generations, represented by the children present, for "posterity must not be ignorant of the names of those brave men who, without knowing it, served it so well."[139]

Names, then, serve a dual function: for the community gathered before the newly dedicated monument, they trigger emotion—Lalfert referred to "the voice choking, the eyes moistening" at the sight of the names; for future generations, "posterity," they transmit knowledge. Lalfert made the distinction clear with another trope that recurs frequently in dedication speeches: "To find them again, those sacred names, as long as we live we need only look in our hearts, forever in mourning." Again and again, speakers associated the inscription of names on monuments with the memories of the heart. The mayor of Landévant (Morbihan) drew an exact parallel: "May the names of our dead engraved on this modest monument also remain engraved in our hearts, and may they be eternally blessed."[140] The phrasing of Le Lannic, mayor of another Morbihan community, Kerfourn, suggests a certain hierarchy in the relationship: "We have engraved their name [*sic*] in marble, but let us do better, let us engrave it in our heart. Let us never forget that it is for us that they died, to ensure our independence and peace." The mayor of Neuville-sur-Orne, in the Meuse, struck the same note in a more affirmative vein: "Thus our debt of gratitude is eternal, and your [soldiers'] names, engraved in marble for future generations, are even more deeply engraved in our hearts."[141]

Thus the parallel implied by the common use of the word *graver*, to engrave or inscribe, serves to link two fundamentally different activities. The idea of inscribing memories "in our hearts" might even be taken as an admonition, to the effect that commemorative transmission does not exempt individuals from the responsibility to harbor their own memories and to reflect on their meaning. In the common discourse, names on monuments beckon the distant future, casting memory into the unknown, while names in the heart represent a bastion of security in an uncertain present. "You did not wish," Maginot told the people of Cousances-aux-Forges (Meuse), "that the names of these valiant among the valiant should one day be forgotten, and that is why you have engraved them in immortal stone." In a similar vein, the editor of *Le républicain de l'est*, Léon Florentin, wrote that "Commercy did not want their names to be unknown; see, then, they are engraved in marble. The passer-by will stop to read them; the child will quit his games to come spell them out."[142]

In order to ensure, however, that personal memories do not escape the context in which commemoration frames and limits their meaning, a certain kind of intervention constructs as inherent the discursive connection between two types of memory, personal and collective, that pivots on names. At the dedication of a school plaque in St. Aignan (Loir-et-Cher), for example, a retired headmaster asserted that "the names of these glorious victims . . . will long remain engraved in this marble, but their memory will remain engraved in our hearts in letters even more enduring, and will be transmitted from generation to generation." Reversing the dynamic, a teacher in Heudicourt (Meuse), M. Lambert, spoke of the way in which the inscribed names would offer "lessons in civics" to schoolchildren, a living symbol of posterity. Addressing the dead, Lambert proclaimed, "If your name is inscribed in perpetuity on the base of this fine monument to your memory, in the name of the whole population your former teacher promises you that your beloved memory will remain deeply engraved in our hearts."[143] The idea of "perpetuity" contrasts with the transience of personal memory, a quality both well known and, in this context, unmentionable. Yet monuments cannot transmit memory in isolation, without making an imprint on individual memories; hence the idea of a kind of complementarity in which inscribed names both prompt individual memories and, in the process, incorporate them into the larger commemorative culture.[144]

For names also effect a different kind of link between personal memory and commemoration, a link at the level of the production of meaning. Take, for example, the teacher Lambert's figure of names as "lessons in civic instruction," which forms part of a broader vision: "The instructors who teach here in the future will not have far to look for lessons in civic instruction, morality, local history, or the history of France, and the page will always be open to the chapter on: Work, obedience, devotion, sacrifice." The mayor of Damvillers (Meuse) told his fellow citizens, "You wished to inscribe the names of these valiant men in stone so that reading them will exert a kind of fascination on the eyes of their juniors, an irresistible attraction toward duty and love of country; you wanted the example of their elders to encourage the young to work in turn to help our Fatherland follow its arduous and glorious destinies."[145]

We have here something other than memory: a set of lessons and exhortations pertaining to the core values of the nation-state. To reassert those values in the wake of war, to attempt to reconstruct the polity around them, is a political act, and like any political process subject to contestation. Rooting such lessons in names, the primary referent for intimate recollections as well as for commemoration, naturalizes this process, casting it as parallel to the apparent spontaneity with which names prompt memory itself. The trope of names as lessons also appropriates personal memories for the purposes of commemoration, enlisting them in the service of reconstructing French politics and society along traditional lines. This appropriation serves to shut down potentially subversive memories by positing the absolute identity of the dead with the ostensible purpose for which they died.

To "remember" and, even more, to "commemorate" thus become synonyms for a host of other terms: to know, to understand, to follow, to act. This should hardly surprise us, since at a basic cognitive level simply reading or repeating a list of names could hardly replicate, for those born after the war, the intimate recollections of those who knew the dead. The very concept of individual memory, moreover, makes it difficult to perceive, and impossible to acknowledge, the way commemorative discourse transforms "memories" of the dead by enfolding them in additional layers of meaning.[146] At most those involved in this process might allude to individuals' lack of control over the transmission of memory, and for this theme names once again provided a useful metaphor. The deputy Maurice Marchais, speaking at the Vannes dedication in 1925, quoted from a poem Victor Hugo addressed to the sons of the dead of Napoleon's Grande Armée, including the following lines:

Soyez nobles, loyaux et vaillants entre tous;
Car vos noms sont si grands qu'ils ne sont plus à vous!
Tout passant peut venir vous en demander compte.
Ils sont notre trésor dans nos moments de honte,
Dans nos abaissements et dans nos abandons!
C'est vous qui les portez, c'est nous qui les gardons!

(Be noble, loyal and the most valiant of all; for your names are so great they are no longer yours! Any passerby can call you to account for them: they are our treasure in our moments of shame, our weaknesses and our neglect. It is you who bear them, we who preserve them.)[147] In what is clearly intended as the ultimate tribute, Marchais unwittingly sums up the way in which commemoration appropriates both the memory of the dead and the memories of remembering subjects. If the commemorated no longer possess their own names, those commemorating do not fully possess their memories either.

Earlier references to *mon Pays* and *la gloire française* in the Hugo poem make clear that the *nous* toward the end refers to the French nation. Leaving aside for a moment Hugo's promise of consolation, let us examine the formulation of this *nous*. The utility of names in the construction of a national community lies in their primary referent, the dead, who are no longer present to describe themselves. But the discursive operation here casts those who still bear these names, the families of the dead, as a *vous*, and arrogate to *nous*, those who "guard" their names, the task of discerning the qualities that constitute a community. Once again, the invocation of names as vectors of memory naturalizes a deeply ideological process. In this context it is worth noting that, according to a distinguished historian of immigration in France, Gérard Noiriel, "in the interwar period, virtually every xenophobic text made some mention of the French sacrifice during the First World War."[148] The *nous* of the French nation thus proves capable of policing boundaries at several different levels.

Another portrait of the French nation emerges in the remarks of Senator Pierre Pichery at the dedication of the monument in Lamotte-Beuvron (Loir-et-Cher, fig. 4.42), where Jean Renoir was later to film his mordant 1939 classic *La règle du jeu*. According to a newspaper summary, Pichery "recalled those whose names, cast to the ages a few moments ago, conjured up in his memory a physiognomy and, so to speak, a family portrait, so much is our race always equal to itself, as splendid in its humble toil as [when it is] confronted with the humble death of the trenches."[149] The cultural work this passage performs goes beyond the troubling but nonetheless fairly general construction of the nation as a "race." For Pichery not only links soldiers' attitudes toward death in combat and peacetime work, he uses a word, *labeur*, which implies pain and endurance, avoiding the more modern *travail* preferred by working-class groups.[150] Note also that the senator's formulation, *devant l'obscure mort*, applies not only to soldiers who died, but also to those who survived, including the "numerous veterans present at the ceremony." But the passage not only ignores, it refuses to contemplate the bitterness and anger many poilus expressed about the conduct of the war. Pichery's inclusion of veterans, moreover, only serves to return them to their "humble" *labeur*, and implicitly rejects any claims they might make to something better. Through a discursive connection to soldiers' deaths, the familiar becomes timeless, the traditional sacred.

Like any ritual, dedication ceremonies point to the sacred in a variety of ways. We have seen officials, veterans, and children laying wreaths at the monument; speakers and guests sometimes bowed or inclined their heads in the direction of the monument or of bereaved families. Both gestures signaled the sacred status of the names of the dead: "Let me bow low," cried one Breton mayor, "before their names, forever immortal."[151] Speakers also made explicit reference to the sacred: Marchais in Vannes called monuments "altars of the Fatherland"; Poincaré in Bar-le-Duc referred to the "sacred cause"; the mayor of Woinville (Meuse) promised the dead a "sacred cult of memory."[152] As a moment of consecration, moreover, a dedication ceremony offered speakers an opportunity to instruct listeners in appropriate behavior, for example, instructing children to bare their heads and refrain from play in front of the monument.[153] For a veteran in Haudainville (Meuse), however, the sacred itself led naturally to pedagogy. The fence around the monument, declared M. Gascon, would preserve the monument enclosure as "a sacred space, doubly sacred by the name it will bear and by those it will evoke. A sacred place where future generations will come in turn to learn that one can truly be a man only by, as they did, in whatever situation one finds oneself, fulfilling one's duty unto death."[154]

Monuments teach lessons by presenting the honored dead as examples to be imitated. Names in this dynamic become signs less of distinct individuals than of the qualities they shared, qualities rhetorically extolled as sources of inspiration to the living. As Pichery's reference to "the race" and Gascon's to "a man" suggest, these qualities limn a composite sketch, not so much of the ideal soldier, but of the model citizen of the postwar period. For on most lists of these qualities the martial virtues occupy a fairly minor place. Dr. Hurault, the mayor of Savigny-sur-Braye whom we encountered in chapter 3, claimed that the pensive soldier sculpted as part of the town's monument (fig. 3.2) more accurately represented the poilu than the "bellicose" model on so many monuments. Mayor Hurault's vision of the war experience emphasized suffering and survival, qualities he summed up as follows: "This is the Poilu who, through his tenacity, his endurance, with only the idea of victory in his heart, held out a quarter of an hour longer than the enemy and drove him off the French soil he defiled."[155]

Some speakers, of course, notably orators with experience on the national stage, used terms from the traditional storehouse of aggressive masculinity. Poincaré described the poilu as "the one who brought together, at the appointed hour, all the qualities of his race, and whose swagger [*crânerie*] and tenacity earned him universal admiration."[156] But "tenacity," the crucial notion of mayor Hurault's speech, had far more currency than swagger. At the dedication ceremony in Ménil-sur-Saulx, a member of the Meuse general council placed his emphasis squarely on endurance, saying, "Our soldiers needed not only courage but patience to endure without weakness demoralizing [periods of] inaction and to bear the harshest physical and moral sufferings with resignation."[157] Again and again these terms recur. A mayor speaking at the dedication in Le Sourn (Morbihan) attributed France's victory to soldiers' "endurance" and "tenacity." In Jouy (Meuse), where the teacher Lalfert distinguished between different types of memory, a veteran recalled an earlier tribute to soldiers' "fine qualities of courage, endurance, and abnegation." Crystallizing this lexicon of patient suffering, the deputy René Chavagnes (Loir-et-Cher) claimed that "the highest virtue of the peasant poilu was silence."[158]

The notion of the "peasant poilu" introduces another important element to this rhetorical portrait: the overwhelming emphasis on poilus' roots not only in rural France, but in the land. The significance attached to this love of the land extended beyond the common courtesy or local boosterism one might expect of ceremonies that took place in small rural communities. At least until World War II small-scale agriculture retained in the French imagination, and in its dominant political culture, a predominance that far exceeded its shrinking share of the French economy.[159] Often, the trope of attachment to the land elides with the more overtly political "love of the native soil," a quality speakers clearly did not intend to restrict to farmers.[160] But many references had far greater specificity. "The dead we honor today, our dead," declared the mayor of Vaux-les-Palameix (Meuse), "were landowners, winnowers, who loved their sky, their fields, in freedom." The president of the Commercy district council (*conseil d'arrondissement*), Morel, described the dead of Ville-Issey as

sons of this land, attached to the earth, this good earth of Ville-Issey, so familiar with its horizons of rich fields, of slopes ribboned with crops, their ridges crowned with forests. Their ambition was limited to doing their best at the task they learned from their fathers, a task they would have taught by example to their children: the humble and sacred task of the peasant of France, always bent over a plot that only his labor makes fertile.[161]

Pichery offered an even more lyrical description as the town of Dhuizon (Loir-et-Cher) dedicated its monument, beginning with the observation that few soldiers had left their native villages before the mobilization, and concluding that "work took them whole, like the earth, and they asked only that they might go on working, and that the earth continue to nourish them."[162]

Centuries of unthinking, uncomplaining work on the land; weeks, months, years of patient suffering at the front: the parallel has little need of elaboration, though it also involves the obvious contrast between the peace and beauty of the countryside and the horrors of the front. Drawing on both the parallel and the contrast in remarks addressed directly to the dead, a member of the Meuse general council "imagined" that "it was this love of your native soil that gave you this tenacity, this will" to hold out in battle.[163] But the implications of the peasant-soldier type encompass more than reflection on the past. Another local politician in the Meuse called the dead "simple souls, in love with the flowering meadows and plains."[164] Simple, silent, hardworking, asking nothing better than to return to the work they had done for centuries, the dead offered a model of citizenship in a country facing massive debt, huge reconstruction costs, and considerable social and political upheaval. Speaking at a dedication ceremony in Fresnes (Loir-et-Cher), the deputy Victor Legros recalled that 90 percent of the wounded he had treated as an army doctor came from the countryside, "men of the fields, those men of good sense and reasoned progress on whom our social order rests."[165] A commonplace of what Stanley Hoffmann has called the republican synthesis, such a view had little to say about the changes the war had brought about. Indeed, in the postwar world it amounted to a form of denial.

If the sense of loss Dr. Legros expressed in Fresnes is palpable and unfeigned, so is the sense of anxiety about the future, the almost wistful hope that the dead as constructed in this discourse could somehow influence the course of French politics. The lyricism and emotion of these passages make it difficult to understand that the dead, and the age-old agricultural traditions for which they are made to stand, were not so much the *objects* of that anxiety as *figures* for its larger scope. For more than a century France had been becoming less of an agricultural country as its cities and industries expanded.[166] Many regarded these changes as themselves a kind of loss. The children of Dompcevrin (Meuse), declared the deputy Taton-Vassal, would learn from the newly dedicated monument that "the life of the fields is superior to that of the city, that our existence there is more intimate, and, more fortunate than the peasant of antiquity, they will come to know how happy they are."[167] A tall order indeed, and one beyond the scope of any ritual space or commemorative monument to carry out. This unlikely vision of happiness suggests that postwar politicians were seeking, with an ideal past constructed in the image of the dead, not to stop the clock but to turn it back, to return not to the status quo ante but to a past one could truly call immemorial.

The twin poles of memory, familiarity and transmission, emerge in this discourse as a sequential process, with the presence of the dead as a crucial median term. The names of the dead conjure up images, a kind of presence that not only allows but virtually obligates the dead to transmit lessons and values to their survivors. The mayor of St. Claude-de-Diray (Loir-et-Cher) called "the cult of the dead . . . not a vain tribute rendered to that which no longer exists: it is the fertile union of the dead and the living." Dr. Legros urged the dead to "be always present in our spirits and our souls, continually to tell us that it is enough for us to remain united to be strong and fearless." In a more solemn formulation, Louis Jacquinot, who had defeated Taton-Vassal for a Meuse parliamentary seat a few months earlier, saw the dedication ceremony as a moment of encounter between "the living and the dead," and expressed the hope that "the union of their flesh and ashes will fulfill the destinies of the Fatherland in the dignity of peace."[168]

The figure of the dead and the living united in patriotic labor effects a graceful transition from the "presence" of the dead at the sacred center of ritual to their more limited roles as both consolation and inspiration to the living. For the rites of collective memory seek as much to displace personal memories as to enshrine them, supplanting images of the dead with the kinds of normative concepts we have been tracing. The postwar reconstruction of the Meuse provided especially fertile ground for this discursive operation, but even there it had to be handled with delicacy. When the prefect of the Meuse, Charles Magny, mentioned "energy, tenacity in work, and a profound love of our native soil" at the dedication in St. Mihiel, he was referring not to soldiers but to those who had worked to rebuild the city after the German occupation. Whereas in St. Mihiel the comparison was only implied, André Campion, the subprefect of Commercy, made it explicit at the Boinville dedication in 1928: "You were sustained, during the long, harsh years you lived among the ruins, by the memory of our dead. Like them, you had a duty, a hard duty to fulfill. Like them, you accomplished it without fail, as good Frenchmen and good Lorrainers. You continued the work of your sons, and you remained worthy of them."[169]

While the inspiring example of the dead—the "sons" [*fils*] whose parents, poignantly, must continue their work—remains Campion's essential referent, on other occasions a certain slippage takes place, as speakers focus more on survivors. Speaking at Les Paroches in 1926, Taton-Vassal, mayor of the reconstructed St. Mihiel, declared that "the virtues [of those] who sacrificed themselves for their country, we find them again here: they have flowered in your homes and all around you in your exemplary and fertile efforts at reconstruction." The mayor of Étain defended the town for attending to the needs of the living, namely reconstruction, before honoring the dead. For him mourners were not simply worthy *of* the dead, but "as worthy *as* the dead in their supreme sacrifice."[170] Like Taton-Vassal, Mayor Collin framed his praise in what had become the customary terms—courage, energy, self-sacrifice—and he carefully addressed his tribute not to the townspeople as a whole but, after acknowledging the magnitude of the loss, to the relatives of the dead. In both places, however, reconstruction becomes a metaphor for the transfer of soldiers' model qualities to their survivors, and the community honors not only the dead, but itself.

A few highly unusual monuments evoke the sufferings of civilians and the work of reconstruction, but they do so in ways that circumscribe the connection to soldiers' sacrifice, clearly emphasizing the latter. In Esnes-en-Argonne (fig. 6.1), where civilian deaths outnumbered those of soldiers, the central relief shows a young peasant sowing a field around a war grave, in a heroic gesture reminiscent of Jean-François Millet's epic naturalism.[171] Esnes, at a strategic location in the Verdun theater, had been practically leveled during the war, and the relief panel pictures with stark simplicity the daunting task of renewal

FIGURE 6.1. War monument, Esnes-en-Argonne (Meuse). Photo: Author.

amidst the ruins, symbolized by the monument's jagged edges. The tomb marker and the helmet beneath it, however, call the viewer's attention to the human loss, both military and civilian, that remains the monument's main focus.[172]

In Lacroix-sur-Meuse, a small town in fiercely contested terrain a few miles north of St. Mihiel, the local sculptor Donzelli fashioned an extraordinary tribute to the sufferings of the inhabitants under German occupation (fig. 6.2). The Lacroix monument also records the names of the civilian dead, and behind the monument's central figures a frieze (fig. 6.3) movingly depicts women, children, and the elderly—the familiar noncombatant triad—their expressions ranging from resignation to puzzlement to uncontrolled grief. Here, the monument tells us, the distinction between battlefield and home front lost its meaning. Yet Donzelli does not go quite so far as to collapse the distinction between soldiers and civilians: while he carved the latter in high relief, the former stand as full sculptures, one dead or dying, the other alive, holding a furled flag, prepared to receive tribute from a female figure above. However similar their sufferings and their grief, the poilus clearly serve as protectors and redeemers of

FIGURE 6.2. War monument, Lacroix-sur-Meuse (Meuse). Photo: Author.

the civilians. And however great the civilian loss in Lacroix-sur-Meuse, the dead poilu in front of the monument clearly stands for the higher value of active sacrifice. Civilian deaths reflected, in the common understanding, only German barbarism; the soldier's voluntary death, in contrast, pertained to the story of masculine French virtues that commemoration sought to tell.

CIVILS

Bellocq Joseph
Goujon J.B.Eugène
Henry Emile
Humbert Marie
Jacob Victorine
Lamacque Felix
Vve Lombard-Charles
Lombard Marie Louise
Martinot Delphine
Pètrement Maria
Varin Adélaïde
Villain Julia

FIGURE 6.3. War monument, Lacroix-sur-Meuse: detail of frieze. Photo: Author.

Even in communities that could recount their own stories of bombard-ment, burning, and occupation, such evocations remain relatively rare, even rarer than the plaques commemorating a monument's own construction. The reluctance of communities to appear to celebrate themselves, their insistence on tracing all the qualities they wished to honor to the commemorated dead, evoke what Moore and Myerhoff call the "ultimate danger" of ritual: "that we will encounter ourselves making up our conceptions of the world, society, our very selves."[173] Ritual seeks to wrest order from disorder, to naturalize the constructed, and not simply to restore the values of the status quo ante but to elevate them to a level of unquestioning acceptance; it cannot accomplish all this if its own status as representation is too obvious. The oratorical moment, at once the most variable, the most artificial, and, in the Periclean tradition most self-contradictory portion of the dedication ceremony, exposed that danger most starkly. Hence the tendency for speakers to hew as closely as possible to rhetorical convention and to *idées reçues*.

For the anxiety that lurks just below the surface of many speeches extends beyond the speech act to the whole commemorative process, encompassing the audience, and by implication the wider public, as well as the speaker. This anxiety finds expression and seeks resolution above all through commemoration's admission of its own inadequacy. We have already seen a kind of invidious distinction drawn between inscribed names and memories "of the heart"; this distinction fed into a discourse in which the dedication of a monument both stands for and initiates a whole series of wider obligations. We should not be surprised to find these obligations coded as a kind of memory. "Monuments in stone and bronze," declared the mayor of Sampigny, Godin, "would be but a vain simulacrum if we did not harbor, deep within ourselves, the grateful memory of the brave men who, by giving their life [*sic*], preserved our freedom and independence."[174] As we have seen, however, memories of the dead have multiple functions within the commemorative process: they create images, teach lessons, compel emotion, and, ideally, shape behavior. Within the limits that commemorative culture constructed, the obligation to remember would prove, to use a contemporary term, as "fertile" in producing meaning as the names that provided its symbolic impetus.

The Power of Memory

In seeking to use monument dedications to influence the conduct of their fellow citizens, speakers relied not only on the authority of their positions but on the far more resonant legitimacy of the dead. Dedication ceremonies and the commemorative rituals they initiated offered, as we have seen, an invaluable opportunity for political discourse to cast itself not as exhortation but as exposition, as a commentary on the qualities of the dead that all who mourned them would wish to perpetuate. Thus, for the mayor of Cellettes (Loir-et-Cher), "we must individually acquire the fine qualities that earned our soldiers their victory over a powerful enemy. We need abnegation, patience, discipline; we must work together [*unir étroitement*] toward the common task [*labeur*], the immense task that lies before us." The dead and the living, declared Mayor Tillier, were "actors in the same . . . drama"; in the light of soldiers' heroism, could we allow ourselves to fail?[175] The subprefect Toucas-Massillon continued the speech in which he called names "a cry of patriotic faith and an appeal to toil" by explaining that "it is through labor that their work [*oeuvre*] will be completed, it is by imitating in peace their courage in war that their sacrifice will remain fertile, it is in modeling our soul on theirs that we will make the French Republic immortal, the France of Valmy, the France of the Great War!" In two sentences the subprefect manages to use three different words that can be translated as "work": *labeur* or toil, *travail* or labor, and *oeuvre*, usually the result of productive labor; the last, traditionally the most exalted, he applies to the mission of the dead.[176]

At first sight, neither of these prescriptions appears very specific, but Mayor Tillier's hinges on a concept with enormous resonance during and after the war, that of unity or *union*. The word recalled the *union sacrée*, or sacred union, a term derived from Poincaré's message to the Chamber of Deputies at the outbreak of the war calling for a political truce during the conflict. In fact the *union sacrée* neither ended partisan bickering nor secured a true left-right coalition; months before Georges Clemenceau formed a government with near dictatorial powers in November 1917, Socialist members of Parliament had withdrawn their confidence from the coalition. Throughout the war, successive governments imposed rigorous press censorship, and Clemenceau used the full power of the state to harass politicians suspected of pacifist leanings.[177] As Jean-Jacques Becker has written, "the *Union sacrée* as it has so often been defined— the ideological union of all French people based on patriotic feeling—was never a reality." Although the participation of right-wing Catholics in wartime governments proved little happier than that of their Socialist counterparts, the *union sacrée* did far more to advance their cause, and conservative nationalism in general, than it aided the left.[178]

Yet the association of the term *union* with the selfless comradeship of front-line soldiers to some extent immunized it from potentially pejorative overtones and extended its life as a political desideratum. In the early 1920s *union sacrée* thus came to connote a state of affairs inherently superior to the normal give-and-take of political life. Veterans, with their habitual contempt for partisan politics, espoused the notion of union virtually as a creed. "And if by chance," declared the veteran and journalist Léon Florentin at the dedication ceremony in Euville (Meuse), "we were tempted to break the harmony so beneficial to the welfare of the city, let us come and reflect for a few moments at the foot of this monument; we will draw from this salutary meditation a precious lesson that will carry us effortlessly toward thoughts of kindness and love that will make us better."[179] The suggestion would sound merely platitudinous were it not for the word *cité*, with its evocation of the ancient world and clearly political connotations.

It was but a short step from such platitudes to more sternly political admonitions. A town councillor in Lamotte-Beuvron warned his listeners that if they did not follow his advice to put aside old left-right divisions, they would be "troubled one day by a voice from beyond the grave," that of an angry and uncomprehending soldier. Maginot told students in Commercy not only to remain "united" but also to "accustom yourselves, each time it should prove necessary, to subordinate your own interests to the general interest, for a people's force and patriotism are measured by how well they bear this subordination."[180]

This passage from "union" to "subordination" suggests that the former concept has some implicit content even when, as often happened, speakers presented it as a goal in itself: "On this stone that has been built here by a common piety, let us swear to remain united as they were in the trenches," urged the mayor of Langoëlan (Morbihan). The commitment to "union" facilitates necessary work or effort, the "immense task" evoked by the mayor of Cellettes. In another Morbihan community, Mohon, Mayor Gaudin called on his listeners to "be worthy of their heroic sacrifice, to preserve their memory deeply engraved in our hearts, to remain strong through our union and to work in harmony for the prosperity and greatness of the fatherland."[181] The goals of this effort usually appear in the sketchiest of forms, for example Florentin's editorial reflection that "in the union of all its children France will find the resources necessary to ensure that no such catastrophe ever occurs again."[182] For the most part, however, the concepts of work, union, and obligation led seamlessly to a conservative political agenda. Speaking in Loyat in 1922, the subprefect of Ploërmel expressed satisfaction that communism had no chance of catching on in the Morbihan, where "our farming population has only one concern, work [*travail*], and is satisfied only when their task is accomplished."[183]

It is worth noting that the subprefect made his comments at a banquet following the ceremony, not at the dedication itself. The taboo against the politicization of dedication ceremonies had its self-appointed enforcers in the local press, even though the obvious partisanship of some accounts itself came in for criticism. In the run-up to the 1924 parliamentary elections, one Breton newspaper accused another of exaggerating the applause received by a senator who espoused its politics; a third deplored the politicization in which both speakers and journalists engaged. "We must," thundered an anonymous veteran, "have the civic courage to stigmatize the political and electoral pandering the various parties are carrying out in front of war memorials: it is an abomination, and must cease immediately."[184] Sensitivities extended as far as mere invitations to attend dedication ceremonies. The Catholic newspaper *Le ploërmelais* criticized the town of Guilliers for not inviting a number of right-wing members of Parliament to its dedication, noting acidly that one moderate deputy, Louis Maulion, in his banquet toast "appealed to the *union sacrée* that he and his friends practice in so bizarre a fashion." The radical newspaper *Le progrès du*

Morbihan gave a far more positive account of the ceremony, saying that Maulion spoke "with his customary eloquence . . . and concluded with a vibrant appeal for union. His words made a very strong impression."[185] A few years later, two newspapers published an extended correspondence between one of the senators excluded from the Guilliers dedication, Ernest Lamy, and the mayor of Inzinzac, over a similar omission, which the mayor denied had any political motivations.[186]

Small wonder, then, that elected officials and newspapers sympathetic to them habitually claimed to eschew politics in their dedication speeches. In August 1930, appearing at the dedication of the monument in Chaillon (Meuse), Poincaré denied press reports that he would give a "political speech," saying he wished only to share the memories and the grief of his listeners. Poincaré was now seventy, and had left office for the last time a year before, so his protestation seems credible. Yet the newspaper that published the speech played up his insistence that France should contemplate no further concessions in its enforcement of the Versailles treaty, contrasting it with a "bellicose" speech given by a German minister at the same time.[187] In Poincaré's heyday as prime minister in the mid-twenties, newspapers across the country routinely scrutinized his speeches at dedication ceremonies for political news, and the local press noted with some pride that he was speaking to a "larger public."[188]

Yet the expectation that ministers appearing at monument dedications would allude to the issues of the day did not give them complete latitude. Politicians had to tread carefully if they wished to transfer to their contingent messages some of the sacrality universally attributed to the dead. The discursive imperatives—to pay tribute to the dead and to their survivors, to recall the courage and sacrifice of the war years, to associate oneself with the community, and to extol "union"—made available several rhetorical strategies. One consisted of portraying unity as indispensable for maintaining France's strength and reputation in the international arena. In the fall of 1925, Maginot, then out of power, declared at the dedication ceremony in Lacroix-sur-Meuse that to preserve France's position in the world, "one condition is indispensable, that we be more united, that we support each other, as our soldiers did in the hours of trial and danger." To remain united, Maginot went on, meant not the renunciation of individual beliefs or principles, but "that we should be capable, in circumstances like those that the country is currently going through, to relegate everything that may divide us to the background, and to attach ourselves only to what can serve the interests of the fatherland."[189] For Maginot, those "interests" included an armed intervention in Morocco, the controversial war of the Rif against the indigenous forces of Abd el Krim, but not the collective security arrangements at the heart of the foreign policy of the center-left Cartel des Gauches government.[190]

The recurrent atmosphere of crisis in the twenties, and the "national union" appellation of the essentially right-wing governments formed by Poincaré in 1922 and 1926, lent plausibility to another tactic evident in Maginot's speech. This was the argument that the conditions of the moment replicated those of the war years and required a similar degree of effort and unity from the populace. At the dedication of the monument in Plouharnel (Morbihan) in July 1922, all the speakers, including Poincaré's junior minister Alphonse Rio, "stressed the difficult situation through which France is currently passing, a situation that more than ever calls for unity among all good Frenchmen."[191] A third strategy consisted of characterizing policy choices as in some way fulfilling the wishes or desires of the dead. In the summer of 1923, Poincaré vowed to keep French forces in the Ruhr until Germany paid the reparations required under the Versailles treaty. Not to do so, he declared, would "certainly betray the supreme wishes of the dead."[192] Justifying the same policy, in the same speech in which he set forth the dichotomy of words and deeds, Maginot insisted that France owed the dead not simply praise, but "actions in conformity with their will." Conscious that they were fighting for a just cause, the dead had wanted a peace that punished the aggressors and provided for French security; so, Maginot asserted, "in trying to secure for this country the peace that our dead desired, we are paying them the tribute they would find most satisfying."[193]

It is worth pausing for a moment over the nature and the logic of Maginot's argument. Few among his listeners would have disputed the justice of France's cause in the Great War, or the proposition that German aggression had brought about the conflict. Most would also have agreed that soldiers fought and died in a similar belief, but some may have recalled that confidence in the justice of French war aims had not managed to sustain morale either among soldiers or on the home front for the duration of the war.[194] As a veteran, Maginot could credibly present himself as a spokesman for the dead, but, even for him, to characterize a particular policy as the perfect embodiment of their desires represented a significant act of presumption. Although Poincaré's decision to occupy the Ruhr in January 1923 initially attracted popular support, its cost and dubious efficacy became an issue in the legislative elections of 1924, which Poincaré's supporters lost to the Cartel des Gauches.[195]

Ministers' use of monument dedications to promote a potentially controversial policy nicely coincided with the Poincaré government's claim to be a continuation of the *union sacrée*. The failure of this strategy both symbolizes and embodies the larger rhetorical inadequacy of Poincaré and of the Bloc National governments that preceded his between 1919 and 1922. By the time of its electoral defeat in 1924, according to Jean-Jacques Becker and Serge Berstein, a government conceived as "the prolongation in peacetime of the practice and ideology of the *union sacrée*" had proved to be "a formation dominated by the right and carrying out right-wing policies. It thus revealed after the fact certain characteristics, poorly perceived at the time, of the *union sacrée* itself." For Becker and Berstein, moreover, the Bloc made clear that a wartime consensus could not—whatever Maginot's protestations—serve as the basis of democratic political debate once the war had ended. In peacetime, in other words, "the Bloc National's wager on unanimity was perhaps lost in advance."[196]

Although the right dominated French political life for most of the twenties—the victory of the leftist coalition in 1924 proved short-lived, and Poincaré was back in power two years later—it did not have a monopoly on dedication speeches, or on their coverage in the press. The mayor of Cheverny (Loir-et-Cher), Hardy, began his speech by saying that, out of respect for the bereaved, he ought perhaps to keep his opinions to himself, but "how can we not express our anger toward this horrible, absurd and criminal thing that is war?" Hardy found in the memory of the dead the obligation to support the League of Nations and promote international understanding. In following this course, he told his listeners, "we will have done well by [*bien mérité de*] our dead. In dying, they believed they were killing war forever; so they were told over and over again, and it is for that above all that they gave their blood." Also present in Cheverny was the mayor of a neighboring commune and member of the departmental general council, Mauger, who excoriated war in the same vein. At the dedication ceremony in Candé a few months later, Mauger expressed the hope that the next generation would never know the horrors of war, "for the hard-working people of our countryside, who labor and who suffer, who are firm supporters of the Republic, but of a Republic of social freedom and brotherhood, desire peace with all the nations of the world."[197]

The audience at Cheverny also heard a speech from Senator Pichery, whose considerably more conservative views we have already encountered, and from the department's four deputies in the lower house. All of them outranked Hardy and Mauger, but the Blois weekly *Le nouvelliste* saw fit to reprint none of their speeches; in its account of the Candé ceremony *Le nouvelliste* did not even name the deputy who spoke.[198] In this journalistic version, ceremonies that probably saw the expression of a spectrum of viewpoints become one-sided celebrations of pacifism. What lent this presentation even a surface plausibility, besides the fact that most overtly political newspapers tended to preach to the choir, was the two mayors' use of the standard tropes of commemorative discourse. The ritual setting prevented them from voicing any explicit criticism of the war itself, lest they be accused of demeaning the "sacrifice" of the dead. The mayors could, however, use the "lessons" they drew from the war to plead the cause of pacifism. Like their counterparts on the right, they presented their views as the wishes either of the dead or of the "hard-working populace" whose qualities they most closely shared. In this way they attempted to appropriate the discourse of war "experience," and its logical extension the speech-action dichotomy, for their own purposes.

The Var also had its share of leftist politicians, and one of them, the Radical senator and former minister René Renoult, clearly knew how to shape a political address around the commemorative formulas. Speaking at a dedication ceremony in Aups in September 1922, Renoult praised the "fervent devotion" that had prompted the construction of the monument, and framed his argument with a rhetorical question: "How do our Great War dead advise us to work for the material recovery and the moral greatness of an adored fatherland, for which they, for their part, gave their all?" Renoult reminded his listeners that the dead had fallen under the flag of the Republic, which stood for certain principles of freedom. "Let us not doubt," he declared, "that the shades of our heroes would be indignant if . . . an intolerable effort arose to modify in a regressive, conservative or militarist direction the political orientation of French democracy." The remainder of Renoult's speech consisted of a thinly veiled attack on the Bloc National's security policy, which he accused both of inefficacy and of betraying at least the spirit of the Versailles treaty. He concluded with a call to commitment:

Before this monument that consecrates the memory of soldiers who fell for the sacred cause of Freedom imperiled by brute force, let us state our execration of war which leaves so many French hearts in grief, and let us greet the dawn of a new era in which the friendly settlement of differences among peoples through international law will finally liberate humanity from the fatal violence that, over the course of centuries, has inflicted on it so much appalling misery and eternal mourning.[199]

But if commemorative rhetoric lent itself equally well to overt political messages of either the left or the right, the discourse of commemoration tended to reinforce traditional social and political arrangements that the war had disrupted or put at risk. The set of obligations that commemoration sought to vivify invariably encompassed moments of everyday life, and as such both impinged and relied upon the codes and practices that constitute the social. Just as names conjured up images conforming to a traditionalist notion of citizenship, the ways in which people were enjoined to remember and honor the dead replicated normative constructs and categories of human behavior. Among these constructions gender codes played a crucial role: gender both provided a convenient litmus test for evaluating narratives of the war experience and, at the same time, served as the fulcrum and privileged metaphor for the pervasive cultural anxiety over the war's upheaval.[200]

That traditional constructions of gender underlie even the most politically radical of commemorative discourses emerges quite clearly from a passage in Councillor Mauger's speech in Cheverny. "And you," Mauger cried, "mothers who, as you lean over the cradle of your little ones, shower them with care and love, no more do you want your dearest affections ripped away from you."[201] The "no more" (*vous ne voulez non plus*) forms a connective to the "hard-working people of our countryside," a phrase Mauger used again in his speech at Candé, thus replicating the traditional dichotomy between, on the one hand, the "work" men do and, on the other, the rearing of children as women's "natural" role. Ignoring the many nontraditional duties that women had taken on both in cities and in the countryside during the war, this almost offhand reference does more than simply consign women to the home. By asserting the commonality of women's and men's attitudes toward future conflict, Mauger, whatever his public views on women's suffrage, implicitly endorses the argument of antisuffragists that male heads of household could and did speak for their wives.

It would be a mistake, then, to treat as secondary or as merely conventional the many calls in dedication speeches for attention to the needs of widows and children. Perhaps the most frequently cited obligation for communities in mourning—the care of survivors—responded to a practical problem of considerable magnitude. The president of a Pontivy veterans' group cited the exact amounts of the small pensions received by childless war widows, and, "in the name of the heroes whose names they still bear," called on the politicians present at the dedication to increase them.[202] But many speakers cast the welfare of widows and children as a responsibility of the local community as well. At the dedication of the monument in Grimaucourt (Meuse), a local councillor, Morelle, evoking the familiar speech/action dichotomy, declared, "We must translate our gratitude [to the dead] not only into monuments, but also into daily support for those whose guardianship they have bequeathed to us, their widows and orphans."[203] Speaking as minister of pensions, and as such responsible for the state's assistance to widows, André Maginot told the citizens of Rupt-aux-Nonains (Meuse) that they owed the families of the dead more than condolences. Rather, to the extent possible "we have the duty to replace in their lives those they have lost, to help them, to succor them, to make sure that their existence is not too difficult. The families of our great dead are our families, their mourning is ours, and we share their sadness as we share their pride."[204]

Since he was a skilled administrator and maintained good relations with veterans' groups,[205] Maginot's admonition can scarcely be read as an attempt to let the government off the hook. Rather his remarks suggest that assisting the widows and children of dead soldiers had a fundamental role to play in reconstructing social relations the war had sundered. This attitude undoubtedly had roots in Catholic notions of community. In the observant Morbihan, for example, the mayor of Taupont, Joubaud, called on his listeners to imitate soldiers' "two great virtues: charity and fraternity." Yet Joubaud had more in mind than the cultivation of Christian values. He continued by comparing soldiers to Christian martyrs, whose blood was proverbially the "seed" (*semence*) of Christians, and concluded, "I have the firm hope that the blood of our soldiers will be the seed of good and virtuous Frenchmen."[206] This image recurs in a secular context: addressing the dead at the dedication of a monument in the military cemetery of Revigny-sur-Ornain the mayor, Chenu, said, "Your blood, so generously shed on our beautiful land of France, was like a fertile seed in liberating it from the enemy's yoke, and has caused the idea of sacrifice and devotion to germinate in our hearts as well."[207]

We have traveled some distance from assisting widows to this highly sexualized trope of regeneration. The link between charity and regeneration lies less in Catholic piety or dogma than in underlying notions of a normative masculinity that both serve to reconstruct. Women who during the war had been strong and capable, who had "worked bravely, their energy, their dignity deserving the respect of all," after the war become mournful widows, unable to recover from their losses without the help of men.[208] Again and again speakers and newspapers single out women as mourners or make their grief a synecdoche for the bereavement of the community. *L'avenir de la Meuse* described the monument in Sivry-sur-Meuse, a female figure, as "Grief crying over a soldier's helmet that she presses to her heart, and it is all wives, mothers, and fiancées who are symbolized."[209]

On the other hand, the pronouns in Maginot's speech at Rupt make clear that those seeking to replace lost soldiers are also men, just as the masculinized community of Grimaucourt assumes the "guardianship" of widows and children. Thus the notion of the welfare of widows subtly but unmistakably introduces a gendered distinction into the commemorative process. Mourning imposes responsibilities on the whole community, but it imposes them differently. "Only mothers," declared the mayor of Haudiomont (Meuse), "like this figure who materializes sorrow, have the right to shed their tears before this monument." In contrast, the dead expect "us," a "we" masculinized only by implication, to act, to "complete the sublime work [*oeuvre*] for which they shed their blood and gave their life."[210] This contrastive "we" occurs again in the peroration to a speech in Rouvrois-sur-Meuse by Toucas-Massillon. Anticipating the completion of France's reconstruction, the subprefect predicted that on that day "as we pass before these monuments where the hearts of mothers, widows, and the aged sob, where little orphans quiver in bitter regret, we will be able to say to our beloved brothers: You have saved France by your victory; we have saved your victory for France."[211]

But the salvation of France requires a posterity to secure it and the memories that surround it; hence the references to soldiers' "seed." The language of germination often has, of course, a metaphorical dimension, as in the image of *"restore to the phallus!"*

gender roles during war vs after

soldiers sowing ideas of sacrifice. In rural France, fertilization also has a more literal, agricultural connotation: "Let us devote ourselves," urged the mayor of Rouvrois, "to making good our losses, raising our ruins, and fertilizing our soil, for we must live and grow for the future of France."[212] But the unfamiliar gender roles of the war years had the potential of confusing this imagery both literally and symbolically. A member of the Meuse general council, for example, told women in Louppy-le-Château that during the war they "constituted the main labor force: you were plowing; you were sowing." While, at the front, "death reigned over the furrows. You, you brought life to yours. Thus was the great eternal ritual carried out."[213] Although Cochard's *rite eternel* undoubtedly seeks to evoke no more than the age-old association between agriculture, fertility, and the feminine, his use of the verbs *ensemencer* and *faire germer* with respect to activities carried out by women alone has troubling implications. For if women could generate life on their own, in the absence of able-bodied men, what could compel them to resume their subordinate roles once the men returned? The many references to men's "seed" in other dedication speeches can plausibly be read as an attempt to shut down such potentially subversive meanings, to restore to the phallus its preponderant role in procreation, making women, as it were, once again safe for insemination.

To women inclined to draw strength from memories of the greater independence they exerted during the war, commemorative discourse gently but persistently offers another model. Cochard in Louppy had associated women with children and the elderly, referring to "all your weaknesses joined together," stressing the unnatural aspect of their wartime labors. To the picture of women bravely carrying out unfamiliar tasks the mayor of Selles-sur-Cher, the unfortunately named Dr. Massacré, added an even more familiar image, that of soldiers wresting themselves from the arms of their wives, mothers, and sisters, the latter managing brave smiles as their men went off to war. After that, "they [*elles*] could cry, without risk of softening their courage, now that they [*ils*] had left."[214] At the banquet preceding the dedication in Elven, the prefect of the Morbihan paid tribute to "the French woman, whose devotion over the course of the hostilities never faltered even for a moment." Devotion, however, is an elastic concept, easily transferred to the domestic scene and to relations between men and women generally. In Hennebont (Morbihan) the deputy Pierre Bouligand pitied the widows who, "with beseeching eyes, call out and wait in vain for he who should have trod the paths of life with them as their guide, their protector in the so often difficult moments of existence."[215] And lest there be any doubt about the nature of women's contribution to the war effort, Councillor Morel, speaking at the dedication in Jouy-sous-les-Côtes (Meuse), noted that they had followed the mayor's example in continuing to "dig your vines and plow your fields," and that this work, "though apparently less glorious than the heroism of the poilus, still deserves to be recalled to our national gratitude."[216] Women, in other words, had simply done what they always do in war: follow the example of men, without any foolish hope of equaling men's achievements.

A common feature of dedication speeches, many, if not most of the encomiums to women's effort and "devotion" came thus framed by patronizing qualifications and counterimages of weakness. For the recognition of women's contributions could never be allowed to detract from the main business of commemoration, which was to express gratitude to the poilus, that is, to men. Unlike dead soldiers, women of the home front were never held up as objects of memory, and thus as guides to conduct; they could serve as models only as remembering subjects paying tribute to men. This was the subtext of portrayals of France or one of its provinces as a "grieving mother," or, more elaborately, as "mother of so much heroism, nursemaid to so much sacrifice."[217] Just as women gave birth to heroes and nourished sacrifice, their grief paid tribute to the men who had assumed the ultimate burden of citizenship. To some extent, of course, speakers were here enacting a basic male fantasy, to which a kind of memory suspiciously close to literary formulas gave access. At the dedication in Ménil-la-Horgne, Subprefect Toucas-Massillon described his battalion's arrival in a village during the first battle of the Marne as follows: "And when we entered the village, women, girls, and children, their arms full of roses, decorated my poor soldiers. Not a word, but such looks!" A similar episode appears in Roland Dorgelès's novel *Les croix de bois*.[218] The solemnity and repetition of ritual served in this instance to give substance to the fantasy, to impose as normative the highly artificial notion of commemoration as a tribute rendered by women to men.[219]

To summarize, with the crucial but generally unacknowledged gendering in parentheses: the duty (of males) to render assistance to (female or feminized) survivors of the dead, as it restores men to their capacity as the "guides" and "protectors" (of women), parallels men's return to the dominant position in domestic life. A speech by the mayor of Kerfourn, Le Lannic, shows how the themes of memory, obligation, and the land turn on reproduction, an extraordinarily powerful notion in a country obsessed with declining natality and depopulation:[220]

We have engraved their names in marble, let us do better, let us engrave them in our hearts. Let us never forget that they died for us, to ensure us independence and peace. What would we be without them? So let us not make their sacrifice a vain one. To replace them France needs many young and valiant Frenchmen. It is for us as parents to raise them, for you schoolteachers, men and women, to train them in duty and virtue. In order to survive, France needs intensive production. Peasants of Kerfourn, remain attached to your fields, do not desert the land, for in the land lies the country's salvation.[221]

Le Lannic omits the fertilization, itself a kind of "intense production," that spawns the "young and valiant Frenchmen" he dreams of, but the duty to produce them looms large among the obligations he associates with memory.

The power of memory emerges here, and in so many speeches like it, as a power of suggestion. Commemoration promises that those who remember in a certain way will find in those memories, and in the ritual acts attendant on them, the inspiration to act in ways the dead would have prescribed. What makes the discourse of memory so tempting for postwar politicians is the way it appears to internalize the production of meaning in the citizen. It thus provides an invaluable cloak for the intricate pattern of the interested and the consensual, the particular and the general, that politics within a democracy always weaves. The delicate process through which memory and the discourses of national politics interact resembles a series of dance steps, each with an essential role to play, from the repetition of standard formulas to the tightly constrained references to current events. None, however, has greater significance than the initial casting of memory, not, as Halbwachs would have it, as *itself* collective, but as a fundamentally individual process that collective action can *enable*. Commemoration offers not simply the efficacy of action, but the consolation of memory itself.

One could also say, however, that the power of memory amounts to that of a conjuration, no more, no less, for it relies on both the will and the credulity of those remembering. The incantatory quality of commemoration stems from the constant, pervasive anxiety to which it gives voice, an anxiety about forgetting. "Pas d'oubli, non, pas d'oubli!" (no forgetting, no, no forgetting), cried a school principal, Dambraine, in Ornes (Meuse), asking how a mother could "erase from her memory the sight [*spectacle*] of her son dying far away, murmuring her name without the consolation of her embrace"; how the widow could forget her "broken future, her happiness destroyed"; how the orphan could forget that the war had left him alone in life.[222] For Dambraine "no forgetting" has a distinctly political charge: he urges his listeners not to let down their guard with respect to German militarism. But the very different kinds of memories he adduces, including the peculiar but revealing notion of a memory of the future, point to the fragility of memory that prompts his anxiety. He begins each of his rhetorical questions with the phrase *Comment voulez-vous*, effectively asking the audience to imagine how, possessed of the kinds of "memories" or knowledge he describes, they could "forget," in other words not heed, his admonition. Gender—except for the orphan, his stock figures are all female—reinforces another kind of distinction that undergirds the anxiety over forgetting. This is a distinction between memories based on primary experience, which in this formulation resist forgetting, and another type of memory, here wholly unarticulated but presumably the kind of secondary memory that commemoration transmits. The almost accusatory tone of Dambraine's interrogations implies that for those without the visceral memories he describes, forgetting may be not so much inevitable (this he refuses to admit) as actively desired.

Again in an incantatory vein, most dedication speeches refer to forgetting only in the negative, as something that monuments forestall. "It was your desire, in building this monument in the bosom of the commune, to insure the great dead of the war against forgetting and ingratitude," Taton-Vassal told the people of Dompcevrin in 1925. "By perpetuating their memory in this way, if in the future some were, alas, tempted to forget, this stone would remind them of the sacrifice of our [du pays] children in the general holocaust, surely prompting some remorse."[223] The deputy uses the conditional, not the future, as though reluctant to acknowledge the likelihood of this prospect. Others, however, acknowledged their anxieties more straightforwardly. "Knowing how easy is forgetfulness," declared the mayor of Vineuil (Loir-et-Cher), Marcadet, "we wanted this monument forever to perpetuate the names of those who did not have the happiness to see the day of victory dawn." More pessimistic, Mayor Adol of Cléguer (Morbihan) called monuments a "small thing," saying that the "finest monument" should be built "in our hearts." But he went on, "In these parts forgetting comes quickly: does not experience teach us this grievous lesson? Heroic struggles have quickly given way to petty squabbles."[224] In a few words Adol cuts through the convenient complementarity that commemorative discourse establishes between primary and transmitted memory, casting serious doubt on the potential of commemoration to "perpetuate" any of the values it finds in memory.

Perhaps anxiety over forgetting recurs so often, if only in the form of denial, because it embodies the contradictions at the heart of the commemorative process itself. We return here to Lincoln's paradox, but with a different emphasis, one that recalls the notion of incommensurability enshrined in the discourse of war experience. In this reading, we cannot hallow the memory of the dead because our existence, our interests, our continuing lives, offer too much interference; we cannot wholly remember the dead because we did not "experience" what they did. This is a great taboo, but occasionally a speaker gives it away inadvertently. According to the mayor of Girauvoisin (Meuse), Gabriel:

This monument has been raised on the exact site where the enemy's shells struck. It will, in its simplicity, continue to speak when our voices are silent, when our hearts no longer beat. It will tell future generations of our endurance, our very Lorrainer tenacity, and our faith in France's victory. It will repeat to those who follow us the great lessons of duty and ardent patriotism that we have lived through, our hope in the future. . . . It will, finally, tell of the meaning of our motto, "Forget? Never!"[225]

Gabriel's use of the first-person plural, his celebration of survival, exposes commemoration as, at least in part, a ritual of self-definition, the fear of forgetting as the all-too-human fear of being forgotten.

But the fear of forgetting also encompasses a deeply felt, usually repressed awareness of the contradictoriness of the commemorative process, notably the fact that commemoration involves a host of cognitive processes including forgetting. Indeed, the conjuration of forgetting in memorial discourse projects a certain anguish over memory itself, a desperate desire to make it better than its imperfections, its selectiveness, its stubborn associations and exclusions. Speaking at the dedication of the Blois war memorial (fig. 6.4), the prefect of the Loir-et-Cher, Marcel Bernard, put it this way:

Are all the words we have just uttered only words, will they fly away forever? Will nothing remain when, in a little while, we will all have returned home, of course comforted by this moment of reflection in which we felt our hearts, so close to each other, beat to the same feelings? And when, tomorrow, someone passes by, alone, to meditate in front of this wall, is it possible he will not find here, as he would today, our affection enveloping these immortal names?

Bernard then addressed himself to the trees around the monument, asking if they could not "preserve our devout thoughts and make of them your favorite song?" He concluded with a poetic vision in which "winter and summer, the wind, transformed by your branches into a vibrant lyre, ceaselessly sings your glory, O heroic men of Blois who died for eternal France."[226] Rarely has the desire to construe memory as natural and inevitable found such poignant expression.

Today the trees of the place de la République in Blois, and the monument they continue to shelter, witness children's games, the conversations of furiously smoking students from the nearby lycée, and, on Saturday mornings, a market. Situated between the city's conference center and its courthouse, and just down the street from the prefecture, the square also sees many strangers to Blois, some of whom may occasionally pause to admire the simple but elegant war memorial by Sicard, once deemed virtually the only monument of artistic note in the Loir-et-Cher. Twice a year, on the eighth of May and the eleventh of November, a number of dignitaries, including the prefect and the mayor, since 1989 the Socialist politician Jack Lang, as well as civil servants of high enough rank to compel their attendance, gather in front of the monument. After a wreath-laying and the reading of a short text in the name of the minister of veterans' affairs, the officials escort an aging group of veterans of World War II, Indochina, and Algeria to the prefecture for a reception; they then go on with their lives.[227] To my knowledge, no one has yet deciphered the song of the trees.

FIGURE 6.4. War monument, Blois (Loir-et-Cher). Photo: Author.

EPILOGUE

Because those who rest here and elsewhere entered the peace of the dead only to institute the peace of the living, and because it would be a sacrilege to allow in the future what the dead detested: the peace that we owe to their sacrifice, we swear to protect and to wish it.

OATH OF VERDUN, 1936

Before they die, the survivors of Verdun wanted to leave future generations this testimony to what was the greatest battle in history.

DEDICATION OF THE MÉMORIAL-MUSÉE DE VERDUN, 1967

Now we would have to get used to this redistribution of memory.

JEAN ROUAUD, *Les champs d'honneur*, 1990

An oath, a museum, a novel: it would be too simple to claim that each typifies a particular moment of World War I commemoration, at respectively twenty, fifty, and nearly eighty years' distance. But together these moments suggest that as the forms of commemoration change, the same basic dynamic continues to propel it, the attempt to meld individual memories into a collective version of the past. The durability of commemoration as a type of representation involves both the continuity of its fundamental impetus *and* its ability to change, appropriating newly resonant cultural materials or discarding those that have become either obsolete or overly controversial. Commemoration sets itself an objective it can never entirely attain: to construct a unitary and coherent version of the past that displaces individual memories. While certain configurations of power and knowledge within a society can facilitate that goal, others, such as the bitter internal divisions of the 1930s in France, make it more difficult. Yet commemoration's success cannot be measured entirely in terms of the group, community, or nation that lies at its heart. As an examination of these three moments and their contexts will reveal, commemoration has a life independent of the groups it represents, a life rooted in individuals' paradoxical desire that their memories endure in some collective form.

The Thirties: Dying of the Light

The oath of Verdun originated in a familiar place, the cemetery just below the Ossuary of Douaumont, on the night of 12–13 July 1936. The ceremony in which approximately ten thousand veterans from all over Europe swore to defend the peace also involved a second commemorative practice characteristic of the late thirties, a fascination with light of various kinds, especially torches. At 6 P.M. on the twelfth, four emblematic figures—a war widow, the mother and son of dead soldiers, and a wounded veteran—used a torch lit at the eternal flame under the Arc de Triomphe to light four torchères in front of the ossuary. Four hours later, the giant floodlights that bathed the ossuary and cemetery in a ghostly pallor were switched off for a few moments' private reflection. When the lights came on again, the assembled veterans, led by several representatives speaking into radio microphones, swore, each in his own language, to preserve the peace.[1]

The poignancy of this ceremony is readily apparent, and not only in retrospect. The ceremonies that saw the birth of the oath of Verdun came barely six weeks after Léon Blum became France's first Socialist prime minister. Despite its clear victory in the parliamentary elections of April-May 1936, Blum's Popular Front coalition, with the support of Communists in Parliament, attracted opposition so bitter and venomous that in November it drove his minister of the interior, Roger Salengro, to take his own life. Significantly, Salengro stood accused, in the right-wing press, of desertion in 1914, a charge that was baseless.[2] He committed suicide just eight days after an Armistice Day in which the many calls for unity served only to highlight the country's divisions.

Accounts of 11 November observances in different parts of France in 1936 reveal many continuities with the ritual type we examined in the last chapter. Centering on a procession to the war memorial and cemetery, a wreath-laying, and speeches from the mayor and local veterans' leader, the holiday might also include, depending on the community, a religious service, banquet, sporting events, a concert, even a dance. As at dedication ceremonies, schoolchildren usually played an important part in the ceremony, marching in the procession, reciting poems, sometimes singing patriotic songs.[3] From Commercy, *Le républicain de l'est* reported that "not since 1919 has the anniversary of the armistice been celebrated with as much fervor as it has this year."[4] But many local newspapers reported considerable controversy, much of it stemming from the government's ban, in an attempt to avoid partisan conflict, on group insignia in public processions.

In Lorient, a last-minute meeting at city hall failed to produce agreement among veterans' groups of varying political persuasions to join in a common procession on the eleventh. In Romorantin, scene in the spring of a hotly contested parliamentary race won by the Socialist candidate, veterans boycotted the procession organized by the municipality, which they denounced as a partisan maneuver on behalf of the Popular Front.[5] Both these disputes echoed the sour mood in Paris. The centerpiece of the national observances went off without incident. At 11 A.M., President Albert Lebrun, with Blum and his cabinet in attendance, laid a wreath at the tomb of the unknown soldier; the country then observed the traditional moment of silence. But in the afternoon the long procession of veterans' groups to the Arc de Triomphe led to shouting matches and even minor scuffles between communist veterans, sympathizers of the right-wing leader François de la Rocque, and a group led by the protofascists Maurice Pujo and Louis Darquier de Pellepoix.[6]

In this atmosphere the idea of unity, and even more the now badly dated notion of *union sacrée*, amounted to little more than naked political slogans. One newspaper observed that if everyone had taken seriously the veteran slogan "united as at the front," the country would not be in the position in which it found itself, "the French rising up against each other." The mayor of Chouzy-sur-Cisse (Loir-et-Cher) called on veterans "more than ever to keep up that admirable spirit of brotherhood that united all the social classes of the nation in the trenches," declaring that the country "needs this union to overcome the serious problems that threaten it inside and out."[7] But in Romorantin a newspaper report offered an explicit contrast between "the atmosphere of sacred union" at a memorial mass organized by the Red Cross and the civil ceremony, which it called "the affair of a clan." In both Romorantin and Selles-sur-Cher, following government instructions, mayors recited the oath of Verdun; in the latter, the mayor and the local veterans' president were able to agree on a common ceremony. Yet surface harmony could not dispel the considerable tension: according to one observer, when the mayor asked the people of the crowd to raise their right hands and swear with him, one young man proffered a clenched fist and "was roughed up a bit by a veteran." Nonetheless, the observer called it "a good day of memory and *union*."[8]

The sacralized aura of Douaumont, beloved of the Catholic right, could not immunize the oath of Verdun from the taint of the Blum government's attempt to insert it into official ceremonial.[9] Despite its use of religious terminology (*sacrilège*) and a general distaste for foreign engagement, the oath too obviously corresponded to a particular narrative of the war, one emphasizing its horrors and inhumanity, to attract support across the political spectrum. Rather than affirm a common purpose, then, the oath of Verdun became a symbol of commemoration's inability to forge a unitary narrative in the political climate of the 1930s.[10] Confronting a "unity" that justified sectarianism, the oath, in committing its adherents to an ideal, effectively acknowledged their powerlessness to bring it about. The 1937 sound version of Abel Gance's *J'accuse*, in which an army of the dead rises up from Douaumont to prevent the outbreak of a new war, operates within a similar register of futility.[11] So does the obsession with light that reached its apogee on the twentieth anniversary of the armistice, in 1938. On that occasion, each department, every colony, and most of France's allies in the war dispatched individual torches or *flammes* to Paris. Assembled in the courtyard of the Invalides on the evening of 10 November, the torches were taken on the eleventh to Rethondes, site of the signing of the armistice, and then, near midnight, back to Paris, where each symbolically relit the eternal light under the Arc de Triomphe. The next day the torches set out for their points of origin, and many towns held special ceremonies to mark their return on the thirteenth.[12]

The symbolism of the eternal light had a relatively brief history in French commemoration. Not originally a part of the tomb of the unknown soldier, an eternal flame was added to the gravesite in 1923, on the proposition of a group of conservative veterans. The symbolic relighting of *la flamme* subsequently became the responsibility of a veterans' association solely devoted to the task. The daily ritual also provided a useful photo opportunity for politicians seeking to invoke memories of the war, notably Edouard Daladier on the day after his return from the Munich conference in the fall of 1938.[13] Precedents for the torch "relays" that so dramatized the twentieth anniversary of the armistice included, besides the July 1936 ceremony at Douaumont, a bilateral exchange between Paris and Brussels that occurred each 11 November.[14] But the 1938 relay took place on a wholly unprecedented scale.

What are we to make of this intricately orchestrated ritual, dominating the scene of commemoration with all the suddenness of an emergence? *L'illustration*, which devoted a third of its coverage of Armistice Day to the torches, including four photographs, called them "a pure and burning symbol [of] the presence and the universality of memories [*souvenirs*]." But this simple explanation begs more questions than it answers, especially in the context of the magazine's assertion that a "new, or rather renewed, outlook of the French spirit" had marked the observances, "a tightening of the national instinct, a defensive union against everything that would dissociate or reduce it."[15] Although overt confrontation over commemoration had declined after 1936, the ensuing years produced not so much reconciliation as a cold peace in which different groups went their separate ways. In Lorient in 1938 the municipality authorized, in addition to the civic ceremony, two separate *11 novembre* "demonstrations" at the war memorial, a "unity demonstration" of conservative groups and a "pacifist demonstration" of republicans and antifascists.[16] Speakers at some local ceremonies, moreover, reflected on the momentous events that had taken place just a few weeks before with considerably less confidence than *L'illustration*. Although the subprefect of Lorient, as the representative of the government, defended the Munich accords, he referred openly to the "anguish" with which people had waited for news in late September, a "memory" that largely displaced those the ceremony ostensibly consecrated. In Romorantin, the *Écho de la Sologne* found in the anniversary an opportunity to "measure the ground lost, the vanished victory," and though it pronounced the holiday a successful truce, it blamed France's weakness on the left.[17]

In such circumstances commemoration draws its power from the relative autonomy of its symbolic vocabulary, and from a general willingness to conflate the symbolic and the political. Following the highly contested 11 November 1936, one newspaper observed that "there, under the Arc de Triomphe, the Flame holds its own. That one cannot die; we know it well, and it is that that reassures us."[18] Like the oath of Verdun, the obsession with light and the desire to rekindle symbolically the light of memory thus have an air of conjuration, not affirmation. In Brittany in 1938 the convoy of departmental torches to Paris gave rise to an elaborate series of foot races, deliberately linking the ritual to the ancient Olympics. The runners, 140 of them in twenty-eight teams—the largest such race to date in the region—offered Bretons a reassuring portrait of their own strength, using an ancient ideal of masculine prowess to mask present divisions and displace the sobering memories of the recent past. Speakers throughout the Morbihan urgently appealed for unity, calling on their listeners to "forget our quarrels, to think only of our country."[19] Fulfilling one of the primary if usually unacknowledged tasks of commemoration, the ballet of torches offered France, at least momentarily, the means of such a forgetting.

The refuge that commemoration offered from the present came in many forms, including, suitably enough, personal memories. In honor of the twentieth anniversary of the armistice, the *Nouvelliste du Morbihan* organized a week-long exhibition in its Lorient headquarters of "souvenirs" lent by veterans, and concurrently published letters, memoirs, and other writings about the war submitted by readers. The editor of the series likened his role to that of "a collector, eagerly seeking out the new and the original." Yet he made only modest claims for the texts he presented, saying, "If they do not have the merit of pages of History, and if some narratives seem embroidered, like the chapters of novels, they will at least have the attraction of 'memoirs' gathered . . . in the desire to preserve the spontaneity and sincerity of recalling old memories [*souvenirs*] experienced in suffering." He concludes with a citation from Jean Bernier's *La percée*, the canonical assertion of the uniqueness of the poilu's experience: "He who has not understood with his body cannot speak to you."[20]

If the self-styled collector thus pays tribute to the uniqueness of combatant memories, his comments nonetheless attribute value to memory itself, construed in terms of recollection. For the text finds *spontanéité* and *sincérité* not in *souvenirs*, but in their *rappel*, the act of recalling them. Since these memories conspicuously lack the *valeur* of historical writing, they offer no lessons, no moral imperative, no guide to conduct in the present. Memory, recollection, here takes its distance from the larger stakes of commemoration, presenting itself as a source of comfort, not of responsibility. But the *Nouvelliste* was offering not "memory" itself but memory articulated, objectified, reproduced, and displayed: memory as representation, in other words, or commemoration in masked retreat from its own complexities.

The Sixties: Memory into History?

In June 1963, after four years of planning and fund-raising, a group of veterans, cabinet ministers, and other dignitaries gathered to lay the cornerstone for a new museum, the Mémorial de Verdun. About a kilometer to the south of the Douaumont Ossuary, the Mémorial would, its organizers hoped, allow future generations to "tend the flame" of memories of the Great War and of what many survivors considered its pivotal battle.[21] At nearly a half century's distance, the flame was beginning to flicker. As Gustave Durassié, founder of the building committee, put it,

Little remains of the battlefield of 1916. Tourists, visitors, and pilgrims, ever more numerous, no longer find the places that have been described to them. Villages have been rebuilt, fields returned to cultivation, trenches and mine craters, imbued with martyrs' blood, filled in. The Mémorial will thus be the museum of the battle, retracing its development and reconstituting its atmosphere.[22]

Durassié's elegiac tone recalls the debates over the preservation of war ruins that preoccupied veterans and politicians alike in the early 1920s. But the link he constructs between the museum and the disappearance of living memories points to the specificity of the "museal" as a mode of commemoration.

The museal, in Theodor Adorno's influential coinage, describes "objects to which the observer no longer has a vital relationship and [which] are in the process of dying."[23] In this way the museum as institution fundamentally transforms the practice of collecting, which, as we saw in 1938 Lorient, bears a strong relationship to memory. The founding fiction of the museum holds that an arrangement of heterogeneous objects can constitute a logically consistent representation of the world. It entails ordering, classification, hierarchy, so that the objects it displays together tell a story—in other words, they constitute a historical narrative.[24] Without the institutional imperatives of the museum, objects, either in isolation or as part of a private collection, trigger individual memories in Proustian ways, unpredictably. Thus the museum begins with a notion of memory as a kind of chaos to be both used and tamed: a set of signifieds to be detached from the objects on display, their signifiers, and woven into a new system of signification.

If the collection of objects, or, in one of the word's meanings, *souvenirs*, can facilitate the transition from individual memories to collective narrative, the more austere disciplinary practices of the museum make it less than immediately appealing as a site of commemoration. The museum's *retracing and reconstitution*, in Durassié's words, become attractive to those trying to preserve their own memories when they feel those memories fading, when their own mortality compels them to seek alternative means of telling their stories. Appealing for funds for the Mémorial in 1961, a veteran, Paul Manet, asserted that the museum would allow the "materialization and intact preservation of a Memory that constitutes one of the high points of our national History."[25] The metaphorical extension of the notion of "intact preservation" from a physical artifact to memory, as well as the implied equivalence between memory and history, convey the ambivalence that veterans must have felt in entrusting their memories to a museum. For all their insistence that the Mémorial would keep "memory" alive, they clearly perceived the difference, and the distance, between its modalities and the more personal ones on which they had long relied.

Most of the veterans involved in the Verdun project were presumably familiar with the Bibliothèque et Musée de la Guerre, the first major French institution dedicated to documenting and exhibiting a war. Founded in 1917, the Bibliothèque-musée originated in a collection of documents and artifacts related to the war assembled by a wealthy Parisian industrialist, Henri Leblanc, and his wife.[26] In its original installation in the Leblancs' apartment (and some adjoining ones) on the avenue Malakoff, the new institution evinced some of the charm of a private collection, and the Leblancs' conception of their collection's future purpose clearly included commemoration as well as documentation.[27] Yet once a group of historians headed by the trained archivist and Sorbonne historian Camille Bloch took control of the Bibliothèque-musée and moved it to Vincennes, its documentary purpose quickly took precedence over the memorial. Literature by and about the institution emphasized the seriousness and importance of its scholarly role: the careful organization of the library, exchanges with parallel institutions abroad, and an extensive publication program. A 1927 guidebook to the museum, while paying tribute to soldiers' "sacrifice," emphasized its goal of "making visible, in as methodical an order as the space and disposition of the rooms allow, the main historical lines of a conflict and upheaval that affected the entire world."[28]

If the ordering power of history offered aging veterans a way to perpetuate memories nearly half a century old, history had also altered the memorial landscape in more unsettling ways. Certainly Verdun in 1963 was not what it had been in 1936. Since Marshal Philippe Pétain had died in confinement in 1951, his remaining partisans had clamored for the transfer of his body to Douaumont. (In 1973 a band of particularly fervent Pétainistes even managed to steal the marshal's remains from his grave, but they were found after a few days and returned to the Ile d'Yeu, off the coast of the Vendée, where he had died.) If the Vichy régime originated in Pétain's reputation as national savior, that reputation itself grew out of Pétain's command of the army during the battle of Verdun. While Pétainistes presented his reburial at Douaumont as an act of national reconciliation, those whose political engagement grew out of opposition to the Vichy régime, notably Charles de Gaulle, could only regard such a move as a challenge to their own legitimacy.[29]

At the time of the cornerstone-laying in 1963 de Gaulle was, of course, president of France, and the Fifth Republic, the regime he had founded on his own reputation as leader of the Resistance, was barely five years old. De Gaulle had just weathered a stormy period, including two assassination attempts, a terrorist campaign that marred but did not prevent Algerian independence, and a controversial referendum that approved, at de Gaulle's behest, election of the French president by universal suffrage. An attempted coup by French generals in Algiers in 1961, and the involvement of many officers in the terrorist Organisation de l'Armée Sécrète (OAS), which opposed Algerian independence, also led de Gaulle to undertake a rigorous purge of the military. Although these events coincided with the crucial period of planning and fund-raising for the Mémorial, its documentary record makes no explicit reference to them. But de Gaulle's severity toward those associated with the OAS cost him support in the professional officer corps, a mainstay of veterans' groups like the ones building the Mémorial. More generally, the French far right has long brought together Pétainistes, fanatical proponents of French rule in Algeria, and people hostile to de Gaulle for other reasons.[30] Though he had fought there as a young officer, de Gaulle could never be the "man of Verdun," and Douaumont, where he was captured by the Germans in March 1916, must have signified for him an unmasterable past. Still president, de Gaulle skipped the dedication of the Mémorial de Verdun in 1967, and when his representative, minister of veterans' affairs Henri Duvillard, spoke the general's name, "murmurs" and cries of "Pétain to Douaumont" arose from the crowd.[31]

A few of those involved in building the Mémorial may have regarded it as a gesture of defiance toward de Gaulle. For others, the Mémorial probably represented something like the opposite: a desire to protect memories of the Great War from the interference of more recent history and politics. But whatever the motives of the founders, most of whom probably strove to keep their memories of the two world wars separate, what we might call the musealization of World War I commemoration clearly resembles the formation of a Freudian screen memory.

For Freud, a screen memory "owes its value as a memory not to its own content but to the relation existing between that content and some other, that has been suppressed." In its classic form screen memory consists of an image or images from early childhood that draw their vividness from their connection to a more recent event too painful to remember.[32] Freud observes that in a majority of screen memories "the subject sees himself in the recollection as a child, with the knowledge that this child is himself; he sees this child, however, as an observer from outside the scene would see him."[33] Along these lines, the chairman of the Mémorial building committee, none other than Maurice Genevoix, claimed at its opening in September 1967 that the Mémorial "restores to us, with our common past, our comrades, still alive."[34] For those seeking to shelter their memories of the Great War from more recent recollections, and thus in a sense to recapture their youth, the power of the museal must have seemed both welcome and necessary in the early 1960s. For ritual repetition could by this time, and in this context, no longer secure the transmission of memories tainted by subsequent events: only the ordering models of history could do that.

The rhetoric of the Mémorial's founders nonetheless makes manifest a certain tension between its historical (or museal) and commemorative dimensions. Whatever its historicizing objectives, in an important sense the Mémorial emerged from the memories of its founders rather than from a collection, which barely existed at the museum's groundbreaking in 1963 and never became extensive. Indeed, the search for objects continued for years after the Mémorial opened in 1967.[35] Yet in his opening speech Genevoix asserted the importance of more than individual experience: "What counted here, beyond the pain of the body and their unspeakable suffering, is the spirit of sacrifice." He also supplied an inscription for the Mémorial's entrance, which declares that it was "built by the survivors of Verdun in memory of their comrades who fell in that battle, so that those who come to reflect and meditate at the site of their sacrifice [might] understand the Ideal and the Faith that inspired and sustained them."[36]

Thus objects in the Mémorial serve to illustrate a narrative largely external to them, a narrative about the heroism of common soldiers and civilians with Verdun as its paradigmatic episode. The narrative employs standard historical categories, mostly military but with a smattering of social history as well; most evident in the museum's guidebook,[37] it also appears, summarily, in the form of the huge illuminated map and slide show that occupies an entire wall of the upstairs gallery. The museum consists of two types of exhibit. Upstairs, a chronological arrangement tracing the course of the battle employs objects arranged in the manner of souvenirs, typically in groups framed by photomontages and explanatory text (fig. 7.1). On the lower level, a series of tableaus with life-sized mannequins (fig. 7.2) provides a kind of spatial approach to the battle: one moves from well behind the lines (hospital and supply depot) to auxiliary

FIGURE 7.1. Mémorial de Verdun: daily life vitrine, upper level. Photo: Author.

FIGURE 7.2. Mémorial de Verdun: lower-level reconstruction. Photo: Mémorial de Verdun.

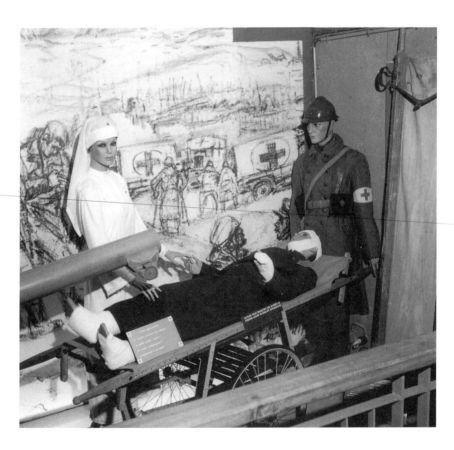

FIGURE 7.3. Mémorial de Verdun: trench landscape. Photo: Mémorial de Verdun.

services near the trenches (field kitchen and an assortment of weaponry). Visible from both floors, a trench and battlefield landscape occupies most of the museum's exhibition space (fig. 7.3) and connects the two sections.

Although some of the Mémorial's organizers worried that such reconstructions would sacrifice history to dramatic effect,[38] they clearly correspond to veterans' desires to "materialize memory." At the same time, the Mémorial's resolute emphasis on Verdun as quotidian experience effectively screens out the political dimensions that subsequent history had made so delicate. Above all, the artifice of Verdun's installation institutionalizes the distinction between memory and history that underlies the Mémorial project. For the reconstructions serve, at the same time that they represent experience and memory, to hierarchize and arrange them. Alone among the principal elements of the museum, the trench landscape, without any human figures, resists incorporation into narrative. This very resistance stands for the incommensurability of the experience represented, thus perpetuating the idea at the heart of veterans' understanding of commemoration itself.

In addition to the historical, another avenue lay open to veterans fearing the imminent disappearance of memory, the aesthetic. A few months before the dedication of the Mémorial, an article in the veterans' magazine *La charte* decried both the banality and the fragility of local war memorials. The author, Georges Pineau, began by declaring that "the dead, the poor dead, deserved better than that!" He mocked the major monument types, including "those soldiers twisting their stomachs, who seem to tell passers-by, 'I shouldn't have eaten so many prunes!'" and deplored the collective expense they had entailed.[39] Such disparagement of monuments as works of art had long since spread beyond artistic circles, and attempts to regulate World War II commemoration only reinforced the critical line.[40] Its sensitivity perhaps heightened by some German destructions of World War I monuments in 1940,[41] in January 1942 the Vichy government issued an ordinance requiring that all commemorative monuments be approved in advance by both the interior minister and the undersecretary for fine arts.[42] Though its primary objective was clearly political—it covered not only design and siting but also inscriptions—the 1942 ordinance provided a useful precedent for a provisional government with quite different preoccupations.

A law of January 1947 restored the authority of prefects to approve monuments, with the notable exception of those containing "any sculptural element such as a statue, medallion bust, bas-relief, detached figure, and so on" and those costing in excess of 500,000 francs—a sum that, because of inflation, probably corresponded to no more than 25,000 francs in 1921.[43] Monuments with any artistic pretension had to be approved by the new Central Commission on Commemorative Monuments, which included officials from both the Interior and the Fine Arts Ministries. As communities and Resistance groups undertook to memorialize the war dead, Resistance heroes, political prisoners, and deportees, one high-level official wrote that it was necessary "to prevent a repetition of the bad old ways of 1919–1924 and not permit the construction of monuments unworthy of French good taste and renown."[44] The very nature of the restrictions along with the severe hardships France suffered after the Liberation help explain why the most common form of World War II commemoration in France was simply the addition of names to an existing World War I memorial.[45] Like its Vichy predecessor, the 1947 law even provided for the removal of monuments erected without the requisite authorization.[46]

Beyond his aesthetic views, our veteran, Georges Pineau, found in the decay of many monuments a presage of the fate of memory itself. "They wanted to mold in stone an exemplary and lasting lesson," he wrote. "And the lesson crumbles away with the cement."[47] Although Pineau's views recall the anxiety in *Ceux de 14* and the cynicism in *La tête brûlée* about commemoration, his article produced a reaction quite different from the conventional pieties of the interwar period. Two months after its publication, a reader from the Isère wrote in with the photograph of a war memorial from Savoie, which he praised entirely in aesthetic terms. Then, the following year, the president of the association that published the magazine, Max Girou, challenged his readers to send in photographs of the monuments "that have best honored their example and their sacrifice." As examples, he offered pictures of two noteworthy memorials, including the Eymet monument by Gabriel Forestier (fig. 4.7) that attracted such praise in the 1920s.[48]

Neither the veteran from the Isère nor Girou fundamentally contested Pineau's argument. The former even agreed that most monuments were "either ugly or ridiculous, or both at once." Girou hoped that *La charte* would be able to establish that "we have more than half-starved roosters, or poilus tortured by stomach pains, to express our country's gratitude to its martyrs." But the terms of his challenge have little in common with communities' early assertiveness regarding the inherent aesthetic status of their monuments. "If," he wrote, "either in your hometowns or in the course of your travels, you are really moved by the beauty of the funerary sculpture, make it a point to send us a good photograph, accompanied by some commentary."[49] Emotion, in this text, comes not from individual memory but from the physical appearance of an object, and *La charte* was seeking not the typical but the exceptional. This is the logical consequence of the Vichy and Liberation ordinances. For even though they follow logically from the critical discourse of the interwar period, in making artistic ambition the exception rather than the rule for commemorative monuments, they suspended World War I monuments in time, transforming them into the artifacts of a vanished culture. As though simply an aspect of monuments' physical decay, the chill of the museal hangs over these articles, for the appearance of a high-art notion of universal beauty responds to the loss of any "vital relationship" to monuments as signs. Like May 1968, however, the month in which it was published, Girou's appeal heralded a change less dramatic, and more rooted in the past, than it first appeared.

The Nineties: Return of the Repressed

Asked in 1992 why a new museum devoted to the Great War had opened only that summer, the institution's first curator, Hugues Hairy, replied succinctly, "There were still too many veterans [earlier] and too much sentimental attachment to the event. Only today can we really begin to take a historical approach [*faire de l'histoire*]."[50] The museum, the Historial de Péronne, built by the department of the Somme with assistance from the state and the European Community, eschewed any commemorative intent; its name represents an amalgamation of the words *histoire* and *pictorial*, not *mémorial*. Instead it offers, in an exhibition program developed by an international team of historians in conjunction with curators and designers, a "comparative cultural history" of the war.[51] A press release for the Historial explicitly differentiates its approach from that of institutions like the Mémorial de Verdun: "This Historial is thus consistent with its etymology: it is a historical narrative. This narrative is not closed [*figée*] (as in the unfortunate galleries of wax) but open. It helps us to see and to think, and enriches us."[52]

The team responsible for the installation of the Historial jointly agreed on a set of basic principles, including a rejection of reconstructions, originals rather than reproductions, and a broad confidence in the communicative potential of objects.[53] The organizers sought to avoid aestheticizing objects, wishing to keep their frame of reference historical rather than art historical.[54] In an airy, light-filled building designed by the architect Henri Ciriani, the installation proceeds chronologically, with two large galleries on the war years preceded and followed by smaller rooms on its origins and aftermath. In the two central galleries, wall cases or vitrines contain objects and documents related to the home front, while sunken areas in the middle of the room present artifacts of the combatant experience (fig. 7.4). Each vitrine displays items from Germany, France, and Britain on a separate horizontal level, though with variations to allow for odd-sized objects and video monitors showing film footage from the period. Some of the display strategies are startling and powerful, such as the juxtaposition of weapons with headless, reclining mannequins, and of weaponry with bandages, medicines, and other artifacts of suffering; others are cooler and more dispassionate. In all cases, however, the installation bespeaks an assumption that the objects displayed no longer derive any meaning from memory, but only from history, that is from the narrative the institution alone supplies.

The last room at the Historial de Péronne (fig. 7.5) places plaster casts, models, photographs, and a video related to the commemoration of the war in the context of the physical and emotional damage, political upheaval, and massive reconstruction that followed the armistice. The installation treats commemoration, including the war museum itself (the video includes a clip of the opening of the Imperial War Museum in London) as a historical phenomenon, a window into the mentality of the war's survivors. More generally, however, in its insistently historical discourse and the emphasis of its master narrative on ordinary individuals, the Historial embraces an anticommemorative spirit characteristic of many recent representations of the Great War. Midway through the Historial's galleries, visitors enter a darkened theater to watch a film that depicts the battle of the Somme from the perspective of a British veteran, Harry Fellowes.[55] As the Historial symbolically aligns itself—and, by extension,

FIGURE 7.4. Historial de la Grande Guerre, Péronne: room 2. Photo: Author.

FIGURE 7.5. Historial de la Grande Guerre, Péronne: room 4. Photo: Historial de Péronne.

history in general—with the personal, symbolized by Fellowes's voice, it gently but firmly consigns commemoration to the realm of historical artifact.

The opposition between commemoration and private lives emerges most clearly in a film and two novels that marked the reappearance of the Great War, long a topic of scholarly inquiry, in mainstream French culture. Bertrand Tavernier's 1989 film *La vie et rien d'autre* (Life and Nothing But), set in northern France in 1920, chronicles the effort to account for the missing on the battlefield. Sébastien Japrisot's *Un long dimanche de fiançailles* (A Very Long Engagement), winner of the 1991 Prix Interallié, revolves around a search for a missing soldier after the war; its resolution turns on the assumption of new identities by characters who have escaped a particularly brutal form of military justice. Jean Rouaud's *Les champs d'honneur* (Fields of Glory, 1990), one of the rare first novels to win France's most prestigious literary award, the Prix Goncourt, concerns a family in southern Brittany in the early 1960s still haunted by its losses in the Great War. All three works valorize the personal, including private memories, in part by contrasting it with a far more mistrustful, even hostile, portrayal of public commemoration. At a time when France's uneasy relationship with its Vichy past had reached the level of an obsession,[56] the Great War once again offered relief in the form of a screen memory.

In one scene in *La vie et rien d'autre*, a sculptor of middling talent exults in the commercial opportunities the war's aftermath has presented him. Another scene has a sheepish delegation from a small village pleading for a slight modification in communal boundaries that would allow them to claim one dead soldier from the war. In its current configuration the commune had lost no one, but the villagers, rather than accept their good fortune, fear the suspicion and hostility of their neighbors. Commemoration in the film thus amounts to mere show: it fills pockets and gives survivors a sense of self-satisfaction, but it is essentially hollow. This attitude extends to the obsession with names at the heart of commemorative practice.

The film's central character, Dellaplanne, an independent-minded army officer in charge of finding and identifying the missing, is haunted by the statistics that frame his task, but he feels ethically impelled to produce a precise record. Numbers constitute the only fitting index to the war's horror; names, both elusive and illusory, provide only false consolation. Dellaplanne discovers that two women he encounters, the aristocratic Madame de Cantil and a local girl called Alice, are in fact searching for the same man, Madame de Cantil's husband, who the two hope is still alive. It seems Monsieur de Cantil had, using an assumed name, had an affair with Alice while serving in the army. No aspect of postwar commemoration escapes the film's skepticism: the main narrative of *La vie et rien d'autre* concludes with the selection, from eight caskets sent from different sectors of the front, of the unknown soldier who would be buried under the

Arc de Triomphe. Set in the Citadel of Verdun, this is an entirely historical scene, staged, except for the presence of the fictitious Dellaplanne, with scrupulous accuracy. But the film has taken a cynical view of the search for these bodies, mocking the army's obsession with finding remains both unidentifiable and certifiably French, and at the ceremony Dellaplanne can barely conceal his disgust.

Un long dimanche de fiançailles, in contrast, begins with an episode that has no known historical basis. In January 1917, five soldiers convicted of self-mutilation in the hope of escaping the war are, on the highly irregular order of a colonel, left as cannon fodder in no-man's-land with their hands tied behind their backs. The novel traces the determined five-year effort by Mathilde Donnay, the fiancée of one of the condemned men, to find both the truth and her beloved, who she believes has survived. Late in the novel, one of the men who secretly escaped his intended death, a foundling known by the nickname "That Man," urges the heroine to forget the past, telling her, "I can promise you this, a name signifies nothing. Mine was given to me by chance. I took someone else's name by chance." For Japrisot, as for Tavernier, the insight that a name signifies nothing leads to a rejection of all collective forms of commemoration. "That Man" cannot, for safety's sake, tell his small son who he really is, but, he says, he can wait: "I'll wait until the flags stop flying in November in front of the monuments to the dead, I'll wait until the Poor Bastards at the Front stop gathering, wearing their damned berets and missing an arm or a leg, to celebrate what?"[57]

Rouaud's narrative differs from those of Japrisot and Tavernier in several respects. Though it includes many flashbacks and two climactic framed narratives, one from 1916, the second from 1929, the novel's present is the period of the narrator's childhood, a few years around 1960. Both spatially and temporally remote from the Great War, the fragmented narrative structure of *Les champs d'honneur* provides another kind of distance from the precise historicism of *Un long dimanche* and *La vie et rien d'autre*. Rouaud nonetheless expresses, through the voice of his first-person narrator, considerable distrust of commemoration, which in the novel falls largely in the domain of the church. The awarding of a medal to his great-aunt Marie, to mark her fifty years of faithful service as a lay teacher in a Catholic school, amounts to little more than a ploy to force her retirement.[58] When the narrator's maternal grandfather dies, the family resents the appropriation of his memory by a Trappist monk whom he had befriended. Similarly, at the funeral of Tante Marie, the family fumes when the priest refers to "our Tante Marie": "still and all, grief wasn't the same for everyone."[59] In the secular realm, the local war memorial stands for the arbitrariness of commemoration: since the narrator's great-uncles died in different years, the monument's list of names keeps them apart.[60]

Beyond these passing references, *Les champs d'honneur* turns on some of the central themes of World War I commemoration. The novel's title comes from a devotional image, discovered in the family attic, that Tante Marie had hoped would help her brother Joseph recover from exposure to poison gas in 1916. The image features a cross surrounded by the names of the major battle sites of the first two years of the war, those of destroyed towns and villages, and those of the French patriotic saints, leaving space for the name of the soldier needing protection. The card, so inscribed in Marie's hand with her brother's name, age, and the date of his death in a hospital in Tours, represents for the narrator the doomed meeting of history and the personal: "the official variety [history], which for once coincides with our own neglected chronicle."[61] In the novel it serves, like other artifacts of the past, to prompt memory and reflection, but it also stands for the powerlessness of conventional narratives to account for individual loss or to provide consolation.

The image "Les champs d'honneur" cost five centimes, which benefited the Catholic charities of Commercy, a subprefecture in the Meuse with which we have become familiar. In the frigid winter of 1929 the narrator's paternal grandfather, Pierre, sets out for Commercy where, a letter has just informed him, his brother Emile, missing in action since 1917, had been buried in secret by one of his comrades. For a few years after the war Emile's wife, Mathilde, had hoped that, through an exchange of identity plaques, he had perhaps survived. The same hope, coupled with the many cases of amnesia among shell-shocked soldiers after the war, fuels both Madame de Cantil's search for her husband in *La vie et rien d'autre* and the complicated plot of *Un long dimanche de fiançailles*. The letter from Commercy puts an end to this hope in *Les champs d'honneur*, however: the nameless comrade had buried Emile in order to spare his body the indignity of collective burial or of decomposition on the battlefield.[62]

After a long car journey, Pierre arrives in Commercy and, with the help of the friend, digs up his brother's body. (The earth is so thoroughly frozen that they must pour boiling water on it to soften it, thus replicating the mud of the trenches.) But when he comes to the remains he finds not one body but two, and the comrade suddenly remembers having thrown another body, unknown to him, in the grave. Unable to distinguish his brother's remains from the other body, Pierre takes them both. Since the transport of a coffin in a private car required special permits, he places the bones in tins normally used to store the products of a local factory: madeleines.[63] Thus this assortment of human remains returns home packaged under the celebrated Proustian sign of memory. Yet the memories that the madeleine boxes symbolically enshrine are, in their physical form, fragmentary and confused. Like memory itself, Rouaud suggests, they comprise signifiers and signifieds in uncertain relationship, a highly unstable system of signs.

In valorizing the personal as an alternative to the commemorative, Japrisot and Tavernier turn to another set of collective meanings, the powerful master narratives of romance.[64] Periodically, and decisively toward the end, both *Un long dimanche* and *La vie et rien d'autre* dissolve into love stories, the latter quite conventional, if thwarted; the former more uncertain but in the end triumphant. In this way the novel and the film, beyond simply representing the tension in commemoration between different levels of meaning, actually enact it. If love does not exactly conquer all, it empowers the characters and frees them from their obsessions with the past. Like commemorative constructions of grief, the narrativizations take an ostensibly private and individual emotion and endow it with social value: ironically enough, the same values of self-sacrifice, idealism, and devotion to others that commemoration routinely celebrates in dead soldiers. Indeed, as we saw in chapter 6, soldiers' love, not only of their country but of their wives, their families, their homes, figured prominently in postwar commemoration.

Rouaud's subtler, denser, and more wrenching book avoids such conventional reassurance. Punctuated by the deaths of its major characters, *Les champs d'honneur* treats the 1959 death of the narrator's father, not yet forty, almost in passing, yet powerfully conveys its crushing effect on the family. Rouaud thus points to the artificiality and sterility of a code of values, whether patriotic or religious, that places higher value on some lives, those "given" in battle, than on others. The passage from the epigraph concerns the rearrangement of the attic by the narrator's other grandfather, bewildered by his daughter's sudden loss and seeking to find the clue to what he views as almost a family curse; his search turns up Marie's devotional image and Pierre's diary of his 1929 journey, which form the basis for the climactic narratives. For Rouaud memory consists of a series of accretions, some of them accessible only through the kind of upheaval represented by the alteration of the attic: not, the narrator observes, a new order, but an unfamiliar disorder. Memories inhere in the body, as the family discovers when comparing the physical features of long-dead relatives to those of the narrator's sisters.[65] At one point Tante Marie discloses to her startled family that she had had her period for only eight years, reaching menopause at the age of twenty-six. The family calculates that she had her last period in 1916, around the time of her brother Joseph's death as she sat by his hospital bed. "This long, secret repression of sorrow, this blood choked back as one chokes back tears," the narrator writes, "and from this death her life forever thrown off course."[66]

For Rouaud, then, memory offers readers not so much consolation, for it carries its own share of pain, but the deeper human understanding that the novel otherwise associates with writing itself. The grandfather's "redistribution of memory" unearths the texts on which the two climactic narratives of

Joseph's death and of Emile's exhumation rest; the narratives come so late in the novel because only the discovery of their written traces can restore them to the family's consciousness. Though its criss-crossing narratives and frequent flashbacks at first seem almost random, the structure of *Les champs d'honneur* corresponds to the complexity, the tortuousness, and the multidirectionality of any group's journey through its own past. Rouaud rejects any and all claims for the larger meaning of memory, but the rich evocativeness of his prose in recreating the past suggests that the journey itself, in bearing fruit, can constitute its own reward.

In Japrisot and Tavernier, the rejected values of commemoration return in the guise of selfless love. In a very different yet parallel way, Rouaud's anti-commemorative novel in the end testifies to the power of representation to make sense of the past. Finally, the terms of memory, deliberately excluded from the operating discourse of the Historial de Péronne, return in visitors' responses to the evocative power of objects.[67] The very ordinariness of many of those objects, the highly personal character of some, such as letters, diaries, and trinkets, seems to provoke some resistance to the narrativizing the institution enacts, a resistance that takes the form of memory. Typical comments in the visitors' book include "Jamais plus! [Never again]" and "A moving thought in memory of my Father who fought *for nothing* in the 350th Infantry Regiment."[68] Despite Hairy's assertion that the museum wanted not to "give a history lesson, but rather to make available to the larger public the means of reflection,"[69] many of the comments in the visitors' book see the Historial as offering a lesson they need to "remember." Like the many critics who characterized the Historial in terms of "memory," visitors may have been responding to the visual clues, some of them required by the competition program, inscribed in the building itself.[70] Architect Henri Ciriani points to a number of symbolic elements in his design (fig. 7.6): the exterior whiteness, intended to evoke the chalky soil of the Somme, and the protruding marble cylinders on the surface, which refer, in their rectilinear alignment, to the numerous Commonwealth cemeteries that now dot the region's landscape.[71] Stéphane Audoin-Rouzeau was only acknowledging the obvious when he wrote that the Historial is "also a memorial."

But the recurrence of memory in spaces constructed under other signs, whether "history" or "fiction," points to a dynamic fundamental to commemoration's endurance as a form of representation. For commemoration in the broadest sense, the active subsuming of individual memories into discourse, does not operate through coercion or deceit. Recognizing, at some level, the importance of their own memories in constituting their identities, individuals can intuit that "memory" plays a similar role in constructing the groups to which they belong, beginning, as *Les champs d'honneur* so poignantly demon-

FIGURE 7.6. Historial de la Grande Guerre, Péronne: pond façade (Henri Ciriani, architect). Photo: Historial de Péronne.

strates, with the family. Commemoration endures because people yearn to construe as natural the solidarities that bring structure to an increasingly fragmented world. Most of the forms that commemoration took in interwar France have by now lost their resonance; they are, for better or worse, the stuff of history. Yet the dynamic on which commemoration thrived remains with us, continually creating new representations of the past that only grudgingly, and never completely, disclose the secrets of their emergence.

NOTES

INTRODUCTION

1. Mary Gordon, *The Shadow Man* (New York: Random House, 1996), xx. See also Andreas Huyssen, *Twilight Memories: Marking Time in a Culture of Amnesia* (New York: Routledge, 1995), 5–6.

2. Ernest Renan, *Qu'est-ce qu'une nation? et autres essais politiques*, ed. Joël Roman, Agora Les Classiques (Paris: Presses Pocket, 1992), 54; Idem, "What Is a Nation?" trans. Martin Thom, in *Nation and Narration*, ed. Homi K. Bhabha (London: Routledge, 1990), 8–22. The relevant passage (p. 19) begins as follows: "A nation is a soul, a spiritual principle. Two things, which in truth are but one, constitute this soul or spiritual principle. One lies in the past, one in the present. One is the possession in common of a rich legacy of memories; the other is present-day consent, the desire to live together, the will to perpetuate the value of the heritage that one has received in an undivided form."

3. Benedict Anderson, *Imagined Communities: Reflections on the Origins and Spread of Nationalism*, rev. ed. (London: Verso, 1991), especially chapter 11.

4. See, for example, Robert D. Kaplan, *Balkan Ghosts: A Journey through History* (New York: St. Martin's, 1993); Tina Rosenberg, *The Haunted Land: Facing Europe's Ghosts after Communism* (New York: Random House, 1995); Ian Buruma, *The Wages of Guilt: Memories of War in Germany and Japan* (London: Jonathan Cape, 1994); Jane Kramer, *The Politics of Memory: Looking for Germany in the New Germany* (New York: Random House, 1996).

5. Richard Terdiman, *Present Past: Modernity and the Memory Crisis* (Ithaca: Cornell University Press, 1993); Matt K. Matsuda, *The Memory of the Modern* (New York: Oxford University Press, 1996); Jacques Le Goff, *History and Memory*, trans. Steven Rendall and Elizabeth Claman, European Perspectives (New York: Columbia University Press, 1992); Patrick H. Hutton, *History as an Art of Memory* (Hanover, N.H.: University Press of New England, 1993).

6. Some of the essays in which Freud adumbrates his theory of the relationship between memory, the unconscious, and conscious behavior include "The Aetiology of Hysteria," in *The Standard Edition of the Complete Psychological Works of Sigmund Freud*, trans. and ed. James Strachey, 24 vols. (London: Hogarth Press, 1953–74), 3: 191–221; "Screen Memories," in ibid., 3: 303–22; and "Remembering, Repeating, and Working Through," in ibid., 12: 147–56.

7. See Hutton, *History as an Art*, 68–72; Terdiman, *Present Past*, 280–82.

8. Maurice Halbwachs, *On Collective Memory*, ed. and trans. Lewis A. Coser (Chicago: University of Chicago Press, 1992), 43, 51–53; *La mémoire collective*, 2d ed. (Paris: Presses Universitaires de France, 1968; orig. publ. 1950), 132, 146–67; in English, *The Collective Memory*, trans. Francis J. Ditter, Jr., and Vida Yazdi Ditter (New York: Harper and Row, 1980), 130, 140–57.

9. Halbwachs, *The Collective Memory*, 48.

10. For the term "social memory," and some of the categories of memory, see James Fentress and Chris Wickham, *Social Memory*, New Perspectives on the Past (Oxford: Blackwell, 1992), ix–x, 15–32.

11. Terdiman, *Present Past*, 8.

12. John R. Gillis, "Memory and Identity: The History of a Relationship," in *Commemorations: The Politics of National Identity*, ed. John R. Gillis (Princeton: Princeton University Press, 1994), 5.

13. Pierre Nora, "Comment écrire l'histoire de France?" in *Les lieux de mémoire*, 3 vols., vol. 3, *Les France*, 3 books (Paris: Gallimard, 1992), 1: 11. For a good summary of the project and its conceptual stakes, see Nancy Wood, "Memory's Remains: *Les lieux de mémoire*," *History and Memory* 6: 1 (1994): 123–49.

14. On this mutation, see Nora, "Comment écrire," 12–13.

15. Ibid., 20.

16. Ibid., 22–25.

17. For example, François Hartog, "Comment écrire l'histoire de France," *Magazine littéraire*, February 1993, 28–32.

18. Jean-François Chanet, "Le passé recomposé" (Interview with Mona Ozouf), *Magazine littéraire*, February 1993, 23.

19. Nora, "La nation-mémoire," in *Les lieux de mémoire*, vol. 2, *La nation*, 3 books (Paris: Gallimard, 1986), 3: 648–51; Idem, "L'ère de la commémoration," *Les France*, 3: 985–88, 997–1006.

20. Maurice Agulhon, "Esquisse pour une archéologie de la République: L'allégorie civique féminine," *Annales* 28 (1973): 5–34; Idem, "Imagerie civique et décor urbain," *Ethnologie française* 5 (1975): 33–57; Idem, "La 'statuomanie' et l'histoire," *Ethnologie française* 8 (1978): 145–72.

21. Agulhon, *Marianne au combat: L'imagerie et la symbolique républicaines de 1789 à 1880* (Paris: Flammarion, 1979); in English, *Marianne into Battle: Republican Imagery and Symbolism in France, 1789–1880*, trans. Janet Lloyd (Cambridge and Paris: Cambridge University Press and Éditions de la Maison des Sciences de l'Homme, 1981); Idem, *Marianne au pouvoir: L'imagerie et la symbolique républicaines de 1880 à 1914* (Paris: Flammarion, 1989).

22. June Hargrove is currently preparing a book-length study of 1870 monuments

in France. In the meantime, see her "Souviens-toi," *Monuments historiques* 124 (December 1982–January 1983): 59–65; Agulhon, *Marianne au pouvoir*, 128–36; Monique Luirard, *La France et ses morts: Les monuments commémoratifs dans la Loire* (St. Etienne: Université de St. Etienne, Centre Interdisciplinaire d'Études et de Recherches sur les Structures Régionales, 1977), 14–17; David G. Troyansky, "Monumental Politics: National History and Local Memory in French *Monuments aux Morts* in the Department of the Aisne since 1870," *French Historical Studies* 15 (1987–88): 121–41; Annette Becker, "Monuments aux morts après la Guerre de sécession et la Guerre de 1870–71: Un legs de la guerre nationale?" *Guerres mondiales* 167 (1992): 23–40; Neil McWilliam, "Race, Remembrance, and 'Revanche': Commemorating the Franco-Prussian War in the Third Republic," *Art History* 19 (1996): 473–98.

23. Antoine Prost, *Les anciens combattants et la société française, 1914–1939*, 3 vols. (Paris: Presses de la Fondation Nationale des Sciences Politiques, 1977), vol. 3, *Mentalités et Idéologies*, 52. An abridged translation has been published as *In the Wake of War: "Les anciens combattants" and French Society*, trans. Helen McPhail (Providence: Berg, 1992).

24. Prost, *Les anciens combattants*, 3: 41–52.

25. Ibid., 50–62; Idem, "Les monuments aux morts: Culte républicain? Culte civique? Culte patriotique?" in *Les lieux de mémoire*, vol. 1, *La République* (Paris: Gallimard, 1984), 195–225. Prost reiterates this thesis in a response to his critics, "Mémoires locales et mémoires nationales: Les monuments aux morts de 1914–1918 en France," *Guerres mondiales* 167 (1992): 41–50.

26. Jean-Jacques Becker, *Les français dans la grande guerre*, Les Hommes et l'Histoire (Paris: Robert Laffont, 1980), 304–5; in English, *The Great War and the French People*, trans. Arnold Pomerans (Leamington Spa: Berg, 1985), 326–27.

27. Prost, "Les monuments aux morts," 195; Stéphane Audoin-Rouzeau, *14–18: Les combattants des tranchées*, L'Histoire par la Presse (Paris: Armand Colin, 1986), 214; in English as *Men at War 1914–1918: National Sentiment and Trench Journalism in France during the First World War* (Providence: Berg, 1992).

28. Prost, *Les anciens combattants*, 3: 118–19, 174–85, 205.

29. Not least with respect to combatant morale and the relationship between soldiers and officers: see Leonard V. Smith, *Between Mutiny and Obedience: The Case of the French Fifth Infantry Division during World War I* (Princeton: Princeton University Press, 1994), 246–58.

30. Prost, *Les anciens combattants*, 3: 52; Agulhon, "La 'statuomanie,'" 146–47.

31. Jay Winter, *Sites of Memory, Sites of Mourning: The Great War in European Cultural History* (Cambridge: Cambridge University Press, 1995), 2–6, 115; Annette Becker, "From Death to Memory: The National Ossuaries in France after the Great War," *History and Memory* 5: 2 (1993): 32–49; Idem, *La guerre et la foi: De la mort à la mémoire, 1914–1930* (Paris: Armand Colin, 1994).

32. Michel Foucault, *The History of Sexuality*, vol. 1, *An Introduction*, trans. Robert Hurley (New York: Vintage, 1990), 94–96.

33. Michel Foucault, *The Archeology of Knowledge and the Discourse on Language*, trans. A. M. Sheridan Smith (New York: Pantheon, 1972), 115–17.

34. For a lucid summary of Peircian semiotics, see Keith Moxey, *The Practice of*

Theory: Poststructuralism, Cultural Politics, and Art History (Ithaca: Cornell University Press, 1994), 32–37.

35. Henry Rousso, *The Vichy Syndrome: History and Memory in France since 1944*, trans. Arthur Goldhammer (Cambridge: Harvard University Press, 1991), 4.

36. "Mourning and Melancholia," in *The Standard Edition of the Complete Psychological Works of Sigmund Freud*, 14: 243.

37. Jane Tompkins, *Sensational Designs: The Cultural Work of American Fiction, 1790–1860* (New York: Oxford University Press, 1986), xi, xvii, 135, 200.

38. Joan Wallach Scott, "Gender: A Useful Category of Historical Analysis," in her *Gender and the Politics of History* (New York: Columbia University Press, 1988), 44.

39. Mary Louise Roberts, *Civilization without Sexes: Reconstructing Gender in Postwar France, 1917–1927*, Women in Culture and Society (Chicago: University of Chicago Press, 1994), 19–45. I am here summarizing the argument in my article "Monuments, Mourning, and Masculinity in France after World War I," *Gender & History* 8 (1996): 82–107.

40. Steven C. Hause with Anne R. Kenney, *Women's Suffrage and Social Politics in the French Third Republic* (Princeton: Princeton University Press, 1984), 191–251; James F. McMillan, *Housewife or Harlot: The Place of Women in French Society 1870–1940* (New York: St. Martin's, 1981), 101–92; Françoise Thébaud, "La grande guerre: La triomphe de la division sexuelle," in *Histoire des femmes en Occident*, vol. 5, *Le XXe siècle*, ed. Thébaud (Paris: Plon, 1992), 31–74; in English, "The Great War and the Triumph of Sexual Division," trans. Arthur Goldhammer, in *A History of Women in the West*, vol. 5, *Toward a Cultural Identity in the Twentieth Century* (Cambridge: Harvard University Press, 1994), 21–75; Roberts, *Civilization without Sexes*.

41. Mary Poovey, *Uneven Developments: The Ideological Work of Gender in Mid-Victorian England* (Chicago: University of Chicago Press, 1988), 2.

42. Michel Foucault, "Nietzsche, Genealogy, History," in his *Language, Counter-Memory, Practice: Selected Essays and Interviews*, ed. Donald F. Bouchard, trans. Donald F. Bouchard and Sherry Simon (Ithaca: Cornell University Press, 1977), 144.

43. Ibid., 151.

44. One such book, international in scope, is Richard Cork, *A Bitter Truth: Avant-garde Art and the Great War* (New Haven: Yale University Press, 1994).

45. This is not the case of perhaps the classic study of 1940, in my view never surpassed, Marc Bloch's *Strange Defeat: A Statement of Evidence Written in 1940*, trans. Gerard Hopkins (New York: Norton, 1968; orig. publ. 1946).

46. Omer Bartov, "Martyrs' Vengeance: Memory, Trauma, and Fear of War in France, 1918–1940," *Historical Reflections/Réflexions historiques* 22 (1996): 47–76.

CHAPTER ONE

1. See Patrick H. Hutton, *History as an Art of Memory* (Hanover, N.H.: University Press of New England, 1993), 27–28.

2. Henri Bergson, *Matter and Memory*, trans. Nancy Margaret Paul and W. Scott Palmer (New York: Zone Books, 1988; orig. publ. 1896), 103.

3. Martin Jay, *Downcast Eyes: The Denigration of Vision in Twentieth-Century French Thought* (Berkeley: University of California Press, 1993), 192–202. On Bergson's use of the cinematic metaphor, see Matt K. Matsuda, *The Memory of the Modern* (New York: Oxford University Press, 1996), 163–64, though Matsuda does not consider its pejorative connotations.

4. George Johnson, *In the Palaces of Memory: How We Build the Worlds inside Our Heads* (New York: Knopf, 1991), xi, 83, and passim.

5. Joan W. Scott, "The Evidence of Experience," in *The Lesbian and Gay Studies Reader*, ed. Henry Abelove, Michèle Aina Barale, and David M. Halperin (New York: Routledge, 1993), 398.

6. See Chris Jenks, "The Centrality of the Eye in Western Culture: An Introduction," in his *Visual Culture* (London: Routledge, 1995), 1–2.

7. This is the purport of Jay's discussion of the impact of photography in the nineteenth century (*Downcast Eyes*, 125–46), as well as his treatment of Bergson cited above.

8. W. J. T. Mitchell, *Iconology: Image, Text, Ideology* (Chicago: University of Chicago Press, 1986), 12–13.

9. Scott, "The Evidence of Experience," 399.

10. Ibid., 401.

11. Stéphane Audoin-Rouzeau, *14–18: Les combattants des tranchées*, L'histoire par la Presse (Paris: Armand Colin, 1986), 20, 40–47.

12. These included René Benjamin's *Gaspard*, winner of France's premier literary award, the Prix Goncourt, for 1915; Henri Barbusse's *Le feu*, still the most celebrated of French war novels and recipient of the Prix Goncourt for 1916; and the first three volumes in Maurice Genevoix's series of war narratives, *Sous Verdun* and *Nuits de guerre* (1916) and *Au seuil des guitounes* (September 1918), later collected under the title *Ceux de 14*.

13. Dean MacCannell, *The Tourist: A New Theory of the Leisure Class*, 2d ed. (New York: Schocken, 1989; orig. publ. 1976), 68.

14. Ibid., 13.

15. See, for example, Gérard Canini, "Le témoignage de Norton Cru à Jules Romains," in *Mémoire de la grande guerre: Témoins et témoignages*, ed. G. Canini (Nancy: Presses Universitaires de Nancy, 1989), 12. Although the literary scholar Maurice Rieuneau occasionally quibbles with the rigidity of Norton Cru's approach, he rarely differs profoundly with the latter's assessments: *Guerre et révolution dans le roman français de 1919 à 1939* (Paris: Klincksieck, 1974), 22, 170, 193–94, among many possible examples.

16. Jean Norton Cru, *Témoins: Essai d'analyse et de critique des souvenirs de combattants édités en français de 1915 à 1928* (Paris: Les Etincelles, 1929; reprint ed., Nancy: Presses Universitaires de Nancy, 1993).

17. There is a detailed account of the controversy in Hélène Vogel, "Jean Norton

Cru," in Norton Cru, *Du témoignage* (Paris: Éditions Allia, 1989), 155–206. *Du témoignage* was a partial abridgement of *Témoins* published by Gallimard in 1930, consisting of portions of the introduction to *Témoins*, revised and expanded, as well as selections from some of the texts Norton Cru considered the finest examples of war literature. The 1989 edition consists of the introductory chapters by Norton Cru, the table of contents of the anthology, and a biographical essay by Vogel, who was Norton Cru's sister, originally published in a 1967 reprint of *Du témoignage*. See "Note de l'éditeur," in *Du témoignage*, 207, 219.

18. *Témoins*, vii, 26.

19. Ibid., 14.

20. Shoshana Felman, "Film as Witness: Claude Lanzmann's *Shoah*," in *Holocaust Remembrance: The Shapes of Memory*, ed. Geoffrey H. Hartman (Oxford: Blackwell, 1994), 92.

21. *Témoins*, 9.

22. Jay, *Downcast Eyes*, 197.

23. Ibid., vii–viii, 3–5, citation from p. 7; *Du témoignage*, 120–21.

24. *Témoins*, 24, 66; citation from p. 24.

25. Ibid., 27–35.

26. Ibid., 15 (*vue de haut*).

27. Ibid., 24 (*sincérité, fidélité de l'image*).

28. Ibid., 20.

29. *Du témoignage*, 99–110.

30. One of the best of the recent contributions to the "new military history," basically a history of warfare from the combatant's perspective, Leonard V. Smith's *Between Mutiny and Obedience: The Case of the French Fifth Infantry Division during World War I* (Princeton: Princeton University Press, 1994), uses a citation from *Témoins* as an epigraph.

31. *Du témoignage*, 119. Cf. Bergson, *Matter and Memory*, 101: "Memory thus creates anew the present perception, or rather it doubles this perception by reflecting upon it either its own image or some other memory-image of the same kind."

32. M. Genevoix, *Ceux de 14* (Paris: Flammarion, 1950), 129: "Assis devant la table, fumant ma pipe, j'écris, je note des souvenirs."

33. *Du témoignage*, 129.

34. Ibid., 122, 129.

35. *Témoins*, 661.

36. Norton Cru places both Barbusse and Dorgelès in his fourth class, which he defines as "médiocre."

37. Charles Delvert, *Carnets d'un fantassin* (Paris: Albin Michel, 1935). This edition incorporates the principal text considered by Norton Cru, *Histoire d'une compagnie* (Paris: Berger-Levrault, 1918), as well as some other writings.

38. Delvert, *Histoire d'une compagnie*, 5–9. In his discussion of Delvert, Norton Cru contrasts Delvert's own text with the borrowings from it in two articles and a subsequent book on the battle of Verdun by the well-known writer Henry Bordeaux, a staff officer. (Delvert had lent his notebooks to Bordeaux and did not publish them

until two years later.) He concludes that "les livres de certains combattants, celui de Delvert en particulier, sont la reproduction presque textuelle de leurs carnets; . . . qu'un texte vigoureux, coloré et vrai emprunté à un combattant par un publiciste comme Henry Bordeaux, subit un travail d'adaptation au goût du public d'où il sort émasculé, travesti et dénaturé" (*Témoins*, 122–26, citation from p. 125).

39. *Témoins*, 144. Genevoix's war narratives were originally published as five separate but consecutive volumes: *Sous Verdun* and *Nuits de guerre* (1916), *Au seuil des guitounes* (1918), *La boue* (1921), and *Les Éparges* (1923); as Norton Cru writes, "Ces 5 volumes ne sont pas 5 oeuvres différentes; ils sont à proprement parler les 5 tomes d'une même oeuvre." I have used the definitive one-volume edition that Genevoix published in 1950: *Ceux de 14* (Paris: Flammarion, 1950); for that edition, the section title "Au seuil des guitounes" was removed, and the material it contained redistributed among the four remaining sections, which remain in the same order.

40. Jean Bernier, *La percée* (Paris: Albin Michel, 1920). On the types of novels Norton Cru included in his study, see *Témoins*, 61: "souvenirs un peu transposés, où l'auteur s'est effacé ou fait représenter par un personnage fictif qui lui ressemble plus ou moins"; on Bernier: "C'est l'oeuvre d'un vrai poilu, qui connaît son sujet et qui le prouve par une abondance de petits détails typiques" (573).

41. On the importance of rumor and soldiers' general ignorance of battle plans, see, e.g., Genevoix, *Ceux de 14*, 119, 221, 455–56, 468–69; Bernier, 162.

42. Bernier, 52–55, 173, 255; Genevoix, 30–31, 562, 594.

43. Bernier, 191–94; Delvert, 100–101, 138; Genevoix, 67, 479, 492; cf. Audoin-Rouzeau, 37–38.

44. Genevoix, 115, 596.

45. Bernier, 33–34, 98; Delvert, 25, 132–33, 158; Genevoix, 365, 432; Audoin-Rouzeau, 50–56.

46. Delvert, 21–22, 169.

47. Genevoix, 295; Bernier, 86.

48. Delvert, 75, 93, 101–2, 225–27, 246–48, 280.

49. Bernier, 46, 232; Genevoix, 654.

50. Delvert, 242; cf. Audoin-Rouzeau, 107–17, 125–37.

51. Genevoix, 644; Bernier, 217; cf. Audoin-Rouzeau, 129: "La pire épreuve des soldats est de n'être pas compris."

52. Bernier, 136, 68. The latter is one of the rare passages in *La percée* in which the narrator appears in the first person.

53. *Témoins*, 575–76, citation from p. 575.

54. Instances of hostility toward noncombatants: Roland Dorgelès (pseudonym of R. Lécavalé), *Les croix de bois*, Le Livre de Poche ed. (Paris: Albin Michel, n.d.; orig. publ. 1919), 69, 90–92, 243–44, 275–77; Henri Barbusse, *Le feu: Journal d'une escouade* (Paris: Flammarion, 1965; orig. publ. 1916), 34–35, 60, 93–104, 244–50. On poilus (the character uses the synonym *biffins*) as the only true soldiers, Dorgelès, 268.

55. Barbusse, 248; see also 93.

56. *Témoins*, 557, 564–65, citation from p. 557.

57. Ibid., 588.

58. *Témoins*, 69; *Du témoignage*, 103–4 (on pacifism and accuracy), 188–204 (biographical essay by Hélène Vogel).

59. See, e.g., Audoin-Rouzeau, 68.

60. Details on backgrounds and military service from *Témoins*, 122, 142–43, 572–73.

61. Audoin-Rouzeau, 11–15.

62. Delvert, 158; Bernier, 172; Genevoix, 215.

63. Genevoix, 96; Bernier, 206.

64. Genevoix, 364; Delvert, 124; Bernier, 37.

65. Genevoix, 364, 432 (class solidarity), 213 ("obscure souffrance"); Bernier, 14.

66. Genevoix, 281, 610; see also Delvert, 49, paying tribute to one of his sergeants, the regimental boxing champion.

67. *Témoins*, 558, 564, 37.

68. Audoin-Rouzeau, 146; Mary Louise Roberts, *Civilization without Sexes: Reconstructing Gender in Postwar France, 1917–1927*, Women in Culture and Society (Chicago: University of Chicago Press, 1994), 34.

69. Dorgelès, 208–10, 243–44, 273–74; see also Roberts, 38–39.

70. Barbusse, 131–33; Genevoix, 210, 310, 324–25, 429.

71. Bernier, 9, 55, 111–15, 120–25, 147, 186; citation from p. 186.

72. Ibid., 184–86, 229–30.

73. Maurice Rieuneau, "Le romancier dans *Ceux de 14*," in *Maurice Genevoix 1890–1980: Colloque pour le centième anniversaire de la naissance de Maurice Genevoix, 15 et 16 décembre 1990*, ed. Jean Dufournet and Jean Dérens (Paris: Bibliothèque Historique de la Ville de Paris, 1992), 31–39. Norton Cru also recognizes (*Témoins*, 145) that "aucun récit de guerre ne ressemble plus à un roman," but instead of pursuing this insight, he devotes himself to supporting Genevoix's assertion that the work involves no invention.

74. *Témoins*, 15–17. Norton Cru insists that this "paradox" does not represent Stendhal's own view but those of later readers.

75. Barbusse, 179–80; Dorgelès, 203.

76. Genevoix, 127, 33, 95.

77. Ibid., 42, 242, 485, 487–88, citation from p. 242.

78. Ibid., 119.

79. Bernier, 98; Dorgelès, 28, 73.

80. For example, in Genevoix, the story a soldier tells of having to abandon his dying brother in the woods (p. 98); in Barbusse, the story cited above of Poterloo, the soldier who slips into occupied Lens (pp. 131–33); and rival accounts of earlier shelling during an ongoing bombardment (pp. 179–80).

81. Dorgelès, 176; *Témoins*, 590.

82. Barbusse, 171.

83. Genevoix, 65–66; Bernier, 149.

84. Genevoix, 58–59; Bernier, 65.

85. Genevoix, 467, 533–34; ellipsis in original.

86. Ibid., 425, 460; see also 256: "Les souvenirs se lèvent sous chacun de mes pas."

87. Genevoix, 296; Bernier, 188, 237.

88. S. Freud, "Screen Memories," in *The Standard Edition of the Complete Psychological Works of Sigmund Freud*, trans. and ed. James Strachey, vol. 3 (London: Hogarth Press, 1962), 320, 308.

89. Genevoix, 589–91.

90. Ibid., 252.

91. Bernier, 35; Genevoix, 210, 383–84.

92. Dorgelès, 149. *Souvenirs* is the term Genevoix most frequently uses for "memory," and it often refers to visual images or impressions. For instances where Genevoix uses the term *images* to mean, essentially, memories, see pp. 323, 631, and arguably 589, though there the *images fièvreuses* also have the character of hallucinations. For a striking passage in which memories are presented as a series of images, see p. 322.

93. Genevoix, 262. This passage is dated 20–21 October 1914.

94. Bernier, 68, 133.

95. Dorgelès, 282.

96. Bernier, 222–23. I have simplified the paragraph divisions.

97. Joseph Jolinon, *La tête brûlée* (Paris: F. Rieder, 1924).

98. Norton Cru's assessment of *Le valet de gloire* (*Témoins*, 622–23) is unfavorable, calling the entire book "tendentious," deformed by Jolinon's vigorous opposition to the war, but of course this critique postdates the publication of *La tête brûlée*.

99. Jolinon, 36. In the end, Lunant asks the gardener, La Fiarde, to help him farm a parcel of land owned by his father, and is content to work under the latter's direction.

100. Ibid., 30, 89, though on another occasion, 142, she is more tentative and girlish.

101. Ibid., 206.

102. Ibid., 225. On fashion, see Mary Louise Roberts, "Samson and Delilah Revisited: The Politics of Women's Fashion in 1920s France," *American Historical Review* 98 (1993): 657–84.

103. Maurice Genevoix, *La joie* (Paris: Flammarion, 1924). For a slightly fuller discussion of the novel, see Daniel J. Sherman, "Monuments, Mourning, and Masculinity in France after World War I," *Gender & History* 8 (1996): 86–89.

104. Genevoix writes of the two opposing veterans' groups in the village, the *Combattants* and the *Mutilés* (p. 159): "Andrianne belonged to both associations, and for that reason was in good odor in neither. Even had he tried, he would not have been able to choose: despite the fierce battles in which he had risked his life, he was a poor postwar 'combatant'; despite his smashed foot, he was not truly one of the 'disabled.'"

105. See Antoine Prost, *Les anciens combattants et la société française 1914–1939*, 3 vols. (Paris: Presses de la Fondation Nationale des Sciences Politiques, 1977), vol. 3, *Mentalités et Idéologies*, 124–51.

106. Genevoix, *La joie*, 237, 250.

107. Ibid., 222, 207; Jolinon, 89.

108. Roberts, *Civilization without Sexes*, 37–38.

109. Genevoix, *La joie*, 186.

110. Ibid., 265.

111. Ibid., 282.

112. Ibid., 171, 271–72.

113. Genevoix, *Ceux de 14*, 677.

114. On the importance of this theme in war literature, see Roberts, *Civilization without Sexes*, 31.

115. Jean Schlumberger, *Le camarade infidèle* (Paris: Gallimard, 1922); cf. Rieuneau, *Guerre et révolution*, 147. On Genevoix and nature writing, see Françoise Chenet, "Le paysage dans l'oeuvre de Maurice Genevoix," in *Maurice Genevoix 1890–1980*, 137–50; Rieuneau, "Le romancier dans *Ceux de 14*," in ibid., 38.

116. Schlumberger, 11–23.

117. Ibid., 94.

118. Ibid., 117–24, citation from p. 117.

119. Ibid., 185–90. Though the narrative does not relate Clymène's response to the proposal, it is clear that she will accept Vernois out of a similar sense of duty.

120. Ibid., 160.

121. Ibid., 169.

122. Ibid., 174–77.

123. "Nouvelles du tourisme," *RTC* 31 (1921): 197.

124. MacCannell, *The Tourist*, 110–11.

125. "Conférence de M. le Chanoine Collin," *Echo de l'ossuaire de Douaumont* 16 (March-April 1924): 53; see also "A travers la zone rouge: Une visite à la côte 119," *La voix de Notre-Dame de Lorette* 56 (April-May 1929): 142–45.

126. "Visite aux champs de bataille," *Indicateur du tourisme* 1921, fasc. 13, *De Paris aux Vosges*, ii.

127. Barbusse, 34–35; cf. Audoin-Rouzeau, 112–14.

128. Dr. Péquart, *Une visite à Verdun (9 Octobre 1917)* (Nancy: Imprimeries Réunis de Nancy, 1917?), 4; pamphlet reprint excerpted from *La reconstruction Lorraine* 6 (1917).

129. Charles and Géralde Sax, *The English Tourist in France: Grammar, Conversation, Vocabularies, Useful Information, Sports, Clubs, Excursions, Aviation, Army, etc.* (Paris: Delagrave, 1916), 247–50.

130. "Visite au champ de bataille de l'Ourcq," *RTC* 27 (1917): 103. The Verdun volume was published in a German translation in 1929; many of the titles were translated into English, and Michelin also published guides to the Italian front, in Italian, in 1919.

131. "Le mouvement touristique," *RTC* 29 (1919): 20.

132. "Comité de tourisme scolaire," *RTC* 29 (1919): 82; AN, 53AS165, Touring-Club de France scrapbook from 1919, article by Marcel Violette, "Les pèlerinages à la voie sacrée: Faire appel aux pèlerins c'est bien; les loger et les nourrir serait mieux."

133. "Pour les familles des morts," *La voix du combattant*, 28 March 1920; *Le Chemin des Dames*, Guides Illustrés Michelin des Champs de Bataille (Clermont-Ferrand: Michelin, 1920), 19; "Vers Douaumont," *Echo de l'ossuaire de Douaumont* 2 (November-December 1921): 156; "Service de visite des Champs de Bataille," *Bulletin du souvenir* 9 (June 1922): 348.

134. Figures from Jean-Jacques Becker and Serge Berstein, *Victoire et frustrations, 1914–1929*, Nouvelle Histoire de la France Contemporaine 12 (Paris: Seuil, 1990), 150; see also *Reconstructions et modernisations: La France après les ruines, 1918 . . . 1945 . . .*, catalog of an exhibition at the Archives Nationales, Paris, 1991, 22. Although this section of the catalog was written by Becker, in one instance the figures do not coincide: the catalog refers to "350,000 hectares of built property," not 350,000 houses; 350,000 hectares equals 864,500 acres.

135. "Le tourisme et les régions dévastées," *AFC* 10–11 (February-March 1920), article reprinted from the *Télégramme de Boulogne* distinguishing between pilgrims and the merely curious.

136. Louis Fontenaille, "A propos des cimetières militaires," *La France mutilée*, 7 December 1924.

137. Editorial, *Echo de l'ossuaire de Douaumont* 1 (September-October 1921): 2.

138. "Visite au champ de bataille de l'Ourcq," *RTC* 27 (1917): 103; *Champs de bataille de la Marne*, 3 vols., Guides Michelin pour la Visite des Champs de Bataille (Paris: Berger-Levrault, 1917), vol. 1, *L'Ourcq: Meaux—Senlis—Chantilly*, n.p.

139. Léon Auscher, *La prospérité de la France par le tourisme* (Bar-le-Duc: Comte-Jacquet, 1920), citations from pp. 5, 6, and 8. On Auscher lectures to promote tourism in the former war zone, see AN, 53AS165, Touring-Club scrapbook, article by Marcel Violette, June 1919.

140. AN, 53AS165, Touring-Club scrapbook, article by Marcel Violette, June 1919.

141. "Hôtels et hôteliers," *RTC* 33 (1923): 320–21.

142. "Nouvelles du tourisme," *RTC* 31 (1921): 72; AN, $F^2$2127, Préfet Nord to Ministre Intérieur, 22 July 1920.

143. A 1932 article in a veterans' newspaper, picking up on a newspaper account of scantily clad tourists at Douaumont during a heat wave, is ambiguous in this regard. Certainly the article takes a disapproving tone, and refers to the distress caused the parents of the dead by this "sad spectacle." But only the visitors' clothing (or lack of it), not their behavior, brings to mind a beach, and the indignation has a somewhat ritualized quality, suggesting that there was nothing more serious to complain about. "De la tenue devant nos morts," *La voix du combattant*, October 1932.

144. *Champs de bataille de la Marne*, 1: n.p.

145. Ibid. Unless otherwise indicated, subsequent translations from the Marne guidebooks, like this one, are taken from *Michelin Guide to the Battlefields of the World War*, vol. 1, *The First Battle of the Marne, including the Operations on the Ourcq, in the Marshes of St. Gond and in the Revigny Pass, 1914* (Milltown, N.J.: Michelin, 1919); I have inserted in brackets words from the original French when the translation strays too far from their meaning. My readings are based in all cases on the French text, and references will be given to the French original, hereafter abbreviated *Marne* (French) as well as to the American edition, abbreviated as *Marne* (English). Note that the American edition incorporates the three French volumes in one book.

146. *Marne* (French), 1: n.p.; *Marne* (English), 7. The translation rearranges the French sentences; I have followed the French word order and replaced the English "ef-

forts" with the word "effects," both a more literal and more accurate rendering of the word *effets* in this context.

147. *Témoins*, 27–28.

148. *Marne* (French), 1: n.p.; *Marne* (English), 7.

149. *Marne* (French), 3: 4; *Marne* (English), 25.

150. *Marne* (French), 1: 84; *Marne* (English), 94.

151. *Marne* (French), 1: 41, 51, 43, 47 (caption); *Marne* (English), 52, 62, 54, 58 (caption).

152. *Marne* (French), 1: 51–54, citation p. 53; *Marne* (English), 62–65, citation p. 64.

153. *Marne* (French), 1: 23; *Marne* (English), 35.

154. *Marne* (French), 1: 94–95, 108; *Marne* (English), 104–5, 118–19.

155. *Marne* (French), 1: 110–11; *Marne* (English), 120.

156. *Marne* (French), 1: 16; translation mine.

157. Audoin-Rouzeau, 129.

158. *La bataille de Verdun 1914–1918*, Guides Illustrés Michelin des Champs de Bataille (Clermont-Ferrand: Michelin, 1919), 66–67, 98.

159. Ibid., 100–101; *Le Chemin des Dames*, Guides Illustrés Michelin des Champs de Bataille (Clermont-Ferrand: Michelin, 1920), 56–57.

160. *Strasbourg*, Guides Illustrés Michelin des Champs de Bataille (Clermont-Ferrand: Michelin, 1919), 5–13.

161. *Marne* (French), 1: n.p.; *Marne* (English), 7.

162. Delvert, 215–16; Genevoix, 274.

163. Audoin-Rouzeau, 130, 136.

164. *The Somme*, vol. 1, *The first battle of the Somme (1916–1917) (Albert— Bapaume—Péronne)* (Clermont-Ferrand: Michelin, 1919), 98–99; *St. Quentin— Cambrai—La Ligne Hindenburg*, Guides Illustrés Michelin des Champs de Bataille (Clermont-Ferrand: Michelin, 1921), 77.

165. Gustave Babin, "Un anniversaire," *L'illustration*, 30 September 1916, 312.

166. For summaries of the work of this commission and its initial report, see *JO* CD/A, document 3506, 7 December 1921, 319–26 (citations from p. 319); Paul Léon, "Les nouveaux monuments historiques," *L'illustration*, 23 February 1918, 175–78.

167. The report on the proposed bill by the deputy André Fribourg (*JO* CD/A, document 3506, 7 December 1921, 319–26) was reprinted in *La voix du combattant*, 19 March 1922.

168. A. Thomasset, "Conservons 'nos' vestiges de guerre," *La voix du combattant*, 26 November 1922.

169. Brochures include G. Crouvezier, *Itinéraires pour la visite des champs de bataille: Champagne, Aisne, Argonne, Verdun* (Reims: L. Michaud, 1930), 18 pages including illustrations; and *Ce qu'il faut avoir vu sur les champs de bataille de Verdun*, jointly produced by the Touring-Club de France, the Automobile Club de France, and the Office National du Tourisme in 1920 and sold for one franc (see "Itinéraires spéciaux pour les Champs de Bataille," *RTC* 30 [1920]: 181). The least expensive of the Michelin guides, covering only cities, cost around 2.50 francs, and the battlefield guides cost 5 francs.

170. Antoine Champeaux, "Les *Guides Illustrés des Champs de Bataille* 1914–1918," in *Mémoire de la grande guerre*, 341–54, especially 346–48.

171. Gabriel Hanotaux, *Circuits des champs de bataille de France: Histoire et itinéraires de la grande guerre* (Paris: Édition française illustrée, 1920), 5, 254.

172. *Verdun, Metz et les champs de bataille*, Series Les Guides Bleus (Paris: Hachette, 1934), 24–25.

173. See *Témoins*, 33–35; on the Rand donation, *JO CD/A*, document 3506, 7 December 1921, 319; Antoine Prost, "Verdun," in *Les lieux de mémoire*, ed. Pierre Nora, 3 vols., vol. 2, *La nation*, 3 books (Paris: Gallimard, 1986) 3: 120–21. The protective roof and gateway were dedicated in December 1920; in an article on the dedication, *L'illustration* noted that the shelter transformed the site considerably in the name of protecting it, but says that it "conserve tout ce qui raisonnablement pouvait être conservé en ce lieu: un aspect, un signe, un symbole": "Le monument de la Tranchée des Baïonnettes," *L'illustration*, 11 December 1920, 478.

174. *Témoins*, 9.

175. "La vie de l'U.N.C.: A travers nos sections," *La voix du combattant*, 25 June 1922.

176. "Chronique de l'ossuaire," *Echo de l'ossuaire de Douaumont* 34 (March-April 1927): 24; 40 (March-April 1928): 21–22.

177. "Chronique de l'ossuaire," *Echo de l'ossuaire de Douaumont* 46 (March-April 1929): 130–31.

178. Paul Galland, "La guerre tue encore," *La voix du combattant*, 13 April 1929.

179. "Un artificier est horriblement déchiqueté par un obus," *BM*, 30 March 1929.

180. "Département," *RM*, 18 December 1921.

181. "Conservons 'nos' vestiges de guerre."

182. The cited phrase is from Henry Defert, "Visite aux pays dévastés," *RTC* 29 (1919): 161–63.

183. For an example of a school exhibition of souvenirs, see H[enry] D[efert], "Souvenirs de guerre," *RTC* 28 (1918): 35–36; on the Bibliothèque-musée de la Guerre, see Daniel J. Sherman, "Objects of Memory: History and Narrative in French War Museums," *French Historical Studies* 19 (1995–96): 54–56, and the Epilogue below.

184. See Karal Ann Marling and John Wettenhall, *Iwo Jima: Monuments, Memories, and the American Hero* (Cambridge: Harvard University Press, 1991).

185. Elaine Sciolino, "A Painful Road from Vietnam to Forgiveness," *New York Times*, 12 November 1996, section 1.

186. Roland Barthes, *Mythologies*, trans. Annette Lavers (New York: Noonday Press, 1972), 114, 113.

187. Émilie Carles, *A Life of Her Own: The Transformation of a Countrywoman in Twentieth-Century France*, trans. Avriel H. Goldberger (New York: Penguin, 1992; orig. publ. as *Une soupe aux herbes sauvages*, Paris, 1977), 55–57; Simone de Beauvoir, *Mémoires d'une jeune fille rangée* (Paris: Gallimard, 1958), 39–40; in English, *Memoirs of a Dutiful Daughter*, trans. James Kirkup (New York: Harper and Row, 1974), 27–28.

188. "Transformation d'une capote d'infanterie en un manteau pour dame," *Petit echo de la mode*, 25 January 1920, supplément p. 3; Colette, *Les heures longues* (Paris:

Fayard, 1917), 69–75; see also Roberts, *Civilization without Sexes*, 30; and Sherman, "Monuments, Mourning, and Masculinity," 89–91.

189. On postcards, Marie-Monique Huss, "Pronatalism and the Popular Ideology of the Child in Wartime France: The Evidence of the Picture Postcard," in *The Upheaval of War: Family, Work, and Welfare in Europe, 1914–1918*, ed. Richard Wall and Jay Winter (Cambridge: Cambridge University Press, 1988), 329–67; on children's games, S. Audoin-Rouzeau, *La guerre des enfants 1914–1918: Essai d'histoire culturelle* (Paris: Armand Colin, 1993); on devotional images, Annette Becker, *La guerre et la foi: De la mort à la mémoire, 1914–1930* (Paris: Armand Colin, 1994); on images d'Épinal, Jay Winter, *Sites of Memory, Sites of Mourning: The Great War in European Cultural History* (Cambridge: Cambridge University Press, 1995), 122–31; on posters, Peter Paret, Beth Irwin Lewis, and Paul Paret, *Persuasive Images: Posters of War and Revolution from the Hoover Institution Archives* (Princeton: Princeton University Press, 1992).

190. On another level of memory, the card was sold to benefit a planned monument to the defenders of the nearby fort of Troyon.

191. *La guerre: Documents de la section photographique de l'armée*, fasc. 1–20 (Paris: Armand Colin). The fascicules are not dated on the cover, but some of the text articles introducing each one are dated 1916. Bound inside fascicule 20 is a notice saying that publication of the series was being "momentarily suspended."

192. *L'illustration*, 6 January 1917, 9; 1 July 1916, 10. Cf. Barbusse, 229–43.

193. *L'illustration*, 20 November 1915, 534; 27 May 1916, 503.

194. *L'illustration*, 17 July 1915, 69.

195. On the ambiguous artistic status of posters, see Paret et al., *Persuasive Images*, vi–xiii; and, on a slightly earlier period, Marcus Verhagen, "The Poster in *Fin-de-Siècle* Paris: 'That Mobile and Degenerate Art,'" in Leo Charney and Vanessa Schwartz, eds., *Cinema and the Invention of Modern Life* (Berkeley: University of California Press, 1995), 103–29. Statistics from Martin Hardie and Arthur K. Sabin, eds., *War Posters Issued by Belligerent and Neutral Nations 1914–1919* (London: A. & C. Black, 1920), 3 (Imperial War Museum); and *Le musée de la grande guerre (Château de Vincennes)*, a brochure in the archives of the Bibliothèque de Documentation Internationale Contemporaine, the current title of the Bibliothèque-musée; and Guy-Charles Cros, "Le musée de la Guerre," *Mercure de France*, 1 July 1925, 114.

196. Cros, "Le musée de la Guerre," 114.

197. *L'illustration*, 12 October 1918, 333.

198. It is also the case that some significant deaths in the war narratives go unseen, notably that of Genevoix's closest friend, Porchon: see *Ceux de 14*, 595–96.

199. *La guerre*, fasc. 14: *Les étapes du blessé*, 110, plate 24.

200. *Marne* (French), 1: 106, 110–11; *Marne* (English), 116, 120–21; *Ypres et les batailles d'Ypres*, Guides Illustrés Michelin pour la Visite des Champs de Bataille (Clermont-Ferrand: Michelin, 1919).

201. *L'illustration*, 16–23 November 1918, 488.

202. Photographs of tombs appear in *L'illustration*, 26 September 1914, 219, 223; 24 October 1914, 309; 5 December 1914, 429; 20 February 1915, n.p. but around 182; 31 July 1915, 99; accounts and illustrations of ceremonies, 24 October 1914, 300–301; 11

December 1915, 620–21. On the first battlefield monuments, see "Les monuments aux morts de l'Ourcq et de la Marne," *L'illustration*, 18 September 1915, 295.

203. Genevoix, *Ceux de 14*, 63–64.

204. Ibid., 128, 262, 326, 519.

205. Paret et al., *Persuasive Images*, 96.

206. Barthes, *Mythologies*, 114.

CHAPTER TWO

1. Maurice Genevoix, *Ceux de 14* (Paris: Flammarion, 1950), 552, ellipses in original.

2. Claudine Boulouque with Jean-Paul Avice, *Maurice Genevoix et le métier de l'écrivain*, catalogue of an exhibition at the Bibliothèque Historique de la Ville de Paris, December 1990–February 1991, no. 122, illustrated p. 32.

3. Joseph Jolinon, *La tête brûlée* (Paris: F. Rieder, 1924), 37.

4. Philippe Ariès, *Western Attitudes toward Death from the Middle Ages to the Present*, trans. Patricia M. Ranum (Baltimore: Johns Hopkins University Press, 1974), 78–82; Ariès, *The Hour of Our Death*, trans. Helen Weaver (New York: Oxford University Press, 1991; orig. publ. 1981), 548–50; George Mosse, *Fallen Soldiers: Reshaping the Memory of the World Wars* (New York: Oxford University Press, 1990), 9–10; Joanna Bourke, *Dismembering the Male: Men's Bodies, Britain, and the Great War* (London: Reaktion, 1996), 228.

5. M. Sturken, "The Wall, the Screen, and the Image: The Vietnam Veterans Memorial," *Representations* 35 (Summer 1991): 126.

6. Thomas W. Laqueur, "Memory and Naming in the Great War," in *Commemorations: The Politics of National Identity*, ed. John R. Gillis (Princeton: Princeton University Press, 1994), 160.

7. Arno Mayer, "Memory and History: On the Poverty of Remembering and Forgetting the Judeocide," *Radical History Review* 56 (Spring 1993): 9.

8. Sturken, "The Wall," 138, n. 6; Vincent Scully, *Architecture: The Natural and the Manmade* (New York: St. Martin's, 1991), 366. Lin first learned of the Thiepval memorial through Scully's lectures at Yale.

9. Jay Winter, *Sites of Memory, Sites of Mourning: The Great War in European Cultural History* (Cambridge: Cambridge University Press, 1995), 105–6, citation from p. 105.

10. "Villerbon," *RLC*, 6 March 1921.

11. *JO* CD/A, 1919, document 6024, 1216.

12. Winter, *Sites of Memory*, 3, 29.

13. See Stanley Hoffmann, "Paradoxes of the French Political Community," in Hoffmann et al., *In Search of France* (New York: Harper and Row, 1965), 3–18; Theodore Zeldin, *France 1848–1945*, 2 vols., vol. 1, *Ambition, Love, and Politics* (Oxford: Oxford University Press, 1973), 570–93, 601–4; David Thomson, *Democracy in France since 1870*, 5th ed. (London: Oxford University Press, 1969); for a more recent

discussion, see Sudhir Hazareesingh, *Political Traditions in Modern France* (Oxford: Oxford University Press, 1994), 80–83.

14. Two excellent compendia of photographs of World War I memorials, with stimulating commentary, are J.-M. de Busscher, *Les folies de l'industrie* (Brussels: Archives d'Architecture Moderne, 1981); and Annette Becker, *Les monuments aux morts: Mémoire de la grande guerre* (Paris: Errance, n.d. [1987]).

15. *JO* S/A, 1916, document 184, 240. Senator Henry Chéron was proposing that the government award a certificate to the families of all those killed in the war.

16. J. Ajalbert, *Comment glorifier les morts pour la patrie?* (Paris: Georges Crès, 1916), i–ii.

17. *JO* CD/A, document 948, 21 May 1915, 638. Petitjean reintroduced this bill, using exactly the same language, in December 1919, shortly after the election of the first postwar Parliament: *JO* CD/A, document 71, 19 December 1919, 75–76.

18. Such items were offered in *La voix du combattant*, the weekly newspaper of the Union Nationale des Combattants, the largest veterans' association, in its issues of 13 July 1919 (insignia), 11 January 1920 (helmet case), and 10 September 1922 (figurine), among others.

19. *JO* S, 29 July 1920, 1572.

20. *JO* CD/A, document 917, 18 May 1915.

21. For example, *JO* CD/A, document 1119, 20 July 1915, 747–48; *JO* CD/A, document 2129, 18 May 1916, 687; *JO* S/A, documents 184, 20 April 1916, 240; and 255, 29 June 1916, 388 (the basis of the eventual law).

22. See *JO* S/A, document 222, 23 May 1918, 226–27; and document 92, 18 March 1919, 417.

23. *JO* CD/A, 1918, document 5267, 20 November 1918, 1837–38. In rejecting this obligation a second time, the committee argued that though gratitude would surely move every commune to some form of commemoration, some might have legitimate reasons for not erecting a monument within their own territory, as the Senate would have required. A commune might, for example, choose to join with others to build a larger monument in the cantonal seat than any of them singly could have afforded. See *JO* CD, 12 December 1918, 3341–45; *JO* CD/A, 1919, document 6964, 25 September 1919, 2890–91.

24. The final text of the law, dated 25 October 1919, is in *JO*, 26 October 1919, 11910.

25. Michelin *Marne* (French), 1: 86; *Marne* (English), 96; the reference is to the "Grande Tombe de Villeroy," where among others the writer Charles Péguy was buried.

26. ADM, 2 O 35/6, CM/D Caro, 18 December 1919, with a lengthy citation from an earlier meeting of 8 November 1914; Vendôme considered a similar proposal in August 1916: cf. ADL, 274 O⁶ VII/37, CM/D Vendôme, 31 May 1919.

27. ADM, O Moréac, plan by J. Caubert, Vannes, 26 February 1916; and CM/D, 3 September 1916; CM/D, 5 July 1920, in which the mayor declares that the city can proceed to inscribe the names *maintenant connus;* estimate for the inscriptions, 7 September 1922.

28. A description of the project, with a rendering, can be found in "De Bar-le-Duc à Verdun," *La voix du combattant*, 4 June 1922. Another project, for the placement of small markers at each kilometer of the 56-kilometer route between Bar-le-Duc and Verdun, did bear fruit. The density of monuments in the Verdun theater is probably smaller than, for example, at Gettysburg: see Edward Tabor Linenthal, *Sacred Ground: Americans and Their Battlefields* (Urbana: University of Illinois Press, 1991), 87–126.

29. The figures on state support come from Antoine Prost, "Verdun," in *Les lieux de mémoire*, ed. Pierre Nora, 3 vols., vol. 2, *La nation*, 3 books (Paris: Gallimard, 1986), 3: 124; the article provides a good concise history of the construction of the Douaumont Ossuary.

30. Bishop Tissier of Châlons-sur-Marne was the president, and Cardinal Luçon of Reims the honorary president, of the Dormans committee, but its guiding spirit seems to have been the Duchesse d'Estissac, who was co-president of the committee. See Fernand Laudet, "Rapport sur l'oeuvre de la Chapelle de la Reconnaissance de Dormans (Marne)," *Bulletin du comité de la Chapelle de la Reconnaissance de Dormans (Marne)* 1 (May-June 1920): 1–3.

31. René Rémond, ed., *Société séculaire et renouveaux religieux (XXe siècle)*, Histoire de la France religieuse, vol. 4 (Paris: Seuil, 1992), 116–22.

32. Annette Becker, "The Churches and the War," in Jean-Jacques Becker, *The Great War and the French People*, trans. Arnold Pomerans (Leamington Spa: Berg, 1985), 178–91; Rémond, *Société séculaire*, 123–26.

33. *JO* CD/A, document 1593, 17 December 1915, 1417.

34. AN, $F^2$2125, dossier "Entretien des sépultures militaires," report entitled "Résumé du fonctionnement du Service des Inhumations entre le 2 août 1914 et le 10 janvier 1919," 10 May 1919.

35. AN, $F^2$2125, dossier "Entretien des sépultures militaires," ministerial arrêté, 25 November 1918. The creation of this office seems also to have been prompted by a British request for a single interlocutor on issues of burial: see ibid., minutes of an interministerial meeting, 3 October 1918. The Office des Sépultures was later transferred to the Ministry of Pensions.

36. AN, $F^2$2125, dossier "Entretien des sépultures militaires," "Rapport sur le fonctionnement du Service de l'État Civil aux Armées entre le 10 janvier et le 10 mai 1919," 12 May 1919.

37. Genevoix, *Ceux de 14*, 256. Although in the single-volume edition this passage is located in part 2, "Nuits de Guerre," first published in 1916, according to Jean Norton Cru it would originally have appeared in the third volume, *Au seuil des guitounes*, first published in September 1918 and suppressed from the definitive edition: see Norton Cru, *Témoins: Essai d'analyse et de critique des souvenirs de combattants édités de 1915 à 1928* (Paris: Les Etincelles, 1929; reprint ed, Nancy: Presses Universitaires de Nancy, 1993), 143.

38. See AN, $F^2$2125, dossier "Entretien des sépultures militaires," letters regarding clandestine exhumations, July 1919.

39. "Respect à nos morts!" *La voix du combattant*, 27 July 1919; "On profane toujours les tombes de nos camarades," *La France mutilée*, 9 October 1921; "Autour du scan-

dale des exhumations," *La France mutilée*, 9 November 1924; AN, F²2125, dossier "Violations de sépultures: Incidents," regarding reports of "indecent" behavior by visitors (although it is worth noting that in this archival record none was confirmed), 1919–20.

40. "Transfert des corps des militaires tués aux armées," *Bulletin de l'Union fédérale*, 21 November 1920; "A propos des exhumations: Respectons la volonté des morts," *La voix du combattant*, 7 May 1922.

41. One prominent proponent of burial at the front was General de Castelnau; see "Où nous en sommes," *AFC* 10–11 (February-March 1920).

42. *La voie sacrée*, issues of November 1920, December 1920–January 1921, and March-April 1921.

43. "La grande manifestation nationale," *L'avenir, moniteur de Loir-et-Cher*, 4–5 August 1919.

44. *JO* CD, 19 September 1919, 4440, statement of Léon Abrami.

45. *JO* CD/A, document 5642, 4 February 1919, 479–80. In *Sites of Memory, Sites of Mourning*, 25, Jay Winter suggests that the ban on exhumations took effect with a military instruction of 15 June 1919 (text in AN, F²2125, dossier "Entretien des sépultures militaires"). But this decree simply replaced and generalized long-standing military policies; it was necessitated by the government's temporary withdrawal of its bill as discussed below.

46. "Pour les familles des morts au champ d'honneur," *LeT*, 10 May 1919.

47. AN, F²2125, dossier "Entretien des sépultures militaires," PV Commission Nationale des Sépultures, 31 May 1919. Winter refers to this debate in *Sites of Memory*, 24–25, but his discussion is marred by several factual errors (the meeting was of the Commission des Sépultures Militaires, not the Conseil d'État; Barthou did not become minister of war until 1921) and does not mention Doumer.

48. *JO* S, 16 October 1919, 1696.

49. AN, F²2125, dossier "Entretien des sépultures militaires," PV Commission Nationale des Sépultures, 31 May 1919.

50. *JO* S, 16 October 1919, 1696; see also *JO* CD, 19 September 1919, 4441.

51. *JO* S, 29 July 1920, 1571–74. The proposal that the state fund relatives' travel to battlefield cemeteries was considered in a report on a number of proposed bills related to burials and transfers. Though endorsed, it was not adopted because of financial constraints; the report reprinted a letter from the minister of public works guaranteeing reduced fares for close relatives in straitened circumstances. See *JO* CD/A, document 831, 28 April 1920, 790. The law providing annual travel at state expense was promulgated on 29 October 1921; cf. AN, F²2125, dossier "Sépultures militaires: Textes (Voyages gratuits des familles)."

52. Compare the language of Simonet in his bill proposing immediate exhumations at state expense, *JO* S/A, document 759, 18 December 1919, 892–93, with that of Maginot in his appearance before the Senate, *JO* S, 29 July 1920, 1574. For a typical article criticizing the government, though in fairly moderate terms, see "Respectons nos morts et songeons à leurs familles," *La voix du combattant*, 7 September 1919, 2.

53. "Notre pétition," *AFC* 5–6 (September-October 1919); "Où nous en sommes," *AFC* 10–11 (February-March 1920).

54. "Atavisme," *AFC* 8 (December 1919), attack on Abrami; "Les morts de la guerre," *AFC* 8 (December 1919), criticism of the playwright François de Curel; "Le retour des morts," *AFC* 10–11 (February-March 1920). In the latter two cases *L'art funéraire* was commenting on news items from other publications.

55. *JO* CD, 19 September 1919, 4440, remarks of the deputy Pacaud: "C'est pour nous un devoir impérieux que de les ramener dans leur village, à proximité de leurs parents," as well as another mention of "leurs villages"; *JO* S/A, document 759, 18 December 1919, 892, Simonet's proposal for immediate exhumations: "Les familles étaient en droit de compter que leurs morts leurs seraient rendus et que leurs glorieux restes pourraient revenir au pays natal."

56. On Barrès's "organic nationalism," with its emphasis on the collective determinants of individual character, irrationalism, and cult of the land, see Zeev Sternhell, *Maurice Barrès et le nationalisme français* (Brussels: Complexe, 1982; orig. publ. 1975), 269–90.

57. See, for example, the comments of the deputy Pacaud, *JO* CD, 19 September 1919, 4442.

58. *JO* CD, 19 September 1919, 4441; *JO* S, 16 October 1919, 1697.

59. *JO* S, 16 October 1919, 1696.

60. AN, F^{2}2125, dossier "Entretien des sépultures militaires," PV Commission Nationale des Sépultures, 31 May 1919, statement of de Mouy.

61. *JO* S, 16 October 1919, 1696.

62. AN, F^{2}2125, dossier "Entretien des sépultures militaires," PV Commission Nationale des Sépultures, 31 May 1919; cf. his comments in *JO* S, 16 October 1919, 1698.

63. "Triptyque," *La voix du combattant*, 5 September 1920; "Pour le repos de nos morts: Histoires lamentables," *La France mutilée*, 19 November 1922; "Les exhumations: La plainte d'une mère indignée," *La voix du combattant*, 5 March 1922; "A la recherche des tombes," *La voix du combattant*, 14 and 21 September 1924, the latter articles describing the experiences of family members who had gone to the original gravesites only to find the bodies missing.

64. "Les cimetières militaires," *La voix du combattant*, 11 April 1920; "Le front misérable: Tombes perdues, cimetières oubliés," *AFC* 12 (April 1920), reprinted from *L'intransigeant*; *JO* S, 16 October 1919, 1692, comments of Senator Touron on the deficiencies of cemeteries.

65. "L'administration de la guerre retient prisonniers les corps de nos soldats," *AFC* 4 (August 1919). The provision for uniform tomb markers with optional religious emblems was part of the omnibus bill on military cemeteries proposed by the Chamber of Deputies' Committee on General, Departmental, and Communal Administration: *JO* CD/A, document 831, 28 April 1920, 791. This bill was never passed: its main elements were incorporated into the budget (*loi des finances*) for 1921, and this provision was included in the decree of application issued on 25 September 1920, article 5: *JO*, 30 September 1920, 14435.

66. Serge Barcellini, "Les monuments en hommage aux combattants de la 'Grande France' (Armée d'Afrique et Armée coloniale)," in *Les troupes coloniales dans la grande*

guerre, ed. Claude Carlier and Guy Pedroncini (Paris: Institut d'Histoire des Conflits Contemporaines/Economica, 1997), 121–23.

67. See, e.g., "A propos des exhumations: Respectons la volonté des morts," *La voix du combattant*, 7 May 1922; Louis Fontenaille, "A propos des cimetières militaires," *La France mutilée*, 7 December 1924.

68. *JO* CD/A, document 4235, 4 April 1922, 557–58.

69. SEACVG/SM, box 1C, sector head to interdepartmental director, Lille, 24 May 1983, on a *fichier* at Lorette dating from 1925.

70. See, e.g., SEACVG/SM, box 95C, Fleury-devant-Douaumont, dossier "Aménagement générale," deputy sector head, État Civil, Meuse, to director, État Civil, 6th region (Metz), 14 August 1925; head, Service des Sépultures Militaires, to sector head, État Civil, Meuse, 2 April 1929.

71. See, on Lorette, SEACVG/SM, box 1, Ablain St. Nazaire, fiche de controle (number of bodies) and section head, État Civil français de Belgique, to head, Office des Sépultures, 3 February 1922, enclosing a list of ninety-four cemeteries in forty-eight Belgian towns from which it was proposed that bodies be transferred to Lorette; on Douaumont, see SEACVG/SM, box 95, Fleury-devant-Douaumont, dossier "Historique," Note au sujet du Monument et du Cimetière de Douaumont, 19 July 1932, and box 95B, dossier "Découverte d'un cimetière militaire dans le zone rouge de Verdun," 1949–50.

72. *JO* S/A, document 759, 18 December 1919, 893.

73. *JO* S/A, document 114, 25 February 1922, 83–84. The bill received a favorable report from the relevant committee on 30 June 1922 (*JO* S/A, document 462, 573), but seems to have gone no further, an indication that the always sensitive Maginot had provided assurances that the Senate's views would be heeded.

74. The ossuary committees seem to have had little difficulty obtaining effective control over unidentified remains, which were technically the responsibility of the state. The provisional ossuary built at Douaumont had been receiving remains since before the end of the war, but this seems to have been a purely informal arrangement, which was duly made official. See SEACVG/SM, box 95, Fleury-devant-Douaumont, letters from the head, Office des Sépultures Militaires, to undersecretary for administration, Ministère de la Guerre, 18 July 1919; and letters from undersecretary to Ginisty and to head, État Civil, Châlons-sur-Marne, 29 July 1919.

75. SEACVG/SM, box 95A, Fleury-devant-Douaumont, minister of pensions to Ginisty, 24 September 1921; minister to General commanding the 6th Region, 16 November 1921.

76. *Echo de l'ossuaire de Douaumont* 4 (March-April 1922): 124–25.

77. SEACVG/SM, box 95, Fleury-devant-Douaumont, Note au sujet du cimetière militaire de Douaumont, 11 May 1922.

78. SEACVG/SM, box 95A, Fleury-devant-Douaumont, sector head, État-Civil, Meuse, to minister, 1 July 1925; and director, État-Civil, 6th region, to minister, 17 August 1925.

79. SEACVG/SM, box 95A, Schleiter to minister, 26 July 1926; box 88, Pétain, Ginisty, Polignac, and Schleiter to minister, 24 September 1926.

80. SEACVG/SM, box 95, Fleury-devant-Douaumont, Marin to Ginisty, 29 November 1926; Note au sujet du monument et du cimetière de Douaumont (Meuse), 19 July 1932. Some documentation gives the number of dead represented by the remains in the Douaumont Ossuary as 130,000, not 32,000; the figure seems plausible, but I have not been able to verify it. See SEACVG/SM, box 95, Fleury-devant-Douaumont, fiche de contrôle; and box 95A, dossier "Doléances diverses, familles et associations," Pierre Boillon, Bishop of Verdun to director of statutes and medical services, 10 April 1978.

81. "L'hommage des communes à leurs enfants tombés pour la patrie," *L'avenir de Verdun*, 2 November 1922.

82. For example, "L'inauguration du monument de Cellettes," *RLC*, 11 September 1921, in which the mayor, accepting the monument from the committee that built it, says "Je le place sous la protection de tous les habitants, ils en ont désormais la garde, ils l'assureront sans défaillance"; see also "L'inaguration du monument aux morts de Landaul," *OR*, 19 April 1923, in which the mayor lists the groups now responsible for the monument—mourners, veterans, all the townspeople, and above all children.

83. "A l'hôtel de ville," *Le progrès du Morbihan*, 4 January 1919.

84. See, for example, "Département," *RM*, 3 April 1921, speech of the mayor, Hublot: "Vos noms ne tomberont jamais dans l'oubli; ils seront pour tous le symbole du dévouement et du sacrifice.—Les enfants trouveront en les lisant sur cette pierre, des leçons de patriotisme et de vertus civiques; ils apprendront à aimer la France leur patrie et rêveront de suivre votre exemple et de vous venger."

85. For additional examples and discussion, see Daniel J. Sherman, "Monuments, Mourning, and Masculinity in France after World War I," *Gender & History* 8 (1996): 99 and n. 72.

86. "Mourning and Melancholia," in *The Standard Edition of the Complete Psychological Works of Sigmund Freud*, trans. and ed. James Strachey, vol. 14 (London: Hogarth Press, 1957), 243.

87. "Pour ceux qui recherchent les corps des soldats disparus," *La France mutilée*, 19 November 1922; "Pour les familles des disparus," *La France mutilée*, 29 April 1923; "Soldat identifié," listing the Comité de Lorette as the source of the information and providing its address, *Courrier de la Sologne*, 15 October 1922.

88. *Bulletin du souvenir*, June 1922: 314–18. The actual lists of both named and unidentified remains were in separate sections.

89. Lorette initiated annual pilgrimages by family members in 1928; cf. *La voix de Notre-Dame de Lorette* 49 (February-March 1928): 41.

90. *La voix de Notre-Dame de Lorette* 71 (October-November 1931).

91. *Echo de l'ossuaire de Douaumont* 10 (March-April 1923): 37, 40–41, 46; no. 13 (September-October 1923): 139; *La voix de Notre-Dame de Lorette* 48 (December 1927–January 1928): 28–30.

92. *Echo de l'ossuaire de Douaumont* 6 (July-August 1922): 162; no. 12 (July-August 1923): 98–99.

93. Annette Becker, "From Death to Memory: The National Ossuaries in France after the Great War," *History and Memory* 5: 2 (1993): 32–49; and *La guerre et la foi: De la mort à la mémoire, 1914–1930* (Paris: Armand Colin, 1994).

94. See the discussion of fund-raising for the Catholic chapel in "L'oeuvre de Douaumont," *Echo de l'ossuaire de Douaumont* 65 (January-March 1933): 467–69.

95. See, for example, "Allocution de M. L'Abbé Bergey," *Echo de l'ossuaire de Douaumont* 66 (April-June 1933): 498–511.

96. *La voix de Notre-Dame de Lorette* 49 (February-March 1928): 35.

97. *Echo de l'ossuaire de Douaumont* 63 (July-September 1932): 423.

98. "Lettre pastorale de Monseigneur l'Évêque au clergé et aux fidèles de son diocèse," 2 November 1923, in Mgr. Julien, *Aux glorieux morts de Lorette (1921–1929)* (Arras: Nouvelle Société Anonyme du Pas-de-Calais, 1930), n.p.

99. See the description by the architect, Cordonnier, "La décoration intérieure de la chapelle," *La voix de Notre-Dame de Lorette* 48 (December 1927–January 1928): 23; and a visitor's description in "Lorette . . . L'hiver: Visions et réflexions," *La voix de Notre-Dame de Lorette* 67 (February-March 1931): 282. On the stained glass, see "Vitraux de la chapelle," *La voix de Notre-Dame de Lorette* 57 (June-July 1929): 162–64.

100. See de Busscher, *Les folies de l'industrie*, 246–47.

101. "Lorette . . . L'hiver," 283; on lanterns, see "La lanterne des morts," *La voix de Notre-Dame de Lorette* 93 (January-March 1936): 14; for background, Thomas A. Kselman, *Death and the Afterlife in Modern France* (Princeton: Princeton University Press, 1993), 56.

102. De Busscher, *Les folies de l'industrie*, 173.

103. On the funding of the tower and the chapel, see "L'Amérique et les morts de Verdun," *Echo de l'ossuaire de Douaumont* 29 (May-June 1926): 142–46; and "Chronique générale," *Echo de l'ossuaire de Douaumont* 43 (September-October 1928): 66–67.

104. On the funding of these monuments and the "neutrality" of the main ossuary space, see "L'oeuvre de Douaumont," *Echo de l'ossuaire de Douaumont* 65 (January-March 1933): 467–69. The Jewish monument was dedicated in 1938, six years after the completion of the main ossuary; see "22ᵉ anniversaire de la victoire de Verdun," *Echo de l'ossuaire de Douaumont* 87 (July-September 1938): 8–10.

105. SEACVG/SM, box 95B, Fleury-devant-Douaumont, secretary of the Conseil de l'Ordre, Grand Orient de France to minister of war, 28 July 1924; "Au sujet de l'ossuaire de Douaumont," typescript four-page protest calling for a "neutral" management of the ossuary, undated but post-1932, probably 1934, from context.

106. SEACVG/SM, box 1C, Ablain St. Nazaire, Notes on a meeting between veterans' groups and representatives of the ossuary committee, 8 October 1930; Note au sujet des cimetières militaires, n.d. but after 1931.

107. "Pour le repos de nos morts: L'inutilité et le danger d'immenses nécropoles," *La voix du combattant*, 26 February 1922, emphasis in original.

108. For a particularly revealing debate on this issue, see the account of a meeting of the monument committee in Pontivy (Morbihan), *JP*, 29 May 1921. Mayors frequently put up preliminary lists of the dead, culled from the official notices they received, in town halls, or sent them to local newspapers, inviting townspeople to come forward to make corrections or signal omissions. Examples include a list with notice from the mayor of Commercy, *RE*, 23 December 1922; ADL, 274 O⁶VII/37, Vendôme city council minutes, 15 September 1921, announcing the posting of a list in the town hall.

109. Cf. ADMe, E Dépôt 260/1M3 (Les Monthairons), letter, Veuve Eudot to mayor, 2 September 1920; E Dépôt 357/1M7 (St. Maurice-sous-les-Côtes), letters from a variety of former residents with inquiries and contributions, 1920–21.

110. ADL, 158 O⁶6, letter, Redouin to prefect Loir-et-Cher, 2 December 1922. In a letter to the prefect of 15 December 1922, the subprefect of Vendôme wrote that since the soldier in question had never lived in Morée, his name should be inscribed in the town where his death certificate had been sent, presumably either his birthplace or the town where he was living at the time of his mobilization.

111. "Conférence de M. le Chanoine Collin," *Echo de l'ossuaire de Douaumont* 16 (March-April 1924): 53–57. The talk was given at the École Centrale de Paris on 25 March 1924; for Ginisty's original talk (16 February 1919), see "La première idée du projet lancée au Trocadéro, à Paris," *Echo de l'ossuaire de Douaumont* 1 (September-October 1921): 12–14. Most local monuments do not specify which of the names inscribed were those of soldiers listed as missing.

112. "La première idée," 13.

113. "L'ossuaire de Douaumont," *L'illustration*, 28 April 1923, 403. The ossuary's own journal described this arrangement in much more flowery terms: see "Le monument de Douaumont," *Echo de l'ossuaire de Douaumont* 10 (March-April 1923): 50.

114. *Verdun, Argonne, Metz (1914–1918)*, Guides Illustrés Michelin des Champs de Bataille (Clermont-Ferrand: Michelin et Cⁱᵉ, 1926), 97; "L'inauguration officielle de l'ossuaire de Douaumont, le 18 septembre," *L'illustration*, 24 September 1927, 314–16. The main photograph is reproduced in Prost, "Verdun," 126–27.

115. "Discours de la princesse de Polignac à la séance patriotique de Verdun, le 17 février 1924," *Echo de l'ossuaire de Douaumont* 15 (January-February 1924): 15.

116. Ibid.

117. See Winter, *Sites of Memory*, 54–77, especially 63–64; A. Becker, *La guerre et la foi*, 87–94.

118. De Busscher, *Les folies*, 246–47. De Busscher does not provide dates either for his childhood visits or for the subsequent closing of the coffin, implying only that the latter occurred sometime between his childhood and the period, presumably the late 1970s, when he was photographing and writing about the monuments. From various indications in the book it seems likely that de Busscher's childhood visits took place either just before or just after World War II.

119. Mayer, "Memory and History," 10–11. It is worth pointing out that the observances at Douaumont could not invariably be called nationalistic in the interwar sense of the term, that is, as a discernibly right-wing movement hostile to the republican regime.

120. M. Foucault, "Two Lectures," in *Power/Knowledge: Selected Interviews and Other Writings, 1972–1977*, ed. Colin Gordon (New York: Pantheon, 1980), 82.

121. Michel de Certeau, *The Practice of Everyday Life*, trans. Steven F. Rendall (Berkeley: University of California Press, 1984), 133; original citation in *L'invention du quotidien*, vol. 1, *Arts de faire*, rev. ed., ed. Luce Giard, Folio Essais (Paris: Gallimard, 1990), 198.

122. "Les inscriptions sur les monuments aux morts," *La voix du combattant*, 18 December 1921.

123. ADMe, E Dépôt 353/1M7, letter Linarez (?) to mayor, 23 May 1921: "Voyant ce monument aux morts avec ces inscriptions, mon fils n'y étant pas, me serait très pénible."

124. De Certeau, *The Practice*, 149; cf. *Arts de faire*, 218. The word *récit*, which Rendall translates as "story," can also mean "narrative."

125. See, for example, Hubert Pérès, "Identité communale, République et communalistation: A propos des monuments aux morts des villages," *Revue française de science politique* 39 (1989): 666–71.

126. *OR*, 3 June 1923.

127. *Le ploërmelais*, 30 October 1921. The poem is signed only with the initials "A. H." A literal prose translation might run: "I sing to you, o sacred names engraved in stone . . . / They are written in haloes of glory / For you were, without fear, the modest heroes / Who will shine endlessly in the sun of history / That will light up your tombs with its very pure rays."

128. "Les Meusiens honorent leurs morts," *RE*, 22 October 1921.

129. Examples include "L'inauguration du monument de Verdun," *BM*, 10 November 1928 (Sparta and Rome); "Les cérémonies du souvenir: Arzon honore ses morts de la grande guerre," *OR*, 6 September 1923 (Celts); "La fête de Fains," *RM*, 2 December 1920 (Gauls); "L'inauguration du monument de Droué," *Le carillon de Vendôme*, 29 September 1921 (d'Artagnan and Revolutionary soldiers); "Inauguration du monument aux enfants d'Houdelaincourt morts pour la France," *RE*, 9 July 1921 (Grande Armée); "Inaugurations de monuments aux enfants de Pagny-la-Blanche-Côte et de Chalaines morts pour la France," *RE*, 30 July 1921 (soldiers from the middle ages to 1870).

130. "Rouvrois-sur-Meuse a honoré ses grands morts," *La Meuse*, 18 April 1925. He used the same image in his speech at Pagny-la-Blanche-Côte cited in the previous note.

131. "A la Haute Chevauchée," *RE*, 5 August 1922; "En l'honneur de nos morts glorieux," *RE*, 19 May 1923.

132. "Ploërmel fête ses enfants morts pour la patrie," *Le ploërmelais*, 23 October 1921; "Deux ministres à Quiberon et Auray," *Le progrès du Morbihan*, 13 November 1921.

133. Josette Rey-Debove and Alain Rey, eds., *Le nouveau Petit Robert: Dictionnaire alphabétique et analogique de la langue française*, rev. ed. (Paris: Dictionnaires Le Robert, 1993), 386: "Manifester (ses sentiments, ses convictions) en termes violents, par des cris."

134. "Les inscriptions sur les monuments aux morts," *La voix du combattant*, 18 December 1921.

135. *JO* CD/A, document 2324, 11 July 1916, 1081.

136. *JO* CD/A, document 2360, 18 March 1921, 1097.

137. *JO* S/A, document 327, 8 April 1922, 329–30.

138. *JO* S, 1 June 1922, 786–88; 8 May 1923, 860–63. The definitive text of the law, dated 2 July 1923, is in *JO*, 3 July 1923, 6350.

139. *JO* S, 1 May 1923, 862.

140. "Informations Parlementaires: Morts pour la France," *La France mutilée*, 18 June 1922.

141. Mary Louise Roberts, *Civilization without Sexes: Reconstructing Gender in Post-war France, 1917–1927*, Women in Culture and Society (Chicago: University of Chicago Press, 1994), 10–12, 89–147; Siân Reynolds, *France Between the Wars: Gender and Politics* (London: Routledge, 1996), 18–37.

142. *JO* S, 8 May 1923, 862.

143. *JO* S, 8 May 1923, 861–62; the discussion of fiscal legislation and its consequences comes largely from the remarks of Gourju in the same debate.

144. The original proposal, by Henri Connevot, is *JO* CD/A, document 1624, 16 November 1920, 255; the committee report is *JO* CD/A, document 2308, 21 January 1921, 103–4. Connevot's bill would have extended article 106 of the law of 31 July 1920, which gave widows, parents, children, or grandchildren the right to reclaim bodies, to include other relatives or friends. The notion of the family in article 106 is, of course, far more restrictive than the one used for the law on the transfer of names, but this probably has to do chiefly with the greater cost to the state the former entailed.

145. For example, "L'inauguration du monument aux morts de Troyon," *La Meuse*, 2 May 1925, speech of Taton-Vassal, deputy: "les simples qui rendirent leur dernier souffle en pensant au champ paternel." See also "La cérémonie du 11 novembre," *Le progrès du Morbihan*, 15 November 1925, the mayor of Vannes's remarks on soldiers' attachment to their native towns: "C'est elle aussi qu'ils défendaient, parce que leur clocher avait pour eux la valeur d'un drapeau et qu'ils avaient appris qu'en défendant la France c'était le clocher de leur pays qu'ils défendaient."

146. "Inauguration du monument de Thenay," *RLC*, 30 July 1922 (the ceremony took place on 16 July).

147. See "La crise monumentale," *La voix du combattant*, 26 June 1921 (excerpted from an article by Louis Forest in *Le matin*): "Elles [monuments, but the antecedent is *choses*, thus feminine] porteraient à rire si elles n'étaient pas sanctifiées par les interminables listes de noms qui y sont gravés." Inscribed names are compared unfavorably to an anthology in Henry de Jouvenel, "Quelques livres: Le plus beau monument," *La France mutilée*, 27 January 1924; see also M. Randoux, "Pour les écrivains morts à la guerre," *La France mutilée*, 7 December 1924.

148. Until a few days before this ceremony, plans had called for the unknown soldier to be buried at the Panthéon after a ceremonial passage through the Arc. When the Chamber of Deputies and the Senate voted, on 8 November 1920, to give the soldier a permanent resting place under the Arc, there was not sufficient time to create such a grave before the ceremony. The remains of the unknown were thus kept in a crypt beneath the Arc and then definitively buried in January 1921. See the following articles from *La voix du combattant*: "Au soldat inconnu," 7 November 1920; "La sépulture du 'soldat inconnu,'" 19 December 1920; "La cérémonie du 28 janvier: L'inhumation définitive du soldat inconnu," 30 January 1921. For the actual bill and debate, see *JO* CD/A, document 1542, 8 November 1920, 5–6; *JO* S, 8 November 1920, 1740–42. On the specific political context of the burial of the unknown soldier, see Annette Becker, "Du 14 juillet 1919 au 11 novembre 1920: Mort, où est ta victoire?" *Vingtième siècle* 49 (January-March 1996): 31–44.

149. "Notre enquête: Un seul poilu inconnu? ou plusieurs?" *La voix du combattant*, 16 October 1921.

150. Laqueur, "Memory and Naming," 163.

151. Jouvenel's speech is in "Au monuments des volontaires morts pour la France," *La France mutilée*, 7 September 1924; Méric's article is reprinted in "Notre enquête."

152. Hans-Jürgen Lüsebrink, "Les troupes coloniales dans la guerre: Présences, imaginaires et représentations," in *Images et colonies: Iconographie et propagande coloniale sur l'Afrique française de 1880 à 1962*, ed. Nicolas Bancel, Pascal Blanchard, and Laurent Gervereau (Paris: Bibliothèque de Documentation Internationale Contemporaine and Association Connaissance de l'Histoire de l'Afrique Contemporaine, 1993), 82; Jacques Thobie, Gilbert Meynier, Catherine Coquery-Vidrovitch, and Charles-Robert Ageron, *Histoire de la France coloniale*, vol. 2, *1914–1990* (Paris: Armand Colin, 1990), 103.

153. Thobie et al., *Histoire de la France coloniale*, 2: 77–78; Barcellini, "Les monuments en hommage," 119–20, 123–24; [France], Ministère des Anciens Combattants et Victimes de Guerre, Délégation à la Mémoire et à l'Information Historique, "1914–1918: L'armée coloniale, les soldats d'outre-mer: Monuments et sépultures," brochure, 1996. One of the most celebrated of these monuments, a figural group in Reims dedicated in 1924 to soldiers from "l'Afrique noire," was destroyed by the Germans in 1940, and is now itself commemorated by a simpler monument dedicated in 1963: see Barcellini, "Les monuments en hommage," 132–33.

154. Thobie et al., *Histoire de la France coloniale*, 2: 101–2, 119–32; Lüsebrink, "Les troupes coloniales," 79–85. The recent revival of French interest in colonial monuments, signaled by the publication of several pamphlets devoted to them in the Veterans' Ministry's series "Les chemins de la mémoire," as well as the construction of new ones, may signal a gradual integration of the colonies into France's national self-image; see, for example, Maryse Michel and Raymond Michel, "A Carpentras, un monument aux africains morts pour la France pendant la guerre de 1914–1918," *Études vauclusiennes* 50 (1993): 27–31, on a monument built in the late 1970s.

155. Elaine Scarry, *The Body in Pain: The Making and Unmaking of the World* (New York: Oxford University Press, 1985), 127. One meaning of the body in its "most extreme form" is the corpse.

156. Ibid., 128.

157. The tomb of the unknown became the focal point not only for official ceremonies, as it still is, but for a number of antimilitarist and generally leftist demonstrations. In 1927 the right-wing press charged that communists protesting the execution of the Italo-American anarchists Nicola Sacco and Bartolomeo Vanzetti had desecrated the tomb of the unknown by urinating on it; see "Le soldat inconnu outragé," *Le cri du poilu de l'Union Nationale des Combattants* (Lorient), October 1927, reprinting a story from *Le Gaulois*.

CHAPTER THREE

1. Jean-Jacques Becker, *The Great War and the French People*, trans. Arnold Pomerans (Leamington Spa: Berg, 1985), 126, 147–48.

2. "Oeuvre des Pépinières Nationales," *RTC* 27 (1917), 76–78.

3. On the controversy provoked by nursing, see Margaret H. Darrow, "French Volunteer Nursing and the Myth of War Experience in World War I," *American Historical Review* 101 (1996), 80–106.

4. *JO*, 26 October 1919, 11910.

5. *JO* S/A, 1919, document 92, 18 March 1919, 417; *JO* S, 30 July 1919, 1196–97.

6. See my *Worthy Monuments: Art Museums and the Politics of Culture in Nineteenth-Century France* (Cambridge: Harvard University Press, 1989), 35–36.

7. *JO* S, 29 September 1919, 1497.

8. Karl Marx, *Economic and Philosophical Manuscripts of 1844*, in *The Marx-Engels Reader*, 2d ed., ed. Robert C. Tucker (New York: Norton, 1978), 105.

9. Prior to the summer of 1922, according to an ordinance dating back to the Restoration, all local monuments had to be approved by the president of the Republic. A decree of 15 July 1922, however, derogated to prefects the authority to approve the construction of local monuments. For a list of relevant legislation and administrative texts, see Philippe Rivé, Annette Becker, Olivier Pelletier et al., eds., *Monuments de mémoire: Les monuments aux morts de la première guerre mondiale* (Paris: Mission Permanente aux Commémorations et à l'Information Historique, 1991), 306–7.

10. ADV, 9T4–4, prefectoral questionnaire, 24 August 1923.

11. Data compiled by the author from questionnaires in ADV, 9T4–4: fifty-eight communes listed a committee as responsible. In addition, two communes gave ambiguous answers, such as *oui* (Rougiers); and one, Callian, listed a single individual as having provided all the funds for the monument.

12. For examples, see Jean Bernard Vazeilles, "Histoire du monument aux morts de Saint-Quentin-la-Poterie," *Rhodanie* 24 (1987): 17–18; AM Ligny-en-Barrois, M1–3, dossier "Comité du monument."

13. ADL, 45 O⁶6, CM/D Chaumont, 26 June 1921.

14. ADM, O Ploërmel, CM/D, 8 June 1919; *Le petit Var* (Toulon), 16 July 1920, a notice summoning residents of the Toulon district of Le Morillon to a meeting to form a committee to put up a memorial plaque; *Le progrès républicain* (Brignoles, Var), 8 December 1918, on such a meeting in St. Maximin.

15. *Le petit Var*, 8 July 1922. This was a new committee for the Champ de Mars and La Collette *quartiers;* the previous committee had been dissolved.

16. AM Vannes, 1M199, membership list from 1921–22.

17. *Le progrès républicain*, 8 December 1918.

18. *Le ploërmelais*, 22 June 1919.

19. ADL, 48 O⁶3, CM/D, 16 February 1936, in which the mayor reads a letter from the president of the local veterans' group asking for authorization to build a monument. There is a similar case in Baudonvilliers, in the Meuse: see ADMe, E Dépôt 22/1M2, Trouchard, adjoint to prefect, 17 February 1932.

20. ADM, 2 O 40/4, Prefectoral dossier, received 1 August 1921; ADL, 211 O⁶5, CM/D, 15 June 1920.

21. ADM, 2 O 62/5, CM/D, 6 November 1921.

22. See Antoine Prost, *Les anciens combattants et la société française, 1914–1939*, 3

vols. (Paris: Presses de la Fondation Nationale des Sciences Politiques, 1977), vol. 2, *Sociologie*, 54.

23. Prost, *Les anciens combattants*, vol. 1, *Histoire*, 115–57; vol. 3, *Mentalités et idéologies*, 187–223.

24. Prost, *Les anciens combattants*, 3: 219–23, citation from p. 219.

25. Robert Coustet, "Le mémorial aux morts de la guerre de 1914–1918 de la ville de Bordeaux," *Bulletin et mémoires de la Société Archéologique de Bordeaux* 75 (1989): 95.

26. On the Levallois-Perret affair, see my "The Nation: In What Community? The Politics of Commemoration in Interwar France," in *Ideas and Ideals: Essays on Politics in Honor of Stanley Hoffmann*, ed. Linda B. Miller and Michael Joseph Smith (Boulder: Westview Press, 1993), 281–83 and nn. 22 and 29.

27. See ibid., 284–86.

28. AM Ligny, M1–3, CM/D, 10 February 1923.

29. ADMe, E Dépôt 289/1M2, statement signed by the mayor, 8 January 1921.

30. ADV, 9T4–4, report by the committee, 2 June 1922.

31. Prost, *Les anciens combattants*, 3: 124–51.

32. ADV, 9T4–4, Colle, committee chairman, to prefect, 13 December 1920; prefect to mayor Ste. Maxime, draft, April 1922.

33. Ibid., committee chairman to prefect, 15 May 1922.

34. Ibid., prefect to mayor, 20 May 1922; mayor to prefect, 15 July 1922. The mayor also accused the committee of having refused to accept his proposal that the prefect himself arbitrate. In fact, however, the prefect had foreclosed that possibility by declining to order the committee to turn over its funds to the town, thus rejecting the mayor's position.

35. Though there are no documents specifically setting out this arrangement, it is evident in ADV, 9T4–4, CM/D, 14 February 1925.

36. SAVT, minutes of meeting of 28 December 1918, letter from secretary-general, Mairie de Toulon, 26 December 1918.

37. Ibid., minutes, meeting of 21 January 1919.

38. The most grandiose rival project, which was never realized, was for a "pantheon" for the Toulon dead, combining a cemetery, mausoleum, and war memorial. See "Le panthéon des héros toulonnais: Transformation de la caserne blindée," *Le petit Var*, 29 January 1920, and "Le panthéon toulonnais des morts de la guerre," *Le petit Var*, 7 February 1920.

39. SAVT, minutes, meetings of 17 December 1919, 10 May 1920, and 29 October 1920.

40. Ibid., Castel's summary of the meeting in minutes, meeting of 26 November 1920.

41. Ibid., Letter Book, letters requesting meetings of 6 March, 15 November, and 22 December 1921; clippings from *Le petit marseillais*, 10, 12, 15, and 17 January 1922.

42. Ibid., minutes, meeting of 15 February 1922; clippings file, *Le petit Var*, report on session of 15 March 1922; AM Toulon, 10M7, CM/D, 20 December 1922.

43. SAVT, minutes, meeting of 8 December 1922; see also clippings scrapbook, *Le petit marseillais*, December 1922.

44. Ibid., Clippings scrapbook, *Le petit marseillais*, December 1922; and 26? February 1923.

45. This was the term the mayor used in his meeting with the committee in February 1922.

46. ADM, O Ploërmel, CM/D, 8 June 1919; *Le ploërmelais*, 22 June 1919.

47. ADM, O Gueltas, CM/D, 21 September 1919.

48. ADL, 175 O⁶12, CM/D, 14 November 1920; ADM, 2 O 66/8, CM/D, 28 August 1921.

49. ADM, O Guern, subscription list, 18 December 1921; O Guénin, subscription list and list of the dead, 24 March 1924.

50. ADM, O Kerfourn, list of the dead, 10 October 1921; subscription list, n.d. The exception may well have been the married sister of a dead soldier.

51. *Le progrès du Morbihan*, 26 February and 10 July 1921.

52. ADV, Deposited AM Brovès, 1M16, subscription list, 1 September 1923.

53. *L'avenir de Verdun*, 10 May 1923, 5 March 1925 (on Étain), 17 August 1923 (on Damvillers); *Le ploërmelais*, 7 September 1919.

54. *OR*, 3 June 1923.

55. ADM, O La Trinité, CM/D, 2 March 1919; O Kerfourn, subscription list, n.d.

56. Lists appeared in the *Journal de Pontivy:* on St. Gonnery, 24 April; 8, 22, and 29 May 1921; on Kergrist, 20 and 27 February; 13 March; 3 April; 22 and 29 May; and 7 August 1921; on Bieuzy, ADM, 2 O 16/7, subscription list, 29 October 1924.

57. AMV, 9T4–4, CM/D, 4 June 1922, and prospectuses of the four monuments, all dated 15 July 1922. There are a number of communes in the Vaucluse with multiple monuments: see Jean Giroud, Raymond Michel, and Maryse Michel, *Les monuments aux morts de la guerre 1914–1918 dans le Vaucluse* (L'Isle-sur-la-Sorgue: Scriba, 1991), 107–9.

58. *RM*, 3 February and 19 September 1920 (wedding banquets in Vaubecourt and Montiers-sur-Saulx); *Le progrès républicain* (Brignoles), 2 April 1921.

59. *Le petit Var*, 9 April 1921; *L'avenir de Verdun*, 5 June 1924 (the collection was for Étain).

60. *L'avenir de Verdun*, 5 June 1924. The brief note does not specify the nature of the *litige*.

61. ADL, 1Z430 (Romorantin), undated sheet headed "Montant des souscriptions recueillis"; *Le petit Var*, 5 August 1921 (on La Londe); 3 January 1922 (on Bormes, but this is a claim made in a discussion of the subscription in Hyères, so may be exaggerated).

62. ADMe, E Dépôt 22/1M2, Trouchard to prefect, 17 February 1932.

63. Examples from *Le petit Var*, 15 September 1921 (a benefit concert in Le Lavandou), 27 March 1920 (free use of a theater in Toulon).

64. *Le petit Var*, 8 and 16 May 1920.

65. *Le ploërmelais*, 21 September (citation) and 28 September (list of activities) 1919.

66. Ibid., 5 October 1919.

67. *Le petit Var*, 30 July and 3 August 1921.

68. *L'avenir de la Meuse*, 31 March 1927.

69. *Le petit Var*, 3 January 1922.

70. AMV, CM/D, 15 February 1922.

71. *RM*, 18 January 1925.

72. Jean-Jacques Becker and Serge Berstein, *Victoire et frustrations, 1914–1929*, Nouvelle Histoire de la France Contemporaine 12 (Paris: Seuil, 1990), 359–61.

73. *Le reveil de la Meuse*, 19 June 1924.

74. *RE*, 16, 23 April 1921.

75. *Le petit Var*, 3 January 1922.

76. ADM, 2 O 7/15, CM/D, 11 November 1920; SAVT, clipping from *Je dis tout*, 21 January 1922.

77. *RM*, 7 February 1924.

78. Ibid., 19 June 1924.

79. *OR*, 5 November 1922.

80. AMV, CM/D, Report of Pleyben, 15 February 1922.

81. On the figure of the profiteer in the trench press, see Stéphane Audoin-Rouzeau, *14–18: Les combattants des tranchées*, L'Histoire par la Presse (Paris: Armand Colin, 1986), 131.

82. *Le progrès républicain*, 8 January 1921.

83. *Le progrès du Morbihan*, 22 January 1921.

84. *RM*, 8 August 1920; *Le petit Var*, 8 February 1920.

85. For examples of appeals to former residents of a commune, see, for example, AMV, Deposited AM Montferrat, series M, model letter of 18 February 1919, and *L'avenir de Verdun*, 20 March 1924, appeal of Fresnes-en-Woëvre.

86. For a striking example, see ADV, Deposited AM Brovès, 1M16, subscription list, 1 September 1923. Those subscribers who resided outside the commune did not actually sign the list themselves.

87. *Le poilu de la Loire*, November 1936, quoted in Monique Luirard, *La France et ses morts: Les monuments commémoratifs dans la Loire* (St. Etienne: Université de St. Etienne, Centre Interdisciplinaire d'Études et de Recherches sur les Structures Régionales, 1977), 23.

88. AN, F^{21}4770, minister to prefects, 10 May 1920. In 1922, the power to authorize monuments was delegated to prefects, but the documentation remained the same; see note 9 above. It is worth noting that this procedure was in theory entirely independent of the one established a few months later for the awarding of state subsidies to monuments, though in practice the same documentation seems to have done double duty. The disappearance of the files containing these documents from the archives is one of the great frustrations for historians of commemoration in interwar France.

89. The first systematic use of statistics to establish a political "typology" of war memorials can be found in Prost, *Les anciens combattants*, 3: 41–52; Prost's categories remain influential. The statistical approach is at its most elaborate in unpublished theses, typically at the level of the *maîtrise* (the fourth year of postsecondary studies), for example, Myriam Baron, "La symbolique des espaces mortuaires: Les monuments aux morts de la guerre 1914–1918 dans le Département du Morbihan," Mémoire de maîtrise

(géographie), Université de Paris VII, 1988. But see also Bernard Cousin and Geneviève Richer, "Les monuments aux morts de la guerre 1914–1918 dans les Bouches-du-Rhône," in *Iconographie et histoire des mentalités* (Paris: Éditions du CNRS, 1979), 124–30; and Alain Sauger, "Les monuments aux morts de la grande guerre dans la Drôme," *Études drômoises* 1 (1990): 17–25.

90. Figures from Institut National de la Statistique et des Études Économiques, *Annuaire Statistique de la France*, vol. 66 (n.s. 8): *Rétrospectif* (Paris: Imprimerie Nationale and Presses Universitaires de France, 1961), 253–54. The mean hourly wage for an *imprimeur-compositeur* in a departmental *chef-lieu* (prefecture) in 1921 was 2.32 francs, for a *plombier* 2.36 francs, and for a *maçon* 2.39 francs. Wages in Paris (listed separately) were higher; wages in small provincial towns and villages, and for women, were lower.

91. Giroud, Michel, and Michel, *Les monuments aux morts*, 64.

92. ADL, 243 O⁶6, CM/D, 1 October 1922 (on the gift) and 26 November 1922 (on the loan); undated biographical statement on the artist, Herant-Bendérian; letter from the artist to the mayor, 26 January 1922, and from the mayor to the prefectoral review board, 7 April 1922.

93. ADM, O Pont-Scorff, monument sketch, dated September 1917, and balance sheet for the monument, 12 June 1921.

94. ADM, O Ploërmel, CM/D, 7 November 1920; *Le ploërmelais*, 16 January 1921.

95. *Le ploërmelais*, 6 March 1921; ADM, O Ploërmel, CM/D, 26 June 1921.

96. ADM, 2 O 178/16, CM/D, 6 April 1919 (misdated 1918); *JP*, 6 April 1919, expressing doubts about the opportuneness of a municipal grant; 20 April 1919, on the beginning of a subscription.

97. *JP*, 11, 18, and 25 May 1919 (on site preferences); 13 June 1920 (citation).

98. Ibid., 28 November 1920; ADM, 2 O 178/16, CM/D, 31 May 1921. The councillor proposing the supplement was the same one who had two years before worried about putting the cart before the horse.

99. *JP*, 28 November 1920.

100. It is also the case that on a per capita basis the municipal contributions were not strikingly different: 2.65 in Pontivy (with a population of 9,424 in the 1911 census) and 1.79 in Ploërmel (population 5,370). The difference is that in Ploërmel the contribution represented just over 16 percent of the total cost, in Pontivy nearly 57 percent.

101. ADM, O Port-Louis, CM/D, 13 June 1920 (original vote) and 3 July 1921.

102. Ibid., prefect to mayor, 10 October 1921.

103. Ibid., CM/D, 3 July 1921.

104. ADL, 226 O⁶6, CM/D, 13 June 1920; prefect to mayor, 19 June 1920; and reply, 20 June; prefectoral ordinance approving loan, 1 July 1920.

105. ADM, O La Trinité-Porhoët, CM/D, 17 June 1923. The record indicates that by 1925 the loan, contracted from the Caisse Nationale des Retraites pour la Veillesse, had still not been paid, but does not indicate why.

106. ADM, O Rohan, prefect to mayor, 11 June 1921; bank director to prefect, 7 September 1921, with marginal note on disposition; CM/D, 15 September 1921; prefect to mayor, 5 October 1921; decree approving loan, 22 November 1921. In the amount of

some 20,000 francs, the loan was meant to cover another public works project as well as the monument.

107. *Le ploërmelais*, 16 January 1921. This is the issue in which the second subscription is announced.

108. ADM, 2 O 67/4, cahier des charges, 4 December 1920.

109. ADM, 2 O 34/9, adjoint to prefect, 12 April 1920.

110. ADV, 9T4–4, financial statement, 21 April 1921.

111. ADMe, E Dépôt 181/157, minutes of committee meeting, 9 October 1928; and correspondence with suppliers, December 1928–January 1929.

112. *JO*, *Lois et décrets*, 1920, 10940–1.

113. *JO* S, 30 July 1919, 1197.

114. On the Morbihan, see ADM, O Taupont, prefect to mayor Taupont, 12 July 1920; and O Guillac, undated press clipping, probably spring 1920, on departmental and state subsidy programs, the latter still in preparation. On the Vaucluse, Giroud, Michel, and Michel, *Les monuments aux morts*, 75–76. Departmental subsidies were far from universal; on the decision of the Loire-Inférieure (now Loire-Atlantique) *conseil général* not to provide them, see Yves Pilven le Sevellec, "Les monuments aux morts de la Loire-Atlantique, 2ème partie: Les monuments aux morts de la guerre de 1914–1918," *Visions contemporaines* 4 (1990), 31–32.

115. See Alexandre Israel's objection to a committee proposal to delay the subsidy program until it could devise alternative criteria: *JO* CD, 31 July 1920, 3392.

116. *JO* CD/A, 1918, document 5267, 1837; *JO* S/A, 1919, document 92, 417.

117. ADMe, E Dépôt 353/1M7, duplicated prefectoral circular, 14 September 1920.

118. AM Ligny, M1–3, minutes of committee meeting, 12 October 1920.

119. ADM, O Trédion, prefect to mayor, 29 June 1921; and reply, 2 July 1921.

120. ADV, 9T4–4, prefect to mayor La Londe, via subprefect Toulon, 2 June 1923; ADM, 2 O 50/4, prefect to mayor La Croix-Helléan, 20 January 1921; *JO* S, 30 July 1919, 1199.

121. ADL, 158 O⁶6, CM/D, 12 June 1921.

122. ADV, 9T4–4, prefect to Jules Roustan, architect and a member of the prefectoral review board, 29 January 1923.

123. *JO* S, 19 October 1919, 1828.

124. SAVT, letter, chairman to minister, 16 February 1923; ADM, O Taupont, mayor to prefect, 13 June 1919 (well before the state subsidy program had been determined); and O Pluméliau, mayor to prefect, 13 February 1920 (this inquiry was made before the town had voted or raised any money at all for the monument). In Toulon, Castel was seeking a subvention not tied to the municipal contribution; there is no indication that he obtained what would have been an exceptional derogation of the rules.

125. ADL, 17 O⁶4, CM/D, 25 December 1920 (the circular was dated 20 December); ADMe, E Dépôt 93/1M2, prefectoral circulars of 25 October and 27 November 1924; prefect to mayor Contrisson, 7 January 1925; ADL, 8 O⁶4, prefectoral circular of 3 November 1924; prefect to mayor Avaray, 26 November 1924; and CM/D, 7 December 1924.

126. For examples of requests for subventions that predated the official beginning

of the program, see ADL, 39 O⁶6, CM/D, La Chapelle–St. Martin-en-Plaine, 31 August 1919; and Ministry of the Interior to prefect, 26 September 1919; ADM, O Gueltas, CM/D, 21 September 1919, as well as the case of Taupont already cited. On monuments in reconstructed villages, to be discussed more fully in a subsequent chapter, see for example *BM*, 3 November 1928, on dedication ceremonies in Maucourt, Boinville, and Warcq; and *RE*, 11 October 1930, on Béthincourt.

127. ADL, 247 O⁶13, Pichery, senator, to prefect, 16 August 1921; and response to a later missive, 12 October 1921.

128. ADM, 2 O 66/8, prefectoral decree, 15 June 1922; mayor to prefect, 21 November 1922 and 22 August 1923; prefect to mayor, 25 August 1923.

129. ADM, 2 O 11/13, mayor to prefect, 25 August 1919, 8 October 1921, and 15 January 1922.

130. ADM, O Plumelin, mayor to prefect, added note on a letter originally sent 9 February 1925. This letter was actually pleading for quick approval of a loan agreement, but two weeks before, on 27 January 1925, the mayor had sought information on the subventions the town could expect, not realizing that the program had expired.

131. ADL, 39 O⁶6, CM/D, La Chapelle–St. Martin-en-Plaine, 7 August 1921.

132. The ministry replied that such an addition to the monument posed no problems as long as it received the approval of the town council, which the new mayor assured the subprefect of Pontivy would be forthcoming. ADM, O Gueltas, Veuve Brient to minister, 18 June 1921; ministry to prefect, 29 June, transmitted to subprefect Pontivy, 2 July; subprefect to prefect, 4 July.

133. An example is the commune of Neulliac.

134. The incident is reported in *L'avenir de la Meuse*, 15 December 1927, with the frosty observation that the worker, Ferdinand Develtian, "avait déjà été envoyé il y a un mois par son chef de chantier parce qu'il dévissait les obus."

135. ADV, 9T4–4, letters from Chauvin, deputy mayor and chairman of the committee (whose actions he disavowed), to the prefect, 30 January 1923 (misdated 1922).

136. M. Genevoix, *La joie* (Paris: Flammarion, 1924), 163–64, 172–73.

137. ADM, O Gueltas, Madame Brient to minister, 22 August 1921. During the war the couple had survived entirely on Madame Brient's salary as the mayor's secretary—an illegality that, as a marginal note pointed out, she ought not have admitted.

138. Ibid. The full sentence reads in French: "J'en serais désoler [*sic*] Monsieur le Ministre si je ne pouvais mettre son nom sur ce monument dont son mort si cruel est venu le surprendre en faisant son devoir."

139. S. Freud, "Mourning and Melancholia," *The Standard Edition of the Complete Psychological Works of Sigmund Freud*, trans. and ed. James Strachey, vol. 14 (London: Hogarth Press, 1957), 244–45.

CHAPTER FOUR

1. ADL, 9T2ᵇⁱˢ, G. Niox to prefect, 2 February 1939; and draft reply, 26 February. The last quoted phrase reads in French "qui porte la marque originale de son auteur,

le maître Bourdelle." The prefect of the Loire-Inférieure (now the Loire-Atlantique) mentioned nine monuments in his reply; see Yves Pilven le Sevellec, "La Loire-Atlantique," in *Monuments de mémoire: Les monuments aux morts de la première guerre mondiale*, ed. Philippe Rivé, Annette Becker, Olivier Pelletier et al. (Paris: Mission Permanente aux Commémorations et à l'Information Historique, Secrétariat d'État aux Anciens Combattants et Victimes de Guerre, 1991), 50.

2. Antoine Prost, *Les anciens combattants et la société française, 1914–1939*, 3 vols. (Paris: Presses de la Fondation Nationale de Sciences Politiques, 1977), vol. 3, *Mentalités et Idéologies*, 41.

3. Janet Wolff, *The Social Production of Art* (Houndmills: Macmillan Education, 1981), 139.

4. See Terry Smith, "Modes of Production," in *Critical Terms for Art History*, ed. Robert S. Nelson and Richard Shiff (Chicago: University of Chicago Press, 1996), 257.

5. Foucault, "What Is an Author?" in his *Language, Counter-Memory, Practice*, trans. Donald F. Bouchard and Sherry Simon (Ithaca: Cornell University Press, 1977), 124.

6. The monument is unsigned, and in fact was only conceived, not personally executed, by Bourdelle: see documents in ADL, 270 $O^6 4$, and further discussion below.

7. Foucault, "What Is an Author?" 124.

8. For a good summary, see June E. Hargrove, "The Public Monument," in *The Romantics to Rodin: French Nineteenth-Century Sculpture from American Collections*, ed. Peter Fusco and H. W. Janson (Los Angeles: Los Angeles County Museum of Art, 1980), 21–35.

9. See Daniel J. Sherman, "Art, Commerce, and the Production of Memory after World War I," in *Commemorations: The Politics of National Identity*, ed. John R. Gillis (Princeton: Princeton University Press, 1994), 187–88.

10. See Antoinette Le Normand-Romain, *Mémoire de marbre: La sculpture funéraire en France, 1804–1914* (Paris: Bibliothèque Historique de la Ville de Paris, 1995).

11. Kenneth E. Silver, *Esprit de Corps: The Art of the Parisian Avant-Garde and the First World War, 1914–1925* (Princeton: Princeton University Press, 1989), 89–111, 185–200, 205–14, 227–30; Nancy J. Troy, *Modernism and the Decorative Arts in France, Art Nouveau to Le Corbusier* (New Haven: Yale University Press, 1991), 197–98.

12. Troy, *Modernism and the Decorative Arts*, 52–55, 101–2, 162–68; Molly Nesbit, "What Was an Author?" *Yale French Studies* 73 (Winter 1987): 229–37.

13. Prost, *Les anciens combattants*, 3: 42.

14. On the emergence of professional art criticism, see Michael R. Orwicz, ed., *Art Criticism and Its Institutions in Nineteenth-Century France* (Manchester: Manchester University Press, 1994); for the period under discussion, see Yves Chevrefils Desbiolles, *Les revues d'art à Paris, 1905–1940* (Paris: Ent'revues, 1993).

15. See, for example, "Les Salons de 1921: Le Salon des Artistes Français," *LeF*, 29 April 1921, in which Arsène Alexandre observes that there are only four or five war scenes in the entire painting section of the exhibition, of which he finds only two worth mentioning; and more generally, Philippe Dagen, *Le silence des peintres: Les artistes face à la grande guerre* (Paris: Fayard, 1996).

16. The proportion of works of sculpture on war-related themes also declined over the course of the 1920s, but more gradually than in paintings. It is impossible to be certain exactly how many exhibited works related to the war, since the Salon catalogues list only titles and contain few illustrations.

17. "Les 'Salons' de 1919 et l'art de se faire peindre," *RDM*, ser. 6, 51 (May-June 1919): 587.

18. "La vie artistique: Le Salon des Artistes Français, la sculpture," *Le T*, 20 June 1920; Etienne Bricot, "Les Salons de 1920," *GBA*, ser. 5, 2 (July-December 1920): 21.

19. On the origins and character of *L'amour de l'art*, founded in 1920, see Chevre-fils Desbiolles, *Les revues d'art*, 157–61.

20. "Monument de la Réformation à Genève," *L'amour de l'art* 2 (1921): 73.

21. "Les Salons de 1922 (Premier article)," *GBA*, ser. 5, 5 (January-June 1922): 286. On monuments as dominating the sculpture sections, see, e.g., "Le Salon de 1923," *Le T*, 1 May 1923.

22. "Yvonne Serruys," *L'art et les artistes*, n.s. 2–3 (1920–21): 397.

23. "Le Salon des Artistes Français: La sculpture, la gravure et l'architecture," *LeF*, 2 May 1922. The formal title of Rude's sculpture, which dates from 1833–36, is *The Departure of the Volunteers*.

24. "L'art en 1919, L'Exposition du Grand Palais," *LeF*, 4 May 1919. The monument in question honored a senator from the Loire, Dr. Reymond, who was killed in action in the air corps, but also functioned as the Montbrison communal war memorial. It was while en route to dedicate this memorial the following year that President Deschanel had his famous "fall" from the presidential train, later attributed to a nervous disorder that led to his resignation: see "Le monument à la mémoire du sénateur Reymond, Les discours," *LeF*, 25 May 1920. The bas-reliefs are also praised in, among others, "Les Salons de 1919," *GBA*, ser. 4, 15 (1919): 163.

25. "Les 'Salons' de 1919 et l'art de se faire peindre," 589–90; on the Perrault-Harry work see also "Les deux salons," *L'art et les artistes*, n.s. 1 (1919–20): 88.

26. "Les Salons de 1920 (Troisième et dernier article), La Société des Artistes Français (Suite)," *GBA*, ser. 5, 2 (July-December 1920): 21.

27. Ibid.

28. "Yvonne Serruys," 397–98.

29. "Yvonne Serruys, sculpteur: A propos d'une inauguration récente," *GBA*, ser. 5, 4 (June-December 1921): 352.

30. "La vie artistique." The work, no. 2888 in the Salon catalog, had the subtitle "A la mémoire de mes camarades tombés." The artist exhibited the work in bronze at the Salon of 1921, no. 3556; the bronze was listed as belonging to the city of Paris.

31. "Les Salons de peinture," *L'amour de l'art* 4 (1923): 550–51.

32. Ibid; "La vie artistique."

33. George, "Les Salons de peinture," 550.

34. "Le Salon de 1923: Salon des Artistes Français; Société Nationale des Beaux-Arts," *Le T*, 1 May 1923; "Les Salons de 1923," *Le T*, 20 May 1923.

35. "Les Salons de 1923," *Le T*, 20 May 1923; "La sculpture aux Salons," *GBA*, ser. 5, 15 (1928): 360.

36. "La sérénité dans l'art et les *Salons* de 1929," *RDM*, ser. 7, 51 (May-June 1929): 700.

37. "Les *Salons* de 1926 aux Champs-Élysées," *RDM*, ser. 7, 33 (May-June 1926): 688.

38. "Echos des Arts," *L'art et les artistes*, n.s. 4–5 (1921–22): 367.

39. "Les Salons de 1922: Le Salon des Artistes Français," *LeT*, 14 May 1922.

40. "Les Salons de 1923," *LeT*, 20 May 1923.

41. See Silver, *Esprit de Corps*, 236–46; Romy Golan, *Modernity and Nostalgia: Art and Politics in France between the Wars* (New Haven: Yale University Press, 1995).

42. "Les Salons de 1922," *LeT*, 14 May 1922.

43. "Echos des Arts," *L'art et les artistes*, n.s. 4–5 (1921–22): 367, 405.

44. Thiébault-Sisson, "Les Salons de 1925: Le Salon des Artistes Français: La Sculpture," *LeT*, 10 May 1925; see also "L'actualité et la curiosité: A travers les Salons," *L'art et les artistes*, n.s. 8–9 (1923–24): 356.

45. On the crisis in sculpture, see, e.g., Pierre Mille, "Le Salon de 1918," *GBA*, ser. 4, 14 (1918): 211–16; Thiébault-Sisson, "La vie artistique"; Waldemar George, "Le Salon d'automne: Suite," *L'amour de l'art* 2 (1921): 363–64.

46. "Notre monument aux morts," *RE*, 20 May 1922; "Les Salons de 1922: Le Salon des Artistes Français," *LeT*, 14 May 1922.

47. "Les monuments commémoratifs," *RE*, 11 June 1921. The comments on artists were secondary to the article's major themes, a political commentary on the pacific character of French war memorials.

48. *RE*, 15 October 1921.

49. "Grandiose manifestation patriotique à Vaucouleurs," *RE*, 14 October 1922.

50. AN, F^{21}4770, dossier 2i, Draft of minister of public instruction and fine arts to Chaulet, deputy, 14 January 1919; the quoted passage is crossed out and replaced with a reference to the importance of "l'inspiration locale et individuelle."

51. AN, F^{21}4770, dossier 2i, copy of minister to mayor Périers (Manche), 31 July 1919. See also my "Art, Commerce, and the Production of Memory," 191. It is worth noting that this reply came only after the minister had requested from Armand Dayot, one of the ministry's inspectors, a report on possible monument models at the Salon, as the mayor of Périers had requested. Dayot's report decried the overall quality of monument projects in the Salon, and recommended that local monuments be limited to simple markers or *bornes*: AN, F^{21}4770, dossier 2i, report of Dayot, undated typescript copy, draft dated 20 June 1919.

52. AN, F^{21}4770, dossier 2i, minister of the interior to minister of public instruction (Direction des Beaux-Arts), 25 September 1919; and reply, 9 October 1919.

53. AN, F^{21}4770, dossier 2i, circular, 10 May 1920.

54. The members of the Morbihan commission are listed in ADM, O 93, folder "Commission Départementale chargée d'examiner les projets"; those of the Var commission in ADV, 9T4–4, minutes of commission meeting, 7 July 1922; on the Loire-Atlantique, see Yves Pilven le Sevellec, "Une étude des monuments aux morts de la Loire-Atlantique, 2ème partie: Les monuments aux morts de la guerre de 1914–1918," *Visions contemporaines* 4 (1990): 124.

55. ADL, 9T2^{bis}, circular, 12 June 1920; ADV, 9T4–4, Commission Spéciale des monuments Commémoratifs, report on meeting of 15 October 1920.

56. ADM, PV, Commission Départementale, 1 July 1920. The commission considered a total of twenty-seven monument projects, of which twelve were accepted and fifteen sent back for revision or modification.

57. In the case of one project in the Loir-et-Cher, a commissioner who was also the departmental architect redesigned an entire monument, a stela, after the commune involved, Seigy, could not provide the desired corrections to its design: see ADL, 9T2^{bis}, PV, Commission Artistique, 14 June 1923.

58. ADL, 9T2^{bis}, circular, 12 June 1920; ADV, 9T4–4, Commission Spéciale report, 25 October 1920.

59. ADL, 118 O^{6}3, CM/D Lestiou, 14 June 1923; 136 O^{6}2, Grenouillot, architect to prefect, 31 August 1923, concerning the projected monument in Méhers.

60. ADV, 9T4–4, Mazaugues: Délibérations de la Commission Artistique, 28 July 1921; Aups: report of Poupé (curator of the Draguignan museum), quoted in ED, Commission Artistique, 7 July 1922.

61. ADV, ED Commission Artistique, 7 July 1922.

62. See my "Art, Commerce, and the Production of Memory," 194 and n. 29.

63. ADM, CM/D Guénin, 17 February 1924. I could find no record of the commission's action concerning this monument.

64. ADL, 276 O^{6}4, "Copie d'une note rédigée par le sculpteur Antoine Bourdelle au sujet du projet de monument de la commune de Trôo," October 1920.

65. AN, F^{21}4770, dossier 2i, interior minister to minister of public instruction and fine arts, 18 May 1920. For the actual circular, see n. 53 above.

66. For examples of the *homme de l'art* phrasing, see ADL, 9T2^{bis}, Procès-Verbaux de la Commission Artistique, 21 April and 2 June 1921 (Averdon); 3 August 1921 (Souday, Plessis-Dorin); 10 October 1921 (La Fontenelle, St. Hilaire-la-Gravelle); 9 March 1922 (Méhers); 9 O^{6}5, mayor Averdon to prefect, 3 May 1921.

67. The *Petit Robert* defines *l'homme de l'art* (under *art*) as "le spécialiste compétent," with a note of its special medical connotation, but without dating other than "moderne": *Le nouveau Petit Robert: Dictionnaire alphabétique et analogique de la langue française*, new ed. (Paris: Dictionnaires Le Robert, 1993), 129.

68. ADM, O St. Nicolas, prefect to mayor, 15 December 1924.

69. ADM, 2 O 55/5, undated plan and prefect to mayor, 23 September 1921; the commission approved the Etel design in its meeting of 10 September 1921, cf. O 94. The bill from the supplier of the poilu, Veuve G. Chapal, is dated 19 October 1921, and the contractor's bill, submitted to the commission, does not specify the source, but the commercial nature of the design must have been fairly obvious.

70. Nesbit, "What Was an Author?" 234–35.

71. ADM, O Locoal-Mendon, prefect to chief road inspector, Vannes, 6 December 1921; and statements of Mélingue, cantonal road inspector, Plouharnel, 13 December 1921, and of the arrondissement road inspector, 14 December 1921, with additional comments by the chief road inspector, 24 December. This was far from the only such incident.

72. ADL, 118 O⁶3, mayor Lestiou to prefect, 8 September 1923, referring to Ratton as *auteur du projet,* and for his credentials (*entrepreneur à Combs-la-Ville* [Seine-et-Marne]), CM/D, 18 March 1923.

73. ADV, 9T4–4, mayor to prefect, 1 December 1920. See also my "Art, Commerce, and the Production of Memory," 198.

74. ADL, 18 O⁶ VII/45, typescript appeal to artists, winter 1920–21 (Blois); AMV, 1M199, "Programme du concours d'un monument aux morts," January 1921 (Vannes), as well as a list of organizations and newspapers to which this was sent; "La ville de Verdun ouvre un concours pour l'érection d'un monument à ses morts de la guerre," *BM,* 5 February 1927. Competitions limited to natives or inhabitants of the department included Commercy, Toulon, and Toulouse (restricted to residents of the city or graduates of its art school): see "Concours pour l'érection d'un monument aux enfants de Commercy morts pour la France," *RE,* 20 August 1921; SAVT, Comité du Monument Commémoratif des Toulonnais Morts pour la Patrie, 1914–1919, "Programme du concours pour l'érection d'un monument," 1 July 1923; Luce Rivet, "Les monuments aux morts de Toulouse," *Revue de Comminges,* 1987: 593–95.

75. In Toulon the committee consisted of the mayor, the president and treasurer of the monument committee, and two sculptors and two architects from outside the department: SAVT, Correspondence file, no. 206, PV du Jury, 5 November 1923.

76. See, on this theme, Hélène Lipstadt, ed., *The Experimental Tradition: Essays on Competitions in Architecture* (New York: Princeton Architectural Press, 1989).

77. See Daniel J. Sherman, "The Nation: In What Community? The Politics of Commemoration in Postwar France," in *Ideas and Ideals: Essays on Politics in Honor of Stanley Hoffmann,* ed. Linda B. Miller and Michael Joseph Smith (Boulder: Westview, 1993), 283–84.

78. "Mon carnet," *BM,* 11 June 1927.

79. ADL, 274 O⁶ VII/37, CM/D Vendôme, 31 May and 23 August 1919.

80. ADM, O Rochefort, CM/D, 23 March 1924; "Dans l'arrondissement," *JP,* 21 October 1923.

81. The Jacomet monument firm, in the Vaucluse, did, however, offer for sale a book called *100 Discours Variés,* intended for mayors and association presidents "for all the ordinary and extraordinary circumstances in the life of a commune." To preserve confidentiality, the book was sold in a limited edition, only by subscription. I have been unable to locate a copy of it; the citation is from a publicity flyer in ADMe, E Dépôt 498/26.

82. The following is an expansion and elaboration of my argument in "Art, Commerce, and the Production of Memory," especially 195–99.

83. Flyer in ADL, 248 O⁶4, n.d.

84. ADMe, E Dépôt 498/26, deposited AM Lavignéville, bold type in the original.

85. ADL, 248 O⁶4, undated flyer and photograph. The flyer came in several closely related versions; for further references see my "Art, Commerce, and the Production of Memory," 198–99 and n. 47.

86. See my "Art, Commerce, and the Production of Memory," 199 and n. 49.

87. ADV/deposited AM Montferrat, undated circular.

88. AMV, 1M199, printed circular addressed to mayors, 1 October 1920.

89. ADL, 9T2^{bis}, circular addressed to prefects, November 1920.

90. "A nos lecteurs," *AFC* 1 (May 1919): 1.

91. "La sculpture commémorative aux Salons de 1921," *AFC* 25 (May 1921).

92. "L'art commémoratif au Salon de 1924," *AFC* 52 (July 1924).

93. Examples of notices consisting only of a photograph and title: "*Soldat gisant*," *AFC* 7 (November 1919); "Maquette d'un 'monument aux morts' destiné à la Bretagne," *AFC* 24 (April 1921); "*La victoire*," *AFC* 40–41 (August-September 1922). Works available in bronze or stone included a bust, *Le poilu dans les plis du drapeau*, *AFC* 19 (November 1920), and a statue, *Dans la tourmente*, also available in *fonte d'art*, *AFC* 34–35 (February-March 1922); the latter ad lists the dimensions in which it is available but not prices. *La résistance* (see below) was available *en n'importe quelle matière: AFC* 37 (May 1922) and other issues.

94. *AFC* 38 (June 1922).

95. *AFC* 7 (November 1919). This was one of the observations or maxims scattered throughout the newspaper in boxes, to be discussed below.

96. "Contre les mauvais monuments: Notre concours des 'Horreurs de l'après-guerre,'" *AFC* 5–6 (September-October 1919).

97. More concise versions of the appeal appear under the same title in *AFC* 18 (October 1920) and 19 (November 1920); two responses, on monuments in Constantine (Algeria) and Montceau-les-Mines (a monument in the form of an enormous miners' lamp), in *AFC* 16–17 (August-September 1920), without photographs. Several explanations for the lack of response are possible: either that the appeal attracted little interest (I have found no circulation figures for *L'art funéraire*, but it may not have been large) or that many of the examples submitted bore too close a resemblance to the work of Pourquet.

98. "Un article sensationnel de M. Clément Vautel," *AFC* 53 (November 1924).

99. *AFC* 20 (December 1920); 19 (November 1920).

100. Aphorisms attributed to Goethe, *AFC* 16–17 (August-September 1920); and Grimm, 18 (October 1920), the latter reprinted without attribution in 21 (January 1921). Aphorisms published in 2 (June 1919) and 5–6 (September-October 1919) were taken from the introductory editorial, "A nos lecteurs," in 1 (May 1919); the latter was reprinted in 16–17 and in 22–23 (February-March 1921). A fragment from the editorial introducing "Notre concours des 'Horreurs de l'après-guerre'" was published as an aphorism in 21 and in 24 (April 1921). Such examples could be multiplied ad infinitum.

101. *AFC* 5–6 (September-October 1919).

102. ADM, O St. Thuriau, prefect to mayor, 16 December 1921; and reply, 31 December 1921.

103. ADL, 248 O⁶4 (Selommes), undated flyer.

104. ADL, 9T2^{bis}, PV, Commission Artistique, August 1921.

105. ADM, 2 O 12/8 (Beignon), flyer.

106. "Le Salon des Artistes Français: La sculpture, la gravure et l'architecture," *LeF*, 2 May 1922.

107. "La couleur aux *Salons* de 1928," *RDM*, ser. 8, 45 (May-June 1928): 684. The

critic is referring to the veiling of the female figure of *Strasbourg* after the German annexation of Alsace, and to the destruction of the Vendôme column during the Paris Commune of 1871.

108. "En l'honneur de nos morts glorieux," *RE*, 19 May 1923.

109. "Les Salons de 1923," *LeT*, 20 May 1923.

110. "En l'honneur de nos morts glorieux"; this is a different passage from the one cited previously ("sublime in all its horror").

111. Clément-Janin, "Les estampes et la guerre," *GBA*, ser. 4, 13 (1917): 75–94, 361–83, 483–508; André Blum, "La caricature de guerre en France," *GBA*, ser. 5, 3 (January-June 1921): 235–54.

112. Blum, "La caricature de guerre," 235–36.

113. Ibid.; Clément-Janin, "Les estampes," 506, 502.

114. Clément-Janin, "Les estampes," 492.

115. "En l'honneur de nos morts glorieux."

116. "Les 'Automotistes' et les *Salons* de 1921," *RDM*, ser. 6, 62 (May-June 1921): 588.

117. "Le casque de tranchée," *L'illustration*, 3 July 1915, 23; "Le nouveau casque au feu," ibid., 2 October 1915, 344.

118. "Le casque Adrian: Les batailles de Champagne et d'Artois," *L'illustration*, 30 October 1915, 462. I have taken minor liberties with the translation to serve my metaphor, notably translating the pronouns as masculine rather than neuter. The French reads: "Et nous nous sommes habitués si vite à ses formes simples qu'il est bien probable qu'il survivra à la guerre, même comme coiffure de parade."

119. For the organization of the subscription, see the articles in *RTC*, 31 (1921): 342 and 371–72. Moreau-Vauthier exhibited the model for the marker under the title *La borne* in the Salon of 1921; the work is not in the catalog but is illustrated: see *Explication des ouvrages de peinture, sculpture, architecture, gravure & lithographie des artistes vivants exposés au Grand Palais des Champs Elysées, Avenue Alexandre III, le 30 avril 1921*, lxiv.

120. Examples are legion, and include Anne-Louis Girodet's famous allegory of the Napoleonic Wars, *Ossian Receiving Napoleonic Officers* (1802, Musée National du Château de Malmaison), in which the rooster has put the Austrian eagle to flight. For historical background, see Michel Pastoureau, "Le coq gaulois," in *Les lieux de mémoire*, ed. Pierre Nora, 3 vols., vol. 3, *Les France*, 3 books (Paris: Gallimard, 1992), 3: 506–39.

121. See Clément-Janin, "Les estampes," 497–98.

122. See Daniel J. Sherman, "Monuments, Mourning, and Masculinity in France after World War I," *Gender & History* 8 (1996): 85, 92, and n. 13.

123. On the marketing of the type, see Rivé et al., *Monuments de mémoire*, 142. The statue appears in plate 357E accompanying the Rombaux-Roland price list for September 1920; see ADV, deposited AC Montferrat, M4. A type distributed by the Chapal foundry in Auray also evokes *On les aura!* (see fig. 4.11).

124. For the grenadier design from Durenne, see Rivé et al., *Monuments de mémoire*, 142. On the Jean Droit poster, Clément-Janin, "Les estampes," 504.

125. The *poilu mourant* appears with the *poilu victorieux* as number 1013 in the Rombaux-Roland price list for 15 May 1922; see ADMe, E Dépôt 498/26, deposited AC Lavignéville. See also Rivé et al., *Monuments de mémoire*, 142.

126. The Gourdon figure appears as number 2167 in the Gourdon (Marbreries Générales) catalog for October 1920; see AMV, 1M199. For the Breton figure, also distributed by Val d'Osne, see Rivé et al., *Monuments de mémoire*, 142–43.

127. For an illustration of *On ne passe pas!*, see *AFC* 44 (December 1922); for *La résistance*, see *AFC* 45 (January-February 1923). The two are very similar, but in *On ne passe pas!* the soldier holds the gun diagonally and the positions of his left and right feet are reversed. *La résistance* appears more frequently in *L'art funéraire*, suggesting that *On ne passe pas!* may not have been commercialized. Many Gourdon models came with the words "Pro Patria" inscribed just beneath the sculpture; see the catalog in AMV, 1M199; and Rivé et al., *Monuments de mémoire*, 145, fig. 8.

128. "Chronique locale et régionale: Salbris," *Courrier de la Sologne*, 4 June 1922.

129. For Pijoury's letterhead, see ADL, 131 O⁶2, Pijoury to mayor La Marolle-en-Sologne, 13 July 1920; the contract, dated 10 December 1921, is in ADL, 237 O⁶7.

130. "Beignon," *Le progrès du Morbihan*, 15 May 1921; "Ville-Issey et Euville honorent leurs morts," *RE*, 2 December 1921. The comments are those of the anonymous authors of the quoted stories.

131. See Leora Auslander, *Taste and Power: Furnishing Modern France* (Berkeley: University of California Press, 1996), 374–76.

132. "'Les bretons n'oublient pas': M. Rio inaugure le monument aux morts à La Gacilly," *OR*, 29 June 1922; "Une belle fête patriotique à Montiers-sur-Saulx," *RM*, 29 September 1921.

133. "L'inauguration du monument aux morts," *OR*, 15 November 1925.

134. *JP*, April 1923 and 18 November 1923. See also ADM, O St. Caradec-Trégomel, devis descriptif, dated 1 August 1922, describing the monument as "un 'poilu' qui, calme dans sa force, dit, 'On ne passe pas,'" and identifies the sculptor as "L. Maubert, chevalier de la Légion d'honneur à Brétigny sur Orge (Seine et Oise)."

135. *La Meuse*, 7 February 1925, quoting from *L'est républicain* of 5 February 1925.

136. The Rombaux-Roland figures appear in the May 1922 catalog in ADMe, E Dépôt 498/26, deposited AC Lavignéville. The Gourdon types, in AMV, 1M199, include a France, no. 2151; and a Victory with a dead soldier, no. 2042. For some examples of female mourning figures in nineteenth-century French funeral monuments, see Le Normand-Romain, *Mémoire de marbre*, 141–63.

137. ADV, 9T4–4, report of Poupé, 17 July 1921.

138. "L'inauguration du monument de Chouzy-sur-Cisse," *RLC*, 21 November 1920.

139. Alex Preminger, Frank J. Warnke, and O. B. Hardison, Jr., eds., *The Princeton Encyclopedia of Poetry and Poetics*, enl. ed. (Princeton: Princeton University Press, 1974), 612, 12.

140. *RM*, 22 February 1925 (statement of the artist); 2 April 1925, containing the mayor's explanation of the monument at its inauguration.

141. Passed by the Chamber of Deputies for the first time in 1919, women's suf-

frage was blocked in the Senate, and women did not receive the vote until 1945; see Steven C. Hause with Anne R. Kenney, *Women's Suffrage and Social Politics in the French Third Republic* (Princeton: Princeton University Press, 1984), 191–254.

142. *L'avenir de Verdun*, 24 August 1922.

143. "Lamotte-Beuvron: Inauguration du monument aux morts," *RLC*, 28 October 1923. The *Courrier de la Sologne* of the same date offers a slightly different interpretation: "Une victoire aux ailes déployées protège sous les plis de son voile les pauvres petits pious-pious qu'elle a mission de garder."

144. "Inauguration du monument aux morts de St. Rémy-la-Calonne," *BM*, 28 May 1932.

145. On gender anxiety and the figure of the mother, see Mary Louise Roberts, *Civilization without Sexes: Reconstructing Gender in Postwar France, 1917–1927*, Women in Culture and Society (Chicago: University of Chicago Press, 1994), 89–91 and passim.

146. References to France as a *mère commune:* "Commune de Selles–St. Denis: Inauguration du monument aux morts de la grande guerre," *Courrier de la Sologne*, 21 May 1922; "Les Meusiens honorent leurs morts" [the French as *enfants d'une même mère*], *RE*, 22 October 1921; "Nonsard et Heudicourt ont inauguré leurs monuments," *La Meuse*, 24 October 1925 [*belle manifestation de mère reconnaissante*].

147. For further discussion of this point, see my "Monuments, Mourning, and Masculinity," 97–98, and chapter 6 below.

148. "Dans l'arrondissement," *JP*, 3 June 1923; "Séglien," *OR*, 8 April 1923.

149. "Chronique régionale," *RE*, 21 November 1925 (remarks of Thonin); "St. Mihiel a glorifié ses morts," *La Meuse*, 14 November 1925.

150. "Les cérémonies du souvenir: Quistinic rend un pieux hommage à ses héros," *OR*, 30 April 1922.

151. Emile Gilles, "Le granit et nos monuments aux morts," *OR*, 23 April 1922.

152. "La cérémonie d'inauguration du monument aux morts de Bracieux," *RLC*, 11 June 1922.

153. "L'inauguration du monument aux enfants de Vendôme 'Morts pour la France,'" *Le carillon de Vendôme*, 17 November 1921.

154. *RLC*, 27 August 1922.

155. "Romorantin: Inauguration du monument," *Courrier de la Sologne*, 4 November 1923.

156. Ibid.

157. "L'inauguration du monument aux morts de Creuë," *La Meuse*, 28 August 1926; for the date of the Stenay dedication, see "A Marville et à Stenay," *RE*, 18 August 1923.

158. ADL, 9T2^bis, PV Commission Artistique, 2 June 1921; 25 O⁶13, mayor to prefect, 11 June 1921.

159. For the inauguration dates, see "Inauguration du monument aux morts de la Commune de Sambin," *RLC*, 4 June 1922, and "La cérémonie d'inauguration du monument aux morts de Bracieux," *RLC*, 11 June 1922.

160. ADM, 2 O 13/7 (Belz), CM/D, 5 July 1923; devis, 23 June 1923; 2 O 55/5 (Etel), Cadoret devis, 6 May 1921; Chapal devis, 21 October 1921; and prefect to mayor,

23 September 1921; O Locoal-Mendon, devis, 1 November 1921; contract for the statue, 15 January 1922. The controversy in Locoal-Mendon, as discussed in n. 71 above, concerned the role of the *agent-voyer*, and occurred prior to the first mention of the Chapal firm as supplier of the statue.

161. ADM, 2 O 12/8 (Beignon), flyer; contract with Querbouët, Plélan-le-Grand, 27 July 1920; prefect to mayor, 24 March 1921; O 94, PV Commission Départementale, 22 March 1921: the Beignon project is listed among those approved without reservation.

162. ADV, 9T4–4, PV Commission Artistique, 28 July 1921.

163. "Les 'Automotistes' et les *Salons* de 1921," *RDM*, ser. 6, 62 (May-June 1921): 588.

164. See Eric J. Leed, *No Man's Land: Combat and Identity in World War I* (Cambridge: Cambridge University Press, 1979), 208–9.

165. "Inaugurations des monuments aux enfants de Pagny-la-Blanche-Côte et de Chalaines morts pour la France," *RE*, 30 July 1921: the assistant mayor declines to speak in Chalaines (Meuse); "Coulanges: Inauguration d'un monument aux morts," *RLC*, 11 December 1921, where the mayor has trouble continuing his speech; *Le ploërmelais*, 1 October 1922, account of the inauguration in Sérent.

166. For additional examples, see Annette Becker, *Les monuments aux morts: Mémoire de la grande guerre* (Paris: Errance, n.d. [1987]), 70–72; Rivé et al., *Monuments de mémoire*, 184, 186–87, 191.

167. "M. Poincaré à Hattonchâtel et à Ménil-la-Horgne," *RE*, 22 September 1923.

168. ADM, 2 O 50/4, du Halgouët to prefect, 19 September 1921; note on Commission approval, 16 December 1921.

169. "Salbris," *Courrier de la Sologne*, 4 June 1922.

CHAPTER FIVE

1. Michel de Certeau, *L'invention du quotidien,* vol. 1, *Arts de faire,* rev. ed., ed. Luce Giard, Folio Essais (Paris: Gallimard, 1990), 163. I have substantially modified Steven Rendall's translation in *The Practice of Everyday Life* (Berkeley: University of California Press, 1984), 108.

2. See Hayden White, *The Content of the Form: Narrative Discourse and Historical Representation* (Baltimore: Johns Hopkins University Press, 1987), 49–57.

3. Henri Lefebvre, *The Production of Space,* trans. Donald Nicholson-Smith (Oxford: Blackwell, 1991), 57.

4. M. Halbwachs, *The Collective Memory,* trans. Francis J. Ditter, Jr., and Vida Yazdi Ditter (New York: Harper and Row, 1980), 140. In the French original, *La mémoire collective,* published posthumously (Paris: Presses Universitaires de France, 1950), Halbwachs uses a double negative (p. 146): "Il n'est point de mémoire collective qui ne se déroule dans un cadre spatial."

5. Halbwachs, *La mémoire collective*, 147–65.

6. *The Collective Memory*, 48.

7. Ibid., 84.

8. M. Christine Boyer, *The City of Collective Memory: Its Historical Memory and Architectural Entertainments* (Cambridge: MIT Press, 1994), 12–18, citation from p. 17.

9. Lefebvre, *Production of Space*, 47–48.

10. Pérès, "Identité communale, République et communalisation: A propos des monuments aux morts des villages," *Revue française de science politique* 39 (1989): 674–75.

11. ADM, O Inzinzac, prefect to mayor Inzinzac, 21 July 1923.

12. Pérès, "Identité communale," 676, 674; Lefebvre, *Production of Space*, 33.

13. See Benedict Anderson, *Imagined Communities: Reflections on the Origin and Spread of Nationalism*, rev. ed. (London: Verso, 1991); and on the relationship between interwar commemoration and the national community in France, Daniel J. Sherman, "The Nation: In What Community? The Politics of Commemoration in Postwar France," in *Ideas and Ideals: Essays on Politics in Honor of Stanley Hoffmann*, ed. Linda B. Miller and Michael Joseph Smith (Boulder: Westview, 1993), 290–91.

14. ADV, 9T4–4, A. Porre et al. to prefect, 3 July 1920. See also Sherman, "The Nation: In What Community?" 287–88.

15. ADV, 9T4–4, mayor to prefect, 17 July 1920; prefect to Porre, 28 July 1920.

16. "Chronique régionale," *Le progrès républicain*, 20 November and 18 December 1920; 8 January 1921; citations from 18 December.

17. For more devout areas, see Yves Pilven le Sevellec, "Une étude des monuments aux morts de la Loire-Atlantique, 2ème partie: Les monuments aux morts de la guerre de 1914–1918," *Visions contemporaines* 4 (1990): 47–49 (just over 60 percent of monuments in the cemetery); and Florence Regourd, "La Vendée," in *Monuments de mémoire: Les monuments aux morts de la première guerre mondiale*, ed. Philippe Rivé, Annette Becker, Olivier Pelletier et al. (Paris: Mission Permanente aux Commémorations et à l'Information Historique, 1991), 59 (65 percent of monuments in cemeteries or near the church). For traditionally secular areas with a more leftist political orientation, see Alain Sauger, "Les monuments aux morts de la grande guerre dans la Drôme," *Études drômoises* 1 (1990): 19 (22 percent of monuments in the cemetery); and Jean Giroud, Raymond Michel, and Maryse Michel, *Les monuments aux morts de la guerre 1914–1918 dans le Vaucluse* (L'Isle-sur-la-Sorgue: Scriba, 1991), 104–5 (38.2 percent of the principal communal monuments in cemeteries). Annette Becker summarizes some of these results in *La guerre et la foi: De la mort à la mémoire, 1914–1930* (Paris: Armand Colin, 1994), 118; but her figure for the Vaucluse, taken from Giroud, Michel, and Michel, includes duplicate monuments, and she does not mention that, all monuments taken together, a slightly higher proportion of communes had monuments on a public square or roadside than in the cemetery.

18. Giroud, Michel, and Michel, *Les monuments aux morts*, 105.

19. Pilven le Sevellec, "Une étude des monuments aux morts," 47–55.

20. See, on this ambiguity, Antoine Prost, "Les monuments aux morts," in Pierre Nora, ed., *Les lieux de mémoire*, 3 vols., vol. 1, *La République* (Paris: Gallimard, 1984), 200; A. Becker, *La guerre et la foi*, 118.

21. On the "isolation" of cemeteries, largely a nineteenth-century development in other parts of France, see Thomas A. Kselman, *Death and the Afterlife in Modern France* (Princeton: Princeton University Press, 1993), 176–80.

22. Regourd, "La Vendée," in Rivé et al., *Monuments de mémoire*, 59; her figure is 65 percent for monuments in current and former cemeteries.

23. ADM, O Neulliac, CM/D, 18 December 1921.

24. ADL, 154 O⁶6, prefect to mayor Mont-près-Chambord, 25 April 1921.

25. ADL, 152 O⁶7, CM/D, 16 September 1921; notice of *enquête de commodo et incommodo*, 20 October 1921; petition of residents opposed to the site, 29 October 1921; report of commissaire, Guibert, 30 October 1921; CM/D, 2 November 1921, affirming the purchase; Barillet, deputy, to prefect, 3 November 1921; and reply, 15 November 1921. The sale may have been controversial, even though the land cost only 326 francs, because the commune had already had to borrow money for the monument project.

26. "Chronique locale et régionale," *Courrier de la Sologne*, 4 June 1922.

27. "Erection d'un monument aux morts pour la patrie," *Le progrès du Morbihan*, 22 January 1921.

28. "Notre enquête au sujet de l'emplacement du monument aux morts," *NM*, 31 August 1930.

29. ADV, 9T4–4, CM/D, 22 November 1925.

30. "Inauguration du monument aux morts pour la patrie d'Ouzouer-le-Marché," *RLC*, 23 July 1922.

31. See the comments of the mayor of St. Julien-de-Chédon, where the monument was so situated: "Inauguration du monument aux morts de Saint Julien de Chédon," *RLC*, 30 April 1922.

32. "Tribune libre: Les monuments aux morts," *RE*, 6 August 1921.

33. ADL, 274 O⁶ VII/37, CM/D, 21 February 1920.

34. AM Lorient, CM/D (printed), 13 December 1925. For further discussion of the Lorient case, see my "The Nation: In What Community?" 288–89.

35. "Notre enquête au sujet de l'emplacement du monument aux morts," *NM*, 31 August and 3 September 1930.

36. "Le panthéon des héros toulonnais: Transformation de la caserne blindée," *Le petit Var*, 29 January 1920; SAVT, minutes, meeting of 8 December 1922. See also clippings scrapbook, *Le petit marseillais*, December 1922.

37. "Arrondissement," *L'avenir de Verdun*, 10 August 1922.

38. "Aux enfants de Bar morts pour la patrie, durant la guerre 1914–1918," account of a monument committee meeting, *RM*, 24 November 1921; "Le Panthéon toulonnais des morts de la guerre," *Le petit Var*, 8 February 1920 (the *Panthéon toulonnais* was a separate project, distinct from the war memorial, that was never realized). For a similarly blithe proposal to move the statue of Jules Simon, see "Notre enquête au sujet de l'emplacement du monument aux morts," *NM*, 31 August 1930.

39. SAVT, PV Comité, 21 April 1922. On the site controversy in Toulon, see above, chap. 3, nn. 48–49.

40. "Notre enquête au sujet de l'emplacement du monument aux morts," *NM*, 2 September 1930. The definitive choice of the monument site, on the cours de Chazelles a few hundred meters north of the place du Morbihan, was made a few months later; see AM Lorient, CM/D, 27 February 1931. The monument was moved twice subsequently, in 1949 and 1961, but is still in a central location, the place Jules Ferry. See AM Lorient, CM/D, 23 April 1949 and 16 September 1961.

41. See AMV, CM/D, 16 February 1924. The Vannes siting decision was highly contentious, and was resolved only after the mayor threatened to resign if his choice was rejected.

42. ADV, 9T4–4, report of Barla on monument project in Flassans, 24 March 1922.

43. ADM, O Limerzel, CM/D, 7 November 1920. For another example of this attitude, in Pontivy, see *JP*, 11, 18, and 25 May 1919; 13 June 1920.

44. ADM, 2 O 11/13, mayor to prefect, 25 August 1919.

45. "Dans l'arrondissement," letter from Th. Huet, *JP*, 21 May 1922.

46. *L'avenir de Levallois*, 16 January 1925, article by André Delacour while the monument was still in the planning stage. See, on this monument, my "The Nation: In What Community?" 279, 281–88.

47. "L'inauguration du monument de Vallières-les-Grandes," *RLC*, 27 November 1921.

48. "Le monument aux morts," *JP*, 25 May 1919.

49. Ibid.

50. "Montrichard: Inauguration du monument aux morts de la grande guerre," *RLC*, 30 October 1921.

51. "Locminé," *JP*, 22 December 1918.

52. Excerpt of the mayor's speech, in "Souesmes: Inauguration du monument," *RLC*, 6 November 1921. On the role of bells in village life in the nineteenth century, see Alain Corbin, *Les cloches de la terre: Paysage sonore et culture sensible dans les campagnes au XIXe siècle* (Paris: Albin Michel, 1994).

53. An example is the mayor of Theillay, count Jacques d'Orléans, who presented a particular intersection as the site that was "the wish of the population": ADL, 237 O^{6}7, CM/D, 26 June 1921.

54. ADM, O Le Palais, CM/D, 27 August 1922.

55. "Le monument aux morts," *JP*, 11 May 1919; see also ADM, 2 O 67/4, cahier des charges, 4 December 1920; and ADM, 2 O 34/9, adjoint to prefect, 12 April 1920.

56. "Le monument aux morts," *JP*, 25 May 1919.

57. ADMe, E Dépôt 260/1M3, four sheets headed "Désignation, par les souscripteurs, de l'emplacement," n.d. but probably late 1920 or early 1921.

58. "Dans l'arrondissement," *JP*, 21 May 1922. Huet took as a "promise" (*engagement*) the mayor's comment, at a ceremony in 1919, that no site would better suit the monument than the cemetery in which he was then speaking.

59. AM Ligny, M1–3, letters of acceptance of members of the monument committee, April 1920; PV Comité, 17 June 1921.

60. AM Ligny, M1–3, CM/D, 23 June 1921.

61. On the resignation: *RE*, 16 July 1921; on the election, J.-M. Simon, "Département," *RM*, 7 August 1921.

62. AM Ligny, M1–3, CM/D, 10 February 1923, for a summary of the town's dealings with the veterans, the unsuccessful subscription campaign, and discussion leading to the vote on a new site. See also ADV, 9T4–4, committee chairman to prefect, 15 May 1922.

63. ADMe, 2 O 690, poster, late February 1923.

64. "Echos meusiens: Autour d'un monument," *RE*, 10 March 1923. A municipal poster, "Réponse à la protestation," can be found in AM Ligny, M1–3.

65. On the Marbreries Générales project, which was approved at the same meeting at which Husson resigned, see correspondence in AM Ligny, M1–3, CM/D, 25 June 1921, at which Husson used the phrase *un monument unique*. The Broquet-Hardelay project was chosen from among ten projects by five artists in November 1921: see ibid., CM/D, 30 November 1921; and contract, 30 January 1923.

66. AM Ligny, M1–3, CM/D, 10 February 1923.

67. *RM*, 1 March 1923.

68. ADV, 9T4–4, Dougnon to mayor, 6 August 1920; mayor to prefect, 15 August 1920.

69. ADV, 9T4–4, subprefect to prefect, 21 August 1920; and draft reply, with letter to Dougnon, 1 September 1920. See also above, n. 15.

70. See A. Becker, *La guerre et la foi*, 129–39.

71. ADL, 9T2^bis, clipping from *Echo du centre*, 9 November 1920, reprinting the article by Jean Guiraud entitled "Les monuments aux morts de la guerre."

72. A copy of the circular, dated 18 April 1919, is in ADL, 1Z430.

73. ADM, O Néant-sur-Yvel, prefect to mayor, 1 April 1921; O Guer, prefect to mayor, 7 October 1922.

74. René Rémond, ed., *Société séculaire et renouveaux religieux (XXe siècle)*, Histoire de la France Religieuse, vol. 4 (Paris: Seuil, 1992), 116–22.

75. Alfred Cobban, *A History of Modern France*, 3 vols., vol. 3, *France of the Republics, 1871–1962* (Harmondsworth: Penguin, 1965), 131. The analysis of this campaign in Jean-Jacques Becker and Serge Berstein, *Victoire et frustrations, 1914–1929*, Nouvelle Histoire de la France Contemporaine 12 (Paris: Seuil, 1990), 261–64, is somewhat more subtle, but they still blame Édouard Herriot, the Radical party leader and prime minister of the Cartel des Gauches, for having by his policies stirred up Catholic hostility to the left.

76. ADM, O Guer, prefect to mayor, 7 October 1922.

77. ADL, 211 O^6 5, Protestation, St. Denis, 17 August 1920; see also CM/D, 27 June 1920.

78. ADL, 211 O^6 5, mayor to prefect, 8 September 1920; prefect to Moreau, conseiller municipal, 14 October 1920. Moreau was one of two councillors who voted against the cross; he signed the petition and wrote the prefect separately (10 September) urging him not to approve the final project.

79. ADM, O Réguiny, mayor to prefect, 9 August 1919; and reply, 12 August 1919.

80. ADM, O Réguiny, mayor to prefect, 15 June 1921; and reply, 18 June 1921.

81. ADM, O Réguiny, mayor to prefect, 22 June 1921.

82. ADM, O Ploërdut, prefect to mayor Ploërdut, 30 May 1921, emphasis added.

83. ADM, O Plouay, mayor to prefect, 13 April 1921; and prefect to director of departmental and communal administration, Paris, 25 April 1921.

84. ADM, O Locminé, see especially CM/D, 20 April 1920; and correspondence with the prefect about a loan, February-March 1921.

85. "Une émouvante cérémonie à Locminé," *Le progrès du Morbihan*, 11 December 1921.

86. ADM, 2 O 1/12, prefect to mayor, 20 March 1923; and reply, 27 March 1923. The planned site was a former cemetery.

87. "Locminé," *JP*, 22 December 1918. The only other trace of controversy in the press stems from a meeting of the monument committee, its status apparently in doubt, in which a decision was taken to inscribe on the monument the names of contributors as well as of the dead. Roundly criticized in the report, this decision seems not to have been carried out. See "Locminé: Autour du monument," *Le progrès du Morbihan*, 19 February 1921.

88. *Le progrès du Morbihan*, 11 December 1921.

89. "Locminé: L'inauguration du monument aux morts," *JP*, 11 December 1921.

90. ADL, 274 O⁶ VII/37, mayor, Barillet, to prefect, 7 October 1920; and reply, 14 October 1920. The monument was moved to the municipal cemetery in the 1960s.

91. "Leur fête à Thenay" and "A Chissay," *Le progrès de Loir-et-Cher*, 8 August 1919. The paper's masthead described it as the "Organe hebdomadaire de la Démocratie Républicaine et Socialiste du Département, sous le contrôle du Parti"; the "party" would have been on the center-left.

92. "Arrondissement," *L'avenir de Verdun*, 20 November 1924; for an initial report on the incident, see ibid., 13 November 1924.

93. "Béthelainville," *L'avenir de la Meuse*, 9 September 1926.

94. ADM, O Plumelec, Le Gal to prefect, 6 May 1925; and reply, 7 May 1925. This dossier also contains the extensive correspondence leading up to the initial decision.

95. A. Becker, *La guerre et la foi*, 10–12, 103–38.

96. Becker rightly points to the importance of ecumenism, but this was only one of a number of discourses in the church's arsenal likely to appeal to the state: ibid., 116–17.

97. ADM, O 94, PV Commission départementale, 9 June 1921.

98. ADM, O La Trinité, Rivaud to mayor, 30 August 1921.

99. Ibid.

100. ADM, O La Trinité, Rivaud to prefect, 5 November 1921.

101. "Le granit et nos monuments aux morts," *OR*, 23 April 1922.

102. ADM, O 94, PV Commission départementale, 16 December 1921; O Le Sourn, PV Commission spéciale, 24 July 1922.

103. ADM, O Le Sourn, Allias to Agent-Voyer en Chef, 14 November 1921; blueprint, 30 April 1922; contract with Vernery, 26 October 1922. It is possible that the sculpture was an artist-executed work supplied by Vernery, whose workshop in Pontivy seems to have been something of a granite-carving center. The archival records, however, contain no indication of authorship.

104. This is true above all of departmental archives, since technically the prefect's responsibility for a project ended after he had approved it, though he would have had to approve any supplemental appropriations and might well be invited to preside at the dedication ceremony. Some municipal archives have preserved correspondence concerning the building of the monument, though even this documentation is often preparatory in nature.

105. Yves Pilven le Sevellec found only four disputes arising from monument construction out of nearly 250 projects in the Loire-Atlantique: "Une étude," 27–28.

106. "Dans le Var," *Le petit Var*, 16 June and 3 July 1921.

107. AMV, 1M199, Marbreries Générales circular, October 1920. The second paragraph concludes with a note calculated to drive prefectoral commissions to despair: "If additional subscriptions or subsidies come through while the work is proceeding, there will always be a way to apply them to the beautification of the monument without delaying the order, which will thus have profited from the most advantageous conditions."

108. For the prevalence of this practice in contemporary public art projects in the United States, see Robert Atkins, "When the Art Is Public, the Making Is, Too," *New York Times*, 23 July 1995, sec. 2.

109. ADM, O Locminé, CM/D, 20 April 1920; mayor to prefect, 21 August 1921, and other correspondence; for an explanation of the initial payment, see mayor to prefect, 12 March 1921.

110. ADM, O Malguénac, Allias to prefect, 27 June 1928. The contract was signed in December 1924. On Vernery's expertise, cf. "Le granit et nos monuments aux morts," *OR*, 23 April 1922.

111. See ADL, 76 O^{6}5, prefect to mayor Droué, 12 October 1921. To another mayor who asked whether, since the construction of a monument involved "en quelque sorte . . . la fourniture d'une oeuvre d'art," a contract could be dispensed with altogether, the prefect and the subprefect of Romorantin replied in the negative: ADL, 131 O^{6}2, mayor La Marolle to subprefect, 14 January 1921; subprefect to prefect, 15 January 1921; and reply, 21 January 1921.

112. ADL, 136 O^{6}2, Grenouillot to prefect, 14 February 1924; and reply, 24 February 1924; for the initial commission decision, see ADL, 9T2^{bis}, PV Commission artistique, 9 March 1922.

113. ADL, 43 O^{6}5, Thomas, locksmith to prefect, 15 July 1922; mayor to prefect, 28 July 1922; and prefect to Thomas, 23 August 1922; 146 O^{6}4, Kléber, mason to prefect, 20 September 1923; mayor to prefect, 26 September 1923; and prefect to Kléber, 29 September 1923.

114. ADM, O Langoëlan, undated note attached to CM/D, 20 November 1922; for a similar explanation, see ADL, 237 O^{6}7, mayor Theillay to prefect, 11 August 1921. In Theillay, where the monument was to be built at an intersection, the fence was supposed to protect it from cars as well as "pour éviter que des animaux chiens poules etc ne viennent salir le monument."

115. See, for example, AMV, 1M199, "Aux morts pour la patrie: Grille spéciale pour entourage de monument," a brochure from the firm of Guillot-Pelletier Fils. For a fence including shell casings or *obus*, see ADL, 55 O^{6}9, CM/D, 27 May 1922 (Chouzy-sur-Cisse).

116. ADMe, E Dépôt 425/1M5, contracts, 25 April 1921; and CM/D, same date, asking for dispensation from competitive bidding.

117. ADL, 59 O^{6}15, estimate for Contres, 27 September 1920; and PV adjudication, 6 March 1921; 62 O^{6}4, plans and estimates for Couddes, 19 May 1923; and PV ad-

judication, 7 October 1923. The lowest discount, 2 percent, was for the monument; the highest, 16 percent, was for the fence.

118. ADM, 2 O 26/6, initial cost estimate, 25 May 1922; on the adjudication, mayor to prefect, 6 September and 8 October 1922; the second estimate, 12 December 1922 and *gré à gré* contracts, 11 and 16 February 1923. The architect was Prosper Demeret. The mayor's considerable care to respect all procedures, including publicizing the auction, lends credence to the notion of some calculation.

119. ADV, 9T4–4, "Construction d'un monument aux glorieux morts hyérois de la guerre: Convention," 22 February 1922.

120. AMV, 1M199, mayor to Ladmiral, 25 October 1922, with draft contract; Ladmiral to mayor, 18 November 1922; final contract, 13 January 1923.

121. AMV, 1M199, extensive correspondence. Threats to take legal action: mayor to Ladmiral, 12 April 1924, 29 January 1925.

122. AMV, 1M199, Ladmiral to mayor: problems with contractors, 18 January 1923, 2 April 1923, 4 September 1923, 27 March 1924; pleas of ill health, 28 December 1922, 20 February 1924.

123. AMV, 1M199, Ladmiral to mayor, 2 August 1923. After a failed attempt to find a contractor who would supply Ladmiral with granite, the monument committee agreed to substitute *pierre de Lorraine* for the monument base and polished Alésia granite for the inscription plaques: see mayor to Ladmiral, 23 September 1923.

124. AMV, 1M199, Ladmiral to mayor, 3 May 1924, announcing the impending arrival of Coste, the Paris contractor; Ladmiral to Coste, 12 May 1924; Ladmiral to Rousseau, architecte voyer Vannes, on Coste's firing, 29 May 1924; for the recommendation of Paul Lépinard, contractor Vannes, see mayor to Ladmiral, 15 May 1923.

125. ADM, O Melrand, CM/D, 10 November 1923; O La Trinité, CM/D, 1 August 1920; mayor to prefect, 25 May 1921.

126. ADM, 2 O 34/9, assistant mayor to prefect, 12 April 1920.

127. ADL, 155 O⁶14, cahier des charges, 1 June 1920. The town had an architect's rendering which it put up for bidding; it received two bids, one at 2 percent below the estimate, a second at 3, which it accepted. Both bidders came from outside the department.

128. ADL, 51 O⁶6, contract with Beaufreton, entrepreneur Le Mans, 23 May 1921.

129. ADV, 9T4–4, contract, 22 February 1922.

130. "Le granit et nos monuments aux morts," *OR*, 23 April 1922.

131. Examples, all from ADM series O, include Questembert (devis, 2 April 1920), Surzur (devis, 28 March 1921), Le Tour du Parc (devis, 28 April 1922), and Ambon (2 O 2/7, devis, 25 December 1925).

132. ADM, O Limerzel, devis, 10 February 1921.

133. "Concours pour l'érection d'un monument aux enfants de Commercy morts pour la France," *RE*, 20 August 1921; description of competition entrants in "Chronique régionale," *RE*, 8 October 1921.

134. "Chronique régionale: La pierre d'Euville," *RE*, 26 August 1922. The last sentence reads in French, "Un grand nombre de monuments s'érigent partout et partout le 'Marbrier meusien' rivalise de beauté et de durée avec les granits somptueux." As a noun, *marbrier* refers to a stonecutter or contractor; as an adjective, to the stone or

monument business; but as an element in a comparison the term makes sense only as a metaphor for *pierre d'Euville*.

135. "Cléguer rend un émouvant hommage à ses héros," *OR*, 8 June 1922. Five paragraph divisions were removed for concision.

136. In the story, the account cited *follows* a description of the mass and blessing of the monument, which took place in the morning, and the banquet at lunch, and *precedes* the narrative of the afternoon dedication ceremony proper. It is immediately preceded by a description of the monument, and thus forms part of the scene-setting for the dedication.

CHAPTER SIX

1. Garry Wills, *Lincoln at Gettysburg: The Words That Remade America* (New York: Simon and Schuster, 1992), 56–61, text from p. 263.

2. Nicole Loraux, *The Invention of Athens: The Funeral Oration in the Classical City*, trans. Alan Sheridan (Cambridge: Harvard University Press, 1986), 233.

3. Ibid., 230–41, citation from p. 238.

4. For the radicalness of this claim, see Wills, *Lincoln at Gettysburg*, 37–40, 62.

5. "En l'honneur de nos morts glorieux," *RE*, 19 May 1923, dedication of several war memorials in Commercy.

6. On the importance of the classics in French secondary education, and France as inheritor of the classical tradition, see Fritz Ringer, *Fields of Knowledge: French Academic Culture in Comparative Perspective, 1890–1920* (Cambridge: Cambridge University Press, 1992), 142–47; and Clément Falcucci, *L'humanisme dans l'enseignement secondaire en France au XIXᵉ siècle* (Toulouse: Privat, 1939), 10–11, 342, 501. Excerpts from Thucydides were frequently part of the program in rhetoric for the last year of lycée studies; see André Chervel, *Les auteurs français, latins et grecs au programme de l'enseignement secondaire de 1800 à nos jours* (Paris: Institut National de Recherche Pédagogique/Publications de la Sorbonne, 1986), 197–203.

7. Terence S. Turner, "Transformation, Hierarchy, and Transcendence: A Reformulation of van Gennep's Model of the Structure of Rites de Passage," in *Secular Ritual*, ed. Sally F. Moore and Barbara G. Myerhoff (Assen: Van Gorcum, 1977), 61.

8. Frederick Bird, "The Contemporary Ritual Milieu," in *Rituals and Ceremonies in Popular Culture*, ed. Ray B. Browne (Bowling Green: Bowling Green University Popular Press, 1980), 19–20; see also Sally F. Moore and Barbara G. Myerhoff, "Introduction: Secular Ritual," in their *Secular Ritual*, 3–7.

9. Moore and Myerhoff, "Introduction," 10–17, 22; Bird, "Contemporary Ritual Milieu," 22; Turner, "Transformation, Hierarchy, and Transcendence," 60–63.

10. Arnold van Gennep, *The Rites of Passage*, trans. Monika B. Vizedom and Gabrielle L. Caffee (Chicago: University of Chicago Press, 1960), 10–11; see also Turner, "Transformation, Hierarchy, and Transcendence." Although van Gennep regarded rites of passage as "a special category," his insights clearly inform much of the recent anthropological discussion of ritual in general.

11. Victor W. Turner, *The Ritual Process: Structure and Anti-Structure* (Chicago: Aldine Press, 1969), 94–97, 106–7, 127–30; Idem, "Variations on a Theme of Liminality," in Moore and Myerhoff, eds., *Secular Ritual*, 36–52.

12. Michel Verret, "Conclusion," in *Les usages politiques des fêtes aux XIXᵉ–XXᵉ siècles*, ed. Alain Corbin, Noëlle Gérôme, and Danielle Tartakowsky (Paris: Publications de la Sorbonne, 1994), 427–28.

13. Van Gennep, *Rites of Passage*, 147. Ben-Amos has also offered an interpretation of state funerals, in particular that of Victor Hugo in 1885, as rites of passage, incorporating rites of separation (the lying in state), of transition (the procession), and of incorporation (burial in the Pantheon, which "incorporates" the deceased into the company of great men). I believe it is more useful to apply van Gennep's schema, as he did himself, to the survivors rather than to the dead. See Ben-Amos, "The Other World of Memory: State Funerals of the French Third Republic as Rites of Commemoration," *History and Memory* 1: 1 (1989): 100.

14. Ben-Amos, "The Other World of Memory," 95.

15. It is worth noting, however, that it in his own research on funerals van Gennep found, country to his expectations, rites of separation less numerous and less fully elaborated than rites of transition and rites incorporating the deceased into the world of the dead: *Rites of Passage*, 146.

16. On the construction of a secular sacrality, see Moore and Myerhoff, "Introduction," 22–23; on rituals as concerned with the affective or subjective reactions of participants, see T. Turner, "Transformation, Hierarchy, and Transcendence," 63.

17. Van Gennep, *Rites of Passage*, 175; Bird, "Contemporary Ritual Milieu," 22.

18. On the types of diversion associated with public festivals, see Corbin, "La fête de souveraineté," in *Les usages politiques des fêtes*, ed. Corbin et al., 35–36.

19. Jay Winter, *Sites of Memory, Sites of Mourning: The Great War in European Cultural History* (Cambridge: Cambridge University Press, 1995), 93–96, 105–8, citation from p. 115.

20. Moore and Myerhoff, "Introduction," 8.

21. On both the possibilities offered and the limits imposed by topoi, see Loraux, *The Invention of Athens*, 220–30.

22. See Daniel J. Sherman, "Monuments, Mourning, and Masculinity in France after World War I," *Gender & History* 8 (1996): 82–107.

23. Cf. Dean MacCannell, "The Future of Ritual," in his *Empty Meeting Grounds: The Tourist Papers* (London: Routledge, 1992), 275.

24. Ibid., 25–26; see also Moore and Myerhoff, "Introduction," 14.

25. Cf. Winter, *Sites of Memory*, 98.

26. In the Catholic calendar, 1 November is All Saints' Day (in French *Toussaint*); 2 November is All Souls, the customary day for visits to the cemetery, although observances often begin on the evening of 1 November.

27. "Nos morts," *JP*, 27 October 1918.

28. "Pour nos morts," *JP*, 17 November 1918; "Pour la victoire, Pour les morts," *JP*, 24 November 1918. The group organizing the event was the local association of *mutilés* or wounded veterans.

29. Thomas A. Kselman, *Death and the Afterlife in Modern France* (Princeton: Princeton University Press, 1993), 199–204; Philippe Ariès, *The Hour of Our Death*, trans. Helen Weaver (New York: Oxford University Press, 1991), 524–31.

30. "Les fêtes de la victoire," *Le progrès républicain*, 19 July 1919.

31. The schedule of events is listed in "Fêtes du 14 juillet de la victoire," *Le progrès républicain*, 12 July 1919.

32. "Bulletin départemental," *Le progrès de Loir-et-Cher*, 25 July 1919, a letter from the secretary of the Socialist federation in St. Georges-sur-Cher; "La fête nationale à Vendôme," *Le progrès de Loir-et-Cher*, 18 July 1919.

33. "Aux soldats dracénois," *Le Var*, 24 April 1921.

34. For examples of speeches that are mainly eulogies, see "Nos glorieux morts," *Le ploërmelais*, 12 February 1922 (Ploërmel, Morbihan); and "En ville: Émouvante cérémonie," *RLC*, 17 July 1921 (Blois).

35. "Transferts glorieux," *Le Var*, 21 May 1922. In June 1921, *Le Var* noted that the funeral of Julien Labat "was particularly moving because, his family having predeceased him, the entire city served as mourners": "A la mémoire de Julien Labat," *Le Var*, 19 June 1921.

36. "Guilliers: Retour de nos morts," *Le ploërmelais*, 25 June 1922.

37. "Funérailles d'un mort pour la France," *Le progrès républicain*, 26 March 1921; "Chronique régionale," *Le progrès républicain*, 18 June and 30 July 1921.

38. "Fête du souvenir," *Le progrès républicain*, 6 November 1920.

39. "Devant nos morts," *Le Var*, 6 November 1921.

40. "Nos glorieux morts," *Le ploërmelais*, 9 July 1922.

41. "Ploërmel fête ses enfants morts pour la patrie," *Le ploërmelais*, 23 October 1921.

42. Daniel Laumonier, "Les fêtes de Bar-le-Duc: Le symbole, l'individu," *L'écho de l'est*, 28 June 1900.

43. "Trente-neuf ans après: L'inauguration du monument des mobiles de Loir-et-Cher," *L'avenir, moniteur de Loir-et-Cher*, 4–5 October 1909.

44. "L'inauguration du monument des combattants 1870–71," *RLC*, 10 October 1909.

45. Ibid.

46. See D. Sherman, "Les inaugurations et la politique," in *Monuments de mémoire: Monuments aux morts de la première guerre mondiale*, ed. Philippe Rivé, Annette Becker, Olivier Pelletier et al. (Paris: Mission Permanente aux Commémorations et à l'Information Historique, Secrétariat d'État aux Anciens Combattants et Victimes de Guerre, 1991), 277–81. The period from 1880 to 1914 is generally regarded as the golden age of the newspaper press in France, and the war saw the demise of a substantial number of provincial dailies. But the interwar period was a generally healthy one for the provincial press; the increase in circulation of provincial titles between 1914 and 1939 was greater than for the national dailies, as the automobile made prompt distribution possible even to the most isolated rural areas. Local weeklies far outnumbered dailies in the provinces (1,160 to approximately 175 in 1939) and generally offered coverage more clearly linked to a particular political viewpoint. Of the newspapers cited

in this book only two, *Le nouvelliste du Morbihan* and *Le petit Var*, had circulations exceeding 20,000; most probably reached only a few thousand readers. See Claude Bellanger et al., eds., *Histoire générale de la presse française*, 4 vols., vol. 3, *De 1871 à 1940* (Paris: Presses Universitaires de France, 1972), 458–59, 604–05.

47. As Moore and Myerhoff ("Introduction," 18) put it: "Underlying all rituals is an ultimate danger, lurking beneath the smallest and largest of them, the more banal and the most ambitious—the possibility that we will encounter ourselves making up our conceptions of the world, society, our very selves. . . . Ceremonies are paradoxical in this way. Being the most obviously contrived forms of social contact, they epitomize the made-up quality of culture and almost invite notice as such. Yet their very form and purpose is to discourage untrammeled inquiry into such questions."

48. Claude Meusy, "Chronique départementale," *RM*, 1 December 1921; *La Meuse*, 24 October 1925; the prefect claimed to be speaking on behalf of the department's parliamentary delegation as well as himself, and as together they constituted the top of most guest lists, their desires would have carried weight.

49. *L'avenir de la Meuse*, 20 May 1926: "La pluie fait rage à l'arrivée de M. le président Poincaré"; "Plumelec rend hommage à ses glorieux enfants," *OR*, 12 April 1923. In the summer of 1921 a flash flood only delayed the dedication in St. Maximin (Var) by half an hour; cf. "Dans le Var," *Le petit Var*, 16 July 1921.

50. "Inauguration du monument aux morts de Saint-Rémy-la-Calonne," *BM*, 28 May 1932; "Romorantin inaugure un monument aux morts de la Sologne," *RLC*, 4 November 1923; "Chronique régionale," *Le progrès républicain*, 15 May 1920.

51. *L'avenir de la Meuse*, 1 October 1925, report on the dedication in Bras; see also "L'inauguration du monument aux morts de Woinville," *BM*, 22 July 1933.

52. "L'inauguration du monument de Droué," *Le carillon de Vendôme*, 29 September 1921. Chrysanthemums were especially popular as floral decorations. See, e.g., "L'inauguration du monument de Chouzy-sur-Cisse," *RLC*, 21 November 1920: "M. Decault, le distingué horticulteur blésois, avait apporté une magnifique collection de chrysanthèmes, qui formaient autour du monument un ravissant massif fleuri"; "Département," *RM*, 21 November 1920 (dedication of the monument in Chardogne): "une profusion de bouquets, de ces chrysanthèmes rustiques et robustes, aux fortes tiges, aux pétales résistantes, simples fleurs; je voyais en elles s'épanouir l'emblème de l'âme campagnarde."

53. "L'inauguration du monument aux morts de Clermont-en-Argonne," *BM*, 27 May 1933; "Une grande cérémonie à Mauron," *Le progrès du Morbihan*, 2 October 1921. A reporter for *Le ploërmelais* observed that two pylons used for the dedication in Ploërmel were reused in another town, but it is not clear whether this was also the case for triumphal arches: see "A Questembert," *Le ploërmelais*, 20 November 1921.

54. "Les belles cérémonies du souvenir: L'inauguration du monument aux morts de Groix," *OR*, 8 June 1922 (the minister, a local politician named Alphonse Rio, was undersecretary for merchant shipping); "Lorient: La bénédiction du monument des morts de Sauzon," *OR*, 30 August 1923.

55. "Une belle fête patriotique à Montiers-sur-Saulx," *RM*, 29 September 1921; J.-M. Simon, "A Demange-aux-Eaux," *RM*, 25 August 1921; *RM*, 6 October 1921.

56. "Grandiose manifestation patriotique à Vaucouleurs," *RE*, 14 October 1922; on Josselin, "Inauguration du monuments aux morts de la grande guerre," *Le ploërmelais*, 18 June 1922.

57. "L'inauguration du monument aux morts d'Auray," *OR*, 19 November 1925; J.-M. Simon, "A Demange-aux-Eaux."

58. The town council in Auray set its dedication for 11 November 1925 as soon as it heard that the statue was on its way from the foundry—just over two weeks beforehand. See ADM, 2 O 7/15, CM/PV, 27 October 1925.

59. ADMe, E Dépôt 289/1M2, Deposited AC Neuville, Maginot to mayor, 5 July 1921 and n.d.; prefect to mayor, 12 August 1921; *RM*, 6 October 1921.

60. For one politician's schedule of inaugurations, see ADL, 1Z430, Pichery, senator to subprefect Romorantin, 13 and 19 May 1922. On multiple ceremonies in one day, see Claude Meusy, "Chronique départementale," *RM*, 1 December 1921; and on Poincaré, "Quatre inaugurations de monuments aux morts," *L'avenir de Verdun*, 14 August 1924.

61. "Ploërmel," *OR*, 13 July 1922, on the dedication in Réguiny. In May 1923, the same newspaper reported that the prefect of the Morbihan, Guillemaut, had presided over forty-two dedications, a substantial figure considering that the Morbihan also had a minister who frequently filled this function: "L'inauguration du monument aux morts de Noyal-Pontivy," *OR*, 31 May 1923.

62. "Chronique locale," *La Meuse*, 2 October 1926 (on the dedication in Ranzières); "Les inaugurations de la Meuse," *La Meuse*, 1 October 1927 (on the dedication in St. Joire: "selon le programme habituellement consacré à ces pieuses manifestations du souvenir").

63. "Inauguration du monument aux enfants d'Houdelaincourt morts pour la France," *RE*, 9 July 1921.

64. ADMe, E Dépôt 353/1 M7, Deposited AM St. Maurice, L. Legrand to mayor, 13 October 1921.

65. "Les Meusiens honorent leurs morts: A Saint-Maurice-sous-les-Côtes," *RE*, 22 October 1921.

66. Cf. Ben-Amos, "The Other World of Memory," 86, in which he lists "the crowd, the schoolchildren, the wreaths, the speeches, the clergy and the army" as the "important elements" of state funerals during the Third Republic.

67. Citation from "En l'honneur de nos morts glorieux," *RE*, 19 May 1923 (Commercy); officers, boy scouts from "Bar-le-Duc honore ses héros," *RM*, 2 April 1925.

68. Kselman, *Death and the Afterlife*, 51–52, 55, citation from p. 52.

69. A special train brought a band and gymnastic society from Commercy to St. Maurice: "A Saint-Maurice-sous-les-Côtes," *RE*, 22 October 1921; visitors from other communes: "Inauguration du monument aux morts de Jonville," *RE*, 11 October 1924; "Inauguration du monument aux morts pour la patrie d'Ouzouer-le-Marché," *RLC*, 23 July 1922, explicitly mentioning trains, *voitures* and *automobiles;* decorations in every house: "Pontivy," *OR*, 22 October 1922; on a dedication in Le Saint: "Toutes les maisons étaient pavoisées et les plus humbles comme les plus riches étaient couvertes de guirlandes et de drapeaux."

70. On the closing off of streets, see *Nouvelliste, journal d'union républicaine*, 16 June 1923 (Blois). The platform collapsed at the dedication ceremony in Remoiville (Meuse): see *L'avenir de la Meuse*, 13 September 1928.

71. Examples include, in the Loir-et-Cher, Savigny-sur-Braye ("Savigny-sur-Braye," *Le nouvelliste*, 11 August 1923); and, in the Morbihan, Brech, bread coupons ("L'inauguration du monument aux morts de Brech," 20 September 1923); Locminé ("Locminé: l'inauguration du monument aux morts," *JP*, 11 December 1921); and Sérent (*Le ploërmelais*, 17 September 1922). Alain Corbin discusses the distribution of bread as a custom that disappeared at some point during the Third Republic; the evidence here suggests that the custom was still alive in some parts of rural France in the early 1920s. See Corbin, "La fête de souveraineté," 33.

72. On crowds, see, for example, "Ploërmel fête ses enfants morts pour la patrie," *Le ploërmelais*, 23 October 1921; and "Saint-Samson a glorifié ses 54 enfants morts pour la France," *OR*, 27 August 1922: on both occasions there were not enough seats for everyone. In a number of communities, the decoration of the church included a catafalque, emphasizing the resemblance to a funeral; see e.g. "Inaugurations de monuments aux morts," *L'avenir de Verdun*, 23 April 1925, on the dedication in Buzy (Meuse). On visiting clerics, see n. 76 below.

73. On multiple services see "En l'honneur de nos morts glorieux," *RE*, 19 May 1923 (Commercy); "Bar-le-Duc honore ses héros," *RM*, 2 April 1925; "L'inauguration du monument de Verdun," *BM*, 10 November 1928, in which Bishop Ginisty, a Protestant pastor, and a rabbi succeeded each other on the podium. In Vaucouleurs a joint Jewish-Protestant service in the hôtel de ville preceded a mass in the parish church: "Grande manifestation patriotique à Vaucouleurs," *RE*, 14 October 1922.

74. "L'inauguration du monument aux morts de Brech: Une journée d'union sacrée," *OR*, 20 September 1923; Rio was in attendance, along with the prefect, the subprefect of Lorient, a senator, and two deputies. At the dedication in Ruffiac two weeks later, it was the mayor himself who spoke of the universal faith of the dead: see "Inauguration du monument aux morts de Ruffiac," *OR*, 4 October 1923.

75. "Nos morts glorieux!" *Le ploërmelais*, 16 October 1921, an article on the eve of the actual ceremony. At the Ploërmel dedication Rio arrived after the mass, but the subprefect (Ploërmel itself was then a subprefecture) and several members of Parliament attended the service.

76. "Chronique régionale," *Le progrès républicain*, 15 May 1920, on the dedication in Vins.

77. Citation from sermon of the dean of St. Mihiel at the dedication in Euville: "Ville-Issey & Euville honorent leurs morts," *RE*, 3 December 1921. Having remained, according to this report, in occupied St. Mihiel during the German occupation to console his parishioners and the French wounded, this priest was exactly the kind of exemplary figure the church was looking for.

78. Moore and Myerhoff, "Introduction," 20. Though apparently unexceptionable, this formulation represents a major departure from Durkheim's radical opposition of the sacred and the profane.

79. ADMe, E Dépôt 353/1 M7, Deposited AM St. Maurice, L. Legrand to mayor, 13 October 1921.

80. Henri Lefebvre, *The Production of Space*, trans. Donald Nicholson-Smith (Oxford: Blackwell, 1991), 193.

81. For example, flowers were offered to the subprefect of Verdun at Herméville ("Arrondissement," *L'avenir de Verdun*, 2 August 1923); to Poincaré at Mécrin ("Maizey et Mécrin ont célébré leurs morts," *La Meuse*, 13 June 1925), Vigneulles-les-Hattonchâtel ("Vigneulles-les-Hattonchâtel a célébré la gloire de ses morts et sa renaissance," *La Meuse*, 1 May 1926), and many other locations; and to Maginot at Cousances-aux-Forges (*RM*, 6 October 1921). Occasionally a spoken "compliment" or recited verse accompanied the floral tribute, and several girls, or a girl and a boy, were involved, as with Poincaré at Troyon ("L'inauguration du monument aux morts de Troyon," *La Meuse*, 2 May 1925) and two members of Parliament at St. Rémy-la-Calonne ("Inauguration du monument aux morts de St. Rémy-la-Calonne," *BM*, 28 May 1932). In Damvillers, more unusually, children "ne remirent pas de bouquets à notre Premier, mais jetèrent des fleurs sous ses pas" (*L'avenir de Verdun*, 13 September 1923). All these communes are in the Meuse; I have found few traces of this custom in other departments.

82. Arrival ceremony and *remise des drapeaux* by Maginot: "En l'honneur de nos morts glorieux," *RE*, 19 May 1923 (Commercy); also Cousances-aux-Forges (*RM*, 6 October 1921); award of medals to soldiers: Bar-le-Duc (*RM*, 2 April 1925), Caudan (Morbihan, to survivors: "L'inauguration du monument aux morts de Caudan," *OR*, 26 April 1923), Le Saint (Morbihan, "Pontivy," *OR*, 22 October 1922); family medals, in the Morbihan, Ploërmel (*Le ploërmelais*, 23 October 1921), St. Samson ("St. Samson a glorifié ses 58 enfants morts pour la France," *OR*, 27 August 1922), and Crédin ("En souvenir des héros de Crédin," *OR*, 23 September 1923); in the Meuse, Moulainville ("Le monument de Moulainville a été inauguré dimanche dernier," *BM*, 13 August 1933). In Locminé the prefect of the Morbihan awarded both military medals and family medals: *JP*, 11 December 1921.

83. Examples include Chattancourt ("Chronique régionale," *RE*, 19 July 1924), Lacroix-sur-Meuse ("Inaugurations des monuments aux morts de Lacroix-sur-Meuse, Marbotte, Apremont-la-Forêt," *La Meuse*, 26 September 1925), Vigneulles-les-Hattonchâtel ("Vigneulles-les-Hattonchâtel a célébré," *La Meuse*, 1 May 1926), and Cheppy ("Inauguration du monument aux morts de Cheppy," *BM*, 14 September 1929).

84. See Mary Louise Roberts, *Civilization without Sexes: Reconstructing Gender in Postwar France, 1917–1927*, Women in Culture and Society (Chicago: University of Chicago Press, 1994), 32–37, 97–119; for information on the medals, see p. 102.

85. I do not mean to imply that soldiers and veterans did not themselves value courage or think of themselves as patriotic, only that over the course of the war and thereafter they defined these qualities according to their own standards, not necessarily those of professional military men. See, for example, Leonard V. Smith, *Between Mutiny and Obedience: The Case of the French Fifth Infantry Division during World War I* (Princeton: Princeton University Press, 1994), 134–54.

86. On organization by veterans, see ADL, 1Z430, circular announcing the dedication and banquet in Selles-sur-Cher; on banquets held in schools as the largest facilities available, see ADL, 20 O^{6}4, mayor Bonneveau to prefect, 5 November 1923; for a

commune picking up the bill, see ADM, O Malestroit, bill from an innkeeper for twenty-eight lunches at eight francs per head, plus wine for a reception.

87. "L'inauguration du monument aux morts de La Trinité-sur-Mer," *OR*, 29 October 1925; "Une belle fête patriotique à Montiers-sur-Saulx," *RM*, 29 September 1921. The menu in Buléon (Morbihan) was only slightly more modest, omitting the fowl but including both fish and meat as well as two first courses, salad, and dessert: see ADM, 27 Es 50/M, Deposited AM Buléon, menu card, 26 April 1925.

88. Olivier Ihl, "Convivialité et citoyenneté: Les banquets commémoratifs dans les campagnes républicaines à la fin du XIXᵉ siècle," in Corbin et al., *Les usages politiques des fêtes*, 137–57.

89. AN, F⁷13003, undated poster headed "Respect aux morts!" The menu included foie gras, York ham, salmon, bouchées à la reine, poulets de bresse with peas, langouste en bellevue, bombe vanille, and dessert, all for twenty-five francs, including wine and champagne.

90. "A Laheycourt," *RM*, 22 July 1920. In Commercy, there were no speeches and no champagne: "Ce fut un déjeuner et non pas un banquet. On sait que M. Poincaré exige qu'il en soit ainsi chaque fois qu'il préside une cérémonie d'inauguration d'un monument aux morts" (*RE*, 19 May 1923). Poincaré's sensitivity did not forestall the polemic in Bar-le-Duc two years later, where he was also present.

91. Towns following the schedule roughly as outlined, with the banquet or luncheon preceding the dedication, include Bar-le-Duc, Commercy, Ploërmel, and, among smaller communities, Flassans (Var: "Chronique régionale," *Le progrès républicain*, 1 May 1920), Plumelec ("Une émouvante cérémonie du souvenir," *OR*, 12 April 1923), Theillay (Loir-et-Cher: "A Theillay: Inauguration du monument," *Écho de la Sologne*, 4 June 1922), and Clermont-en-Argonne ("L'inauguration du monument aux morts de Clermont-en-Argonne," *BM*, 27 May 1933).

92. Pontivy had to revise its order of procession a week after first publishing it: see *JP*, 8 and 15 October 1922; see also the notice from the UNC in the latter issue. For private correspondence, see AMV, 1M199, dossier "Inauguration"; for a planning meeting on the eve of the ceremony, *RE*, 19 May 1923 (Commercy).

93. This order corresponds most closely to the procession in Vannes: see "Vannes: L'inauguration du monument aux morts," *OR*, 15 November 1925. I have discerned no particular regional pattern to variations in the order of processions.

94. Associations with flags at Le Val ("Dans le Var," *Le petit Var*, 15 June 1921); see also the description of the different helmets of gymnasts and firemen, and other distinctive emblems, in "Inauguration du monument aux morts de St. Julien-de-Chédon," *RLC*, 30 April 1922. In Pontivy the delegations of the *mutilés* and the *anciens combattants* were actually separated, by the widows and children of the dead and by the local women's Red Cross chapter; it is worth noting that the *mutilés*, but not the UNC, had protested the date chosen for the dedication because it coincided with an agricultural fair (*JP*, 8 October 1922). On the formation of the different veterans' movements after World War I, see Antoine Prost, *Les anciens combattants et la société française, 1914–1939*, 3 vols. (Paris: Presses de la Fondation Nationale des Sciences Politiques, 1977), vol. 1, *Histoire*, 47–63.

95. Schoolchildren or *pupilles* lead the procession in, for example, Elven ("Elven: Inauguration du monument aux morts," *Le progrès du Morbihan*, 25 December 1921), Figanières ("Chronique régionale," *Le Var*, 10 April 1921), Vannes, and all the towns cited in n. 96 below. They close the procession in Dhuizon (*RLC*, 6 August 1922). There are exceptions: in Oucques (Loir-et-Cher) schoolchildren came third in the procession, following the band and the *mutilés*.

96. Pignans: "Chronique régionale," *Le progrès républicain*, 4 November 1922; St. Maximin: "Dans le Var," *Le petit Var*, 16 July 1921; St. Julien: *RLC*, 30 April 1922, with reference to *un spectacle impressionnant;* Rilly: "L'inauguration du monument de Rilly-sur-Loire," *RLC*, 27 November 1921.

97. Lefebvre, *The Production of Space*, 38–39, 219; citations from pp. 38–39.

98. Flags fringed with black in Le Val (*Le petit Var*, 15 June 1921); funeral march in, for example, Sampigny, site of Poincaré's country home in the Meuse ("A Sampigny," *RE*, 3 November 1923), though it was played at the end of the ceremony rather than during the procession. On funeral practices and mutual aid societies, see Kselman, *Death and the Afterlife*, 256, 275–77.

99. Van Gennep, *Rites of Passage*, 15–25.

100. This was the case in Pontivy; the second newspaper notice spelled this out. In La Valette, in the Var, the procession included only children attending the public, secular school ("Dans le Var," *Le petit Var*, 24 May 1921); in Sanary, a choral group from the girls' public school is the only children's group mentioned ("Dans le Var," *Le petit Var*, 1 June 1921).

101. Ben-Amos, "Les funérailles de Victor Hugo: Apothéose de l'événement spectacle," in *Les lieux de mémoire*, ed. Pierre Nora, 3 vols., vol. 1, *La République* (Paris: Gallimard, 1984), 515. According to estimates, the "procession" in Vannes numbered some 15,000 people by the time it reached the monument (*OR*, 15 November 1925).

102. For assigned seats for family members and standing room for groups, cf. Ploërmel (*Le ploërmelais*, 23 October 1921) and Verdun ("Le monument de Verdun est inauguré," *BM*, 3 November 1928; the seating area was just below the official platform). In Vendôme, the press of the crowd displaced the families with reserved seating: see "L'inauguration du monument aux enfants de Vendôme 'Morts pour la France,'" *Le carillon de Vendôme*, 17 November 1921. Platforms were common but not universal, and were unlikely to be erected in crowded cemeteries.

103. Examples of ceremonies beginning with the "Marseillaise" include Sanary ("Dans le Var," *Le petit Var*, 1 June 1921), Sampigny (*RE*, 3 November 1923), and Ouzouer-le-Marché (*RLC*, 23 July 1922). The ceremony in Rambucourt both began and concluded with the national anthem: "L'inauguration du monument aux morts et de la Mairie-École de Rambucourt," *La Meuse*, 19 June 1926. In Chouzy-sur-Cisse, the ceremony began with a combination of patriotic and funeral hymns, sung by a chorus and a soloist: "L'inauguration du monument de Chouzy-sur-Cisse," *RLC*, 21 November 1920. The "Marseillaise" was much more likely to conclude than to begin a ceremony in the Morbihan, for example in Ploërdut ("Pontivy et son arrondissement," *Le progrès du Morbihan*, 30 October 1921), Ile d'Arz ("Vannes," *OR*, 13 July 1922), and Melrand ("Dans l'arrondissement," *JP*, 8 August 1924). Although this

may have had to do with the conservative Catholic politics of the Morbihan, instances of ceremonies ending with the "Marseillaise" can be found in other departments as well; the choice seems to have involved emphasis and timing rather than any overt political symbolism.

104. Account of Mont ceremony in *RLC*, 27 August 1922. In Vendôme "les derniers voiles qui recouvraient le monument" were also removed before the ceremony began; see *Le carillon de Vendôme*, 17 November 1921. For examples of unveilings as part of the ceremonial ritual, cf. Elven, where there is a tricolor sheet over the monument (*Le progrès du Morbihan*, 25 December 1921), Cellettes ("L'inauguration du monument de Cellettes," *RLC*, 11 September 1921), Le Castellet ("Dans le Var," *Le petit Var*, 4 July 1922), and St. Tropez ("Chronique Régionale," *Le Var*, 3 September 1922).

105. "Ville-en-Woëvre: Inauguration du monument," *L'avenir de Verdun*, 16 August 1923. An instance of *la foule* as respondent can be found in Bovée (Meuse): "Chronique régionale," *RE*, 3 June 1922.

106. For the numbers, see "L'inauguration du monument de Verdun," *BM*, 10 November 1928; and, on Vannes, "La cérémonie du 11 novembre," *Le progrès du Morbihan*, 15 November 1925. Reports of weeping are invariably gendered; the Vannes account, for example, makes this distinction: "L'un après l'autre, le nom de nos héros tombe sur la foule recueillie, toujours nu-tête; et des mères pleurent; et des hommes qui semblent impassibles frissonnent." In Questembert (Morbihan), "Que de coeurs éprouvèrent un nouveau et douloureux brisement! que de larmes silencieuses dans les yeux des épouses et des mamans!" ("A Questembert," *Le ploërmelais*, 20 November 1921). But an account of the dedication in Quiberon ("Deux ministres à Quiberon et à Auray," *Le progrès du Morbihan*, 13 November 1921) runs: "Des pères, des mères, des soeurs, des femmes, des enfants des disparus sont là, qui, à l'appel des noms, ne peuvent retenir leurs larmes."

107. Accounts do not always specify the names of the poems or songs, but the popular choices for both recitation and singing included Hugo's "Aux morts pour la patrie" (see, for example, "Inauguration du monument des enfants de Tréveray morts pour la France," *RE*, 28 May 1921; "Ploërmel," *OR*, 8 June 1922, on the dedication at Rohan, Morbihan) and works by Bouchor and Garnier (for example, in Chouzy-sur-Cisse, *RLC*, 21 November 1920). Original compositions were also featured, often to familiar music: examples include Quiberon (*Le progrès du Morbihan*, 13 November 1921), Chouzy, and Belleville ("Quatres inaugurations de monuments aux morts," *L'avenir de Verdun*, 14 August 1924).

108. Examples include the Grouëts quarter of Blois ("En ville: Inauguration du monument des Grouëts," *RLC*, 17 July 1921), Six-Fours-Reynier ("Dans le Var," *Le petit Var*, 5 April 1922), Le Castellet ("Dans le Var," *Le petit Var*, 4 July 1922), in all three cases by children at the end of the ceremony; St. Rémy-la-Calonne, by two deputies at the beginning of the ceremony, who had received them from a little girl (*BM*, 28 May 1932); and Nixéville (Meuse: *L'avenir de Verdun*, 14 August 1924, by a veteran and his father-in-law, time not specified).

109. Children's contributions to the ritual program were presumably carefully re-

hearsed, but the audience would only witness the final result, which would thus preserve the ritual's carefully cultivated illusion of spontaneity and "mystery." On this paradox, see MacCannell, "The Future of Ritual," 258.

110. Not all ceremonies, obviously, would have guests of all these ranks. Often the honorary "chairman" and keynote speaker would be the subprefect, even if members of Parliament were also present.

111. Lefebvre, *The Production of Space*, 225. The term "sacred" in this passage is most usefully understood in the context of Moore and Myerhoff's distinction between sacredness and religion (see n. 78 above).

112. "Chronique locale et régionale," *Courrier de la Sologne*, 4 June 1922; on Mont, *RLC*, 27 August 1922; see also the Verdun ceremony, where the filing past is by delegation (*BM*, 10 November 1928).

113. Towns handing out certificates included Inguiniel ("Une émouvante cérémonie à Inguiniel," *Le progrès du Morbihan*, 23 April 1921), Landaul ("L'inauguration du monument aux morts de Landaul," *OR*, 19 April 1923), and, in the Meuse, Laheycourt (*RM*, 22 July 1920).

114. The program in Le Faouët included horse, bicycle, and footraces, and dancing in the evening (*OR*, 21 June 1923); in Neulliac, bicycle races and a quoits competition, both with prizes ("Dans l'arrondissement," *JP*, 24 September 1922); in St. Caradec-Trégomel, bicycle races and dancing (*OR*, 29 March 1923).

115. Examples include a gymnastics display and concert in St. Maurice-sur-les-Côtes (*RE*, 22 October 1921); a concert and illumination of the boulevard La Rochelle, the main avenue leading to the monument, in Bar-le-Duc ("Bar-le-Duc: Inauguration du monument," *RM*, 26 March 1925); and a concert and gymnastics exhibition in Étain ("Étain," *L'avenir de la Meuse*, 16 September 1926). Vaubécourt did hold bicycle races, but its dedication took place on the *14 juillet* ("A Vaubécourt," *RM*, 21 July 1921).

116. ADM, O Pluvigner, mayor to prefect, 30 September 1920. Unfortunately the prefect's letter to which the mayor is responding, explaining that the dedication is scheduled for the day before a village festival, is not present. The dedication in Lanouée coincided with the patronal feast: see *Le ploërmelais*, 11 September 1921.

117. *JP*, 24 September 1922 (a delay in the ceremony until 11 November was under discussion, but did not take place).

118. *OR*, 15 November 1925. The full citation is even more explicit: "Et c'est très bien ainsi, car il ne fallait pas, quoi qu'en pensent les amateurs de bonne chère et les friands des discours d'après-boire, qu'une pareille journée soit entachée par les pensées badines que suggère la 'gaieté communicative des banquets.'" Needless to say, the newspaper does not identify the source of this citation.

119. "Chronique régionale," *Le ploërmelais*, 29 October 1922; information on festivities in "Ploërmel," 26 October 1922.

120. ADM, O Port-Louis, CM/PV, 25 June 1922.

121. Consolation: "M. Raymond Poincaré à l'inauguration du monument aux morts de Chaillon," *La Meuse*, 16 August 1930; final farewell: "A Crédin," *OR*, 23 September 1923 (mayor's speech); tribute and consolation: "Ploërmel," *OR*, 19 October 1923 (mayor's speech in Mohon).

122. "Dans l'arrondissement," *JP*, 28 October 1923 (note that the day is referred to as "une impressionnante fête de la reconaissance et du souvenir"); "Une belle fête patriotique à Montiers-sur-Saulx," *RM*, 29 September 1921.

123. "A Ménil-sur-Saulx," *RM*, 12 May 1921.

124. "Discours de M. André Maginot, ministre de la guerre," *RM*, 1 October 1931.

125. Most notably the Constitution's promulgation of a distinction between free citizens and slaves, with the provision that each slave would be counted as three-fifths of a person for purposes of legislative apportionment.

126. "Un moment de poignante émotion" in Vins (Var: "Chronique régionale," *Le progrès républicain*, 15 May 1920); "L'émotion est intense" in Vannes (*OR*, 15 November 1925); "l'émotion sincère" of the mayor of Melrand ("Dans l'arrondissement," *JP*, 8 August 1924); "la plus grande émotion" in La Trinité-sur-Mer ("L'inauguration du monument aux morts de La Trinité-sur-Mer," *OR*, 29 October 1925).

127. "Malestroit: L'inauguration du monument aux morts," *Le ploërmelais*, 20 November 1921.

128. Speech of Goumy, academic inspector, in Sivry-sur-Meuse, "Deux discours de M. Poincaré," *L'est républicain*, 18 May 1926, clipping in AN, F^{7}13003.

129. Victor Turner, *Process, Performance, and Pilgrimage: A Study in Comparative Symbology* (New Delhi: Concept Publishing, 1979), 127, emphasis in the original.

130. On the link between appropriation and myth, see Robert S. Nelson, "Appropriation," in *Critical Terms for Art History*, ed. Robert S. Nelson and Richard Shiff (Chicago: University of Chicago Press, 1996), 118–19.

131. Thomas W. Laqueur, "Memory and Naming in the Great War," in *Commemorations: The Politics of National Identity*, ed. John R. Gillis (Princeton: Princeton University Press, 1994), 161: "What is being represented, in the absence of some commonly accepted idea, some notion of glory, patriotism, or elation in victory—the purpose of the war had been and in memory remained hotly contested—is thus the thing itself and the democracy of death that this collection of things makes so manifest."

132. Toucas-Massillon: "Ville-Issey et Euville honorent leurs morts," *RE*, 3 December 1921; Diard: "Inauguration du monument aux morts d'Onzain," *Le nouvelliste, journal d'union républicaine*, 17 November 1923.

133. "Neulliac a commémoré ses morts," *OR*, 15 October 1922; "En l'honneur de nos morts," *RE*, 19 May 1923: Maginot was speaking at the dedication of the war memorial at the *collège* in Commercy.

134. "Saint-Mihiel a glorifié ses morts," *La Meuse*, 14 November 1925; "L'inauguration du monument aux morts de Spada," *La Meuse*, 6 August 1927.

135. "Inauguration du monument aux morts de la commune de Noyers," *RLC*, 20 July 1922.

136. "L'inauguration du monument aux morts d'Auray," *OR*, 19 November 1925.

137. The conceptual distinction is close to that between the notions of "repetition" (similar to what I call familiarity) and "recollection" (or transmission) in the work of Patrick Hutton, although his emphasis is different because he is looking retrospectively at the connections between theories of memory and historical writing, while I am seeking to examine a moment when this distinction was fresh, at least for the people under

discussion. See Patrick H. Hutton, *History as an Art of Memory* (Hanover, N.H.: University Press of New England, 1993), xx–xxi.

138. "Inauguration du monument élevé à la mémoire des instituteurs meusiens morts pour la France," *RE*, 16 April 1921.

139. "Jouy commémore ses héros," *RE*, 19 August 1922.

140. "Lorient et son arrondissement," *Le progrès du Morbihan*, 29 May 1921 (Landévant); see also "Inauguration du monument de Thésée," *RLC*, 3 December 1922.

141. "Les belles cérémonies patriotiques: Kerfourn a honoré ses glorieux morts," *OR*, 21 October 1923; "La fête de Neuville," *RM*, 9 October 1921.

142. *RM*, 6 October 1921; "Commercy pendant la guerre," *RE*, 12 May 1923.

143. "Inauguration d'une plaque commémorative à l'École Primaire Supérieure de Saint-Aignan," *Le nouvelliste*, 30 June 1923; *La Meuse*, 31 October 1925.

144. See, for example, the comments of the president of the monument committee in St. Mihiel where, exceptionally, names were for aesthetic reasons inscribed not on the monument itself but in the hôtel de ville. There, asserted M. Thonin, "chacun pourra, dans le recueillement, lire et relire à loisir, pour les conserver dans une mémoire fidèle, les patronymes de nos héros": *La Meuse*, 14 November 1925.

145. *L'avenir de Verdun*, 13 September 1923.

146. This is one of the key observations of Maurice Halbwachs in *La mémoire collective*, 2d ed. (Paris: Presses Universitaires de France, 1968), 29; in English *The Collective Memory*, trans. Francis J. Ditter, Jr., and Vida Yazdi Ditter (New York: Harper and Row, 1980), 45.

147. "La cérémonie du 11 novembre," *Le progrès du Morbihan*, 15 November 1925.

148. Gérard Noiriel, *Le creuset français: Histoire de l'immigration, XIXᵉ–XXᵉ siècles* (Paris: Seuil, 1988), 264; in English as *The French Melting Pot: Immigration, Citizenship, and National Identity*, trans. Geoffroy de Laforcade, Contradictions of Modernity, 5 (Minneapolis: University of Minnesota Press, 1996), 202.

149. "Lamotte-Beuvron: Inauguration du monument aux morts," *RLC*, 28 October 1923. The abundant use of idioms and intricate grammar of this passage make it especially difficult to translate; the original runs as follows: "M. le sénateur Pichery rappela ceux dont les noms lancés tout à l'heure aux échos éveillaient en sa mémoire une physionomie, et, pour ainsi dire, un portrait de famille, tant la race chez nous est toujours semblable à elle-même, splendide en l'obscur labeur comme devant l'obscure mort des tranchées." It is impossible to determine whether the phrasing here is Pichery's or the newspaper's, but it is also irrelevant: for the purposes of this analysis "Pichery" should be taken to refer to the newspaper's construct of him, which in any case is consistent with actual transcripts of speeches he delivered at other ceremonies.

150. The first definition for *labeur* in the *Petit Robert* is "travail pénible et soutenu" (*Le nouveau Petit Robert: Dictionnaire alphabétique et analogique de la langue française*, rev. ed. [Paris: Le Robert, 1993]), 1: 1248. The word *travail* includes such meanings but can also convey the dignity of work and of productive labor; it is incorporated in the name of the first French labor federation, the Confédération Générale du Travail (CGT) and in the word *travailliste*, the French translation for the "labor" parties of the English-speaking world.

151. "Inauguration du monument aux morts de Ruffiac," *OR*, 4 October 1923; other examples include a mayor bowing to the families, "A Ménil-sur-Saulx," *RM*, 12 May 1921; and a district councillor bowing to the monument, "Inauguration du monument aux morts de Saint Julien de Chédon," *RLC*, 30 April 1922.

152. *Le progrès du Morbihan*, 15 November 1925 (Marchais); *RM*, 2 April 1925 (Poincaré); "L'inauguration du monument aux morts de Woinville," *BM*, 22 July 1933.

153. See, for example, "A Selles-sur-Cher: Inauguration du monument aux morts de la grande guerre," *RLC*, 6 November 1921, speech of Goudeau, general councillor, who called the monument *un monument sacré*.

154. "Haudainville," *L'avenir de Verdun*, 13 September 1923.

155. "Inauguration du monument aux morts à Savigny-sur-Braye," *RLC*, 19 August 1923.

156. "Inauguration de la statue du poilu à Metz," *RE*, 10 June 1922.

157. "A Ménil-sur-Saulx," *RM*, 12 May 1921.

158. "Le Sourn et Saint-Gonnery ont rendu hommage aux morts pour la patrie," *OR*, 8 November 1923; *RE*, 19 August 1922; "Le monument de Villebarou," *Le nouvelliste*, 27 September 1924.

159. In 1911, 41 percent of French workers were employed in agriculture, 36 percent in industry, 10 percent in commerce, 4 percent each in domestic service and in public administration, 2 percent in the liberal professions. By 1926 the proportion in agriculture had declined to 38.3 percent and by 1936 to 35.6 percent; in the latter year 14 percent of French workers were employed in commerce and 10.1 percent in the liberal professions and public service. See Colin Dyer, *Population and Society in Twentieth-Century France* (New York: Holmes and Meier, 1978), 11, 68.

160. See, for example, "Chauvoncourt & Les Paroches ont honoré leurs morts," *La Meuse*, 13 November 1926, speech of the mayor of Chauvoncourt, Charles Robas: "C'est de ce passé que nous devons nous inspirer pour perpétuer à travers les générations ce sens de la vraie justice, cet amour du sol natal, cet esprit de dévouement et de sacrifice qui fut l'incomparable apanache [*sic*] de ceux qui, en mourant, nous l'ont laissé."

161. Vaux: *L'avenir de la Meuse*, 7 October 1926 (the text has *vanniers*, which means basket-makers; in the context it should probably be *vanneurs*, or winnowers); "Ville-Issey et Euville honorent leurs morts," *RE*, 3 December 1921.

162. "Dhuizon: Inauguration du monument aux morts pour la patrie," *RLC*, 6 August 1922.

163. "A Louppy-le-Château," *RM*, 22 May 1921, speech of Cochard.

164. "Inauguration du monument des enfants de Ménil-la-Horgne morts pour la France," *RE*, 4 June 1921, speech of Cobus.

165. "Fresnes," *RLC*, 27 November 1921, speech of Dr. Legros.

166. See Jacques Dupâquier et al., *Histoire de la population française*, 4 vols., vol. 3, *De 1789 à 1914* (Paris: Presses Universitaires de France, 1988), 177–213, 243–68.

167. "Inauguration du monument aux morts et de la Mairie-École de Dompcevrin," *La Meuse*, 10 October 1925.

168. "L'inauguration du monument aux morts pour la patrie de Saint-Claude-de-

Diray," *RLC*, 13 November 1921; Legros's speech at St. Julien-de-Chédon, *RLC*, 30 April 1922; Jacquinot's speech at Buxières, "Buxières et Woël ont honoré leurs morts," *BM*, 16 July 1932.

169. *La Meuse*, 14 November 1925; "Les inaugurations de Maucourt, Boinville, et Warcq," *BM*, 3 November 1928.

170. "Chauvoncourt et Les Paroches ont honoré leurs morts," *La Meuse*, 13 November 1926; "Étain," *L'avenir de la Meuse*, 16 September 1926, emphasis added.

171. The term is that of Robert L. Herbert, in *Jean-François Millet*, catalogue of an exhibition at the Hayward Gallery (London: Arts Council of Great Britain, 1976), 75; the sower in the Esnes monument most closely resembles Millet's *The sower* (*Le semeur*), cat. 37.

172. For a similar reading, see Annette Becker, *Les monuments aux morts: Mémoire de la grande guerre* (Paris: Errance, [1987]), 27; on the commemoration (or lack of it) of civilian suffering, see her *Oubliés de la grande guerre: Humanitaire et culture de guerre, populations occupées, déportés civils, prisonniers de guerre* (Paris: Noêsis, 1998), 359–76.

173. Moore and Myerhoff, "Introduction," 18; see also MacCannell, "The Future of Ritual," 274.

174. "A Sampigny," *RE*, 3 November 1923.

175. "L'inauguration du monument de Cellettes," *RLC*, 11 September 1921.

176. Toucas-Massillon's speech at Ville-Issey, *RE*, 3 December 1921. Whether copying Toucas-Massillon's text or using a common source, the deputy Taton-Vassal gave virtually the same speech nearly six years later: "L'inauguration du monument aux morts de Bannoncourt," *La Meuse*, 30 April 1927. The only difference is that where Toucas-Massillon says "que leur sacrifice ne sera pas sterile," Taton-Vassal has "que leur sacrifice demeurera fertile." The three words for work are identical in the two versions, as is the unusual word, *parachevée*, which I have translated as "completed"; it literally means something like "perfected" or "put the finishing touches on."

177. On the derivation of the term and subsequent political maneuvering, see Jean-Jacques Becker and Serge Berstein, *Victoire et frustrations, 1914–1929*, Nouvelle Histoire de la France Contemporaine 12 (Paris: Seuil, 1990), 26–28, 52–69, 86–104; on the political atmosphere in 1917 and the formation of the Clemenceau government, see Jean-Marie Mayeur, *La vie politique sous la Troisième République, 1870–1940* (Paris: Seuil, 1984), 242–50.

178. Jean-Jacques Becker, *The Great War and the French People*, trans. Arnold Pomerans (Leamington Spa: Berg, 1985), 324. I have slightly modified the translation; for the original, see Becker, *Les français dans la grande guerre* (Paris: Robert Laffont, 1980), 302. On the right and the *union sacrée*, cf. Becker and Berstein, *Victoire et frustrations*, 95–99, 241.

179. "A Euville," *RE*, 3 December 1921.

180. *RLC*, 28 October 1923; *RE*, 19 May 1923.

181. Langoëlan: "Pontivy," *OR*, 16 September 1923; Mohon: "Ploërmel," *OR*, 18 October 1923.

182. "Bar-le-Duc honore ses morts," *RM*, 2 April 1925.

183. "Ploërmel," *OR*, 26 October 1922.

184. ADM, O Guillac, undated clipping from an unidentified newspaper, probably *Ouest éclair;* the article is headed "Un scandale: La surenchère électorale et les morts de la guerre" and signed "Un ancien combattant."

185. *Le ploërmelais,* 24 April 1921; "L'inauguration du monument commémoratif de Guilliers," *Le progrès du Morbihan,* 30 April 1921.

186. *OR,* 17 and 24 September 1925; *NM,* 29 September and 8 October 1925. The mayor claimed that he had invited only mayors and members of the departmental general council from the area around Inzinzac, some of whom happened also to hold parliamentary seats; he charged that a number of communes run by conservatives had, without any such rationale, invited only politicians of Lamy's persuasion.

187. "Le bon et le grand Pilote! Assez de concessions! a dit M. Poincaré dans son discours de Chaillon," *BM,* 16 August 1930.

188. "L'inauguration du monument aux morts et de la Mairie-École de Rambucourt," *La Meuse,* 19 June 1926. Accounts of Poincaré's speeches in the Meuse, though obviously not of the ceremonies of which they formed part, appear frequently in newspapers in other departments: see, for example, "Poignée de nouvelles," *JP,* 27 August 1922 and 2 September 1923; "Les combats de l'Argonne: M. Poincaré inaugure un monument à la côte 285," *OR,* 3 August 1922.

189. "Inaugurations des monuments aux morts de Lacroix-sur-Meuse, Marbotte, Apremont-la-Forêt," *La Meuse,* 26 September 1925. Compare Poincaré's more general remarks on the same theme in Bar-le-Duc, *RM,* 2 April 1925.

190. On the Rif war, which was strongly opposed by the Communist party and other segments of the French left, see Becker and Berstein, *Victoire et frustrations,* 256–57; Jacques Thobie, Gilbert Meynier, Catherine Coquery-Vidrovitch, and Charles-Robert Ageron, *Histoire de la France coloniale,* vol. 2, *1914–1990* (Paris: Armand Colin, 1990), 190–91. On cartel foreign policy, see Edouard Bonnefous, *Histoire politique de la Troisième République,* vol. 4, *Cartel des gauches et union nationale (1924–1929),* 2d ed. (Paris: Presses Universitaires de France, 1973), 26–33; Becker and Berstein, 250–56.

191. "Plouharnel inaugure son monument aux morts," *OR,* 6 July 1922. The following month in Port-Louis, a similar group of orators, including Rio, "ont fait un commun et nouvel appel à la concorde dans les circonstances politiques graves que traverse le pays": "Poignée de nouvelles," *JP,* 27 August 1922.

192. "M. Poincaré à Damvillers et à Haudainville," *RE,* 15 September 1923.

193. *RE,* 19 May 1923.

194. On the crisis of morale of 1917, see Becker, *The Great War,* 193–248.

195. This is in some degree to oversimplify the 1924 election campaign, in which Poincaré did not wish to appear as a party leader and left that role, exceptionally, to the president of the Republic, Alexandre Millerand. The results of the election, however, in terms of parliamentary seats if not of the popular vote, clearly represented a repudiation of Poincaré's policies. See Becker and Berstein, *Victoire et frustrations,* 237–46.

196. Becker and Berstein, *Victoire et frustrations,* 241.

197. "Chronique locale: Le monument de Cheverny," *Le nouvelliste,* 28 April 1923; "Le monument de Candé," *Le nouvelliste,* 7 July 1923. Mauger's remarks in Candé are very similar to a portion of his speech in Cheverny.

198. For additional examples, see my "Les inaugurations et la politique," 278.

199. "Un grand discours de M. René Renoult," *Le petit Var*, 29 September 1922.

200. This formulation owes much to that of Mary Louise Roberts: see her *Civilization without Sexes*, 7.

201. *Le nouvelliste*, 28 April 1923.

202. "L'inauguration du monument aux morts," *JP*, 22 October 1922.

203. "Inauguration du monument aux enfants de Grimaucourt morts pour la France," *RE*, 23 July 1921; see also the mayor's remarks in Rilly-sur-Loire, "L'inauguration du monument de Rilly-sur-Loire," *RLC*, 27 November 1921.

204. "M. Maginot à Saint-Dizier, Ancerville, Rupt-aux-Nonains," *RM*, 12 April 1923.

205. See Prost, *Les anciens combattants*, 1: 78–80.

206. "Taupont: Echo des fêtes," *Le ploërmelais*, 5 March 1922.

207. "A Revigny-sur-Ornain: Inauguration d'un monument au cimetière militaire," *RM*, 7 November 1920.

208. Speech of a retired teacher, Garçonnet, at Rupt-aux-Nonains, *RM*, 12 April 1923.

209. *L'avenir de la Meuse*, 3 June 1926. Other examples include Ruffiac (Morbihan), where the mayor called the dedication the *fête* not only of the dead but of all those "qui les ont perdus et qui versent sur leurs cercueils des larmes inconsolées," then went on to describe those mourners as mothers, widows, and orphans ("Inauguration du monument aux morts de Ruffiac," *OR*, 4 October 1923); and Dompcevrin (Meuse), where the mayor, bowing in respect to bereaved families, refers only to mothers as weeping. See also my "Monuments, Mourning, and Masculinity," 93–94 and n. 106 above.

210. Haudiomont: *L'avenir de la Meuse*, 18 August 1927.

211. "Rouvrois-sur-Meuse a honoré ses grands morts," *La Meuse*, 18 April 1925. The repetition of the phrase "we will be able" (*nous pourrons*) follows the original French.

212. Ibid.

213. "A Louppy-le-Château," *RM*, 22 May 1921. For a full discussion of this speech, see my "Monuments, Mourning, and Masculinity," 94–95.

214. "A Selles-sur-Cher," *RLC*, 6 November 1921.

215. "Elven: Inauguration du monument aux morts," *Le progrès du Morbihan*, 25 December 1921; "Les visites de M. Alphonse Rio, sous-secrétaire d'état des ports de la marine marchande et des pêches dans le Morbihan," *Le progès du Morbihan*, 11 September 1921.

216. *RE*, 19 August 1922.

217. "Lamotte-Beuvron: Inauguration du monument aux morts," *RLC*, 28 October 1923, speech of Vrain, dean of the conseil municipal: "Il y a ici une mère en deuil qu'on appelle la France"; *La Meuse*, 19 June 1926, Taton-Vassal's speech in Rambucourt: "dans cette Lorraine mère de tant d'héroïsmes, et nourricière de tant de sacrifices."

218. "Inauguration du monument des enfants de Ménil-la-Horgne morts pour la France," *RE*, 4 June 1921; Roland Dorgelès, *Les croix de bois*, Le Livre de Poche ed. (Paris: Albin Michel, n.d. [originally published 1919]), 197.

219. For a further elaboration of this argument, see my "Monuments, Mourning, and Masculinity," 98–99.

220. On the cultural dimensions of this anxiety, see, for example, Roberts, *Civilization without Sexes*, 93–131; Marie-Monique Huss, "Pronatalism and the Popular Ideology of the Child in Wartime France: The Evidence of the Picture Postcard," in *The Upheaval of War: Family, Work, and Welfare in Europe, 1914–1918*, ed. Richard Wall and Jay Winter (Cambridge: Cambridge University Press, 1988), 329–67. For useful background, and an insightful discussion of the malleability of discourses of fertility, see Joshua H. Cole, "'There Are Only Good Mothers': The Ideological Work of Women's Fertility in France before World War I," *French Historical Studies* 19 (1995–96): 349–72.

221. *OR*, 21 October 1923.

222. *L'avenir de la Meuse*, 8 September 1927. Dambraine was at the time director of a school in Thierville, but he had earlier been assigned to Ornes.

223. "Inauguration du monument," *La Meuse*, 10 October 1925. The end of the quoted sentence reads "le sacrifice des enfants du pays dans l'holocauste général"; Taton-Vassal is using the word "holocaust" in something like its original sense as a burnt offering.

224. "L'inauguration du monument de Vineuil," *RLC*, 17 September 1922; "Cléguer rend un émouvant hommage à ses héros," *OR*, 8 June 1922.

225. "Le monument de Girauvoisin," *RE*, 17 December 1921.

226. "L'inauguration du monument commémoratif," *RLC*, 24 June 1923.

227. This account is based on visits to Blois and on my attendance at *11 novembre* observances not in Blois but in another prefecture of similar size, Vannes, in 1990.

EPILOGUE

1. "Vingt ans après Verdun," *L'illustration*, 18 July 1936, 356–57; "La manifestation des A.C. à Douaumont," *RLC*, 19 July 1936.

2. Salengro, at the same time mayor of Lille, was also depressed by the recent death of his wife and overburdened with work. See Dominique Borne and Henri Dubief, *La crise des années 30, 1929–1938*, Nouvelle Histoire de la France Contemporaine 13 (Paris: Seuil, 1989), 180.

3. "Les fêtes du 11 novembre," *La croix meusienne*, 21 November 1936; "Fête de l'armistice," *RE*, 14 November 1936; "Chronique locale" (schedules of events in various towns), *L'avenir* (Loir-et-Cher), 5, 6, 7, 8, 10, and 11 November 1936.

4. "Anniversaire," *RE*, 14 November 1936.

5. "La fête nationale du 11 novembre," *NM*, 11 November 1936; "Le 11 novembre à Lorient," *NM*, 12 November 1936; "Le 11 novembre 1936," *Écho de la Sologne*, 6 November 1936; "Fête du 11 novembre à Romorantin," *Écho de la Sologne*, 13 November 1936; "A l'occasion des fêtes de la Plisson," *Courrier de la Sologne*, 14 November 1936.

6. "La commémoration de l'armistice," *NM*, 13 November 1936; "Paris a commémoré la victoire," *L'avenir* (Loir-et-Cher), 13 November 1936.

7. "La fête nationale du 11 novembre," *NM*, 11 November 1936; "Chouzy-sur-Cisse: La fête du 11 novembre," *L'avenir*, 15 November 1936.

8. "Fête du 11 novembre à Romorantin," *Écho de la Sologne*, 13 November 1936; "Selles-sur-Cher: Fête du 11 novembre 1936," *Écho de la Sologne*, 20 November 1936.

9. Accounts in the right-wing *Écho de la Sologne* emphasized that the oath was read "following orders received from the government" ("Selles-sur-Cher," 20 November 1936). The more centrist *Républicain de l'est* observed simply that the oath had been recited across the country, without commenting on government instructions; see "Echos meusiens," *RE*, 21 November 1936; this issue also contains an account of Salengro's suicide quite sympathetic to the late minister.

10. For additional examples of the use of war memorials in political demonstrations, see Robert O. Paxton, *French Peasant Fascism: Henry Dorgères's Greenshirts and the Crises of French Agriculture* (New York: Oxford University Press, 1997), 26, 75, 95, 138.

11. On the relationship of this version to the 1919 silent original, see Jay Winter, *Sites of Memory, Sites of Mourning: The Great War in European Cultural History* (Cambridge: Cambridge University Press, 1995), 15–17.

12. "Les flammes du 11 novembre," *L'illustration*, 19 November 1938, 389–91; "Le XXᵉ anniversaire de l'armistice," *NM*, 29 October 1938, for the schedule in Vannes. For the national context see Janine Bourdin, "Les anciens combattants et la célébration du 11 novembre 1938," in *La France et les français en 1938–1939*, ed. René Rémond and Janine Bourdin (Paris: Presses de la Fondation Nationale des Sciences Politiques, 1978), 95–114.

13. On the origins of the practice and the formation of "Les vigiles de la flamme," see Gabriel Boissy, "Comment fut pensée et réalisée la flamme perpetuelle du souvenir sur le tombeau du Soldat Inconnu," *La charte*, November 1963, 8–9; on Daladier's relighting the flame, *NM*, 2 October 1938.

14. See "Le relais des flammes," *L'illustration*, 20 November 1937, 320.

15. "Les flammes," *L'illustration*, 19 November 1938, 390, 389.

16. *NM*, 5 and 11 November 1938.

17. "La Toussaint à Lorient," *NM*, 3 November 1938; "Fête de l'armistice," *Écho de la Sologne*, 18 November 1938. Like many towns, Lorient held commemorative ceremonies on the All Saints' holiday, traditionally a day devoted to the memory of the dead, as well as on 11 November.

18. "Paris a commémoré la victoire," *L'avenir* (Loir-et-Cher), 13 November 1936.

19. "L'armistice sportif," *NM*, 12 November 1938; "Dans le Morbihan," *NM*, 13 November 1938.

20. "Vingt ans après!" *NM*, 6 November 1938. The passage from Bernier is discussed in chapter 1.

21. Paul Manet, "Verdun," *Journal des combattants et de toutes les victimes de la guerre*, 18 February 1961.

22. "Pour le 47ᵉ anniversaire de la victoire de Verdun . . . ," *Journal des combattants et de toutes les victimes de la guerre*, 29 June 1963.

23. Theodor Adorno, "Valéry Proust Museum," in *Prisms*, trans. Samuel and Shierry Weber (Cambridge: MIT Press, 1981), 175.

24. See Eugenio Donato, "The Museum's Furnace: Notes toward a Contextual Reading of *Bouvard and Pécuchet*," in *Textual Strategies: Perspectives in Post-Structuralist Criticism*, ed. Josué V. Harari (Ithaca: Cornell University Press, 1979), 220, 223. I am here summarizing the argument in my "Objects of Memory: History and Narrative in French War Museums," *French Historical Studies* 19 (1995–96): 49–74.

25. "Verdun," *Journal des combattants*, 18 February 1961. The French describes "un Mémorial qui, dans l'avenir, permettra de matérialiser et de conserver intact un Souvenir qui constitue un des sommets de notre Histoire nationale." The use of the verb *permettre*, which allows the writer to avoid the personal object that would be required in English ("permits *us* to materialize"), is crucial to my interpretation of this sentence.

26. On the origins of the Bibliothèque-musée, now called the Bibliothèque de Documentation Internationale Contemporaine, see Joseph Hue, "La Bibliothèque-musée de la Guerre dans les années vingt," in *La course au moderne: France et Allemagne dans l'Europe des années vingt*, ed. R. Frank, L. Gervereau, H. J. Neyer, exhibition cat. (Paris: Musée d'Histoire Contemporaine/BDIC, 1992), 169–75.

27. See Leblanc's remarks in Georges Cain, "Préface," in Collection Henri Leblanc, *La grande guerre: Iconographie, bibliographie, documents divers*, vol. 1, *Catalogue raisonné* . . . (Paris, 1916), ix–x.

28. Société de l'Histoire de la Guerre, *Guide du Musée de la grande guerre (Fondé avec les Collections Henri Leblanc)* (Paris, 1927), 10.

29. See Henry Rousso, *The Vichy Syndrome: History and Memory in France since 1944*, trans. Arthur Goldhammer (Cambridge: Harvard University Press, 1991), 40–49, in which he casts doubt on the story, spread by the Association pour Défendre la Mémoire du Maréchal Pétain, that on returning to power in 1958 de Gaulle was prepared to authorize the transfer of Pétain's remains to Douaumont. On the 1973 episode, see Eric Conan and Henry Rousso, *Vichy: Un passé qui ne passe pas*, Pour une Histoire du XXᵉ Siècle (Paris: Fayard, 1994), 40.

30. See Jean Lacouture, *De Gaulle: The Ruler, 1945–1970*, trans. Alan Sheridan (New York: Norton, 1992), 286, 296–98; and Rousso, *The Vichy Syndrome*, 48. Lacouture notes that in 1961 Jean-Marie Le Pen, more recently the leader of the extreme-right Front National party but then a young deputy, called for the legalization of the OAS.

31. "Le Mémorial de Verdun inauguré," *L'est républicain*, 18 September 1967.

32. "Screen Memories," in *The Standard Edition of the Complete Psychological Works of Sigmund Freud*, trans. and ed. James Strachey, vol. 3 (London: Hogarth Press, 1962), 320. The structure of the screen memory may be reversed, in which case a vivid recent memory screens out a significant memory of early childhood.

33. Ibid., 321.

34. "L'inauguration du Mémorial," *La charte*, October 1967, 6.

35. Archives du Mémorial de Verdun, dossier "Recherche de Matériel."

36. *Guide souvenir, Mémorial-musée de la Bataille de Verdun*, 6th ed. (Verdun: Comité National du Souvenir de Verdun, n.d.), front endpaper.

37. Ibid., 35–39.

38. Archives du Mémorial de Verdun, minutes of Groupe de Travail, 29 June 1965.

39. Georges Pineau, "La grande pitié des monuments aux morts," *La charte*, January 1967, 6.

40. Vichy's attempts to modify existing forms of commemoration, including rituals, seem to have had little lasting effect: see Avner Ben-Amos, "La commémoration sous le régime de Vichy: Les limites de la maîtrise du passé," in *La France démocratique (combats, mentalités, symboles): Mélanges offerts à Maurice Agulhon*, ed. Christophe Charle, Jacqueline Lalouette, Michel Pigenet, and Anne-Marie Sohn (Paris: Publications de la Sorbonne, 1998), 397–408.

41. See Marc Lombard, "Le monument à la gloire des combattants vincennois de la première guerre mondiale (1914–1918)," *Bulletin de la Société des amis de Vincennes* 39 (1988): 4–11; and Serge Barcellini, "Les monuments en hommage aux combattants de la 'Grande France' (Armée d'Afrique et Armée coloniale)," in *Les troupes coloniales dans la grande guerre*, ed. Claude Carlier and Guy Pedroncini (Paris: Institut d'Histoire des Conflits Contemporaines/Economica, 1997), 132–33.

42. AN, F^{21}7079, folder labeled "Loi du 13 janvier 1942: Erections de monuments." The text was also in *JO*, 15 January 1942, 215.

43. AN, F^{21}7079, folder "Erection des monuments aux morts." The basic decree, dated 16 January 1947, contained all provisions except the exact sum of 500,000 francs, which was set in a separate decree of 6 February 1947. Price comparisons drawn from Institut National de la Statistique et des Études Économiques, *Annuaire statistique de la France*, vol. 66 (n.s. 8): *Rétrospectif* (Paris: Imprimerie Nationale and Presses Universitaires de France, 1961), 253–54, 259: the average wage in various mechanical trades in 1947 was between eighteen and twenty-four times the 1921 figure, while prices for basic foodstuffs had in some cases increased by as much as thirty times.

44. AN, F^{21}7079, letter budget director, Ministère des Finances, to director-general of fine arts, 12 September 1947.

45. Other contributing factors, of course, included France's record in World War II and the complexity of the political situation from 1944 through 1947. But World War II gave rise to a much greater number and range of monuments in France than is generally realized: see Serge Barcellini and Annette Wieviorka, *Passant, souviens-toi! Les lieux du souvenir de la seconde guerre mondiale en France* (Paris: Plon, 1995).

46. A 1968 ordinance recalling the statutory requirements suggests, however, that this provision was not enforced. Since the 1982 law on decentralization, commemorative monuments have required the authorization only of the mayor: see Barcellini and Wieviorka, *Passant, souviens-toi!*, 12.

47. Pineau, "La grande pitié," *La charte*, January 1967, 6.

48. J. Filippi, "La grande pitié des monuments aux morts," *La charte*, March 1967, 4; Max Girou, "Les monuments aux morts qui ont le mieux honoré leur exemple et leur sacrifice," *La charte*, May 1968, 5.

49. "Les monuments aux morts," *La charte*, May 1968, 5.

50. "L'historial de la 'grande guerre' à Péronne" (Interview with Hugues Hairy), *Lettre des musées de France* 24 (July-August 1992): 2.

51. On the name "Historial," see Madeleine Bunting, "All Quiet on the Tourist Front," *Guardian*, 20 July 1992; Marina Benjamin, "Eloquent Memorial," *Spectator*, 1

August 1992; for "comparative cultural history" see "L'historial de la 'grande guerre,'" *Lettre des musées;* and Emmanuel de Roux, "La grande guerre au quotidien," *Le monde,* 18 July 1992. The Historial's publicity flyer, "L'histoire autrement," refers to "une vision culturelle comparée du premier conflit mondial tel qu'il a été vécu par ses acteurs: les civils et les combattants."

52. "Historial de la grande guerre: L'histoire autrement," press release, summer 1993.

53. See Archives, Société Repérages (the firm responsible for the museographical program), "Historial de la grande guerre, Concours de maitrise d'oeuvre muséographique, Dossier-programme" [1990].

54. On aestheticization, see Archives, Société Repérages, minutes, Historical Program meeting, 25 September 1990; on the historical discourse, "Concours de maitrise d'oeuvre"; and Hugues Hairy, "L'Historial de la grande guerre au Château de Péronne," *Musées et collections publiques de France* 199 (June 1993): 139.

55. For comment on the film, see Catherine Milner, "Was the Great War a Civil War?" *Times,* 5 August 1992.

56. See Rousso, *The Vichy Syndrome,* chaps. 4 and 5 (the term "obsession" is his); and on attitudes toward the Vichy past in the early nineties, Conan and Rousso, *Vichy.*

57. Sébastien Japrisot, *Un long dimanche de fiançailles,* Folio ed. (Paris: Denoël, 1991), 350–51; see also *A Very Long Engagement,* trans. Linda Coverdale (New York: Farrar, Straus, and Giroux, 1993), 308. I have modified the translation of the first passage.

58. Jean Rouaud, *Les champs d'honneur* (Paris: Minuit, 1990), 82; in English, *Fields of Glory,* trans. Ralph Mannheim (New York: Arcade, 1992), 64.

59. *Les champs,* 44, 64; *Fields of Glory,* 32, 49. The translation of this passage is my own.

60. *Les champs,* 165; *Fields of Glory,* 131. Many monuments, however, listed the dead in alphabetical rather than chronological order.

61. *Fields of Glory,* 129; *Les champs,* 162–63.

62. *Les champs,* 170; *Fields of Glory,* 135.

63. *Les champs,* 178–81; *Fields of Glory,* 141–43.

64. On the ways novels, especially romance novels, convey broad social meanings to their readers, see Janice A. Radway, *Reading the Romance: Women, Patriarchy, and Popular Literature* (Chapel Hill: University of North Carolina Press, 1984), 200–208.

65. Rouaud, *Fields of Glory,* 109–12, epigraph from p. 110; *Les champs d'honneur,* 138–40, epigraph from p. 139.

66. *Les champs,* 146, 151–52, citation from p. 152; *Fields of Glory,* 116, 119–20. I have slightly modified the translation. The word *déréglée,* which Mannheim translates as "thrown off course," in French puns on the word *règles,* or period.

67. This was also true of the Bibliothèque-musée de la Guerre in the 1920s. See my "Objects of Memory," 56.

68. Archives de l'Historial de Péronne, Livre d'Or, November-December 1992. A visitor, presumably English, wrote the following: "Frank FUNTHAM était mon grand-père, soldat englais [*sic*] mort pour la France et je remercie profondément les organisa-

teurs du mémorial rappelant qu'une jeunesse est 'partie' pour le respect des libertés."
There are also comments in English and German; citations in the text are translated
from the French.

69. "En mémoire de la grande guerre," *Le pélerin*, 7 August 1992.

70. Consider the titles of some articles published at the time of the Historial's
opening: "Un monument de la mémoire collective à Péronne," *La voix du Nord*, 7 May
1992; "La mémoire des poilus repose en paix," *Libération*, 3 July 1992; "Souvenirs de la
der des der," *Le nouvel observateur*, 23–29 July 1992; "Lieu de mémoire," *Maison et
jardin*, November 1992; and Martin Meade, "War Memorial," *Architectural Review* 192:
1151 (January 1993): 65–69, as well as a number of articles previously cited. The un-
derstatement of the symbolism prompted the *Spectator* to call the Historial a "monument for our times": see M. Benjamin, "Eloquent memorial."

71. S. Audoin-Rouzeau, "La grande guerre prend fin aujourd'hui," *Historia* 548
(August 1992): 94. On the symbolism and Ciriani's remarks, see Archives, Société
Repérages, "Dossier-Programme, Centre Historique de la grande guerre, Péronne:
Dossier technique," 15; Ciriani quoted in "Faire la lumière, une conversation avec l'ar-
chitecte," *L'architecture d'aujourd'hui* 282 (September 1992): 78; and "L'Historial de la
grande guerre à Péronne: L'absurde en toute gravité," *L'humanité*, 28 October 1992.
See also Frédéric Edelmann's discussion of the symbolism in "Le piano à quai," *Le
monde*, 18 July 1992.

INDEX

Italics indicate page on which illustration appears.
Titles of works of art and literature may be found under the name of the author or artist.

Rombaux-Roland (monument firm), 171, 177, 189, 198, 208

Romorantin (Loir-et-Cher), 117, 313, 315; Sologne monument in, *207–208*; dedicated, 269

Ronvaux (Meuse): war monument in, 187, *188*

Rouaud, Jean: *Les champs d'honneur*, 326, 327–30

Rouquier, Louis (mayor), 111

Roustan, Jules (architect), 164

Rude, François: *La Marseillaise*, 149, *150*, 154, 189, 201; on poster, 56, *58*

Ruhr (Germany): French invasion of, 299

Sabattier, Lucien: cartoons by, 54, *55*

sacrifice: double meaning of, 107, 122, 140–1; male and female, 207–8, 275; for subscriptions, 119, 121

Salbris (Loir-et-Cher): war monument in, *190*, 195, 197, 204, 224

Salengro, Roger (minister of interior), 312

Salons, Paris, 145, 148, 153–4

Savigny-sur-Braye (Loir-et-Cher): war monument in, 124–6, *125*, 288

Schleiter, Victor (mayor), 81, 243–4

Schlumberger, Jean, *Le camarade infidèle*, 34–6

Schweitzer, Gaston (sculptor), 252

Scott, Georges: war scenes by 52, *54*

Scott, Joan, 14–5

screen memory, 29, 318–9, 326

sculptors. *See* artists

Selles-sur-Cher, 313; war monument in, 189, *191*

Sem (artist): poster by, 56, *58*

Senate (French), 72, 98, 132–3

separation of church and state, 244–5; and monument sites, 217, 228, 235–9; and ossuaries, 74, 90; and ritual, 273

Sérruys, Yvonne, 173; war monument for Menin, 151, *153*

Sicard, François: war monument for Blois, 143, 308, *309*

Simonet, Senator Adolphe, 72, 81–2

Sivry-sur-Meuse: war monument in, 303

Skinner, Belle, 210

soldier-civilian gap: in cartoons, 54–5, *55;* gendering of, 26, 32–4, 204, 207, 210; memory and, 31, 306; monuments and, 140, 293; in trench press, 16, 45; in war narratives, 17, 23, 24, 31. *See also* experience, soldiers'

Sommedieue (Meuse): war monument in, 201–*202*

spiritualism, 93

St. Denis-sur-Loire (Loir-et-Cher): war monument in, 110, 237–8

St. Maurice-sous-les-Côtes (Meuse), 271

St. Maximin (Var): war monument in, *200*, 210

St. Mihiel (Meuse): war monument in, 204; dedicated, 291

St. Raphaël (Var), 118

St. Rémy-la-Calonne (Meuse): war monument in, *203*, 208; dedicated, 269

St. Thuriau (Morbihan): war monument in, 176, *177*

Ste. Maxime (Var): monument project in, 113

Steeg, Théodore (minister of interior), 164, 236

Steinlen, Théophile-Alexandre: poster by, *62–3*

stelas (monument type), 171

subscription: as community events, 108, 114, 117, 119; and monument sites, 220, 227; organization of, 114–6, 117, 120; and public opinion, 123–4, 126, 138

subventions, departmental, 132

subventions, state, 107, 132–5

Tanneron (Var): war monument in, 198, *201*

taste, provincial, 157–8, 160, 169, 195, 201, 212–3. *See also* art

Taton-Vassal, Louis (mayor), 283, 290, 291, 307

Tavernier, Bertrand: *La vie et rien d'autre*, 326–7

Temps, Le, 77

Thiébault-Sisson (art critic): on monument projects, 148, 152, 154–5, 181; on popular taste, 157, 181

Thiepval. *See* Lutyens, Sir Edwin

Thomasset, A., 46

tombstones: 62–4, 79–80, 82, 90

torches (in ceremonies), 312, 314

Toucas-Massillon (subprefect): as dedication speaker, 271, 296, 303, 305; on commemorative themes, 96, 282

Toulon (Var): war monuments in, 109, 138, 226; monuments as projects, 113, 114, 226–7

Touring-Club de France, 37, 38, 105, 185

tourism, 16–7

tourism, battlefield, 35–9, 48–9, 316. *See also* war ruins

town councils, 108, 109, 164, 230, 234

Tranchée des Baïonnettes (Verdun), 47

trench press, 16, 25. *See also under* soldier-civilian gap

Trôo (Loir-et-Cher): war monument in, 143, 144–*145*, 164

Turner, Victor, 263, 282

uniform, as monument motif, 51. *See also* helmet, military

union sacrée: and interwar politics, 236, 296, 299–300, 313; at local level, 110, 119, 279

Union Fédérale (veterans group), 111